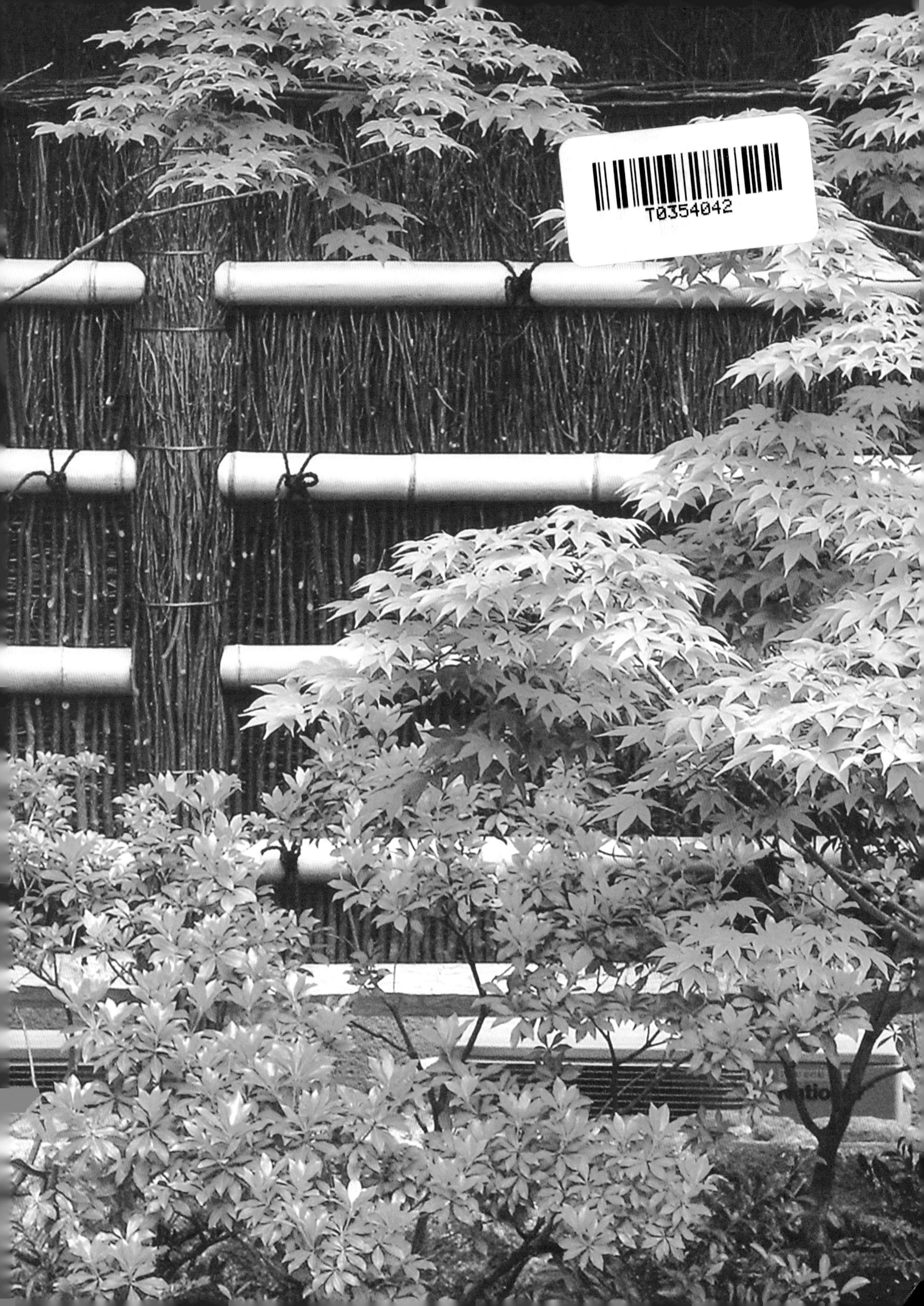
T0354042

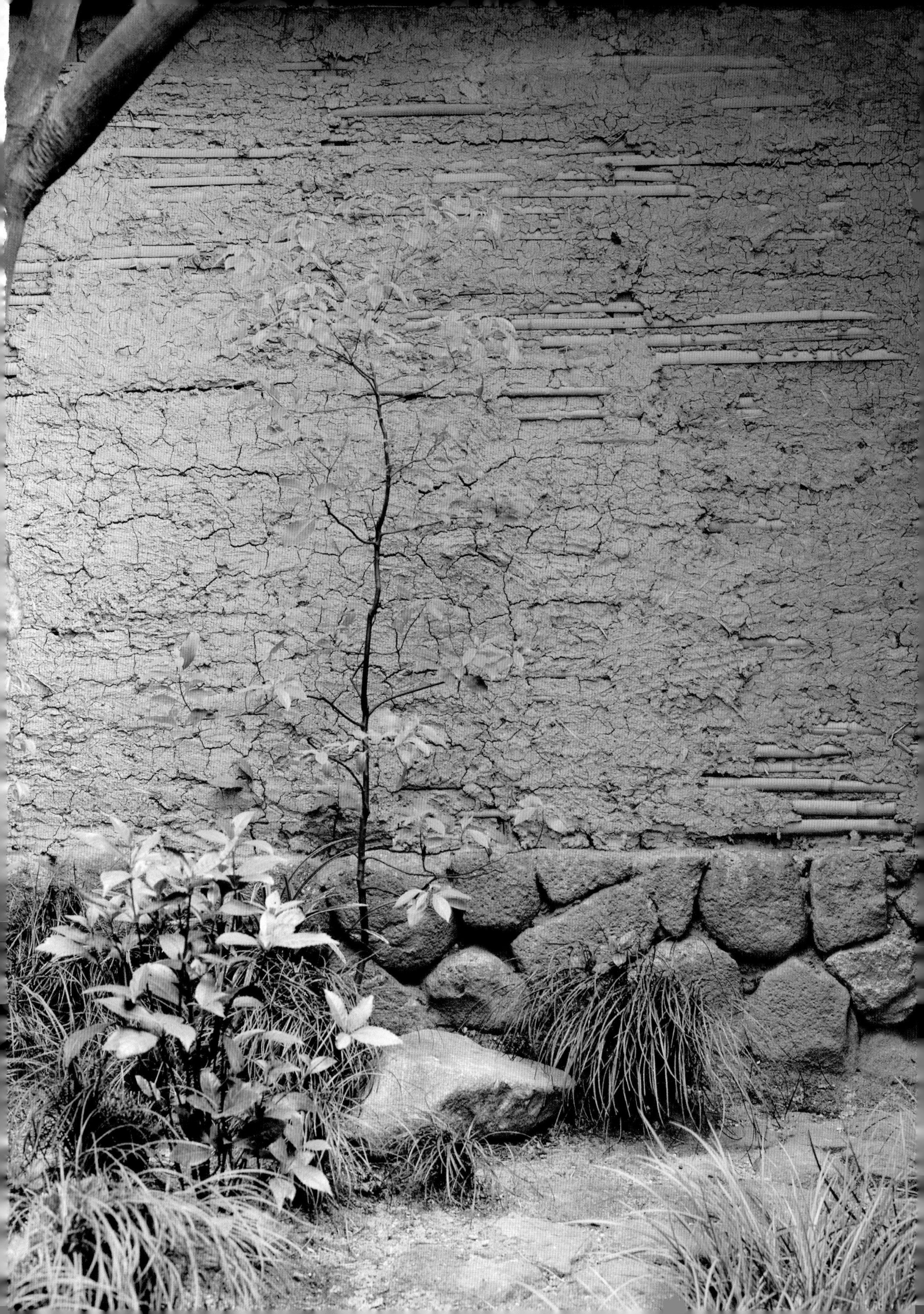

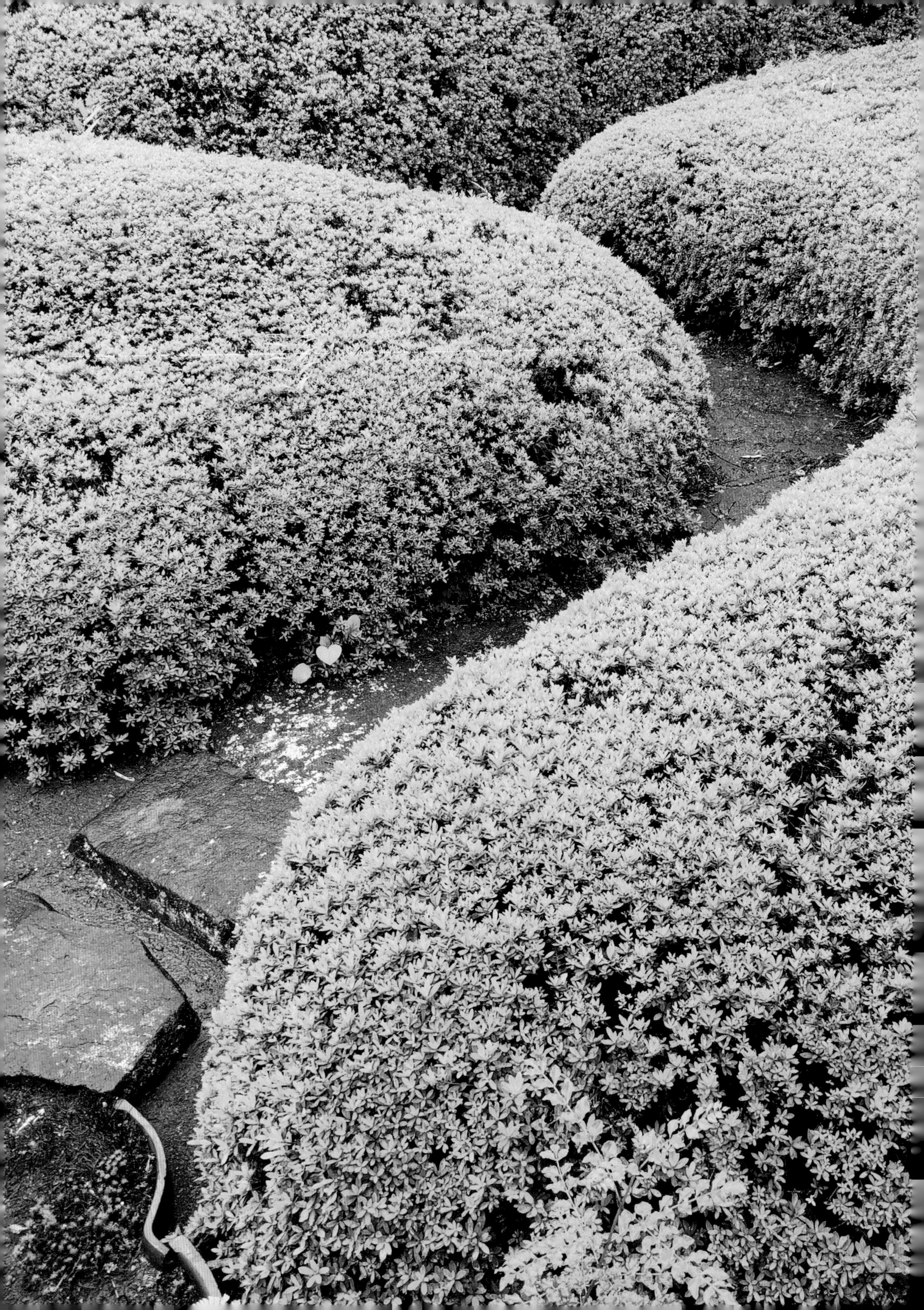

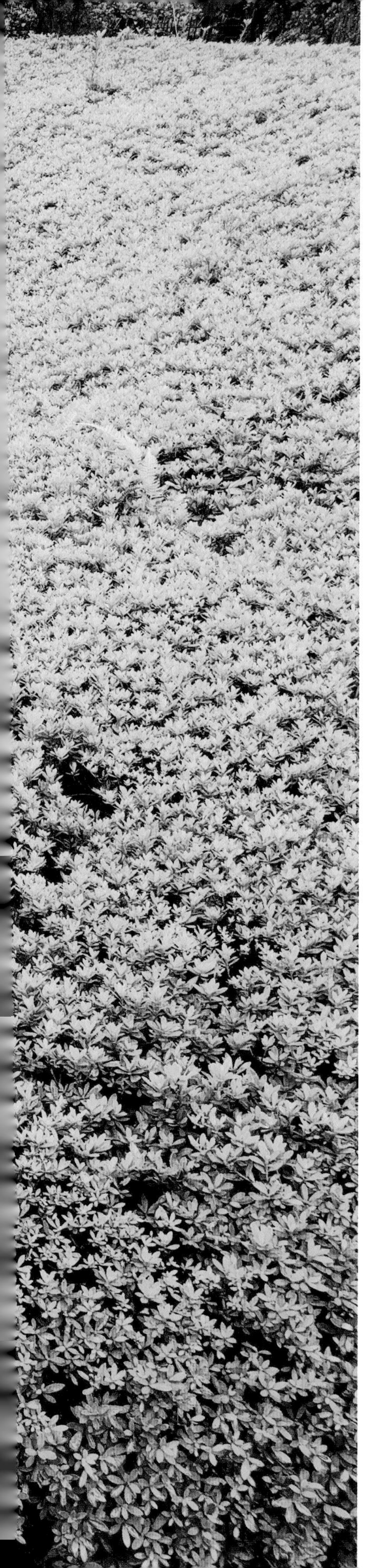

INSIDE YOUR JAPANESE GARDEN

SADAO YASUMORO & JOSEPH CALI

photography by HIRONORI TOMINO

TUTTLE Publishing

Tokyo | Rutland, Vermont | Singapore

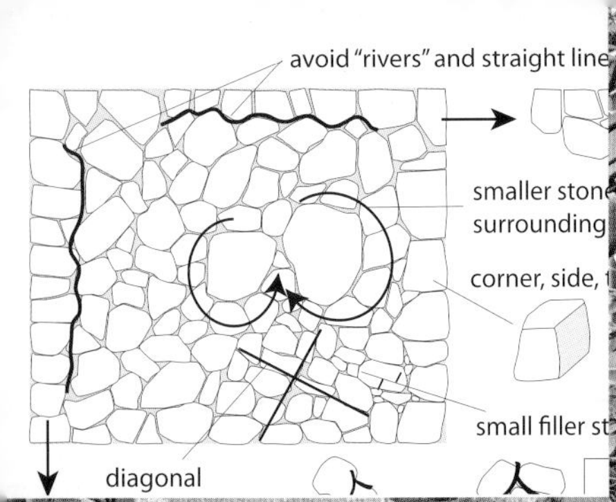

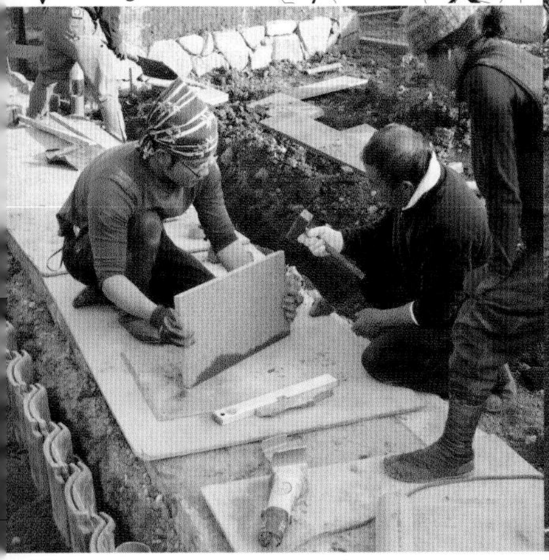

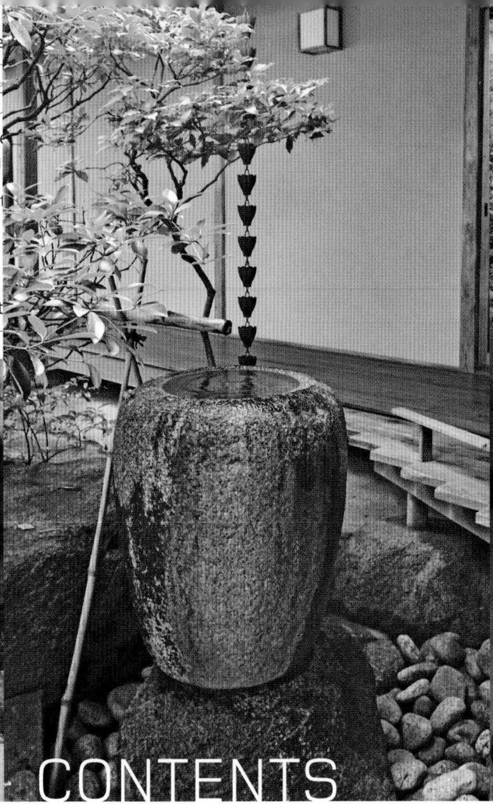

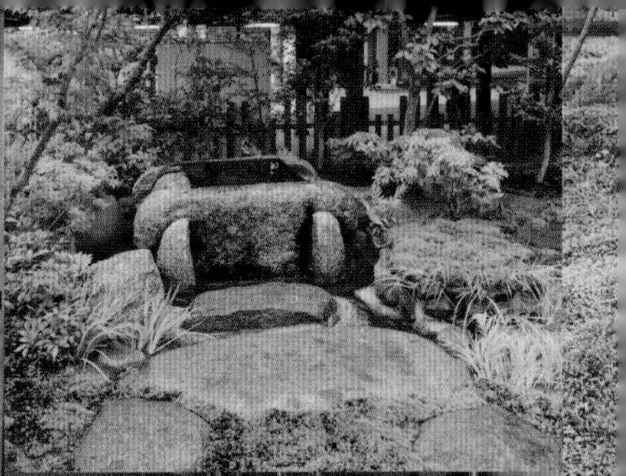

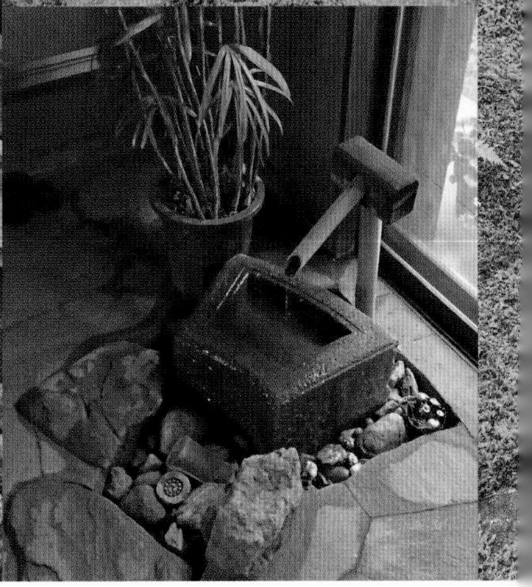

CONTENTS

Getting Started

Don't Follow This Manual *7*

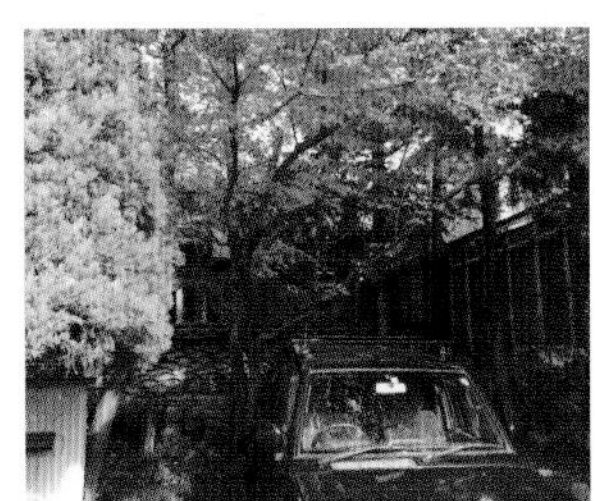

Chapter One

The Garden, the Entrance and the Automobile *19*

A Wall of Memory in a Shady Garden *20*

Garden of the NASA Astrophysicist *24*

A Garden for Lasting Relations *28*

A Professor's Terrace of Stone, Horsetails and Water *34*

The Salaryman's Rice Terrace Garden *38*

The Rustic Elegance of the Amigasa Mon Gate *42*

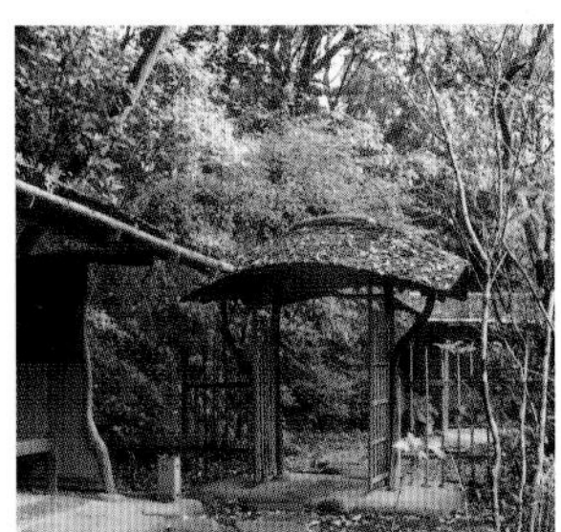

Chapter Two

Backyards and Gardens of the Gods *49*

Paradise in an Urban Jungle *50*

A Stairway up the Mountain *54*

The Landslide That Became a Garden *58*

How to Make a Koshikake Machiai Covered Waiting Bench *62*

The Urban Farmer with a Backyard Stroll Garden *66*

How to Make a Small Dobashira Earthen Bridge *71*

The Garden of Plum Blossoms and Students' Prayers *72*

How to Make a Large Dobashira Earthen Bridge *78*

Buddha's Mountain Retreat of Moss and Stone *82*

The Tatsutagawa River Garden *88*

Garden of the Bell Tower *92*

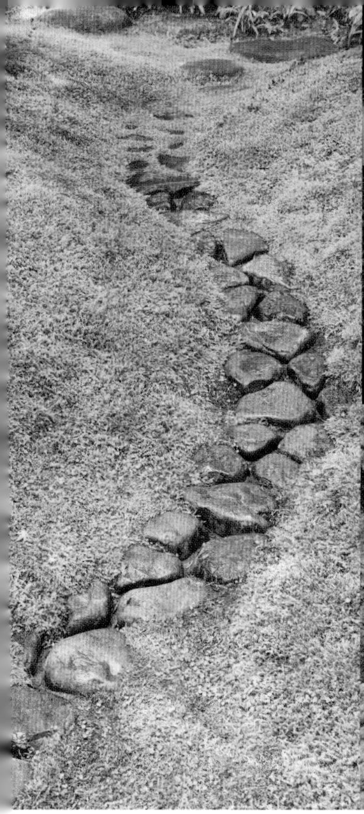

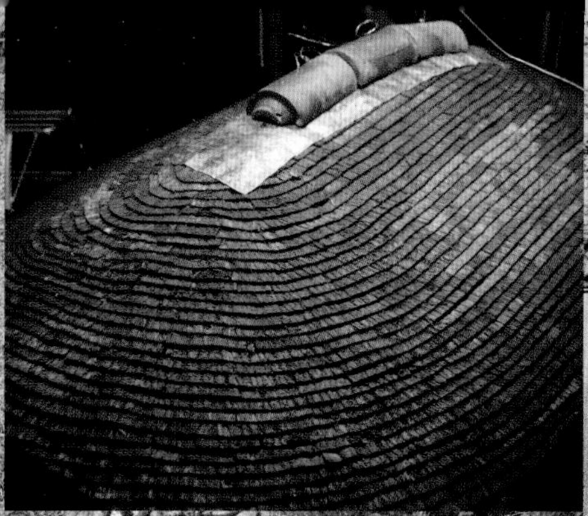

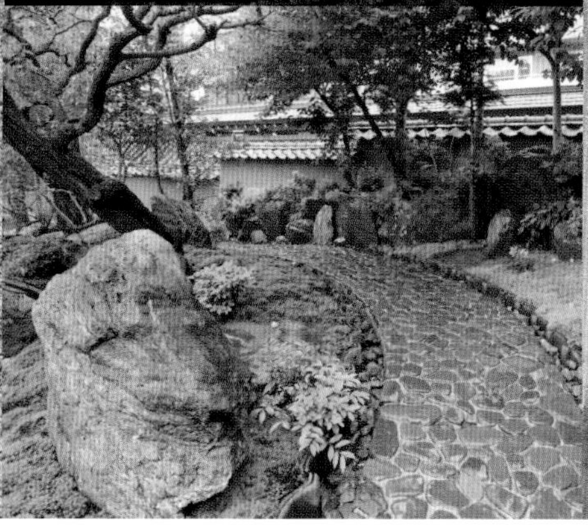

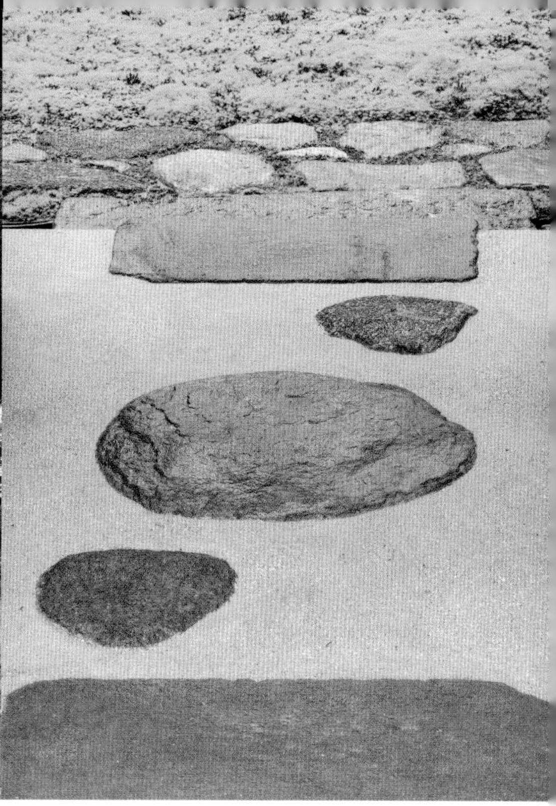

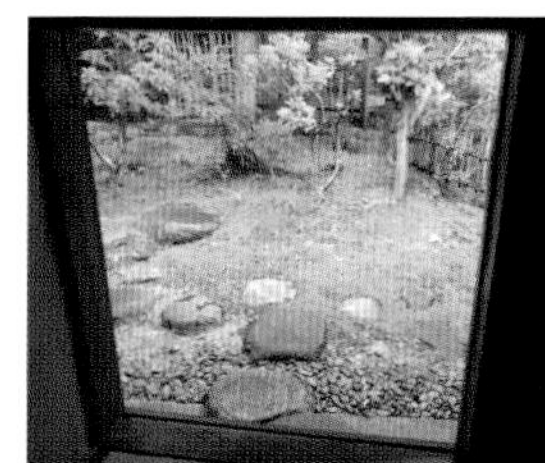

Chapter Three
Small Sanctuaries and Gardens for Refreshment *97*

Garden for a Tea Get-together *98*
Arranging Stones for the Koshikake Machiai Covered Waiting Bench 102
A Tea Garden for an Urban Farmhouse *104*
View of a Tsuboniwa from the Couch *108*
Climb the Stairs to a Private Gem *110*
A Small Garden Made by the Birds *114*
A Tsuboniwa for Visvim *118*
Reconstructing an Old Teahouse 122

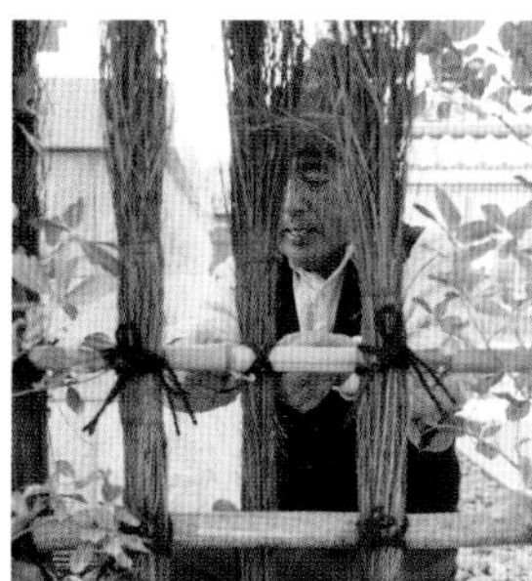

Chapter Four
Some Other Things You Should Know *126*

Handling Stone and Making a Japanese-style Stone Wall *126*
Mud on the Walls, Mud on the Floors *142*
Working with Bamboo *148*

List of plants appearing in this book *156*
Index *157*
Gardens in this book that can be visited *159*
Acknowledgments *159*

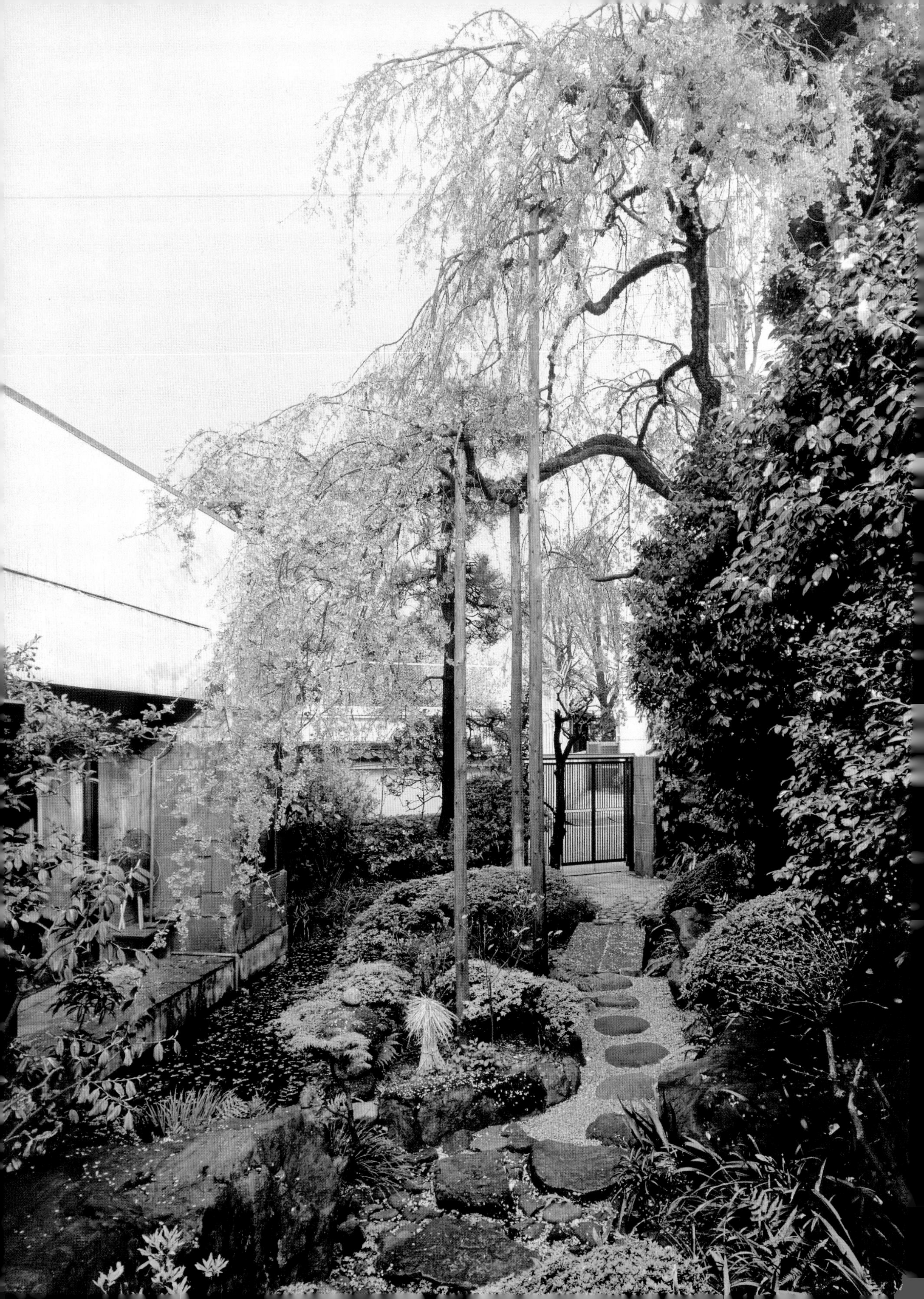

GETTING STARTED

Don't Follow This Manual

Introduction by Joseph Cali

Sadao Yasumoro, now over eighty years old, a Japanese garden designer and builder for sixty years or more, doesn't like manuals. "Most important of all is to put your heart into your work." This is what he told me about twenty years ago when we first met. His work has appeared in many Japanese garden magazines over the years and in a previous work of mine. This is his first book in English and, at my request, it is a "manual."

Just because he dislikes manuals, doesn't mean he's a stranger to teaching. But his world is not that of academia or computer-generated layouts and perspectives. Over the years, he has taught his craft to many who have worked for his company, Yasumoro Teien. He has also taught in many two- or three-day seminars sponsored by the Japanese Garden Society and others. In these hands-on sessions, a group of garden professionals and students create a garden, directed by the teacher (*sensei*).

As a junior high school student, he enjoyed painting. I have seen one piece from this period and it is quite good. But his family was poor and he needed a way to earn money. One of his favorite subjects to paint was the landscape. "When I was fifteen years old, I was sent to Tokyo Metropolitan Horticultural High School [Engei High School]," he says. "Yoshinobu Yoshinaga was my teacher." Yoshinaga went on to become an authority on the history of Japanese gardens. He wrote many books, including *Composition and Expression in Japanese Traditional Gardens*. Yasumoro spent his high school years learning the history and construction of Japanese gardens. "Another teacher, Rikyo Takahashi, sent me to assist Teizo Niwa." Teizo Niwa was a faculty member of the University of Tokyo. He was a leading garden scholar and researcher of his day and also head of maintenance for Tokyo's Shinjuku Gyoen garden. Yasumoro spent between four and five years studying under both men. Niwa-sensei influenced him to travel around the country. After graduating high school, Yasumoro set off on his own to see all the gardens he could. Over the next six years he lived rough, traveled, and worked part-time for other garden designers. He became greatly impressed by the terraced fields and rough stone walls built by unknown farmers. He exhorts students, "Don't look only at gardens: look at the entire landscape."

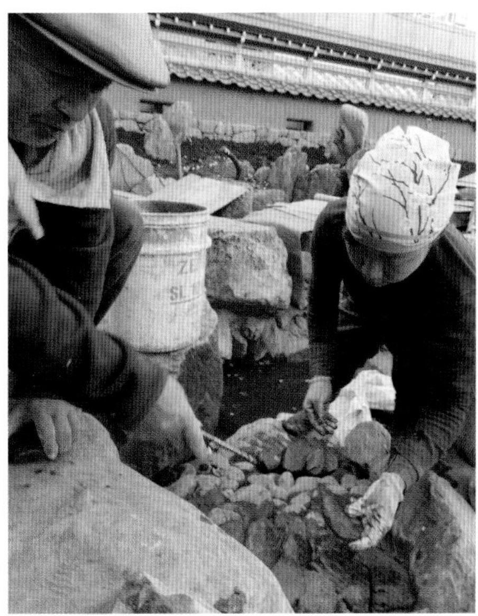

Facing page A large weeping cherry greets visitors from late March to early April, in this entrance garden designed by Katsuo Saito.

Above Selecting small stones that will form the pavement of a pond bottom.

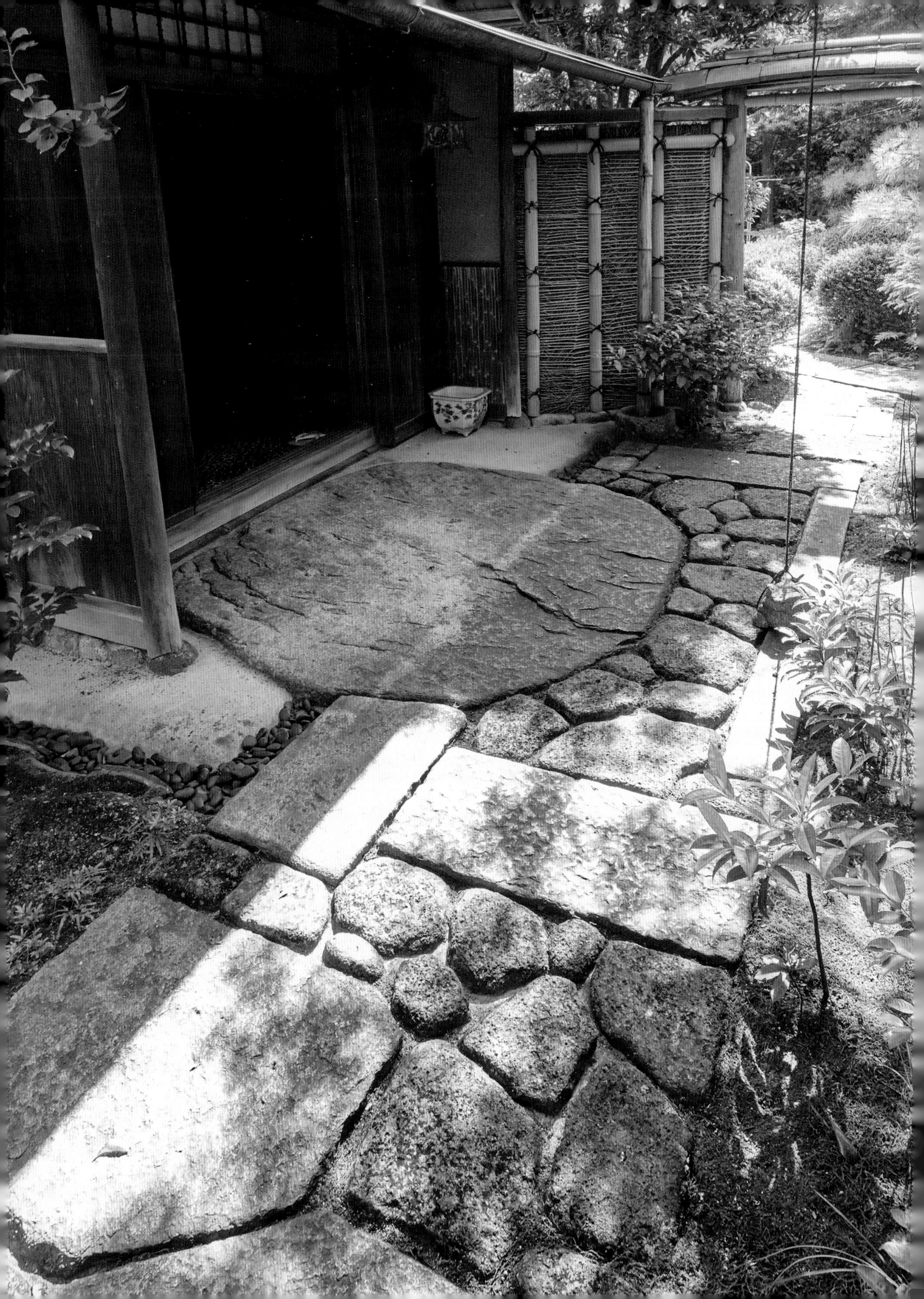

Left A large stone, carefully integrated into a walkway, marks the entrance to this house in Hiroshima.

Yasumoro went on to work for garden designer Katsuo Saito, from whom he learned about the correct form of trees and about making ponds. With Saito's five-man crew he made many gardens, such as the garden for the national broadcaster NHK, a garden for the Japan Railway school for employees, and a garden for the chairman of Fujiya confectionary. Saito is famous in the West for his books *Magic of Trees and Stones* (1964), *Japanese Gardening Hints* (1969), and others. In several of these books Yasumoro's (unaccredited) work appears.

Another piece of his education came when he worked, through a large construction company, for the renowned architect, Antonin Raymond, then in his eighties. He worked on gardens for Raymond's projects such as the Iranian Embassy in Tokyo and a house for the president of Takashimaya department store. He also did some work at the architect's Tokyo office. Yasumoro was in his twenties and he recalls that Raymond and his wife both doted on him. For the home of Takashimaya's president in Minato ward, Raymond wanted a garden that gave a unique view from each room of the house. The architect was very concerned about nature, telling Yasumoro to only cut dead branches, never living ones, and to be careful not to kill the ants when disturbing the ground. He insisted on a garden as natural as possible.

Yasumoro also credits the development of his skills to a study group formed with friends when he was thirty-five. This group included various craftsmen and together they practiced carpentry, plastering and other crafts.

EDUCATION VS. PRACTICE

The typical route for garden designers today is through college. But most schools do not teach traditional garden design and construction. Schools teach landscape architecture, focusing on site drawings for apartment buildings, offices, shopping malls and amusement parks. Students learn standards, regulations, estimates, urban planning and the things that make for getting a license and starting a successful business. Agricultural colleges prepare students for positions in modern farming, nurseries and other agricultural professions. Forestry departments focus on forests, water resources and wildlife management. But there are also many large and small garden-building and maintenance companies. This is the only practical route to learning the craft, in other words, apprenticeship.

It's a time-consuming route, demanding patience and stamina. It is the way of all Japan's traditional crafts, from cloth-dyeing to woodworking. Each year thousands of students from around the world come to this country to learn a craft from a master. The level of experience and teaching ability of the master varies. The traditional system, which is all but gone, saw students working in the master's studio for many years. Students lived in the master's house, received a very small stipend, and gained little in the way of praise. But those who stuck it out got an education they could receive in no other way.

As a homeowner, or someone who just wants to make a garden, none of this applies to you. I include it here for your information. For the average person, it is natural to ask an experienced friend or a clerk at a garden supply store for help, or to pick up a book and start cold. In that case, you might be wondering about the exhortation at the beginning of this introduction: "Don't follow this manual." It refers to Yasumoro-sensei's firm belief that you should develop your own approach to the Japanese garden, not rely too much on the ideas in a book. The only way to study how to make a garden is, as Yasumoro says, "Dig a hole."

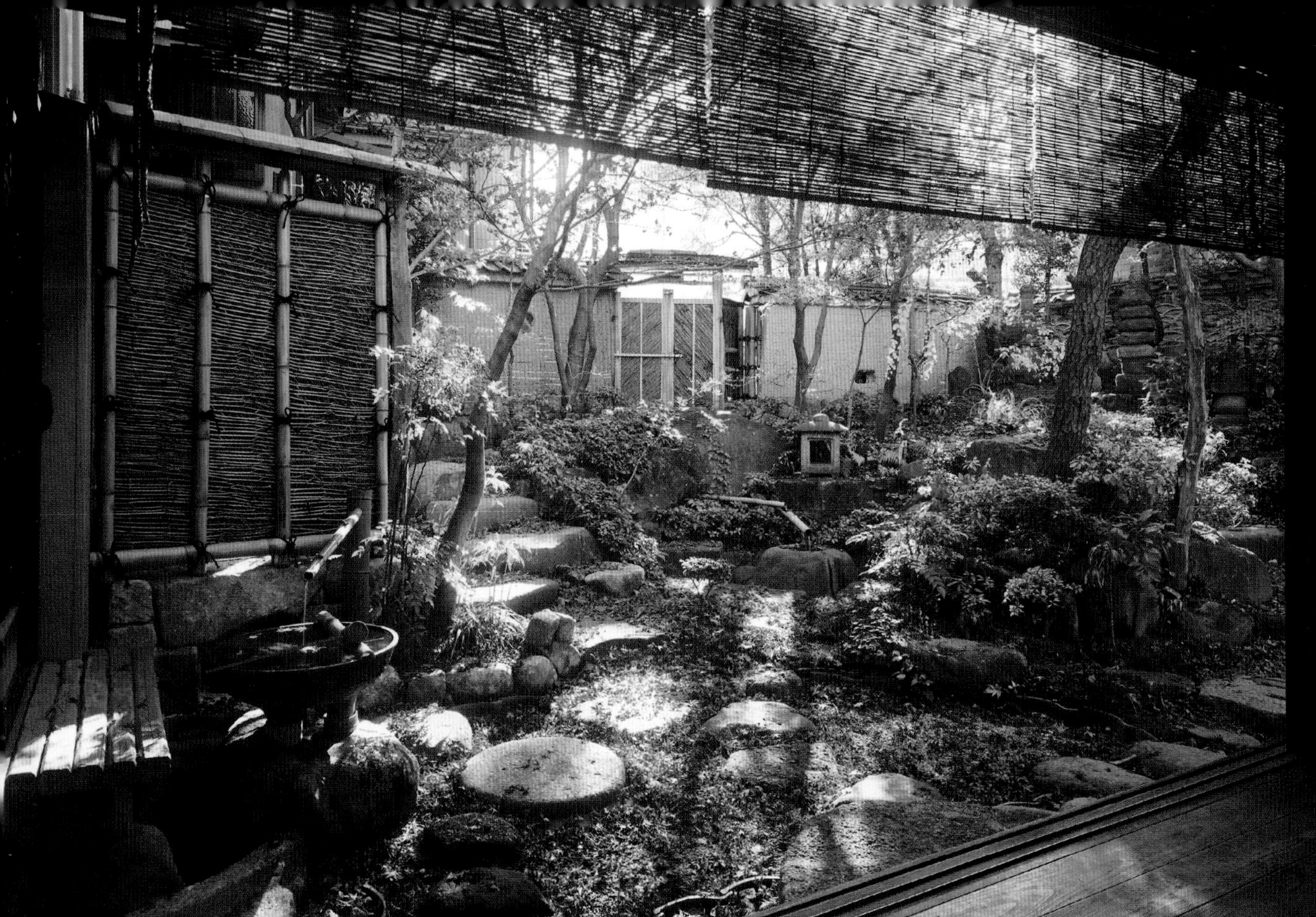

DIG A HOLE

That is how many of the gardens in this book began. Digging a hole in the area where you plan to make your garden tells you several things. It tells you what kind of soil you have. Is it rocky, sandy, clay or even landfill? Dig a hole 5 feet (1.5 m) deep and you will know. Does the hole immediately fill with water? You may need to put in a drain. The kind of drain will depend on where you live and the rules governing runoff. A flexible drainpipe in a sloped trench leading to a municipal sewer system is one possibility. A better way is to improve the absorption of the ground by digging a ditch around the periphery and filling it with gravel (a French drain). Also, mix the soil with wood or coal ash, wood chips and other organic matter. Grading the ground very gently towards the drains helps. It's equally important to understand where excess water is coming from. Sometimes it's obvious: your home is in a low-lying area that easily floods, or the water is runoff from a roof. Sometimes it's not that simple. In this book you will find one garden that was an answer to a total washout (see The Landslide That Became a Garden, page 58).

Is the ground hard with compacted clay? Does it contain a lot of stone? You won't have good plant growth unless you dig it out and replace it with permeable and nourishing soil. Digging out the entire area is best but it can be done in stages. Clay is not good for growing plants, but mixed with cut straw, it's great for making walls. Stone is troublesome when it comes to planting but it can be put aside and used to construct the base of that clay wall. Most gardens in this book use soil and stone dug from the site where they were made.

Digging a hole will also show whether your soil is alkaline or acidic. The standard way to test is to take some soil from various spots and depths in the garden. Take the soil from one spot at a time, put it into a coffee cup with pH neutral water, and stick in a pH meter or litmus paper. Or, add water and white vinegar to the soil in the cup. If the mixture bubbles

Left In a rare case, with the house level lower than the street, good drainage is paramount.

Right Large, flat *tanzaku ishi* "label stones" and a *kutsunugi* shoe-removal stone mark the entrance to an *engawa* corridor.

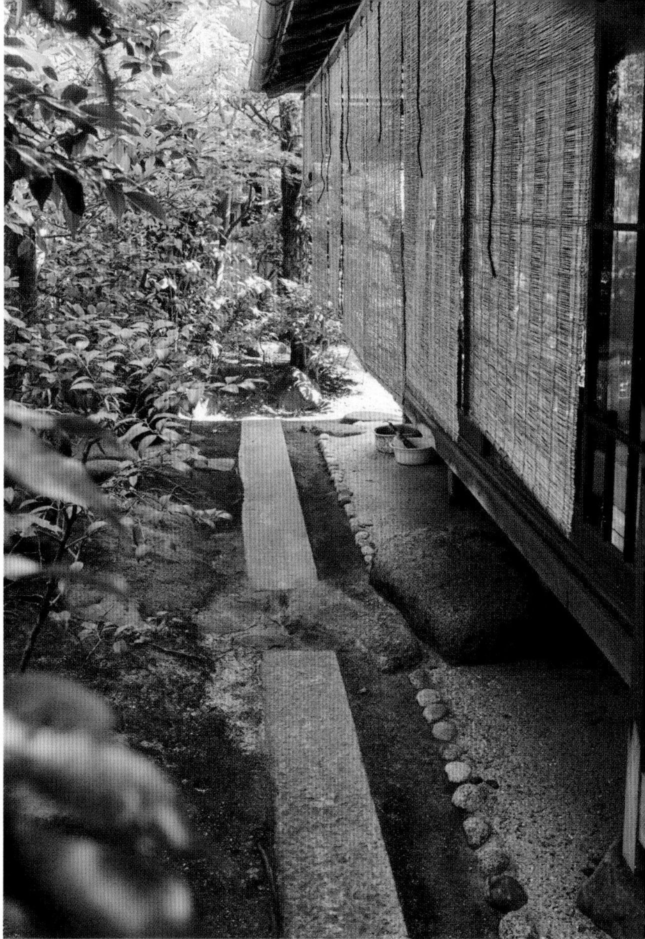

up, your soil may be alkaline. This is good for Japanese garden plants. If there is no reaction, it may mean the soil is pH neutral or acidic. In this case, mixing in lime or wood or coal ash will raise the pH. Yasumoro recommends a combination of volcanic loam (*akatsuchi*) and leaf mulch, which has a pH of 7 or above, as a general-purpose soil. Some plants, like azalea, camellia, and Japanese andromeda, may like a more acidic soil. In that case you can mix in some sphagnum moss, coffee grounds, or vinegar in water. Soil condition, volume, cost and such things all dictate what solution is best for you.

A LITTLE PLANNING

You don't need a teacher to tell you to think about what you want to do before you do it. Hopefully the gardens in this book will give you a reference point. You don't need to be great at drawing to make a plan. Start by writing down general ideas. If you can sketch a rough layout with approximate dimensions, it will be helpful when asking advice from your local garden supply store or DIY shop. It also helps you to think about where to start and what features to work on first. Show the plan to friends. Other sets of eyes can pick up things you missed. Make a list of needed materials along with the drawing.

A plan also helps you think about the time you will need. It may be necessary to build some features bit by bit over a long period, while others can be done in a weekend. A plan will tell you if you need to rent equipment and when. It can help you think about which parts you can do by yourself and which will need another set of hands. Visit some Japanese gardens in your area and photograph or sketch some features that attract you. But keep in mind that the worst gardens are like a junk shop full of all kinds of "interesting" features. Your garden should be simple. Try to project one impression: a deep forest, mountain foothills, a waterfall and pond, a stream meandering through gently rolling hills.

DESIGN PRINCIPLES AND OTHER NOTES

Following is a basic list of design principles to aid in constructing your Japanese garden.

A preference for odd numbers over even numbers: this results in arranging rocks and plants in groups of 1, 3, 5, 7 and 9. There are both physical and language-related reasons for this. The preference for odd numbers pervades Japanese culture.

A preference for asymmetry over symmetry: this relates to the preference for odd numbers and the prevalence of triangular relationships. In fact they are interconnected. Even when there is an even number of things, they are usually distributed so as not to look symmetrical.

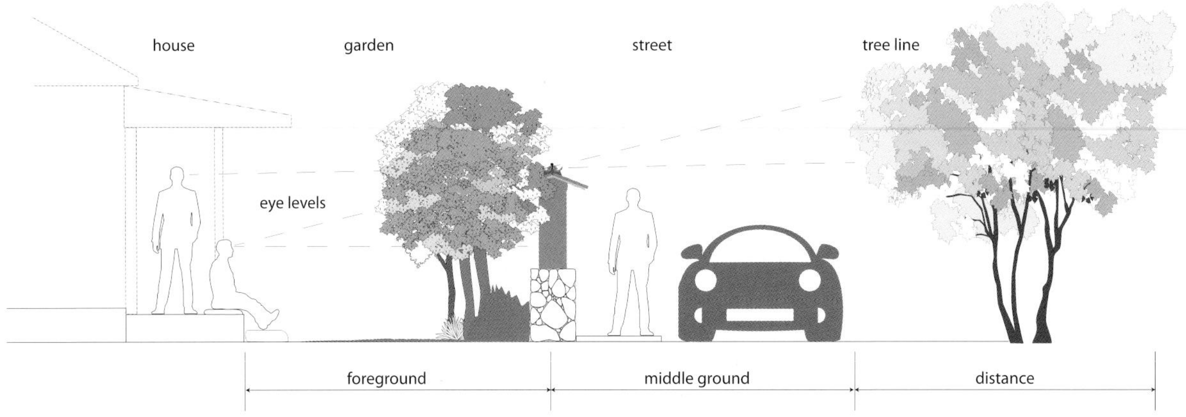

Small, medium, large: a distribution of sizes is important in the design of the garden. This is related to asymmetric balance as well as to the perception of space. For example, three stones in a group are never the same size. Smaller trees—10 to 13 feet (3 to 4 m) tall—are preferred and these are also grouped with taller trees at the back and smaller at the front.

Foreground, middle, distance: controlling the view is important, especially to create a sense of depth or breadth. These concepts are like those governing the composition of a picture in two dimensions. In fact, painting concepts are very much related to garden design. But it's not simply that as in a perspective drawing, a smaller object looks more distant than a larger one. For example, placing a large, dark stone or tree in the foreground can force the eye to compare it to the things in the background. Properly done, the eye will conclude that those things are smaller and farther away than they really are. Or placing a large expanse of gravel in the foreground can give the impression of looking across a lake to a distant landscape.

Miekakure: hide and reveal. This refers to the concept of partially concealing an object to enhance the depth of a shallow space. Think of a shallow stage, which appears deeper due to overlapping flats. The concept also relates to stroll gardens, where various scenes unfold as one walks through the garden. Such gardens create a sequence of scenes controlled by paths, which rise, fall, and turn at the right moment to reveal a new scene. The effect is aided by stones and plantings, which conceal the new scene until the viewer is in the right position. It also relates to controlling distance. For example, a mountain looks all the more distant for having a tree partially blocking its view.

Mitate: the use of double meaning, or representation of one thing by another. The purpose is to add layers of meaning through surprising juxtapositions. This can take the form of a single tree representing a forest, or a stepping stone that was once a millstone. Or, for example, gravel can be used as a stand in for water, or small stones for animals playing in the landscape. Other anthropomorphic representations fall into this category, for example, rocks that resemble turtles and cranes, or tiger cubs crossing a stream. Mitate was originally used in poetry and is often seen in tea ceremony utensils.

Meisho: reference to a real place. Japanese gardens often incorporate references to famous places that can be recognized by people viewing the garden. This is usually a shorthand and not a literal reproduction. This also applies to references from literature, which may or may not be real places, as well as "archetypes." A related term is *shukukei* or miniaturized landscape. References need not be explicit. They can suggest and leave an echo.

Shakkei: borrowed scenery. This means incorporating into the garden a scene that is outside the

Left A cross section of house to street shows a disconnect.

Right The same garden viewed from the house connects seamlessly to the street trees.

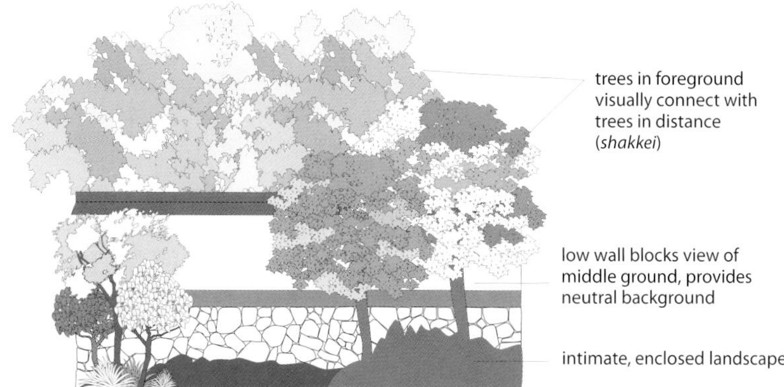

garden. There are several techniques for achieving this. One is replicating shapes in the distance with plantings and stones within the garden. The purpose is to create a continuum from foreground to distant background. By so doing, the garden appears to expand beyond its actual boundaries. Another method, explored throughout this book, is to interrupt the middle ground to create a connection between the foreground and the distant scene. Shakkei also relates to how to conceal the scene outside the garden. Especially in urban areas, this may be more important than incorporation.

Enclosure: a low wall is one way to interrupt the middle ground. This is one reason why Japanese gardens are almost always built inside an enclosure. Another is the idea mentioned earlier of creating a total landscape on a reduced scale (see *shukukei,* under ***Meisho***, facing page). A low wall provides an arena in which to "set the stage." Such an enclosure should provide a neutral and unobtrusive background.

Direction of the sunlight: this will help with determining the size and placement of plantings. For example, trees that tolerate strong light or wind can be used to shelter trees that do not. This also relates to the distribution of small, medium and large, mentioned at the top of the facing page. Generally, large, evergreen trees are kept toward the back of the garden, away from the house. This also relates to enclosure.

Direction of water flow: especially in gardens that draw water directly from a natural source. Always consider the path the water takes as it enters and leaves the garden. When using water from a municipal supply, consider the way water flows in nature from mountains to streams, lakes, and the ocean. The analog in the garden might be having water flow from a waterfall or rock formation at the rear of the garden, to a stream or pond in the foreground, to an unseen drain and recirculation system.

Earth, Water, Fire, Wind, Void *(chi-sui-ka-fuu-kuu)**:*** principles that embody everything in the universe. Beginning in Daoist philosophy, later codified in Buddhism, this concept covers all the elements of existence. In the garden it means taking a comprehensive approach that incorporates nature at its fullest. A direct, physical representation of the concept is the *gorinto*, or stone pagoda, sometimes placed in the garden. Each of its five layers stands for one of the above elements.

Permanent vs. transient: permanent refers to features less likely to change over time, such as stone and evergreen trees and shrubs. Transient refers to garden features that change or deteriorate over time, such as deciduous trees and bamboo features. Transience relates to the joy of renewal, when something old is made new. Permanence relates to the continuity and stability, characteristics that are possessed by evergreens and stone. Both are necessary and both should be present in your garden.

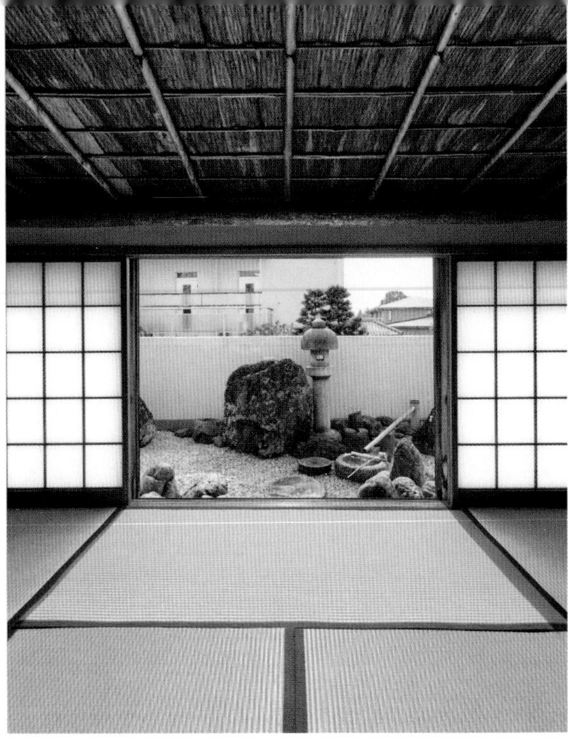

Left A tearoom on the third floor opens onto a stone garden and a tranquil atmosphere.

Below Water is as integral to Japanese gardens as it is to life. Even sand and stone gardens can symbolize oceans and waterfalls.

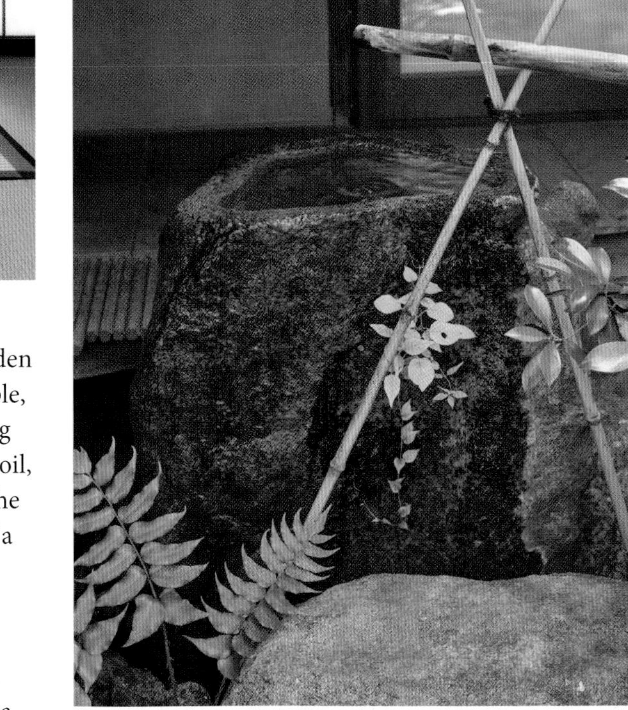

Invisible vs. visible: this refers to parts of the garden that you don't see versus those you do. For example, the buried part of a stone is essential for providing stability and even beauty to the visible part. The soil, eventually hidden by the plants growing in it, is the reason the plants thrive. The interior structure of a clay wall determines its long-term survival.

Connect the garden to the home: this concept is manifested in many ways. Consider, for example, the view of the garden from the main viewing area such as a living-room window or a deck. Orienting the garden scene to present its best face to the main viewing points is an element of the design. This may also include creating an interior space that easily incorporates the exterior. Traditional Japanese homes have an *engawa* corridor that lies between the room and the exterior of the house. Both sides of the engawa have sliding doors, which can be completely opened, allowing an expansive view of the garden and letting sounds and scents into the house. Another method is to construct a narrow exterior deck (*nure-en*) so you can sit outdoors.

The well-being of the family: the garden should promote well-being, enjoyment and a healthy environment. Include space for recreation if you want, or for a kitchen garden (*katei saien*). Yasu-moro-sensei once made a garden for the slightly eccentric chairman of Honda Motors. It had a stream and the chairman liked to stock it with sweetfish (*ayu*). When guests called, he would catch fish and roast them. Traditional garden design also incorporates talismanic stones, like the guardian stone (*shugoseki*) which stands at the heart of the garden. The *fudoseki* is a stone that stands upright and strong as part of a waterfall. The *meotoseki* is a pair of stones symbolizing marital harmony.

Philosophy and history: a Japanese garden is imbued with the philosophy and history of Japan. Studying a little about this may add to the outcome

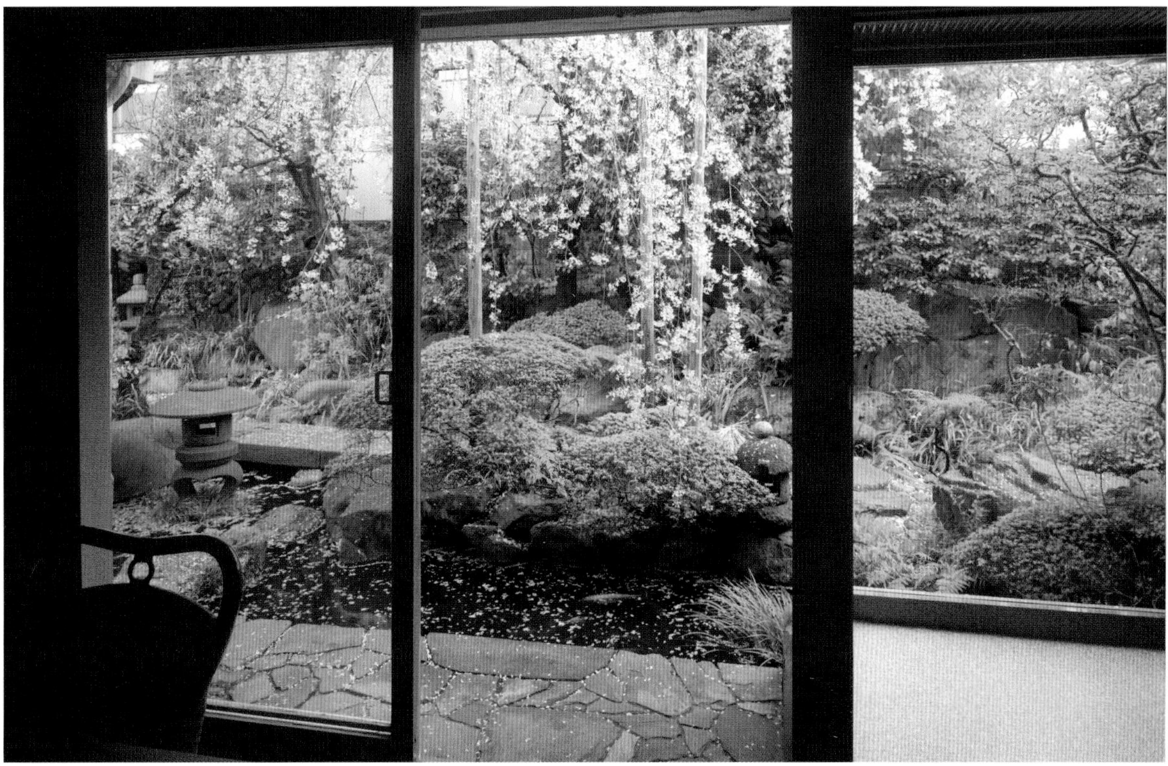

This modern office/home does not have an *engawa* exterior corridor but incorporates the garden through sliding glass doors.

of your work. Looking at images or reading about famous gardens provides ideas for Japanese and foreigners alike. But don't copy and don't be discouraged by a lack of understanding. Be original. True understanding comes from within. For example, try reading old Japanese stories, such as *The Tale of Genji*, and visualizing the scenes in your own mind. This is exactly what garden designers have done in the past. Literature has always been a great source of inspiration for garden designers throughout the world. The resulting garden will be your own interpretation. This is as it should be.

Finished vs. unfinished: this refers to the concept that nothing living can be perfect. It also refers to leaving something remaining to be done. This implies continuation. In times past, craftsmen would go to the extent of intentionally making a "mistake," knowing that it would have to be corrected in the future. A famous example is seen in Shinto shrines dedicated to the spirit of the shogun Tokugawa Ieyasu, where perfection is disrupted by intentionally placing an entrance pillar upside down. In the garden, the implication is to not worry about being perfect and to realize that a garden is always a work in progress.

Spirit vs. technique: spirit comes first. Technique will follow.

Knowing the law: this applies mostly to water runoff, tree overhang, and fence or wall building. Local rules relating to these aspects of the garden should be known at the planning stage. Not only following the rules, but also respect for neighbors' feelings will help assure a successful garden.

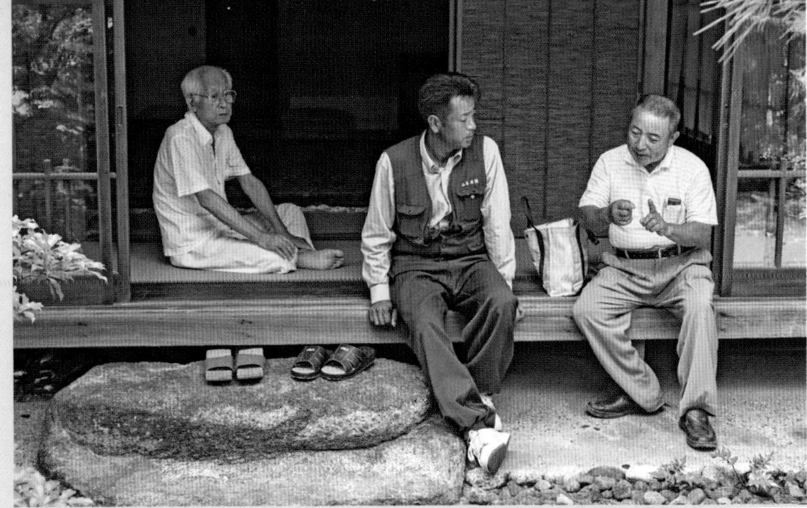

Left Yasumoro sits on the *engawa* corridor and shares a moment with a local carpenter and the homeowner, Mr. Yamamoto.

Right A tall water basin placed close to the *nure-en* deck brings water within easy reach.

SOME QUESTIONS FOR **YASUMORO-SENSEI**

Q. What is one word that describes the Japanese garden?
A. Heart.

Q. What is your theory of garden making?
A. Gardening is not a theory. It is all about learning the various scenes presented by nature.

Q. What is important when making your own garden?
A. Safety: no loose stones or sharp edges. The face of the owner: the garden should reflect your feelings. A place you love: it should be a source of constant enjoyment. A place to enjoy nature: the sounds of birds and insects, and the sound of rain and flowing water. A place to relax: stargazing or watching the moon.

Q. What shrubs would you want to plant in the garden?
A. Japanese enkianthus (*dodan tsutsuji*), azalea (*satsuki*), Japanese andromeda (*asebi*).

Q. What trees would you want to plant in the garden?
A. Red pine (*akamatsu*), birdlime holly (*mochi no ki*), false Japanese cleyera (*mokkoku*), flowering plum (*ume*), Japanese maple (*momiji*).

Q. What is your favorite garden material?
A. Soil and stone dug from the site where the garden will be made. I also like to incorporate local materials wherever possible. Also, moss (*koke*).

Q. When you make a garden, what do you always do?
A. Reuse old materials. Renew an old tradition: bring it into the present.

Q. What do you never do?
A. Use modern chemical-based materials such as vinyl. Use a potentially dangerous material or one that is easily breakable or cannot be replaced.

Q. Is it possible to make a Japanese garden without walls?
A. Yes. For example, you can have a small *tsuboniwa* courtyard garden, maybe surrounded by a deck, open for viewing from all sides. Or some stones standing in a field of moss and some low shrubs. By this definition, a garden is simply arranged nature, no matter how minimal.

Q. Does water always need to be included in a garden?
A. Not physically. Japan has a tradition of stone-and-sand gardens (*karesansui*). But water is always present even when it is only implied, as when gravel is substituted for water, or certain plants found by lakes or streams are used. In my gardens you will often find a stone or ceramic water basin (*chozubachi* or *mizubachi*). Water is not only important for life but is also used for ablution, a basic concept in Japanese culture.

—Joseph Cali

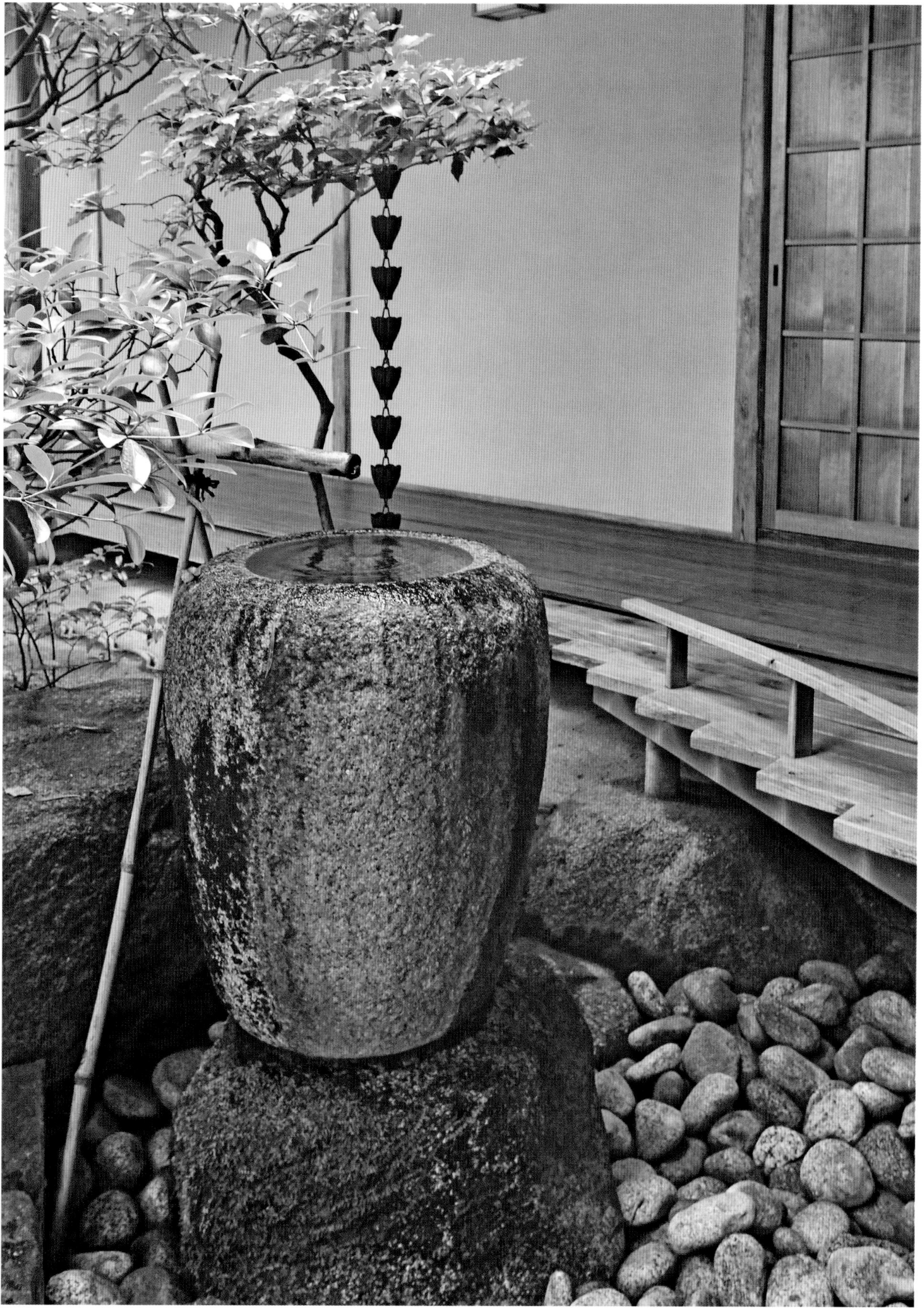

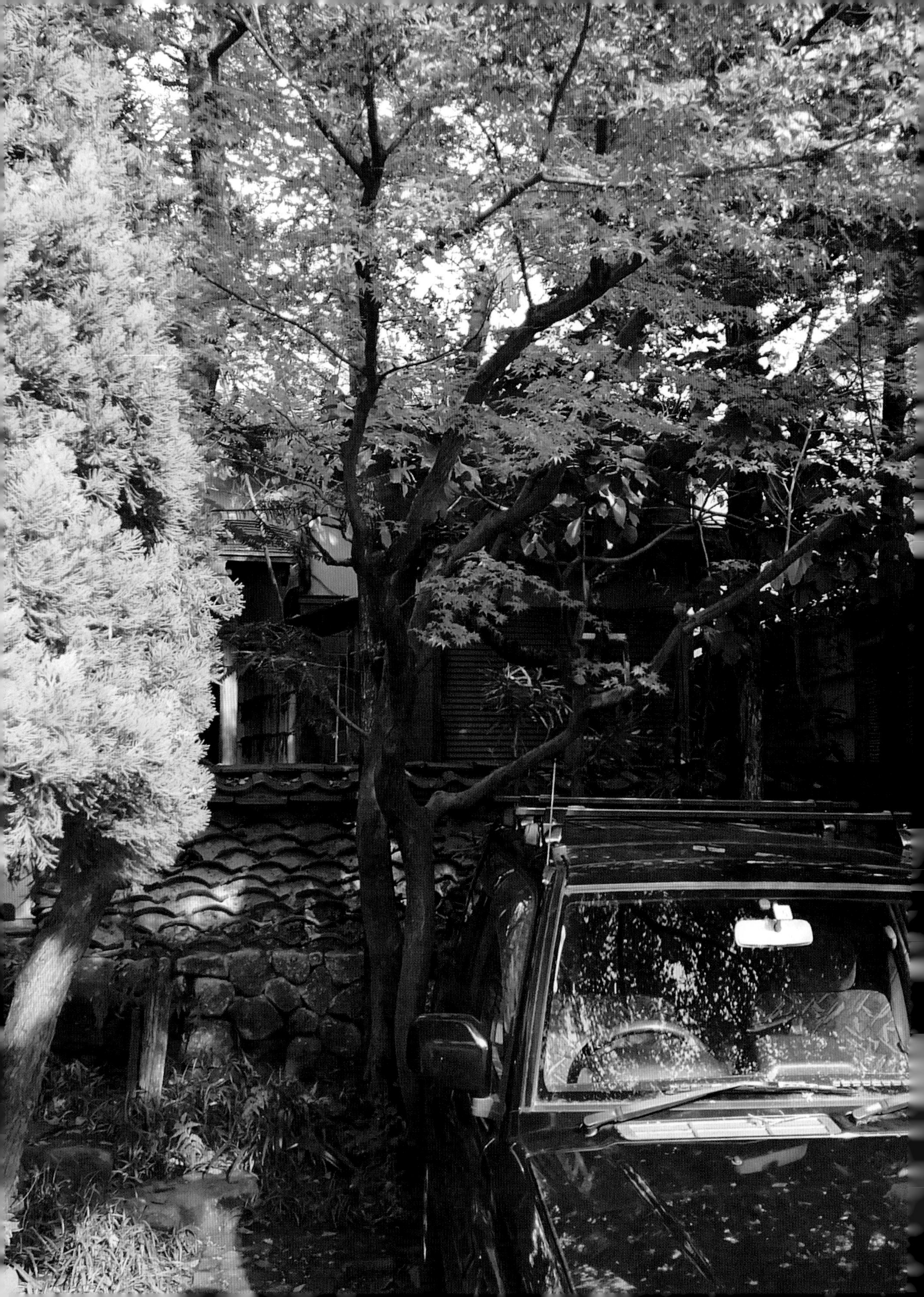

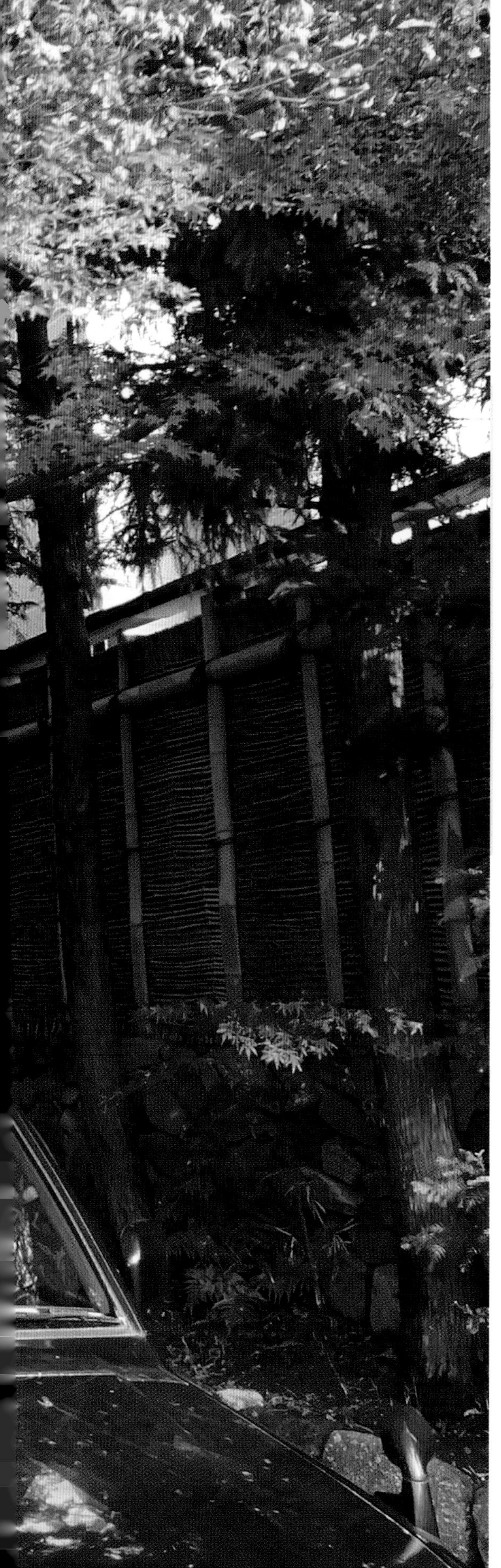

CHAPTER ONE

The Garden, the Entrance and the Automobile

As a gardener and a person who feels at home in nature, I can never be satisfied with the direction of modern cities. I am talking about concrete, asphalt, and the automobile. I have heard that in other countries, many houses include a garage. I have also heard that many of these garages are full of junk, or used for some other purpose, so that the car is left outside anyway. Of course, many people in urban areas park their cars on the street and fill every available space with them.

In Japan, the law requires proof of a parking space in order to register a car, and that space must be within two kilometers (about a mile) of the residence. Most people prefer to park in front of their house but garages are uncommon. Instead, an open space, or a space with a clear plastic roof supported by an aluminum frame, is typical. In other words, the car becomes part of the architecture. As I see it, the front of the house is also the entrance. It should welcome you home in as pleasant a way as possible. It also shares its appearance with the neighborhood and should make a positive contribution.

Whether the house itself has modern lines or traditional, for me, entering the home by walking through or past a garden is enjoyable and relaxing. While the need for automobiles cannot be denied, they can be housed in a natural and pleasing environment. In this chapter I highlight some attractive entrances where cars and nature coexist comfortably.

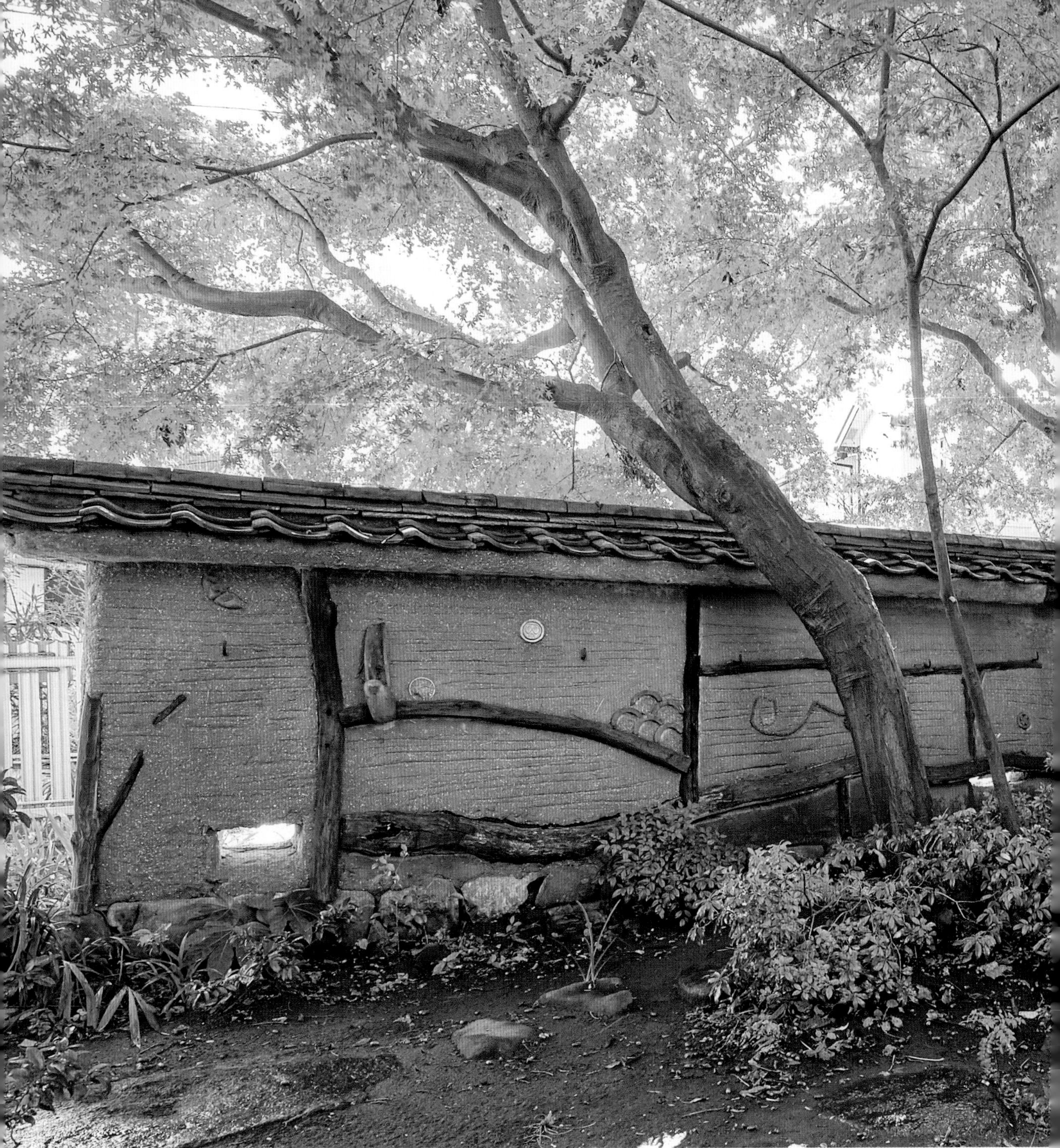

A Wall of Memory in a Shady Garden

A short clay wall provides some privacy from the street but allows the garden to expand into the natural environment next door.

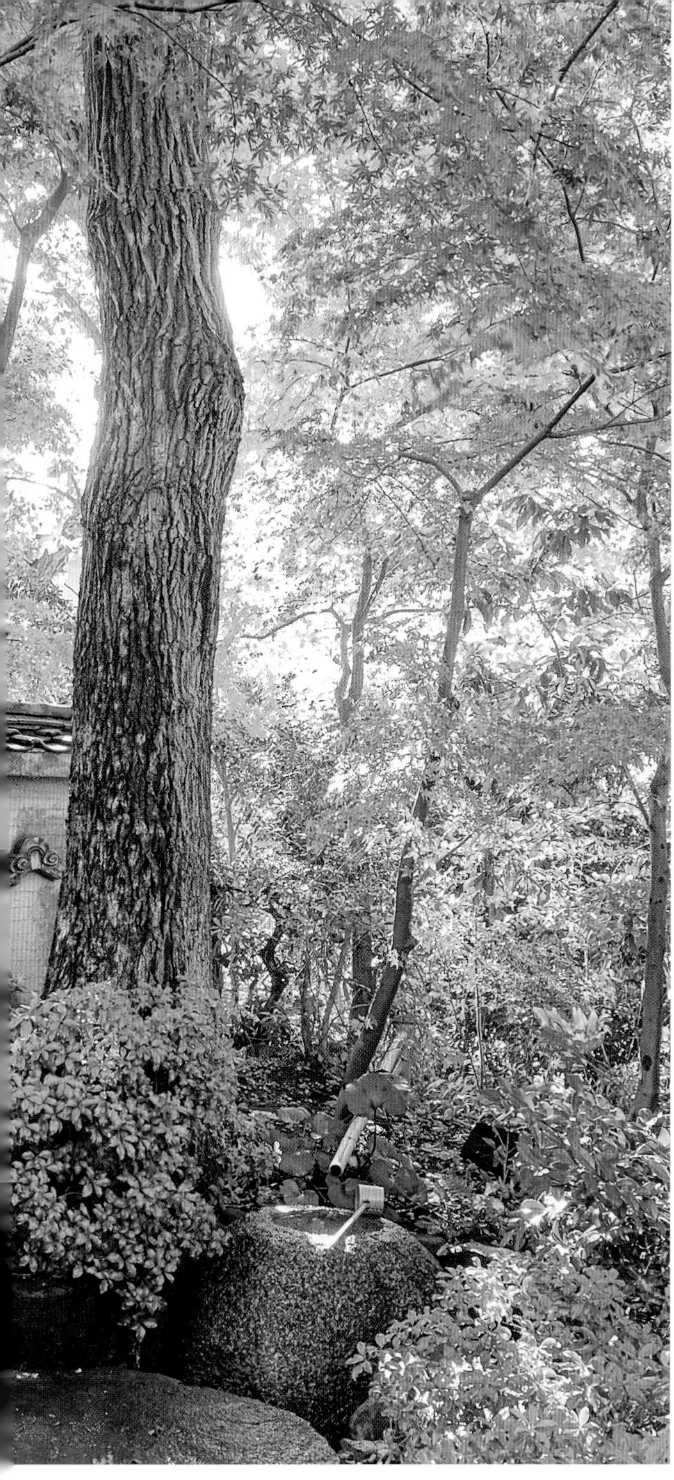

These days, there is a lot of concern about radical shifts in weather. Extreme heat and cold, or droughts followed by flooding are now everyday events throughout the world. In my experience, on a local level, a healthy garden goes hand in hand with a healthy environment. In the area of Tokyo where I live, many houses still maintain gardens. But there is always pressure to sell land to pay taxes, or to reduce the maintenance expenses associated with homes, or because the owner has fallen on hard times or passed away. Houses surrounded by greenery are an endangered species.

The Yusa family has resisted the pressure. Mrs. Yusa inherited a property, which included natural woodland on a steep gradient, adjacent to a larger property that is now a park. It had many deciduous and evergreen trees, to which I added a number of Japanese maples. The house sits on the top of the incline and we turned the level area to the left of the house into the garden. I made a 6½ x 16-foot 5-inch (2 x 5-m) clay wall to separate the car-parking area and the street from the garden. A stone walkway (*nobedan*) to the right of the wall begins at a Western-style gate and leads to the house.

I have already mentioned the main features of this garden: the deciduous woodland (*zokibayashi*), the beautiful Japanese maples, and the clay wall (*dobei*) that blocks the street view from the garden. Traditional gardens are usually surrounded by a combination of walls, hedges and bamboo fences. But in this garden I decided to use only a single wall that is open-ended on both sides. The part of the garden which is on the same level as the house is not large. Completely enclosing it would have made it feel smaller. A single wall is just enough to separate the garden from the two-car parking area and give it an intimacy and privacy enhanced by the adjacent woods.

The garden and the car park are covered in a canopy of bright green in the summer and brilliant red and orange in early winter. Both create a sheltered feeling when standing in the garden or siting on the exterior *nure-en* deck. This character is what I find so wonderful about Japanese maples: cool green in the hot summer, warm red and orange in the winter. The abundance of fine-figured leaves gives good cover when seen from the outside but seen from underneath, their thinness allows light to flicker through.

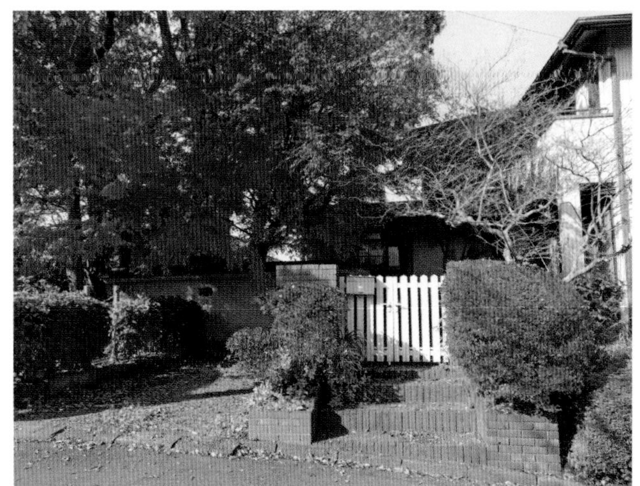

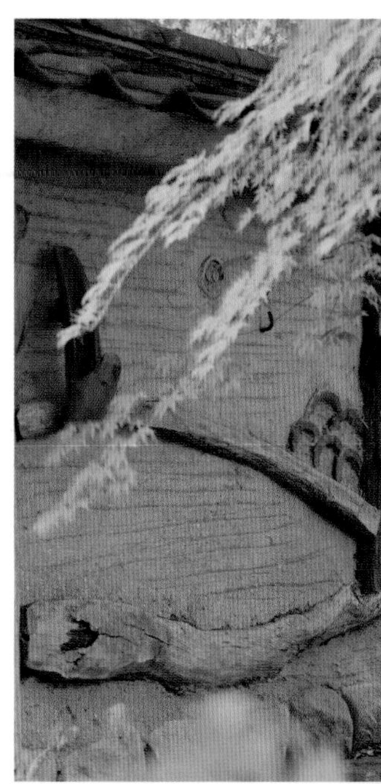

Right The maples and hedge unify the garden and entrance although different people made them at different times.

Below A *tsukubai* water-basin setting creates visual weight and interest at the base of a tall tree.

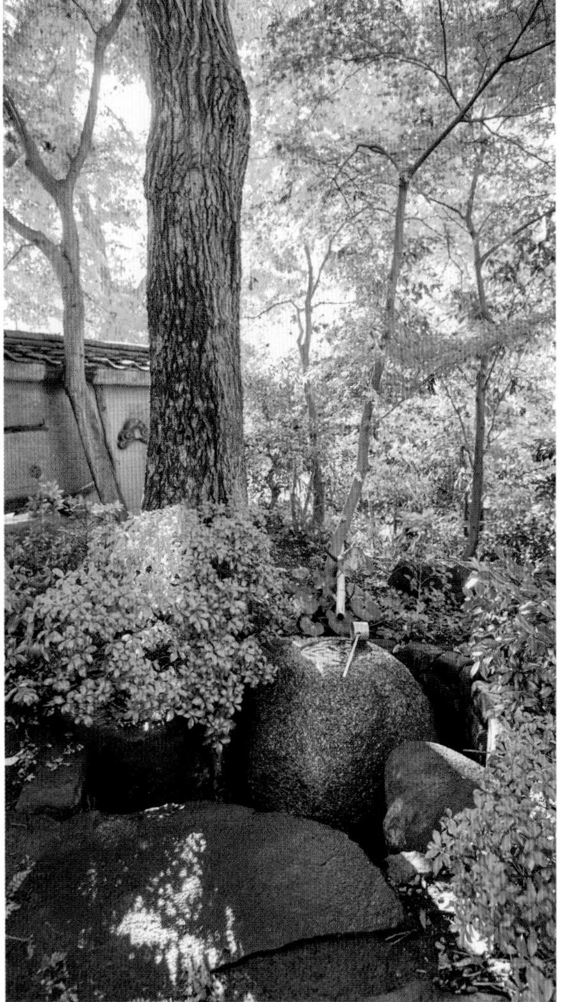

Mr. Yusa has fond memories of Korea where he has spent some time. At his request, on the inside of the wall I created a design using pieces of wood from old construction and other sources. This is my interpretation of Korean cordwood walls. I also scored the inside of the wall and opened several windows in it, to allow air to flow. The result is similar to but different from either Korean or traditional Japanese clay walls.

Again, cars are a necessary evil and this house has parking space for two. As I mentioned, the two-car parking area is isolated from the garden by an open-ended wall but accessible to the street. A hedge separates the car spaces, while the nearside of the area is open for direct access to the house. On foot or bicycle one may enter the garden directly from the street. A few brick steps lead through a white picket gate that existed before the garden was made. The owner did not wish to replace the steps and gate. The overall appearance is unified due to the fact that the existing Japanese enkianthus (*dodan tsutsuji*) hedges along the sides of the steps turn the same shade of red as the maples we planted.

Other than stepping stones, walkways, and a water-basin arrangement (*tsukubai*), there are no

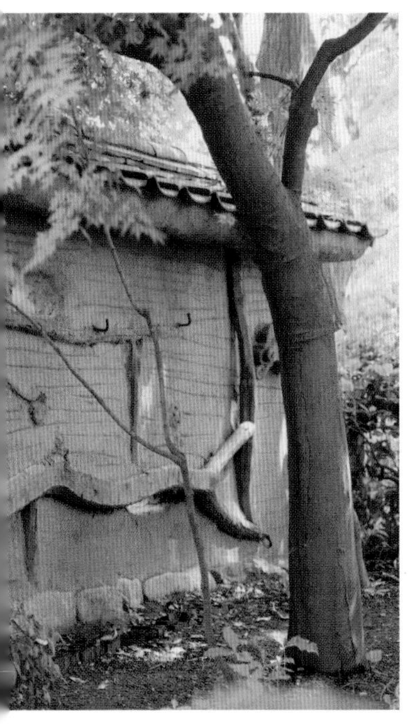

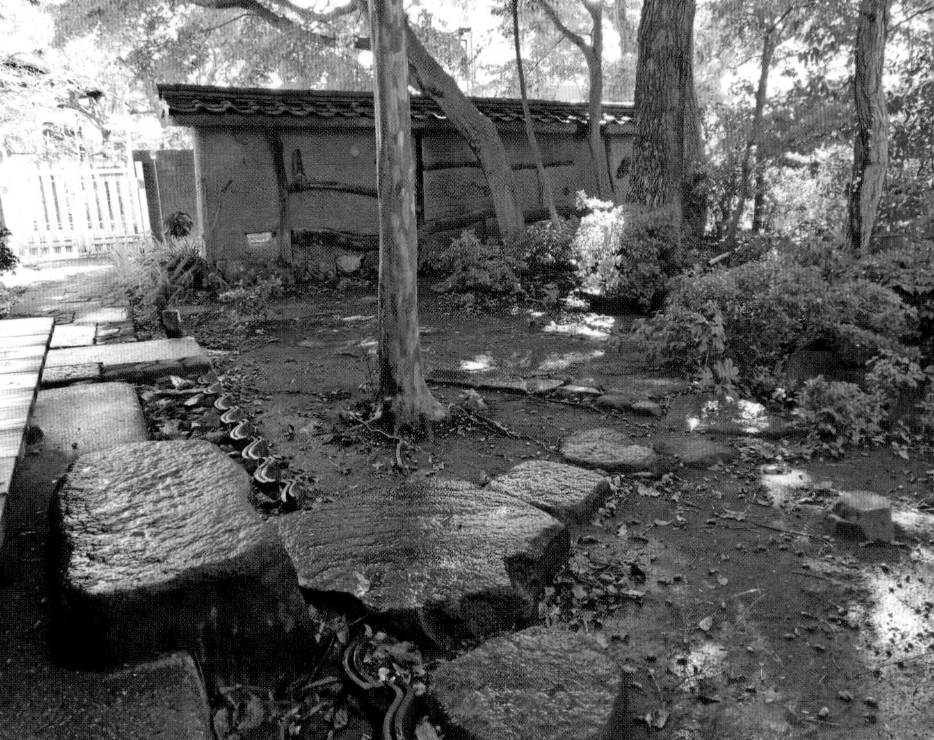

Left Various wood forms in a mud wall recall the owner's experiences in Korea.

Above A large shoe-removal stone and stepping stones add structure in this small tree garden.

large stones here. This is unusual for a Japanese garden. As I mentioned, the actual flat area of the garden is limited and this was one reason to minimize the use of large stones. Another was that this is a tree garden. The trees in the foreground join visually with those outside the garden in the park next door. This technique is called *shakkei* and can be employed if your garden has a view of a landscape. By strategic planting and creating an ambiguous middle ground, the garden appears to join the landscape and extend into the distance. I use this technique in a number of gardens in this book so I think you can get a clear understanding of it.

The tsukubai water basin is at the base of a large tree. Around that, I planted camellia (*sazanka*), coralberry (*manryo*) and Japanese andromeda (*asebi*). These low shrubs add form, and focus attention around the water-basin grouping. They also add color at a low height, which draws the eye to the darker reaches under the trees. The andromeda produces hanging clusters of small white flowers from late winter to spring. The coralberry has a similar flower to the andromeda in summer and bright red berries in winter. After the leaves of the maples turn red and fall in mid-winter, sunlight can penetrate the trees to warm and dry the garden in the coldest season. These are the merits of using deciduous trees—cool shade in the summer, sunlight and warmth in the winter.

We also made a stone stair that leads to the lower level of the garden, where a stone wall helps to support the upper level. The stair also connects with a path to the home of a relative who lives next door. The stair and the grade are very steep and the lower garden has become overgrown and not much used these days. I hope at some point in the future I will have the opportunity to revitalize this area, which would make a great private patio. If not, I hope the next gardener will pick up the thread to both preserve and create the garden anew.

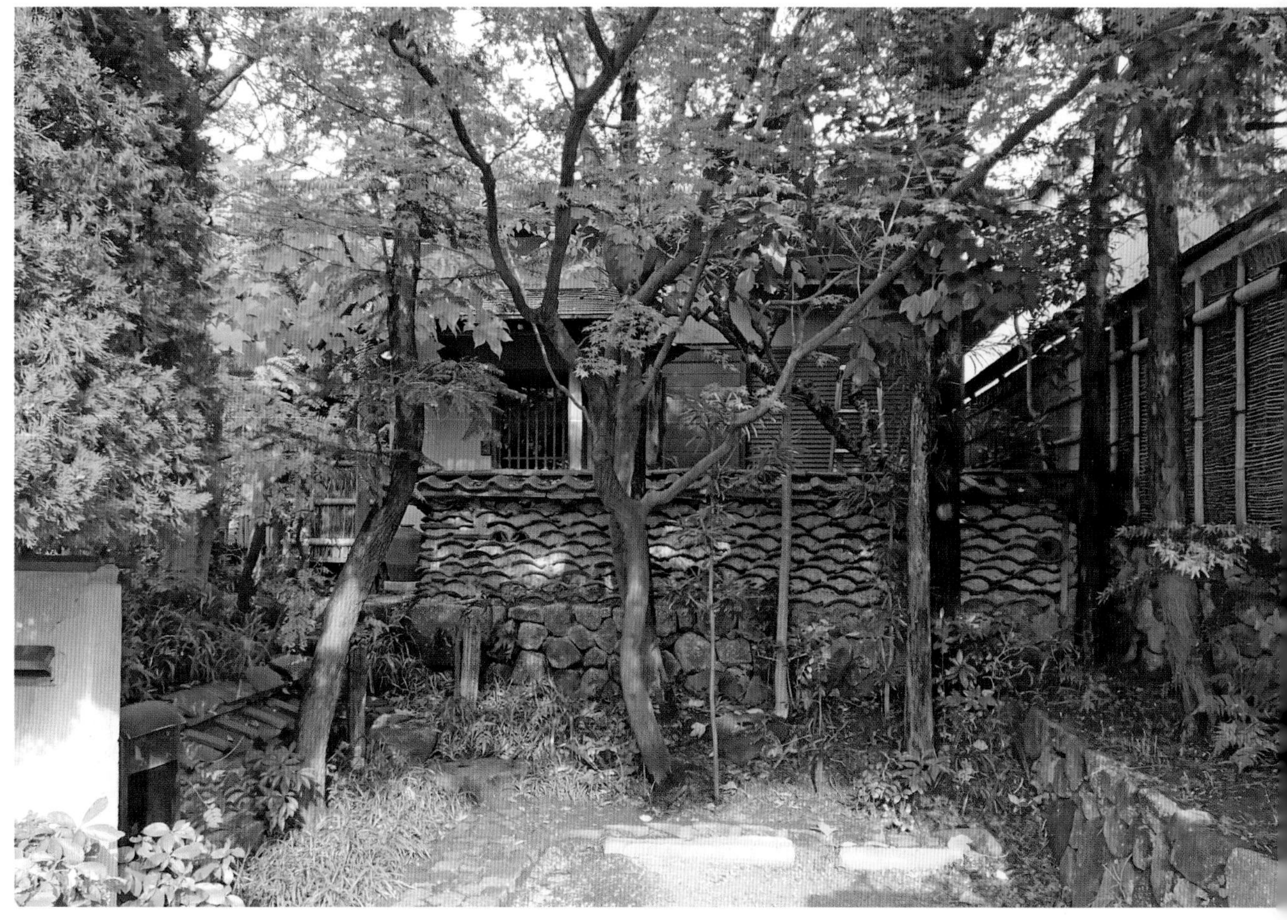

Garden of the NASA Astrophysicist

One of my neighbors, Dr. Koryo Miura, was a professor of astrophysics at Tokyo University until his retirement. He also spent several years at NASA. Dr. Miura is well known for developing a method of folding rigid surfaces, which has been used by the Japanese and American space agencies to deploy solar panels in space. His unique geometric structures have a high strength-to-weight ratio, which is now also used to create thin-walled aluminum cans for beer, soft drinks, and hot coffee. When he and his wife, who is a painter, made an addition to their home they asked me to make a garden.

The two-story house and the front garden are not very large. A 6½-foot (2-m)-tall concrete wall separates the property from the street. Inside this wall, the ground level is just 20 inches (51 cm) from the top edge. We planted a dense row of evergreen Chinese junipers that create an additional 6½-foot-tall enclosure. On the right side of the wall, at street level, are the car park and the entrance to the house. We made a tall *katsuragaki* bamboo fence, over a base of stone, to border the right side of the house along the car park. I lined the space with a combination of maples and bald cypress. The tall, straight cypresses make a year-round windbreak, and help block the view of the neighboring house. They also

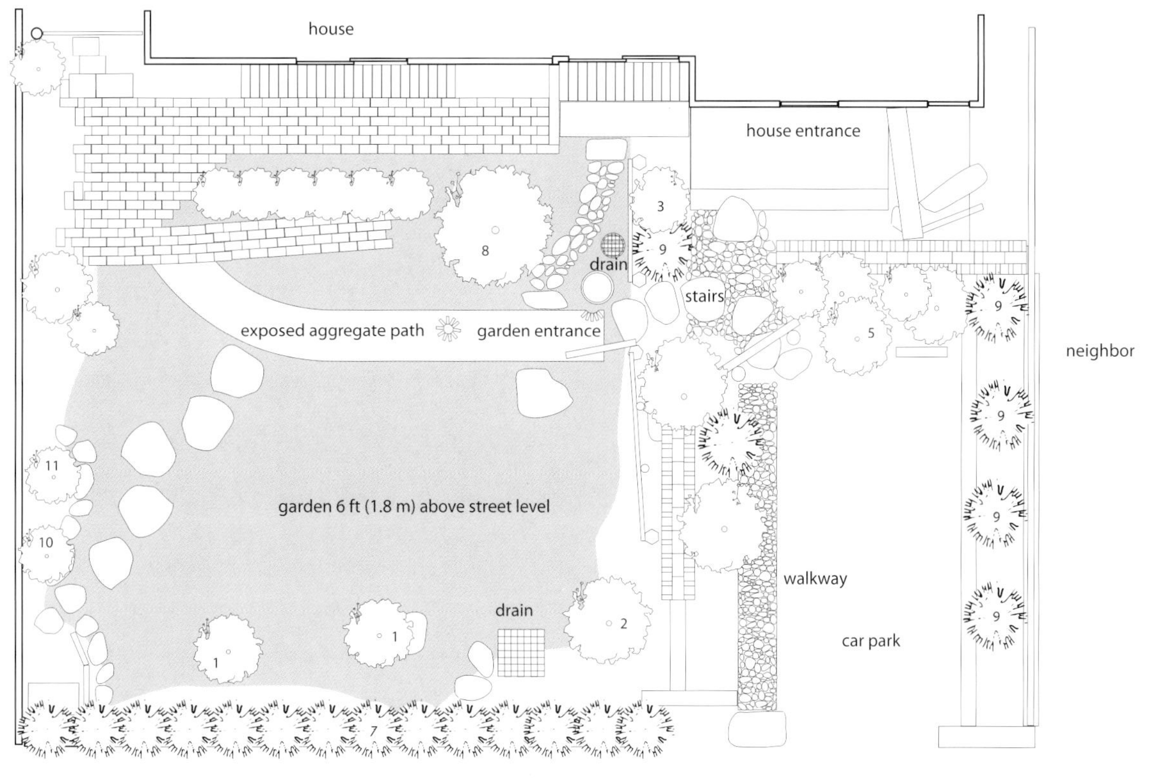

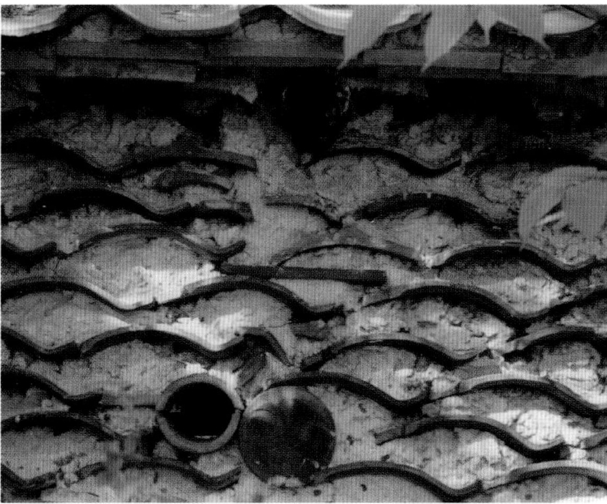

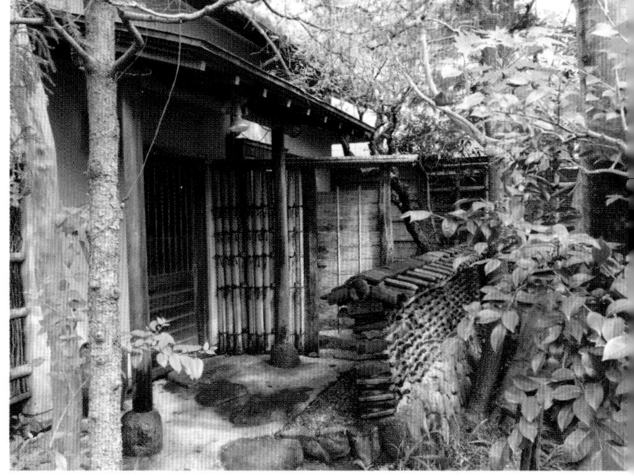

Facing page A car park at the front of the house can be a garden in its own right when the car is gone.

Above left The ceramic tiles from an old roof are combined with clay to make an attractive *neribei* clay-and-tile wall.

Above right The low wall forms a backdrop to the car park and a balustrade for the house entrance.

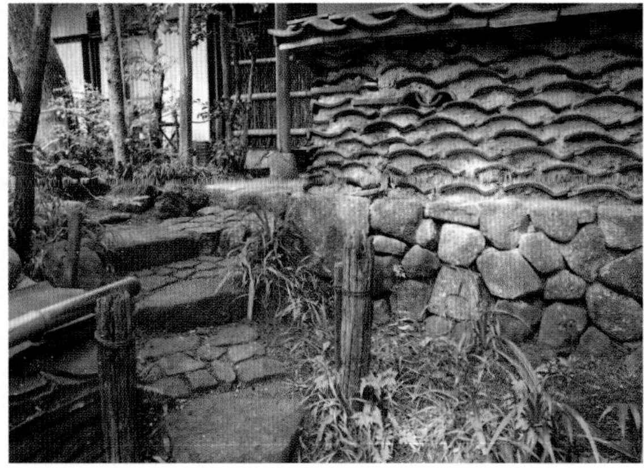

create a background for the maples that form a lovely canopy over the car park. From April to the end of November, they create a welcoming, bright green environment. Then, the hot mix of red and orange leaves warms up the last month of the year. Along the left side of the car park, an informal walkway leads to a stone stairway and the entrance to the house.

I will mention a few points about this garden that may be interesting. First, when the professor added a second floor to his house, he saved the tiles from the demolished roof. He hoped they would be useful in the new garden. I used the tiles in combination with clay on a base of stone to make an attractive wall that separates the house from the parking area. We had enough tiles to make an additional 20-inch (51-cm) retaining wall along the side of the walkway. This traditional-style wall, built with clay and ceramic roof tiles, of which there are many variations, is called a *neribei*. The house is at the same elevation as the garden, about 6 feet (1.8 m) above street level. I made stone steps that wrap around the wall, leading to the garden on the left and to the house entrance on the right.

Another point is that the soil in the garden was basically clay: not the best material for good plant growth. With the help of some of Dr. Miura's college students, we dug out about 4 feet (1.2 m) of soil and replaced it with a combination of volcanic loam (*akatsuchi*) and leaf mulch (*fuyodo*). I also made a drainage system, which helps keep the ground from getting muddy. Getting the soil and the drainage right is fundamental to creating a good garden. A number of the trees were taken from the garden of Mrs. Miura's family home in Odawara, about forty miles (65 km) west of Tokyo. These included magnolia, crape myrtle, persimmon, and others. I added a small weeping cherry tree. Now, forty years later, that magnificent tree is about 13 feet (4 m) tall. It creates a wonderful atmosphere in any season but especially when it blooms in April.

A final point is that Dr. Miura built a garage from plywood, based on the same geometric structure used for aluminum cans. If you imagine an aluminum can cut in half lengthwise and laid on its side, you will have some idea. It was a great success and occupied the space in front of his house for about a year, after which we tore it down to make the open driveway garden. Garages are not common in Japan; tearing one down to make a garden is unheard of. Of course, the space to park a car still exists, but it is much more pleasant now. The beauty of the trees, and of the simple stone, clay, and bamboo structures that harmonize with them, have created a rich environment that even a parked car can't diminish.

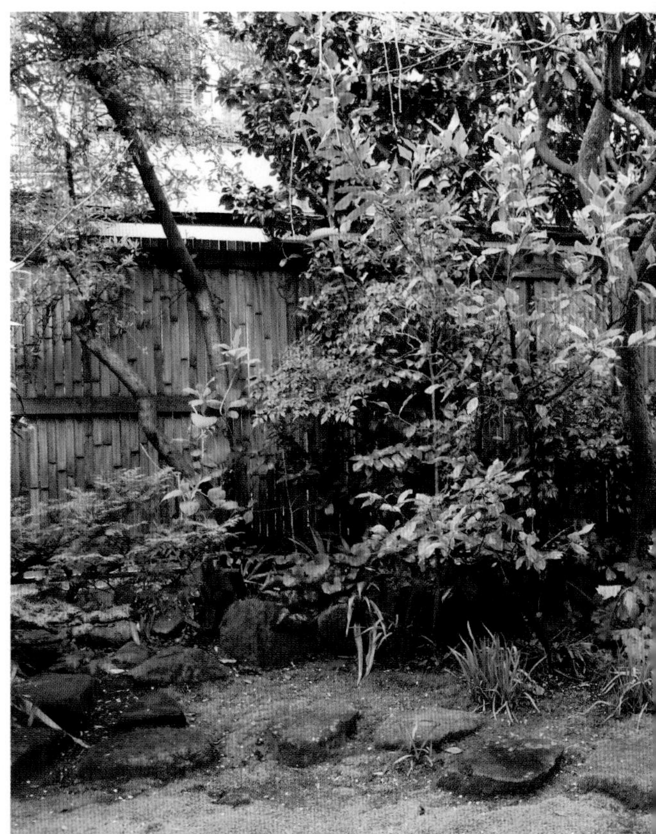

Facing page A stair at the rear of the parking space leads to the garden on the left and the house on the right.

Below The garden, bordered by a *kenninjigaki* fence of vertical split bamboo, named for the Zen temple where it originated.

Right, top A magnificent weeping cherry is a showpiece, especially when in bloom.

Right, bottom A sample of the type of folded surface that Dr. Miura invented; this one is cast in steel.

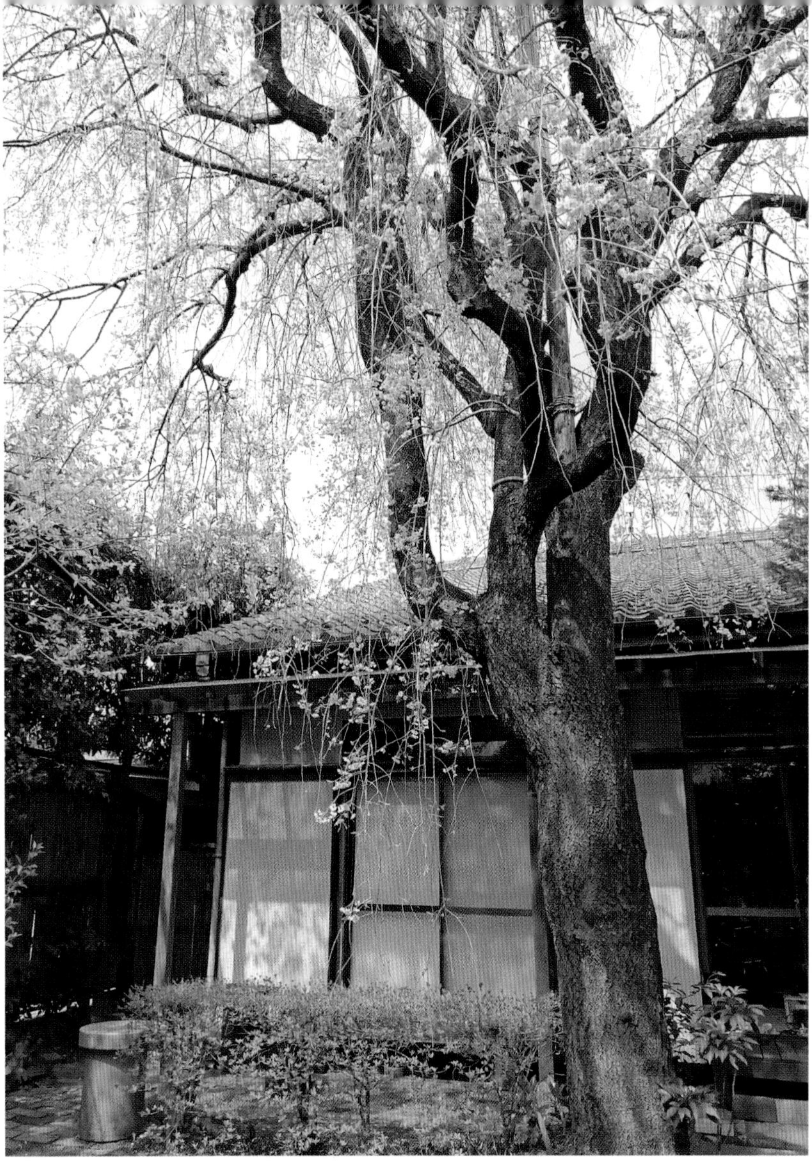

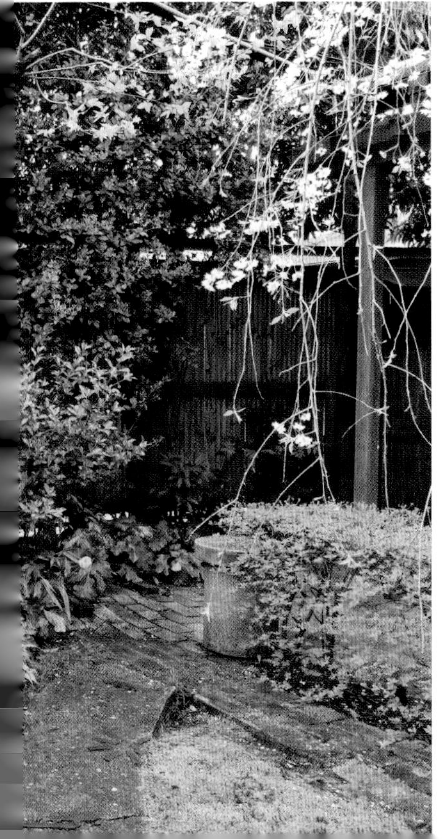

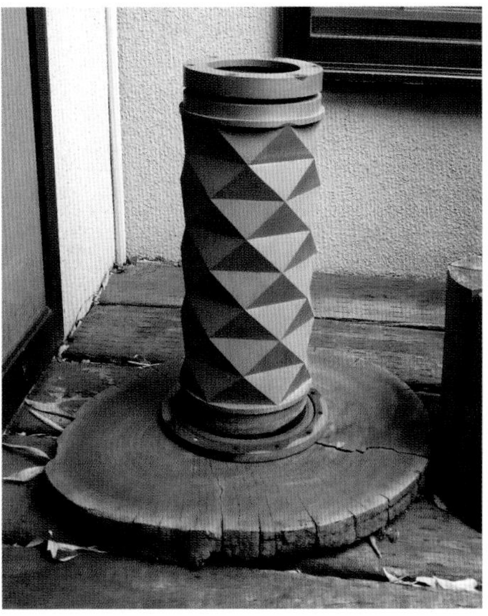

A Garden for Lasting Relations

When I first met the Nagaokas they had recently arrived in the Machida area of Tokyo, where I have lived and worked as a gardener for about sixty years. They are a vigorous and friendly couple that moved from Kyoto where they operated several Chinese restaurants. We created a lovely garden for the first house they built, and modified it when the house was rebuilt many years later. That was about forty-five years ago. We are still friends and we still maintain their garden.

The house has a 9½-foot (3-m) wall with a long shutter on the street side that conceals a parking space for three or four vehicles. Along the right side of the space, we made a 6½-foot (2-m)-tall *katsuragaki* bamboo fence on a base of stone. At the back of the parking space, we made a stone wall with concealed stairs that are the entrance to the garden. The wall is topped with an azalea hedge and above that, several Chinese junipers completely block the view of the garden within.

The main desire of the owner was to keep decorative carp, which we call *koi* in Japan, so I started by digging a hole to create a pond. Japanese gardens have evolved over thousands of years. Physically, they reflect the mountainous and lush landscape of the country. Water, in the form of lakes, rivers, streams, and waterfalls, is a big part of the scenery. But that is not the full picture. Just as

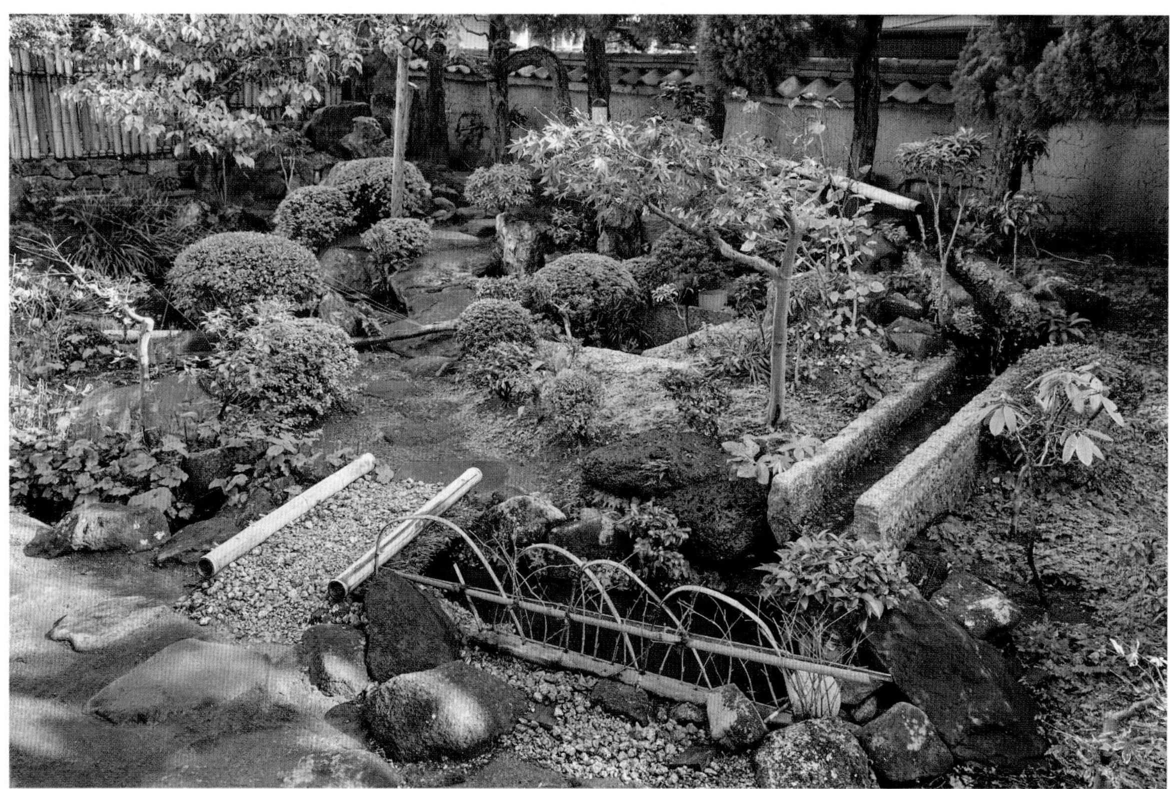

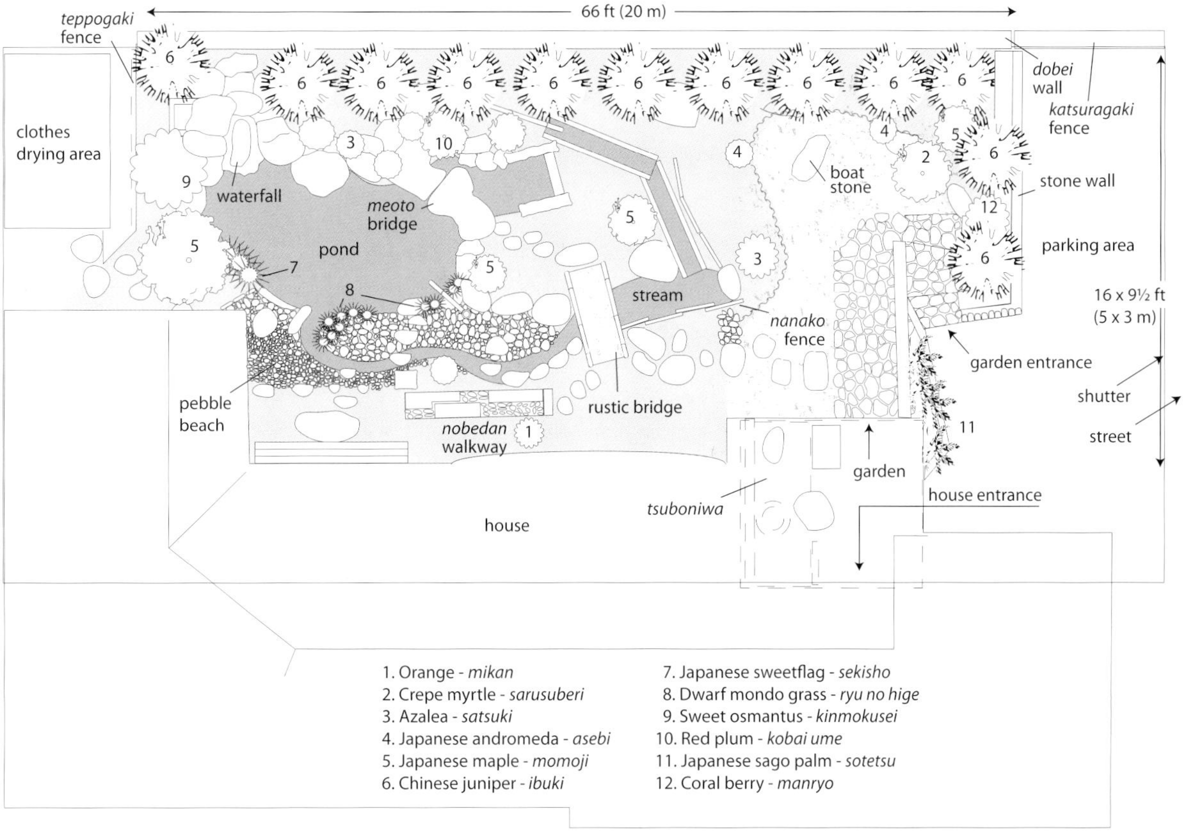

1. Orange - *mikan*
2. Crepe myrtle - *sarusuberi*
3. Azalea - *satsuki*
4. Japanese andromeda - *asebi*
5. Japanese maple - *momoji*
6. Chinese juniper - *ibuki*
7. Japanese sweetflag - *sekisho*
8. Dwarf mondo grass - *ryu no hige*
9. Sweet osmantus - *kinmokusei*
10. Red plum - *kobai ume*
11. Japanese sago palm - *sotetsu*
12. Coral berry - *manryo*

important is the philosophy that underlies every aspect of garden making. For example, although these days people are less mindful of such things, in times past they were concerned with warding off evil and avoiding taboos. That thinking was intimately connected to natural phenomena and many rules for making a house and garden developed from there.

For example, setting a stone horizontally that was found standing vertically in nature, could imply falling down or even dying. This would be an omen of bad luck for the owner. If you are familiar with feng shui, and particularly how it relates to good and bad directions, you get some idea of this concept. Later, garden design came to be influenced by Shinto animism and Buddhism. Next to the hidden entrance, behind the car park, I planted several small Japanese sago palm trees (*sotetsu*). The traditional symbolism here is that the pointed edges of the sotetsu keep the devil away. In the case of ponds, for example, the shape is often based on

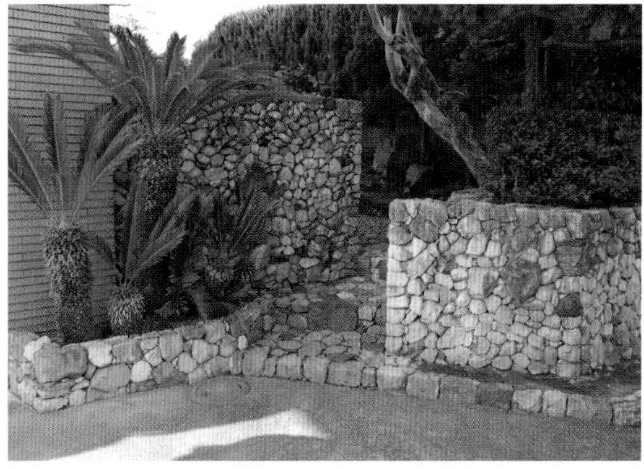

Facing page A rustic bridge made of wood and bamboo crosses a stream that leads deeper into the garden.

Above At the entrance to the garden the pointed edges of the sago palm keep the "devil" away.

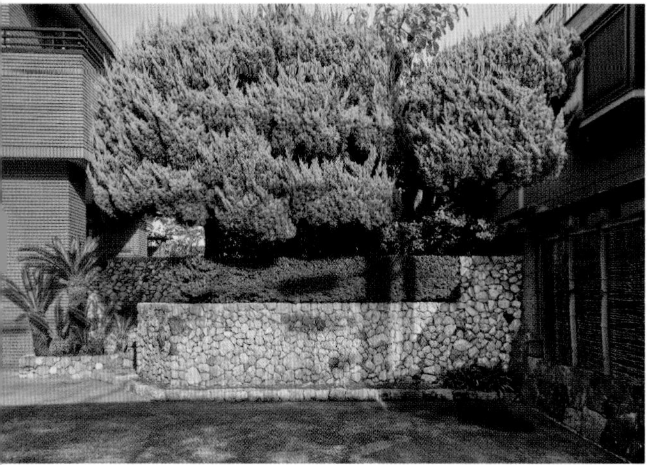

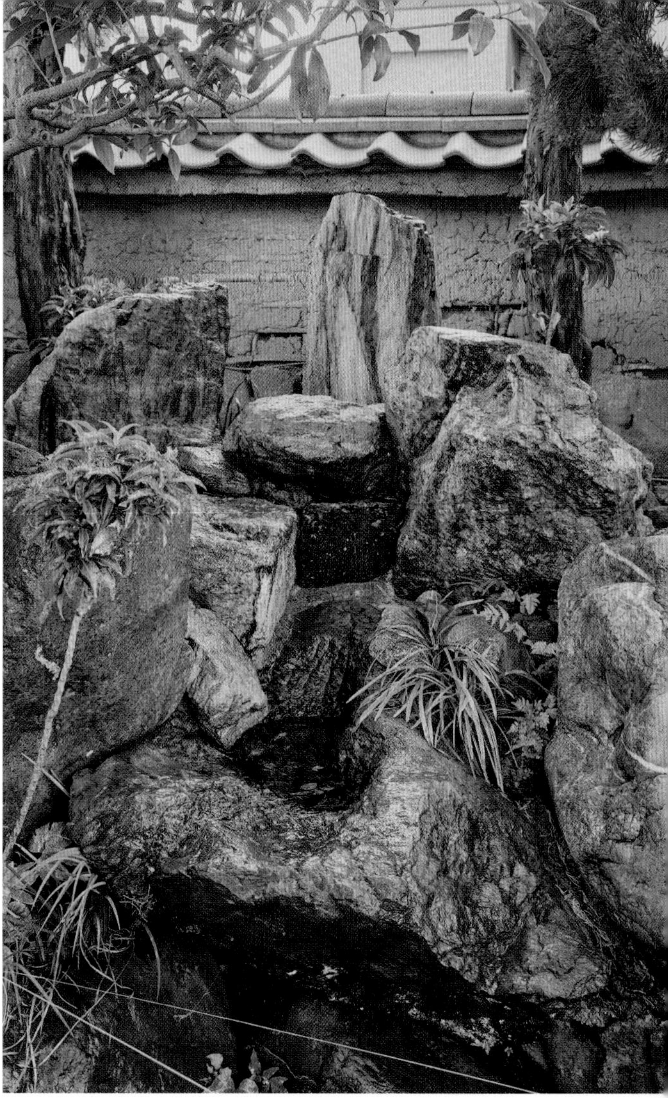

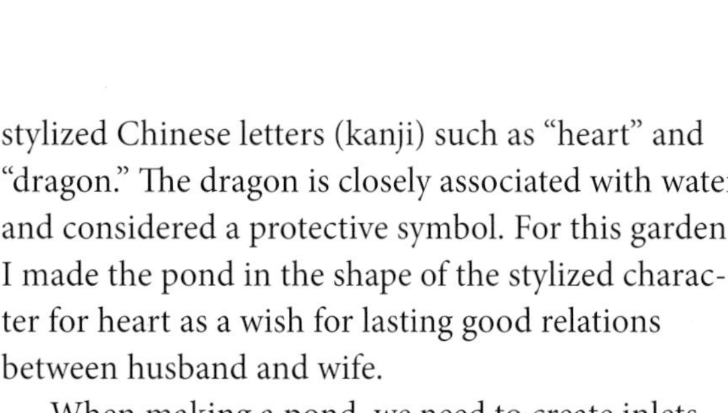

Above A *kuzurezumi* "crumbling" wall of limestone is topped by a hedge and a row of Chinese junipers.

Facing page, left Carp gather in the shade under the *meoto* "husband and wife" bridge. Water streams in from a bamboo pipe.

This page, right A waterfall with a *fudoseki* stone cascades water into the pond from the far right corner of the garden.

Facing page, right Two hand-cut stone gutters become covered with moss, lending them a patina of great age.

stylized Chinese letters (kanji) such as "heart" and "dragon." The dragon is closely associated with water and considered a protective symbol. For this garden I made the pond in the shape of the stylized character for heart as a wish for lasting good relations between husband and wife.

When making a pond, we need to create inlets and outlets for the water. In nature, water flows from the mountains to the sea, so in the garden, stones are piled up in the far corner of the pond and water is made to flow from there to a lower point. In cities, where water is costly, a recirculation system must be devised. The water is captured at a well-disguised outlet, and returned to the high point over the stones, from where it cascades again into the pond. About half of the total volume of water should be recirculated every two hours. The timing and the volume of water in the pond determine the size of the pump. In this garden, water cascading over rocks in the left rear side of the pond is one recirculated source. However, because the pond will support carp, it needs more aeration than a single source provides. So another outlet sends water down a hand-cut stone gutter on the right of the pond, while a third spills water through a bamboo pipe on the pebble beach.

Of course, all this planning takes place before you take the biggest step: digging a hole. For this size pond, we rent a mini digger. First, we lay out the shape with a white powder, such as lime or chalk, and dig to a depth of 5 feet (1.5 m). The bottom and walls of the pond are sealed with tamped clay made up of 1 part limestone (*sekkai*), ⅒ part magnesium chloride (*nigari*), and 1 part soil made up of

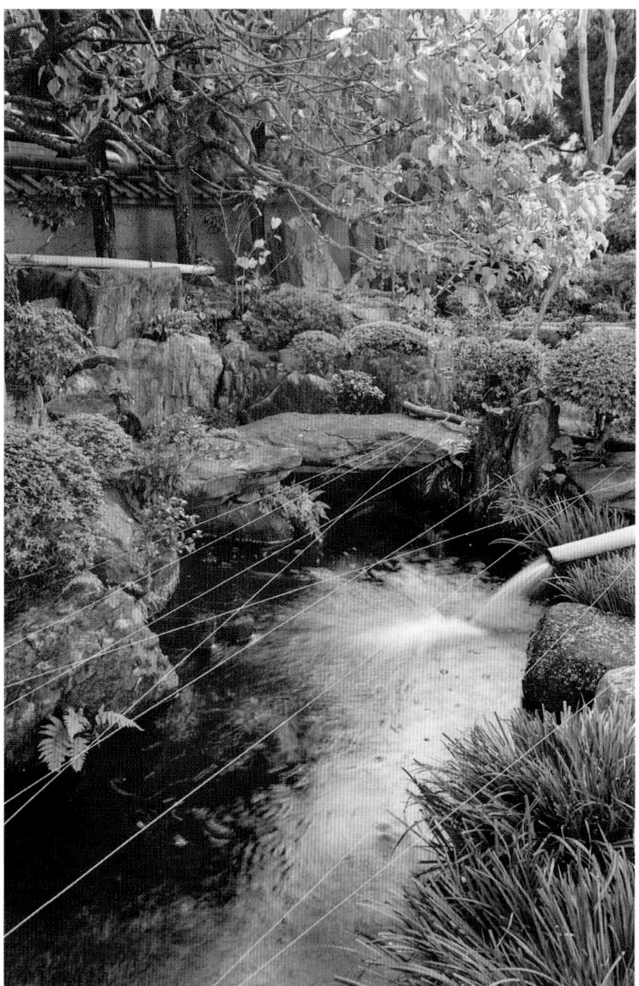

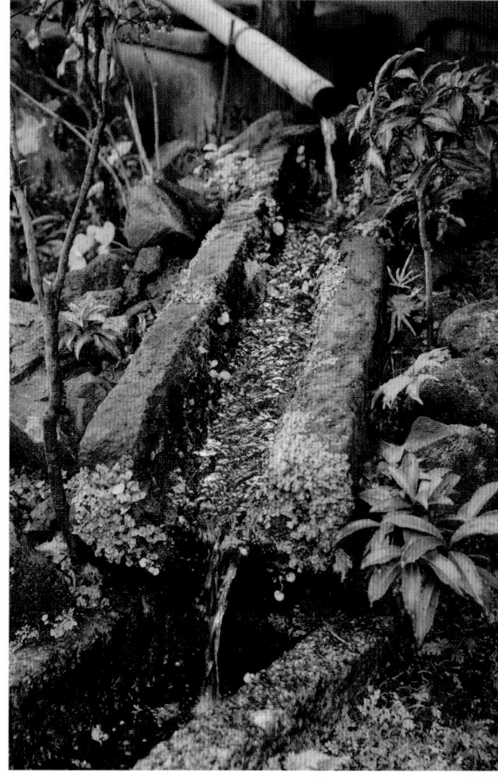

decomposed granite (*masatsuchi*) and volcanic loam (*akatsuchi*) in equal parts. Mixed together with a small amount of water and pounded, it hardens like concrete. Finally, we poured about 6 inches (15 cm) of concrete and sealed it with a waterproof coating. Drains, pipes, and electrical wiring are placed before the pond lining is finished. The pond should be filled and the recirculation pump and water level checked. It is essential to know the final water level before placing the waterfall stones and the stones around the edge of the pond, and for the height of the stone bridge. It is also important for making a pebble beach of rounded river stones. The beach is partly submerged and extends beyond the edge of the pond, giving it the impression of being larger than it is.

We constructed a stone bridge called the *meoto* (husband-and-wife) bridge. This is another symbolic wish for harmony that is often used in Japan. Two irregular-shaped slabs meet in the middle and are supported on stones set into the pond. The most famous example of this philosophy are the *meoto iwa* of Futami Okitama Shrine in Mie Prefecture; these are two large rocks in the bay, connected with a thick rope. Besides its symbolic nature, a bridge serves two practical purposes: it allows easy access to the area of the garden behind the pond, and gives the carp a shady place to hide in the middle of a hot day. A rustic bridge of wood, bamboo, twigs, and gravel provides a place to cross the stream flowing from the stone gutter to the pond. It also gives the impression of a long-forgotten mountain passage.

In some ways this garden is a classic *tsukiyama* hill-and-pond type. The basic physical elements of

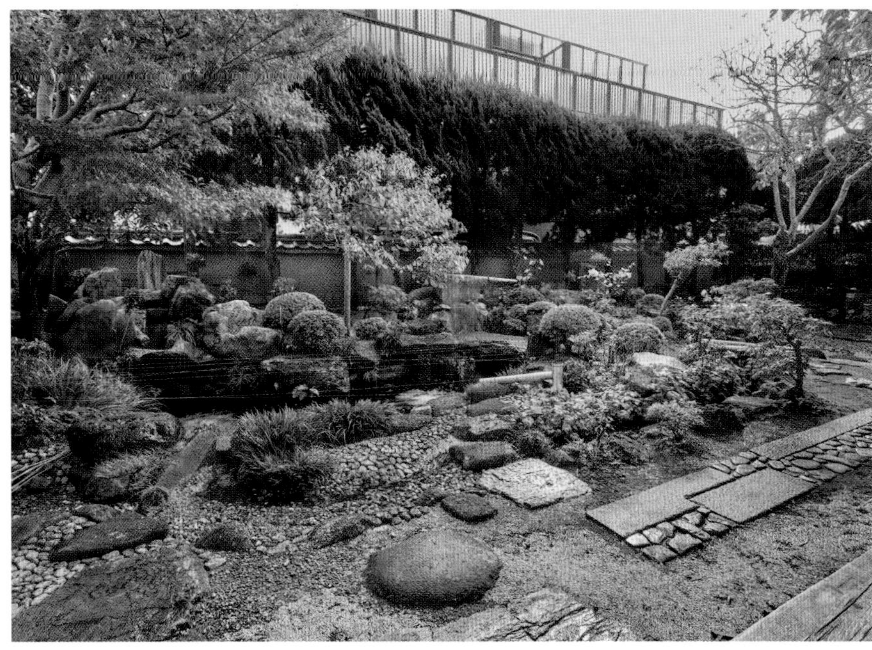

Right A *nobedan* stone walkway and stepping stones define a path to the pebble beach. Chinese junipers block the view of the building next door.

Below Stepping stones cross a trickle of water leading to the pond edge.

the garden are water, stone, plants, and mounded earth. Again, the aim is to create a vision of the natural landscape. In practical terms, when you dig a big hole, you have a lot of soil to dispose of. This is your material for creating hills. Creating a variety of elevations gives the garden a basic structure, which is already visually interesting before any stones or plants are placed. Just as in nature, hills in the distance give a great feeling of mystery and depth. Stones are set for purposes such as waterfalls and bridges, but also serve to keep piled earth from sliding. Imagine rocks tumbling down a mountain and lodging at various critical points in the landscape when you decide where to place your stones. Stones are also used around the edge of the pond to segregate the water from the surrounding soil. These stones are called *gogan*.

This is not a strict order of work, but with pond, hills, and stones in place, it becomes easier to visualize where plants would naturally occur. Trees often grow in the stable soil built up behind stones. Some trees and plants like to be close to water, where they are nourished by the evaporation. But always keep in mind that your garden is *arranged* nature. That means the elements are not haphazard: the viewpoints from which they will be seen help determine their placement. This includes things you

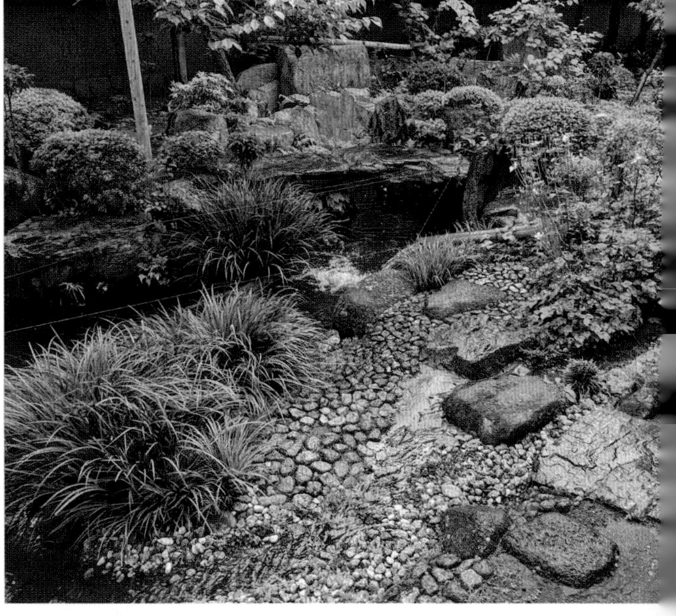

want to highlight as well as things you wish to obscure. The viewpoints here are through the sliding glass doors of the living room and from the garden entrance. In the case of Nagaoka-san's garden, a clay wall (*dobei*) and a row of tall Chinese junipers obstruct the things we don't want to see, such as the view of the neighboring apartment house. On the other hand, the visually dynamic crape myrtle (*sarusuberi*) is placed near the entrance on the right side of the garden. The bark of the tree is interesting in itself when the leaves have fallen in the winter. In the summer months, an abundance of pink flowers presents a stunning appearance. If this tree had been placed in front of the pond it would overwhelm and even block the view.

Visualizing the size and form the plant will ultimately take is important. It is cost prohibitive to begin with fully mature plants, and the original size when planted may be only a fraction of the final dimensions. Of course, cutting and shaping plants is a part of yearly maintenance and this also controls the size and shape. Removing and discarding plants is also an option. But first have an overall vision of how you want your garden to turn out and plan for that. Talk to your nursery to understand how certain plants fare in the local environment. The plant will not grow to its full potential if the soil and weather conditions are not right for it. Take advice where you can and leave the rest to trial and error. Walk around your neighborhood and see which plants are flourishing. Then use some of the techniques in this book to adopt them inside your Japanese garden.

A boat stone glides on a sea of gravel, behind a great crape myrtle with a beautiful bark inside the garden entrance.

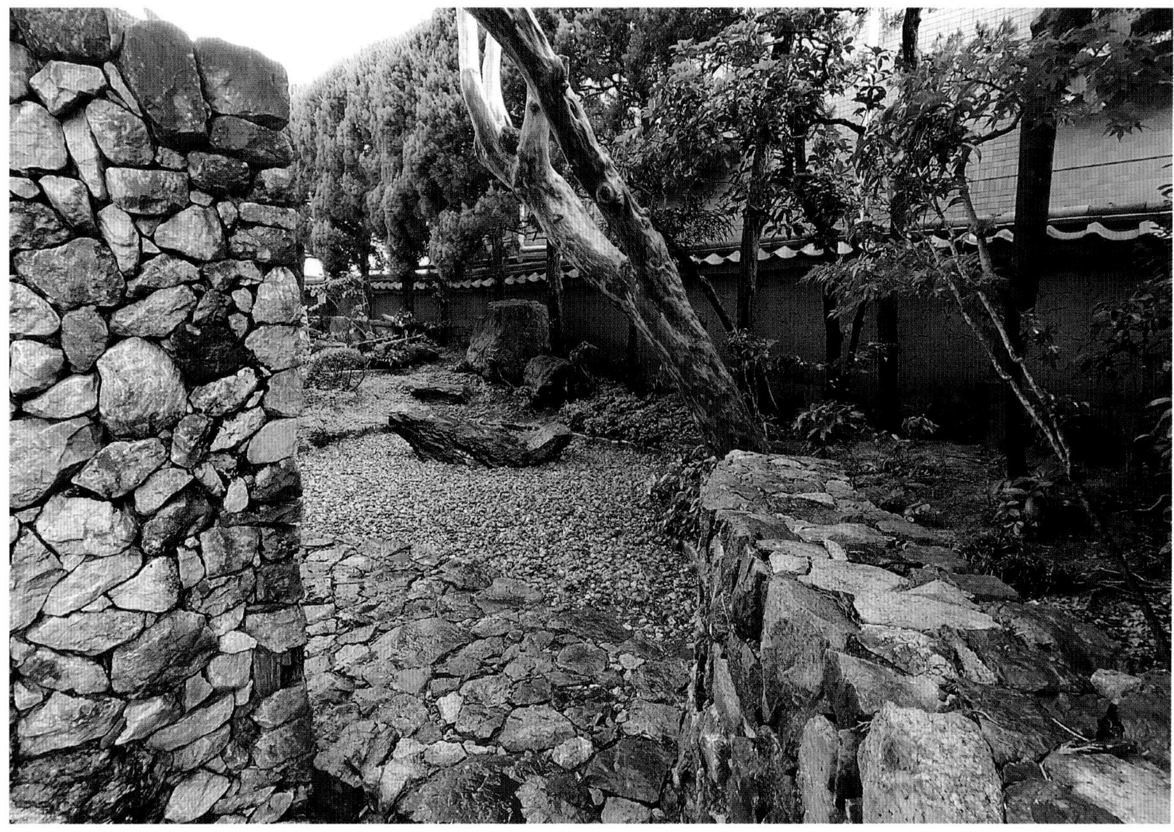

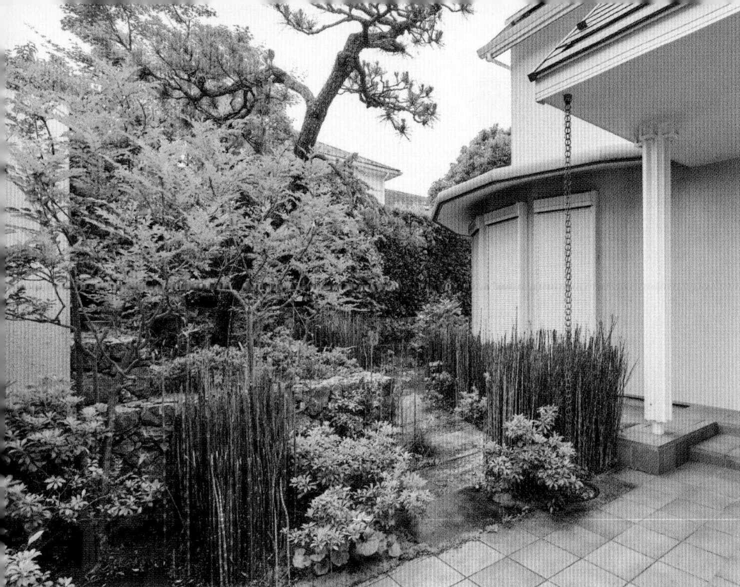

Left A modern tiled entrance gives way to a rich green garden that envelops the left side of the house.

Below A stone path made of *oyaishi* quarried stone echoes the tiled entrance but with a very rich texture.

A Professor's Terrace of Stone, Horsetails, and Water

Morishige-sensei is a former professor of Russian history. When he retired, he rebuilt his father's old house which was vacant at the time. It is now a modern building situated in a cul-de-sac that ends at the Tsurugawa River in Tokyo. He was originally interested in doing some fruit-growing although he never took to the hobby. But based on this idea, I created a terraced field of trees, reminiscent of a grove you might come across in the mountainous countryside. Terracing a mountainside to grow rice, fruits and vegetables is typical in Japan.

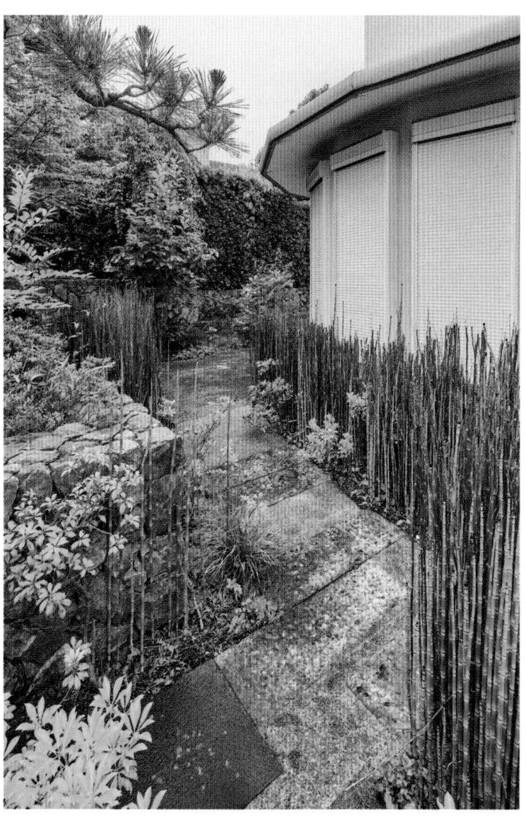

The house occupies most of a 5,000-square-foot (480-m^2) lot with its entrance on the narrow, 54-foot (16.5-m) side facing the street. A modern-style tile walkway leads straight from the fence on the street side to the front door. The car-parking area, with a shelter made of aluminum and plastic, is on the right side of the walkway. These are parts over which I had no control. In a traditional layout, an entryway would weave or turn, to prolong the journey and to keep from having a direct line of sight from the street. On the way to the front door, the entrance to the garden is on the left. We made an informal stone

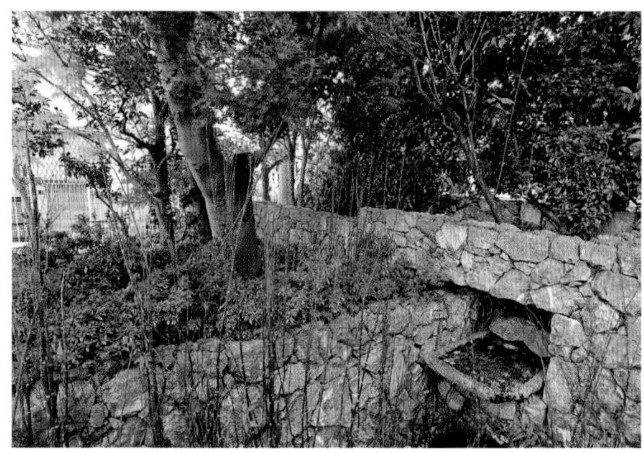

Above Natural granite walls of different heights intersect at a gutter that drips water for the horsetails.

Below Further back into the garden, another gutter extends from the terrace near the large magnolia.

path that wraps around the left side of the house and leads deeper into the garden. We used a combination of tamped clay (*tataki*) and *oyaishi*, which is volcanic tuff cut from mines deep underground in the Utsunomiya area of eastern Japan. It is soft but durable and used throughout the country for walls and floors. Other stone and many of the trees were salvaged from the old garden, and new materials added.

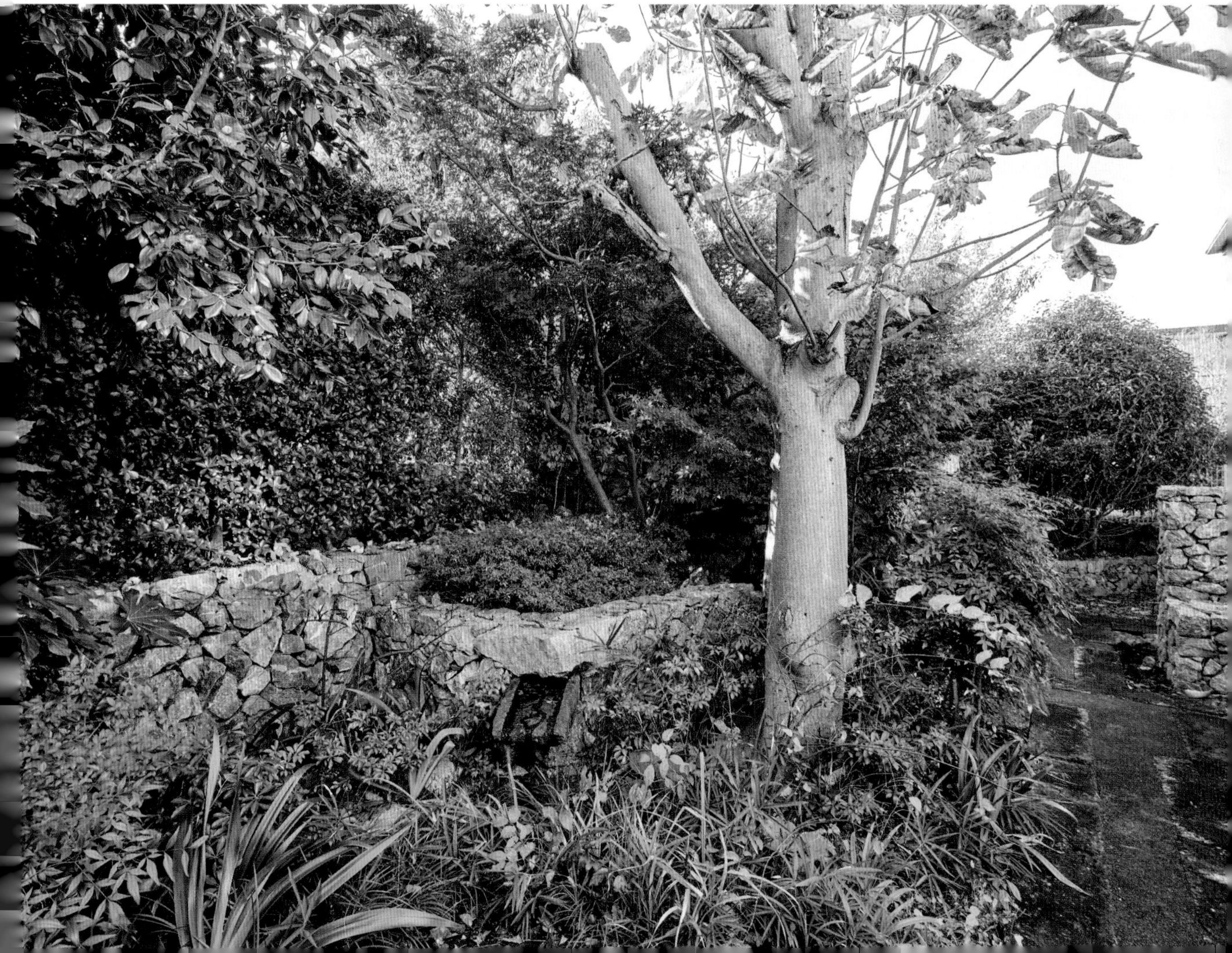

There are a lot of windows on the left side of the house including a rotunda. It is the natural place for the garden but it also faces three of the neighbors' homes. The space is less than 10 feet (3 m) deep at the narrowest part and 17½ feet (5.3 m) at the widest. My first job was to block the view of the neighbors' homes with a tall hedge of ubame oak (*ubamegashi*). I did this by first making a 4-foot (1.2 m) stone wall along that side of the property, and another one inside of and parallel to the first. This created a retainer that I could fill with soil. It also allowed me to make a taller hedge with smaller trees. I used a mix of volcanic loam (*akatsuchi*) and leaf mulch (*fuyodo*). The volcanic loam retains moisture and allows the roots to spread. The leaf mulch provides nourishment.

There was an existing 20-inch (51-cm) curved cement wall with a wire fence mounted to it along the street to the left of the walkway. The low wall provided one side of a planting space. For the other side, I made several taller stone walls attached at 90 degrees to the wall running along the neighbor's property. This extended the planting area and created the garden entrance. Projecting from one of the walls, I made a stone gutter, which drips water to

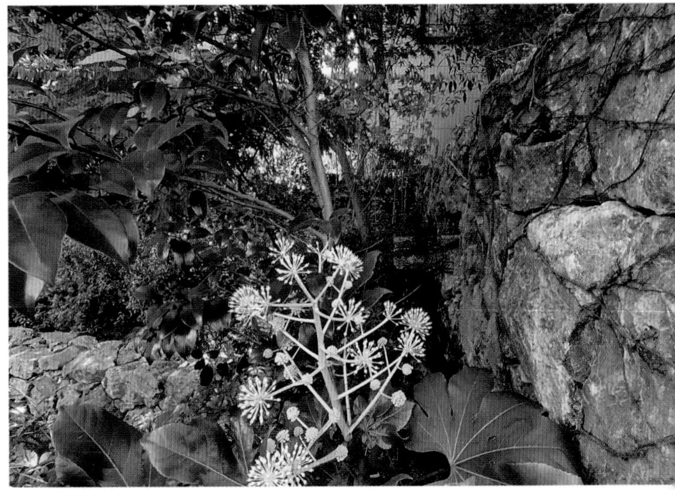

Above Maples and stone make for a wonderful backdrop to the paperplant (*yatsude*) in full bloom.

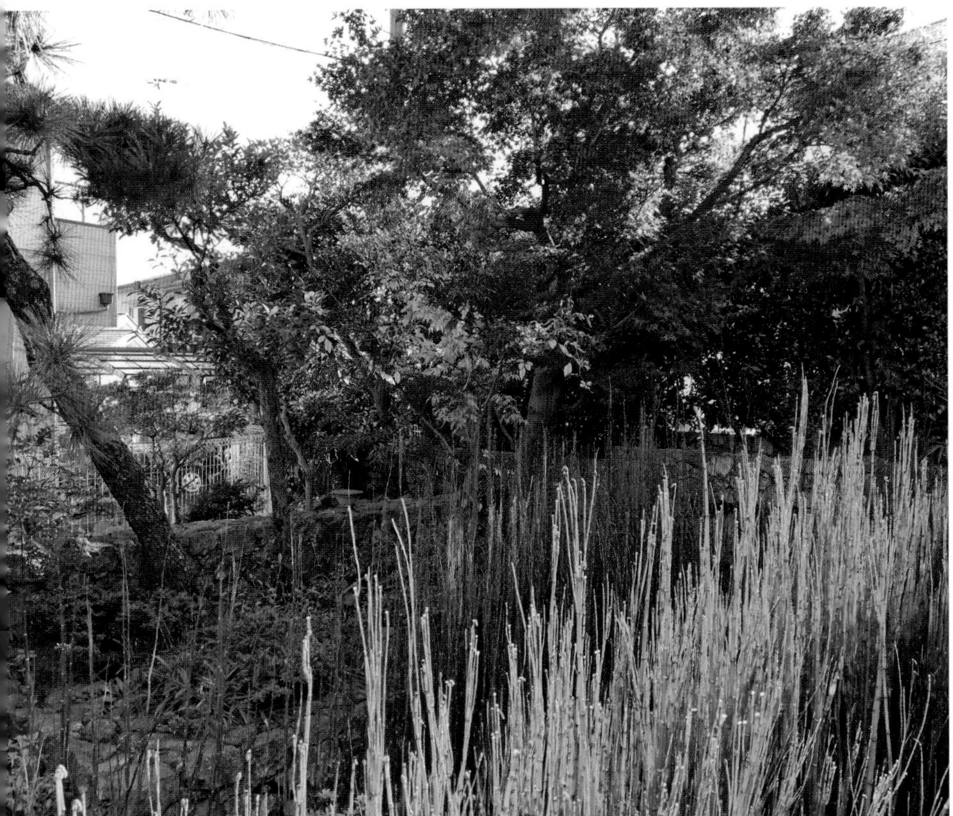

Left Horsetails (*tokusa*) glow bright green in the light against the brilliant reds and yellows of the maples.

Below A stone birdbath highlights the coexistence of nature and the manmade.

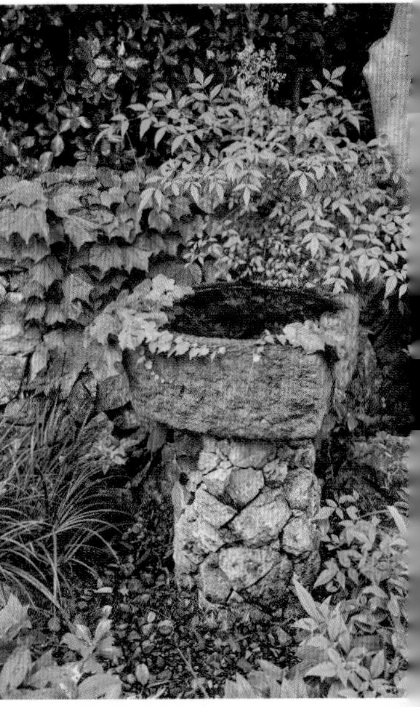

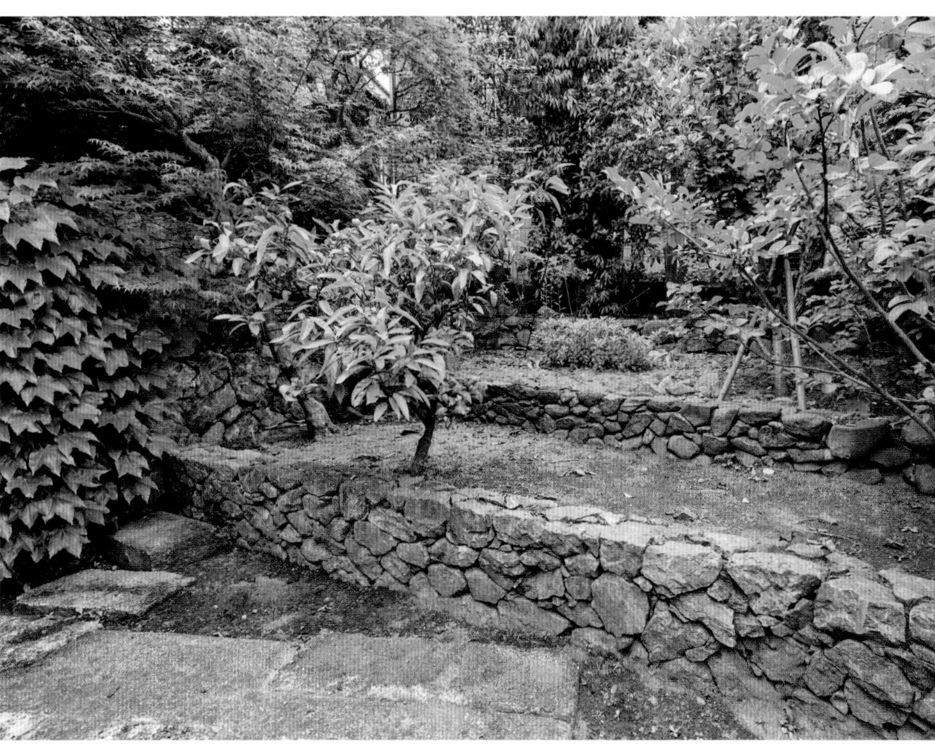

Right Three levels of stone and soil planted terraces extend the depth of the garden beyond easy view.

run along the bottom of the wall. Between the wall and the informal stone entrance path, and between the path and the house, we planted horsetails (*tokusa*). Rivers' edges and flood plains are the natural habitat of this plant. They even grow in standing water to a height of about 4 feet (1.2 m). They also grow wild around rice fields. Horsetail doesn't require any maintenance but will overtake other plants if no barriers are put in place. In this case, the stone wall and stone path are enough to restrain lateral growth. The Japanese name for the plant means "scouring rush" because the dried plant was once used for polishing wood and metal.

Further back in the garden are two more of these gutters and a stone birdbath. The feeling of flowing water along with the terraced stone, gives an image of nature in the foothills—a common scene in mountainous Japan. At the far end of the garden there was a bit more depth, which I emphasized by making a stepped terrace in three levels. Each level is about 1 foot (30 cm) tall and between 2 and 4 feet (60 to 120 cm) deep. Planting trees on each of these levels created a sense of great depth as well as layers of green in different shades and shapes—just like any natural landscape. Some plants cannot even be seen until you climb the terrace. In addition to the ubame oak, I planted many Japanese maples, weeping plum, and black pine. Close to the house I planted hydrangea and mountain camellia for some seasonal color. This garden does not fit neatly into any typical Japanese garden type, but that's okay.

The large existing Japanese magnolia, which both the owner and I wanted to preserve, became a natural limit for the position of the terrace close to the house side. Although I normally keep larger trees further back in the garden, it is an important attribute and part of the history of the land. Modifying the design to accommodate existing features is a facet of Japanese gardens. Cutting out a piece of fence or changing the shape of a path to allow a tree to spread is always preferable to destroying something of value.

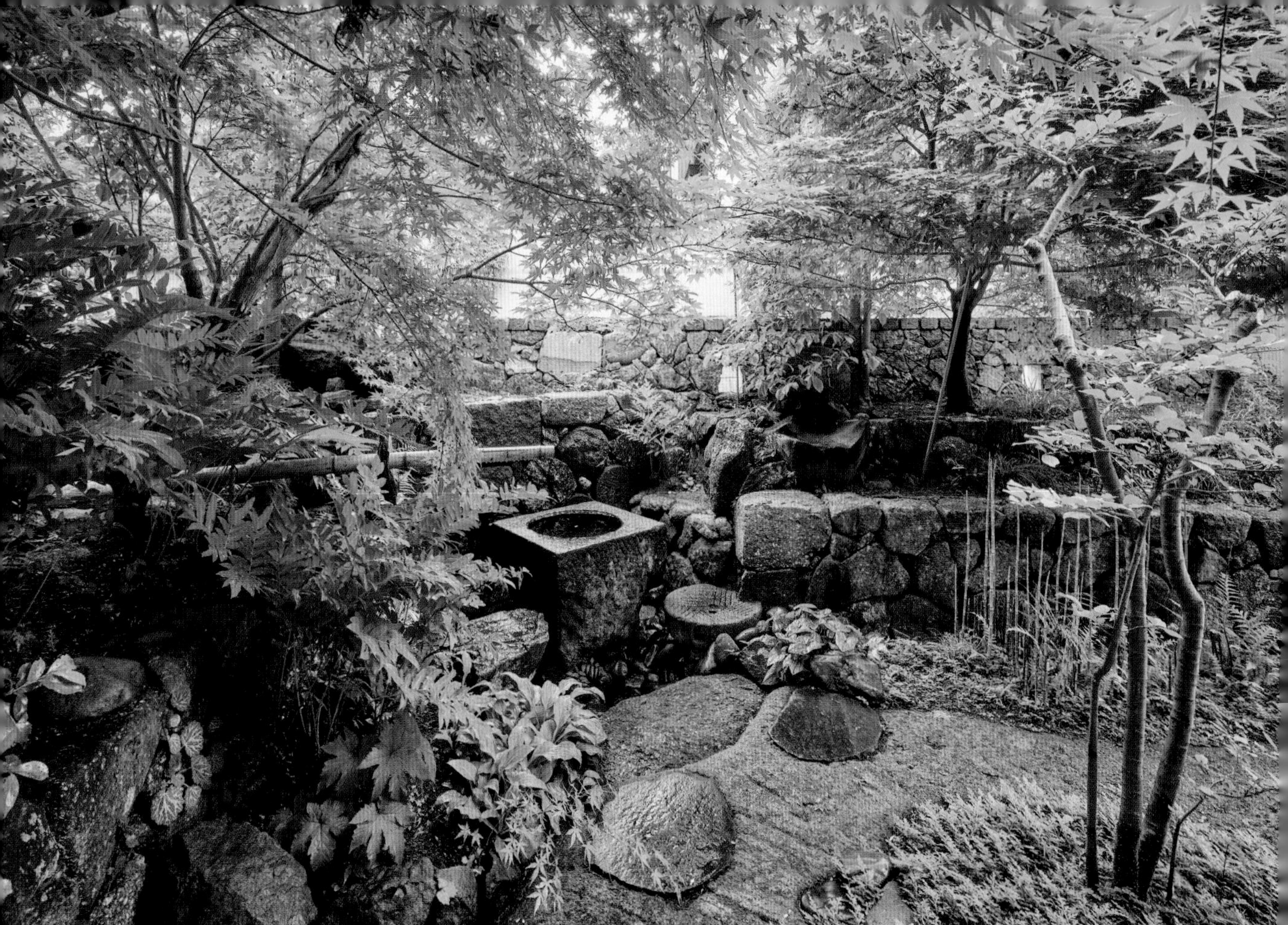

The Salaryman's Rice Terrace Garden

A neighbor of mine is what you call a company employee and we call a salaryman—in this case, a salaried employee of a large department store. He visits clients' homes with a selection of products tailored to their needs, based on expressed preferences. As a result, he must personally acquaint himself with many customers and have a wide-ranging knowledge. He collects statuettes and designed the interior of his home. He is not a wealthy man but he has a nice house and asked me to make a small garden. The garden is at the front of the house behind a 5-foot (1.5-m)-tall cement wall and also runs along one side of the house. The entrance is through a door in the left side of the wall and the car park is next to this at the far left. The thing you immediately notice about the door is the low height, which reflects the owner's interest in the Japanese culture of tea. Behind the house is a good-sized field where he grows fruits and vegetables for his family's use. Recently he has taken to growing flowers too.

The garden can be called rice-terrace style (*tanada fu*), similar to the style I used in the garden of Morishige-sensei (page 34). The reason is the same: to lend greater depth to a space less than 10 feet (3 m) deep. Next to the front of the house is a tiled patio, 4 feet (1.2 m) deep. Between this and the wall at the front of the property, we made a two-step stone terrace, planted with trees only on the step

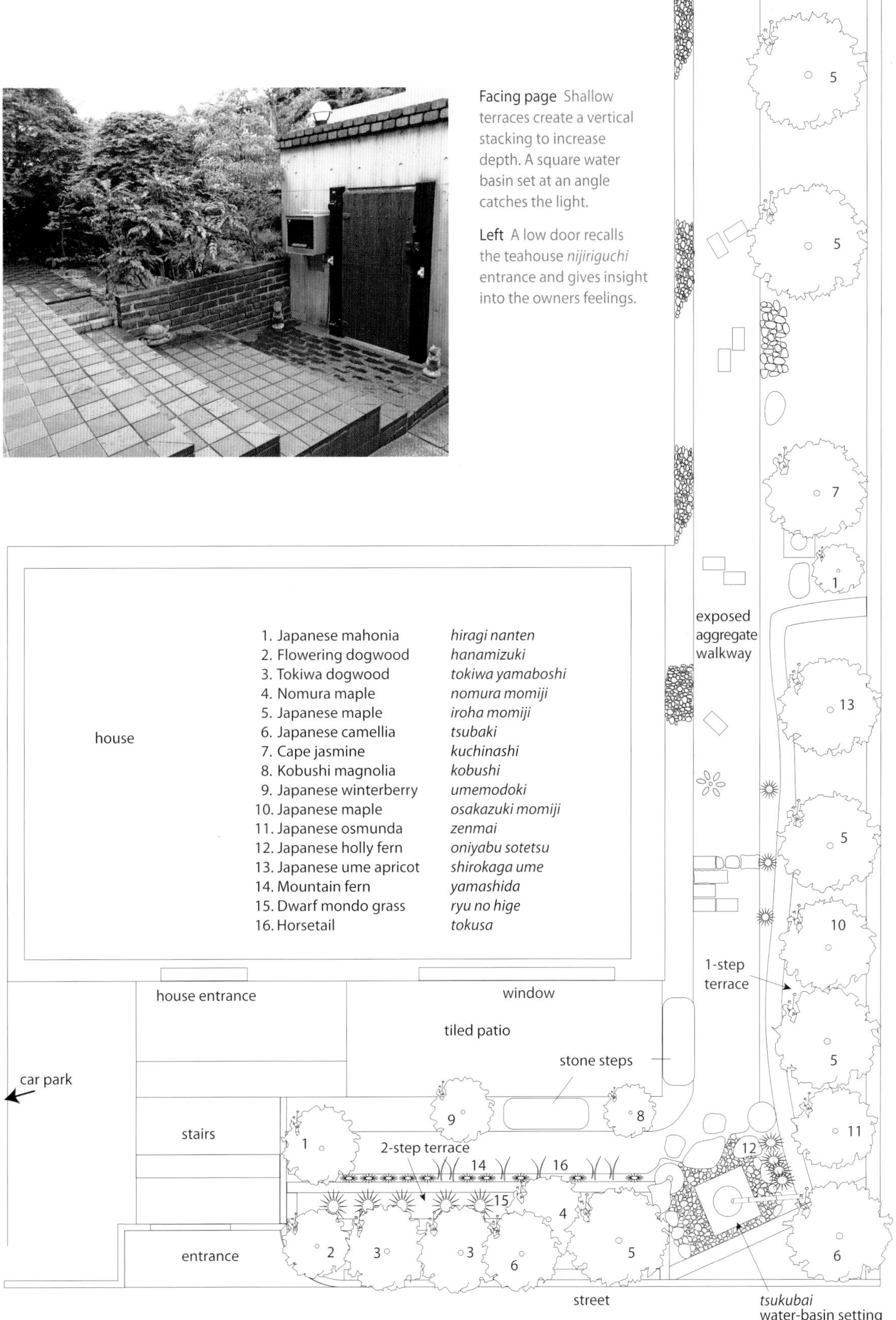

Facing page Shallow terraces create a vertical stacking to increase depth. A square water basin set at an angle catches the light.

Left A low door recalls the teahouse *nijiriguchi* entrance and gives insight into the owners feelings.

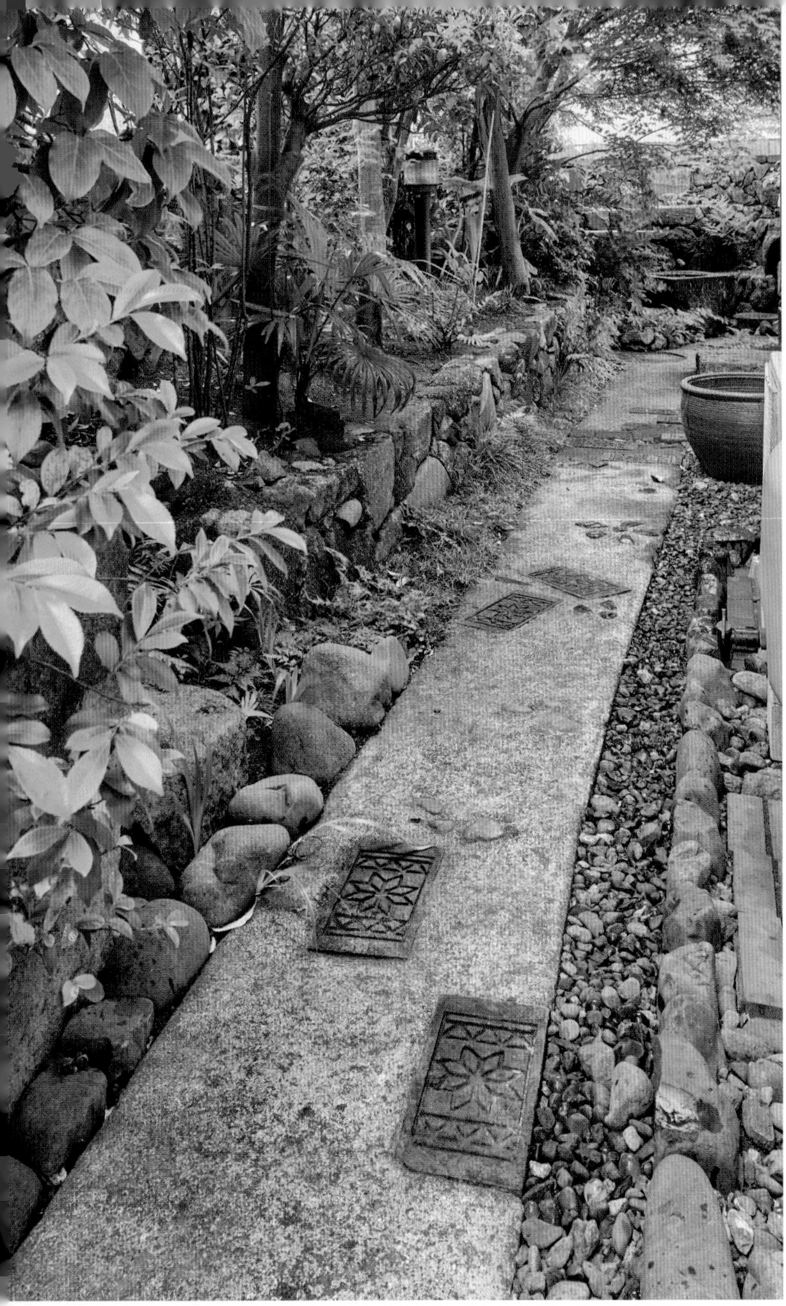

Left The exposed-aggregate (*araidashi*) path at the side of the house is inlaid with tiles collected by the owner.

Below The square water basin (*chozubachi*) seems almost like another terrace, filled with water, as a rice terrace would be in planting season.

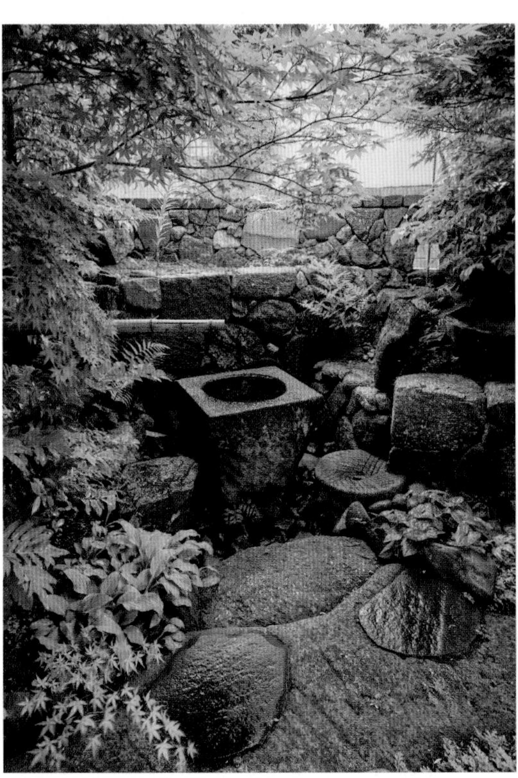

furthest from the house, creating a greater impression of depth than would be expected from such a small space. At about 2 feet (60 cm) tall, the first step of the rough stone terrace is about level with the patio height. The second step is a foot above that and the wall behind that (the back of the cement wall) 2 feet above that. Sitting in a chair on the patio, the top of the cement wall is just above eye level.

We surfaced the wall with a smaller size of the same stone and carried the wall around the side of the property. We also made one 2-foot-tall step around the side of the house. In the corner, we made an angled wall the same height as the second step. In front of this we made a *tsukubai* water-basin arrangement with a square *chozubachi* water basin also set at an angle. The hole made for the tsukubai creates a dark shadow that also magnifies the depth. Along the top terrace we planted two types of Japanese dogwood, Japanese camellia and two types of Japanese maple. The height and positions of the trees were calculated to have the leaf growth begin at the top of the wall. The result is to block the view of

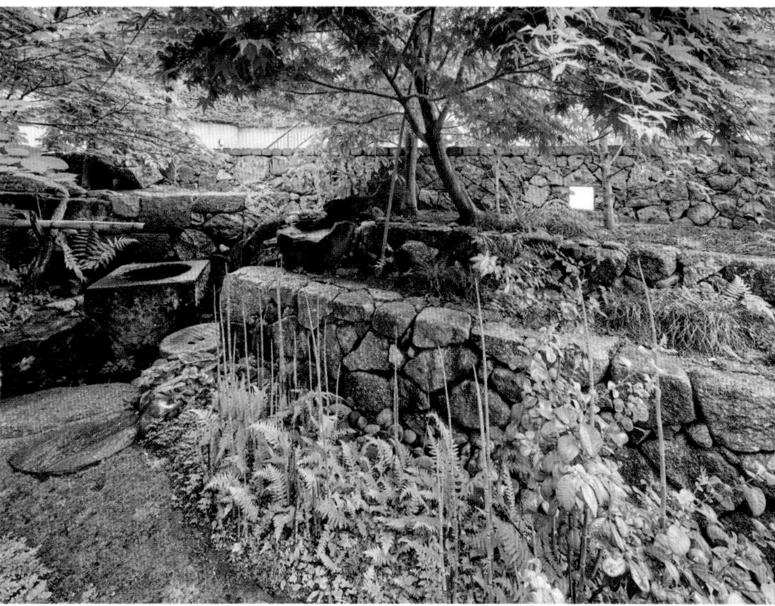

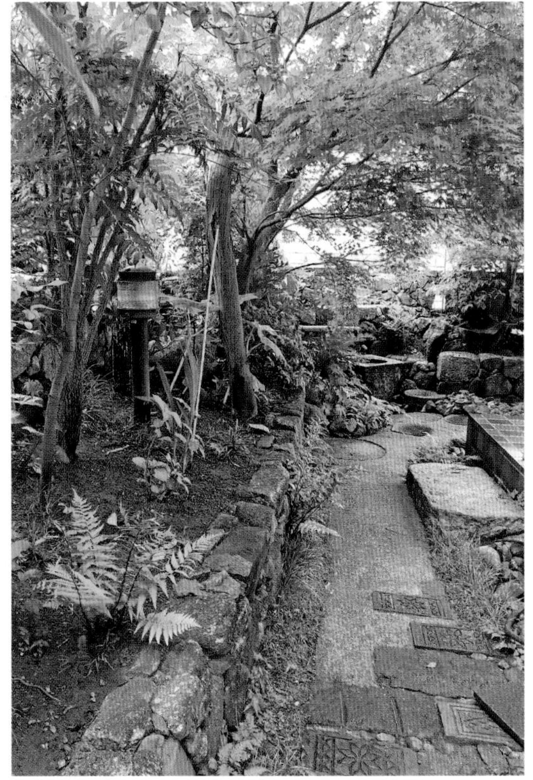

Left The path is lined with trees set in a low terrace, creating a pleasant environment that extends to the back of the house.

Above Holly fern, dragon's beard, sweet flag and other *yama no kusa* mountain grasses found where water is plentiful, give a true feeling of a mountain landscape.

the street to a height well above the wall level. The effect is beautiful from inside and outside the garden. As I mentioned already, an entrance garden should enhance the neighborhood environment.

In the step at the side of the house we planted more Japanese maples, camellia, Japanese mahonia, and flowering plum. The step only extends halfway to the rear of the house but it is about 2 feet (60 cm) deep. Where it curves to an end, we placed a tall chozubachi water basin and continued planting directly into the ground, all the way to the back of the property. We also made an exposed-aggregate (*araidashi*) walkway, about 2 feet wide, and inserted stones and terracotta tiles that the owner had collected. Stones and gravel border the walkway. When the walkway reaches the front garden, it joins with the exposed-aggregate floor that sits between the tiled patio and the terrace.

The first step of the terrace is very narrow. As mentioned, we didn't plant trees there, as it was too close to the patio. Instead, on this level, and around the base of the stone and along the walkways, we planted mountain fern, Japanese holly fern, dragon's beard grass, sweet flag, horsetails, and Japanese (osmunda) royal fern, to project an image of wild weeds (*yama no kusa*) growing in abundant fresh water in the mountains. In keeping with this image, just in front of the patio, separate from the terrace, we planted kobushi magnolia to the left and winter-berry to the right. Both trees will be kept small and the winterberry will probably remain under 10 feet (3 m). Both trees grow in the mountains and both flower and produce a bright red berry in the fall.

THE RUSTIC ELEGANCE OF THE AMIGASA MON GATE

This section is a small departure from the title of this chapter but is in keeping with the theme of "entrance." In my life as a gardener, I have had the opportunity to construct over sixty *amigasa mon* gates. I have also taught many gardeners how to make them. The photos in this section are from one such workshop for about fifty gardeners from around the country. The workshop, which took place in the north of Japan, was led by one of my staff. An *amigasa* is a rain hat, made of straw, worn by monks—also called a *takuhatsugasa*. The shape of the gate's roof recalls that hat. The word *mon* means gate. I first encountered the gate in Kamakura when I was about thirty years old. I have always been struck by its openness and elegance, which beautifully compliments the garden. What I mean is that this is a gate that is at once delicate and rustic. I am attracted to its simple construction and the way it seamlessly blends with nature. It is said that Kobori Enshu, the great sixteenth-century architect, tea master and garden designer, was the originator of the design. Through history it has been used as an entrance to tea gardens (*chaniwa*) and as a separator between the inner and outer tea garden. The most famous examples of these tea gardens are in Kyoto: the Kankyu-an, designed by the founder of the Mushanokojisenke school of tea and the Koho-an, designed by Kobori Enshu. But I have also used it in instances other than tea gardens. I feel that its understated beauty and graceful charm create a warm invitation to enter a garden and be refreshed. Despite my efforts, few gardeners are making this gate nowadays and it has become another endangered aspect of Japanese culture.

The doors of the amigasa mon can be either sliding or hinged. Which you choose will affect the type and position of the lintel and transom as well as other aspects of the construction. The hinged type is easier to make and more appropriate. We often call on the services of a carpenter to make the doors of the gate, especially the sliding variety. That is because square corners are easier to construct on the shop bench than

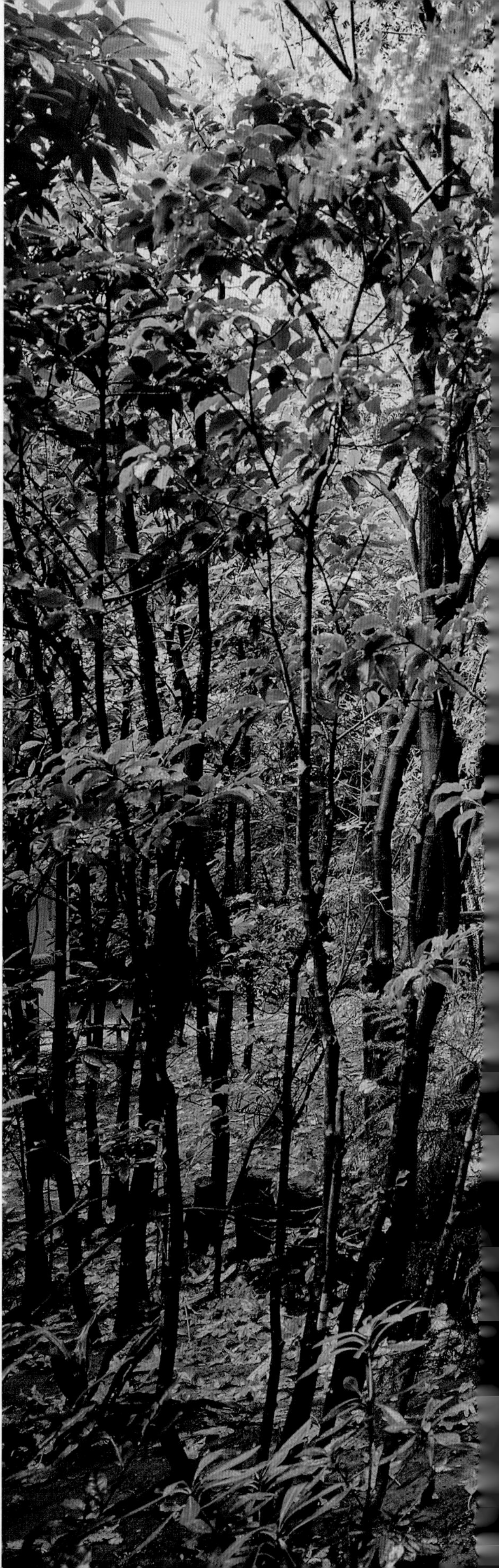

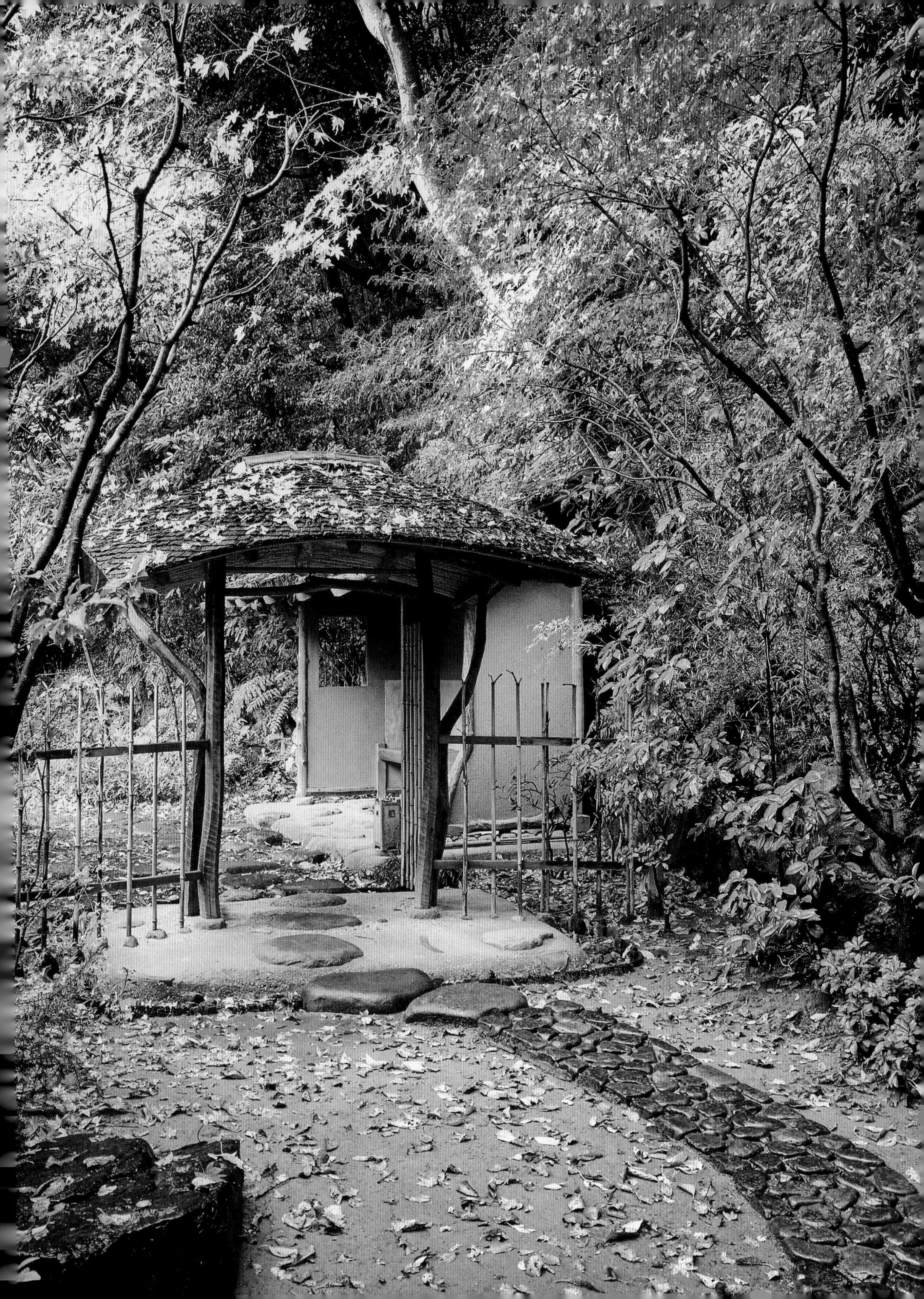

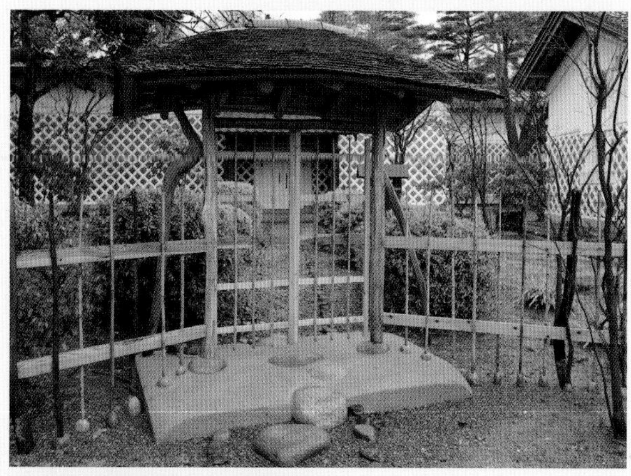

in the field. We always use chestnut or some other wood with good rot resistance to make this or any wooden garden structures. Bamboo is also used in combination with the wood. It too is rot resistant but when using it whole and vertically, be careful to cut it such that the top node is left intact. We don't want water siting inside the culm. Here is a basic primer on how to make this lovely gate. Please refer to the drawings for more details. Note also that dimensions are approximate and should be checked and adjusted to suit your needs.

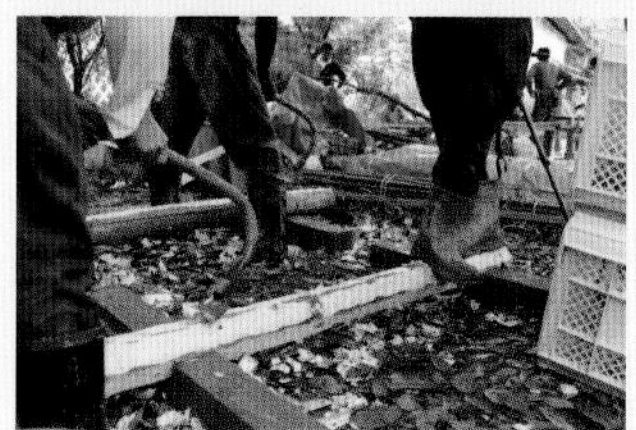

Step 1 Cut the main, vertical gate posts to length, and shave to width. The size is flexible but this lesson begins with two 6½-foot x 8-inch (2-m x 20-cm)-wide posts, shaved to a six-sided form of 6 inches (15 cm) wide. It's also possible to start with a square and cut the corners. For shaving we use an adze, but you can use a tool that is familiar to you.

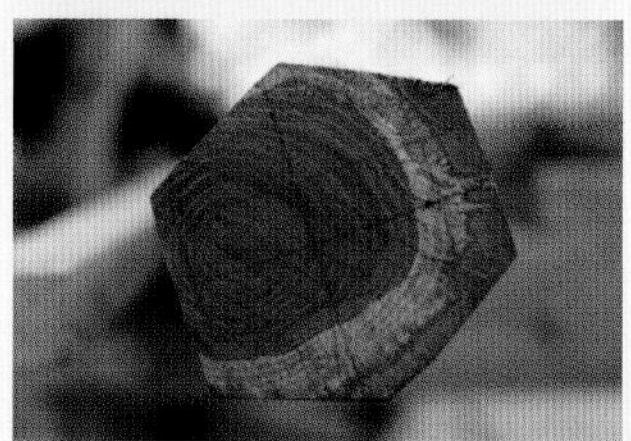

Step 2 Draw centerlines on top, bottom, and side. Draw additional lines at the top of the gate post to cut out a 3½ x 1½ x 8-inch (9 x 4 x 20-cm) tenon.

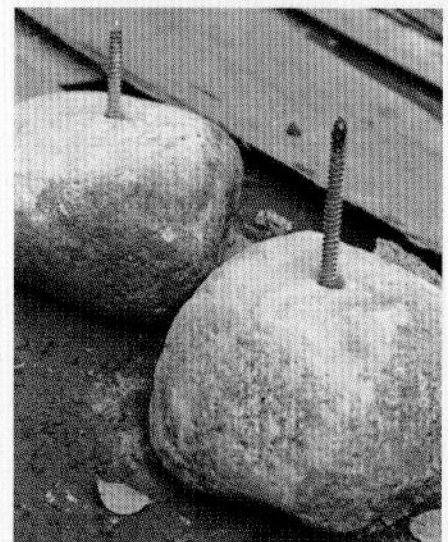

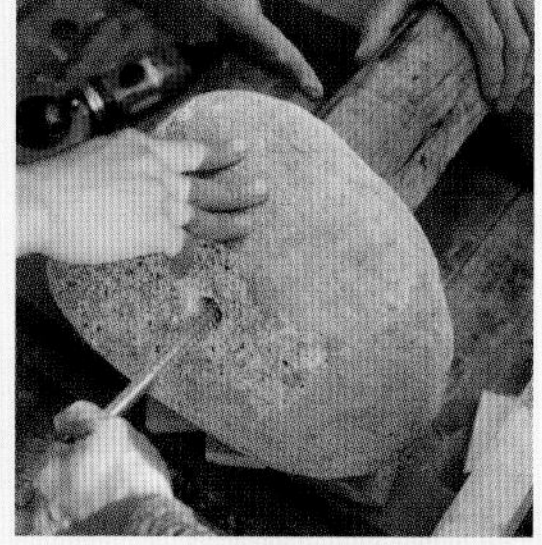

Step 3 Use two naturally rounded stones of about 8 inches (20 cm) diameter. Rounded river stone is best. Drill a 1¼-inch (3-cm) hole through each stone to insert bolts. The bottom side of the hole needs to be countersunk. Leave a minimum of 3¼ inches (8 cm) from the hole to the side of the stone. The bottom of the post will be connected to the stone with a spiral thread bolt (like a sleeper spike).

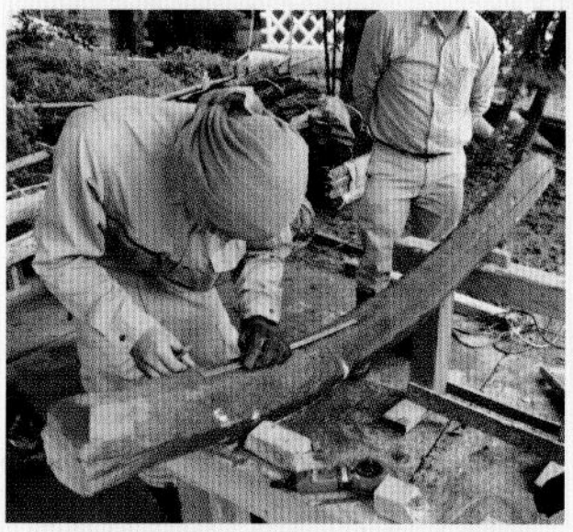

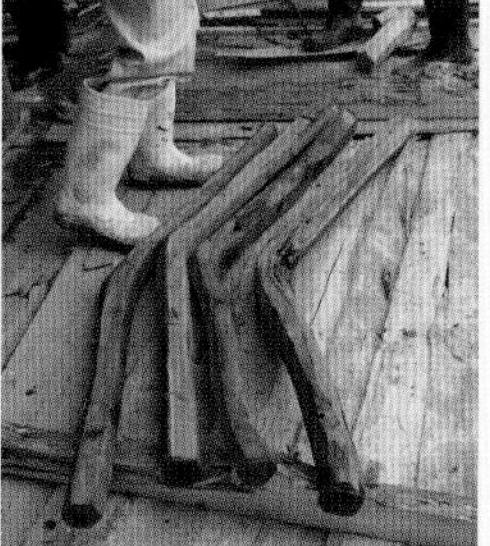

Step 4 Cut a ridgepole 6 feet (1.8 m) long by 6 inches (15 cm) wide. Shave it to roughly six sides. Select a piece with a natural arch of 12 inches (30 cm) minimum to the apex. The gently curving ridgepole will be crossed at right angles by five rafters, which are selected from branches that have a hard bend of about 120 degrees.

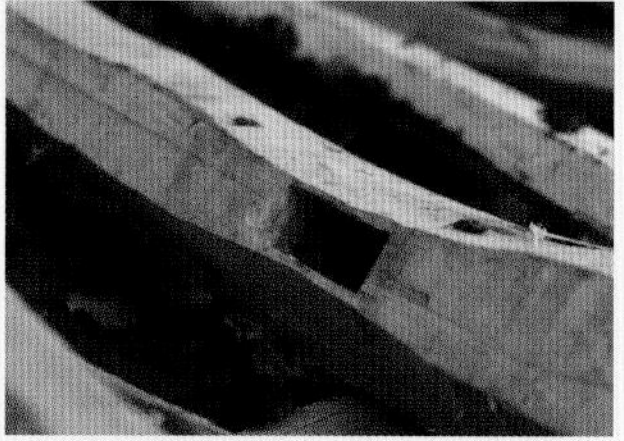

Step 5 Drill holes in the ridgepole and cut mortises to receive the tenons from the gate posts. The dimension from center to center of the mortises is 3 to 4 feet

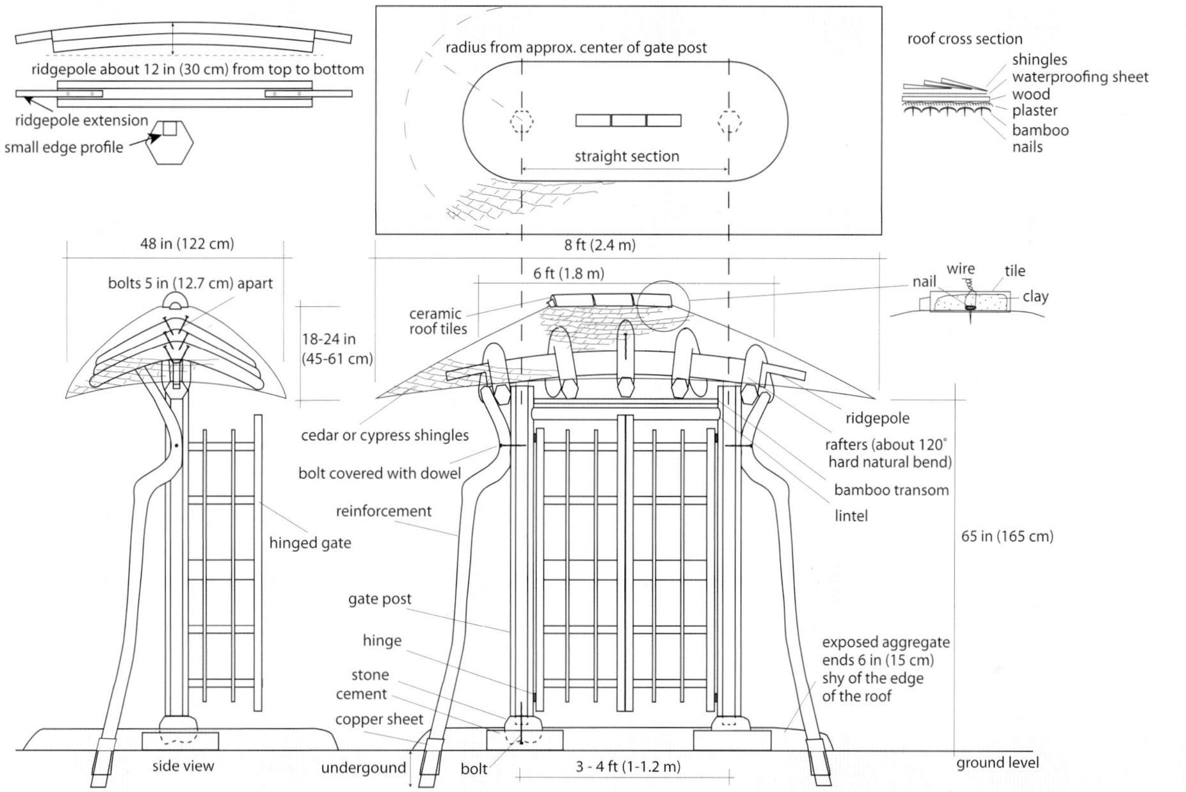

(1 m to 1.2 m). We sometimes add a narrow extension to the ridgepole to lengthen it and give it a smaller edge profile.

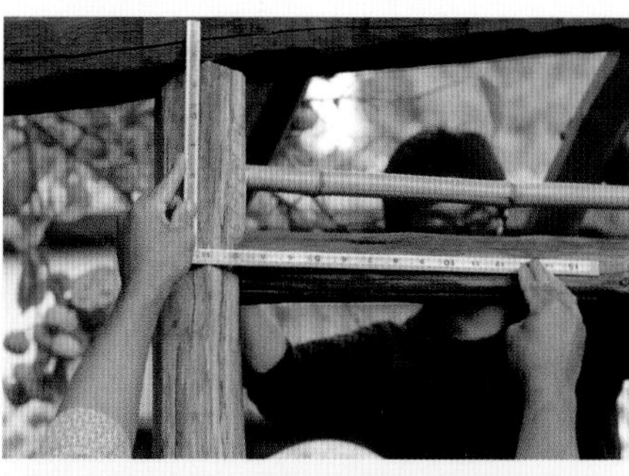

Step 6 Prepare the transom and lintel. Use 2-inch (6-cm) bamboo for the transom. The width of the lintel is slightly less than the gate posts. Holes are drilled in the gate posts to insert the transom. Mortises are cut in the gate posts for the lintel, both to a depth of about half the width of the gate post. The lintel is set at a height to receive the doors, 5 to 6 feet (1.5 to 1.8 m) from the ground.

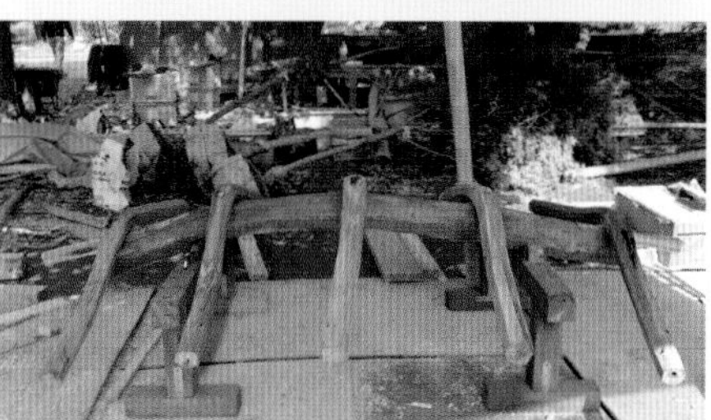

Step 7 With the ridgepole raised on horses, attach the five rafters, with bolts, starting from the center. First, mark the position and drill two bolt holes about 5 inches (12.7 cm) apart on either side of the rafter peak, angled toward the center. Then, notch countersinks in the topside of the rafters. Hold one rafter at a time and use the holes as a guide to drill into, but not through, the ridgepole.

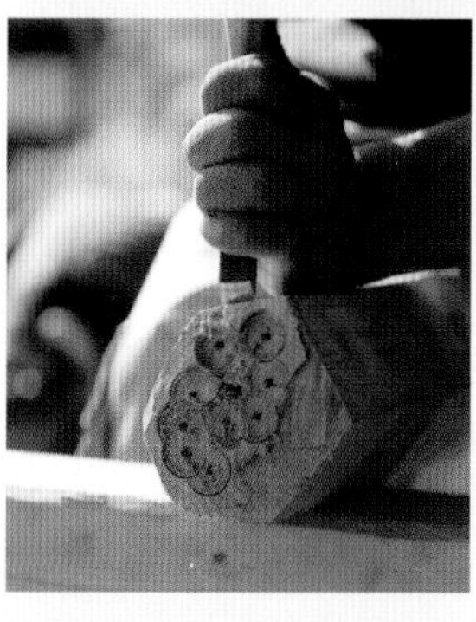

Step 8 Attach the stones to the bottom of the gate posts with bolts. The bottom of the gate post is shaped to fit the stone with no gap. Use a compass, hole cutter and a chisel.

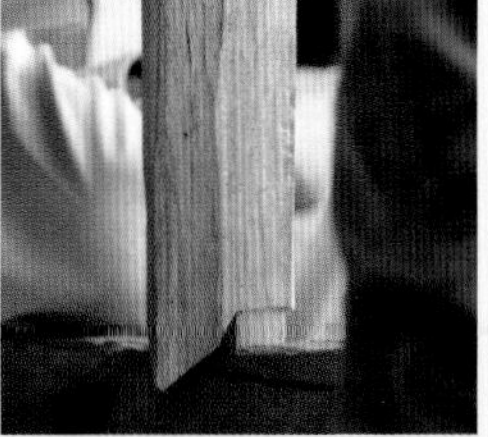

Step 9 Join the gate posts to the ridgepole while inserting the transom and lintel. Pound the ridgepole with a wooden mallet to insert the gate post tenon. You will probably need to shave the mortise but everything should fit tight. The top of the gate post must also be shaped to fit to the ridgepole.

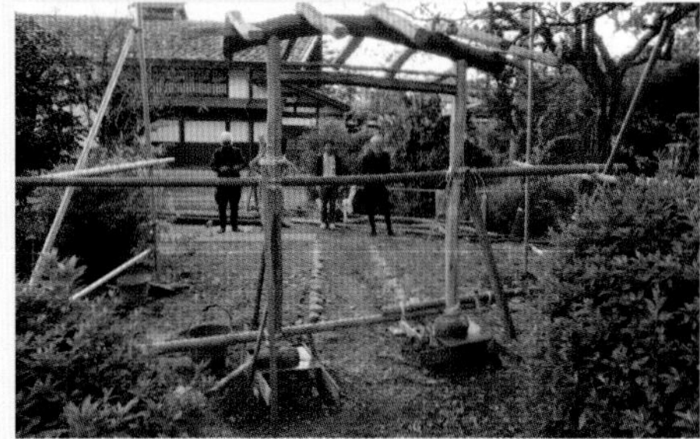

Step 10 With the basic frame of the gate completed and assembled, set it in place and level it. When the position is decided, make wooden forms around the stones to accept concrete. The concrete should be about 4 inches (10 cm) from the edge of the stone and a third to a half of the stone should be embedded. In our case, the ground under the gate will receive a clay, sand, and exposed aggregate (*araidashi*)base. This will determine the thickness of the cement and height of the stone. Continuously check the vertical and horizontal level of the gate and support it with poles while the concrete sets.

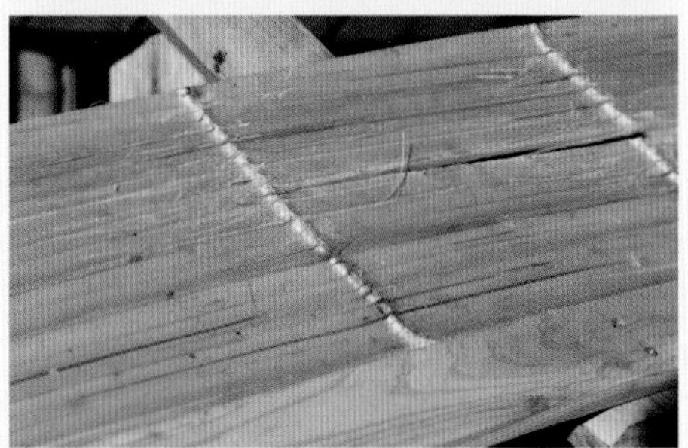

Step 11 Cut 6 to 18 bamboo strips, about ½ inch (1 cm) wide, from one large bamboo. Drill holes to accept nails. Line the strips up across the rafters and attach them with umbrella-headed, galvanized roofing nails. Nail ½ x 4-inch (1 x 10-cm) cedar boards along the rafter edges and align the bamboo to them.

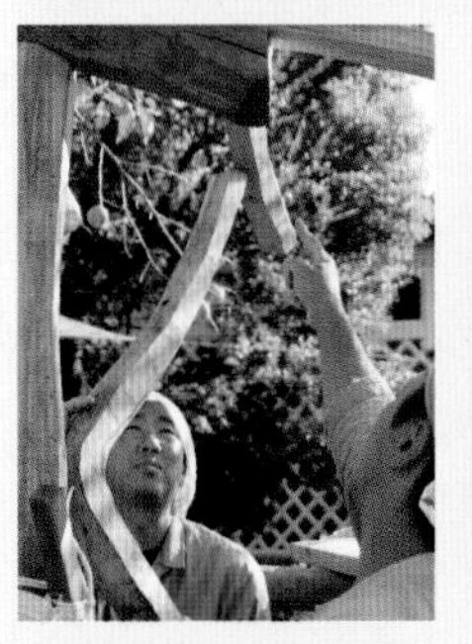

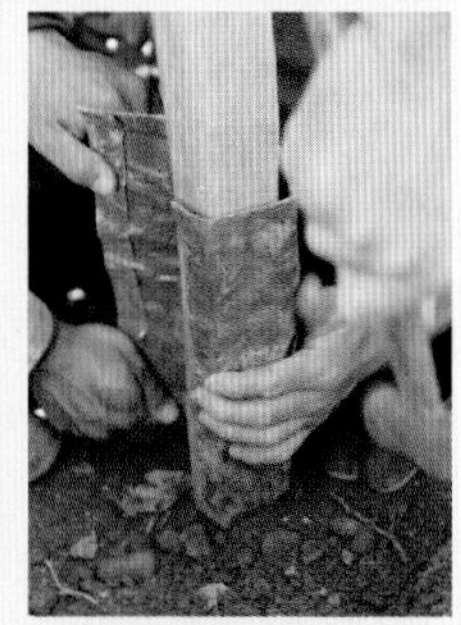

Step 12 Add one reinforcement post for each gate post. Use the same type of wood, slightly slimmer than the gate posts, with an interesting natural curve. Connect the top to the rafter and the side to the gate post. Drill holes for bolts and countersink for bolt heads. Bury the opposite ends about 2 feet (60 cm) in the ground. Wrap copper sheeting around the top half of the buried part to make it rot resistant.

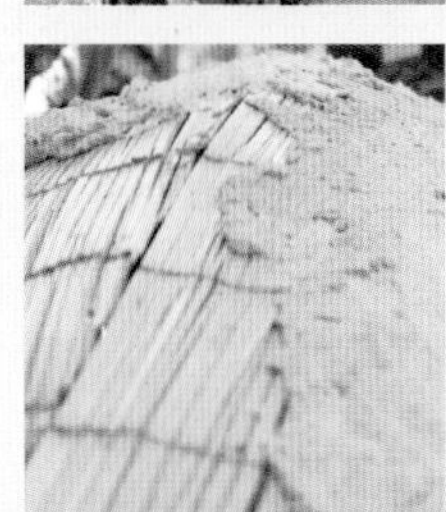

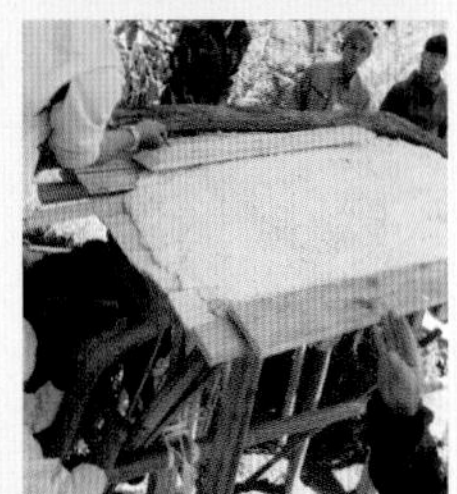

Step 13 Mix seaweed glue (*tsunomata*), or any starch-based glue with plaster and spread it over the bamboo about ½ inch (1 cm) thick (plaster alone is okay). The plaster will drip through the bamboo. This is okay. Add another cedar board of the same size on top of the first ones as a guide for the plaster.

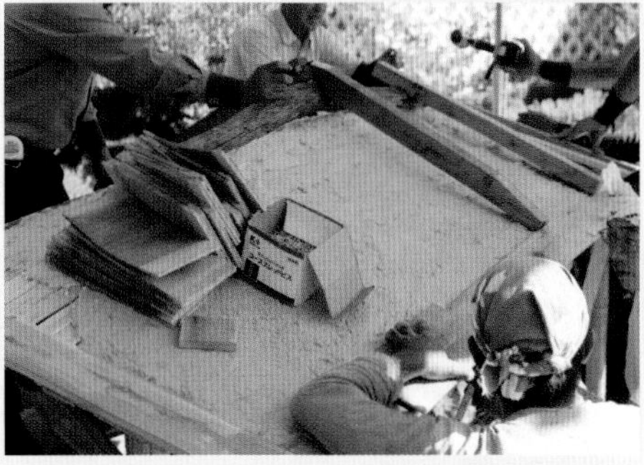

Step 14 If you need to make the roof steeper (if you live in a place with heavy snow, for example), a second roof can be added over the first. This is called a *niju yane*. Begin from the board at the bottom edge of the roof. Add a second ridgepole and rafters above the plaster. If not needed, move to the next step.

Step 15 Cover the bamboo and plaster from Step 13 with ½ x 4-inch (1 x 10-cm) cedar boards secured with screws. Boards can be cut to various lengths to conform to the curved roof shape. They can also be scored with a saw to allow for easy bending.

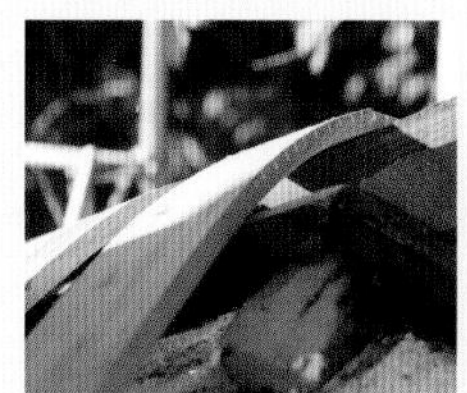

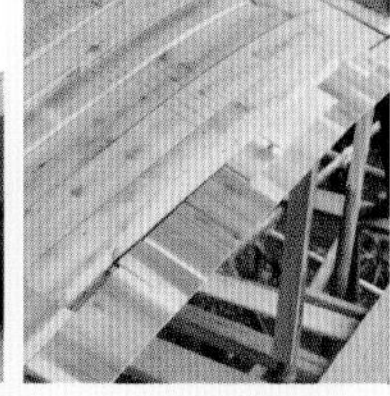

Step 16 A waterproof sheet is applied over this, secured with nails or staples. Copper sheeting may also be added around the edge but it is not required.

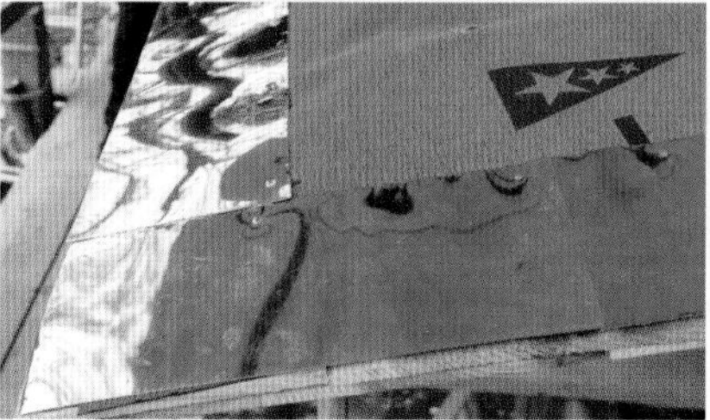

Step 17 Finish the roof with cedar shingles, about 8 inches (21 cm) square. First, soak them in water to make them pliable and resistant to splitting when nailed. Lay them down in an oval pattern and trim with pruning shears. The shingles should overlap by about 6 inches (15 cm). Start from the corners of the roof and work to the ridge.

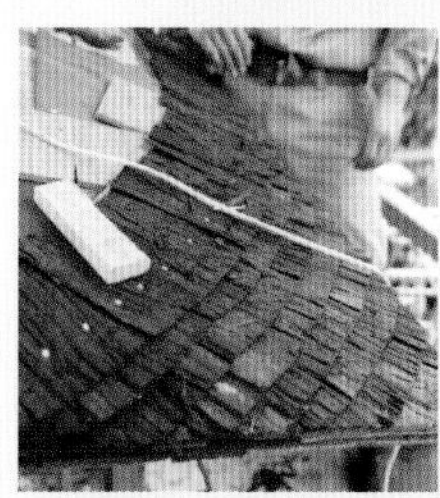

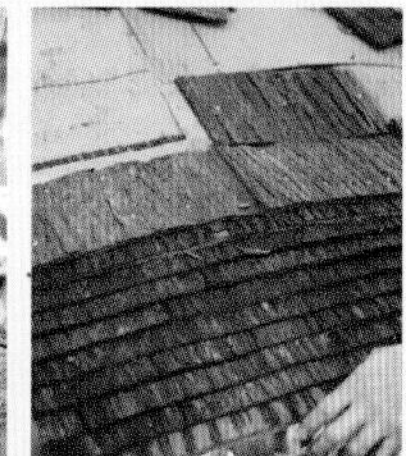

Step 18 Finish the top of the ridge with copper sheet and ceramic roof tiles (*kawara*) or short sections of wide bamboo cut in half. The kawara are wired in place. Attach the wire to large-head nails hammered into the roof. Fill the underside of the tile with clay or plaster before pulling the wire tight and twisting it.

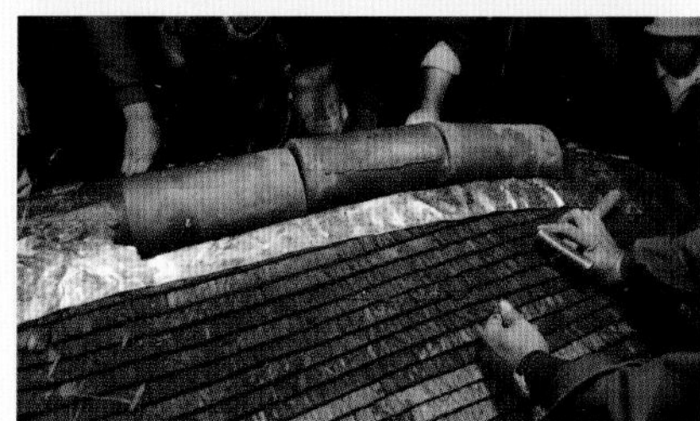

Step 19 Construct the doors. Take two 1½ x 2-inch (4 x 5-cm) lengths to make the vertical frame of each door. The inside lengths are about 6 inches (15 cm) longer than the outside ones. These should hit the lintel and keep the doors from inverting. Cut five mortises in the frame to accept horizontal pieces. The largest piece, about 1 x 5 inches (2 x 12 cm), goes in the center. Two smaller ones, about 1 x 4 inches (2 x 10 cm), go above and below the center. Match the combined finished width of the doors to fit just inside the gate posts. Finish with three narrow, vertical bamboo pieces for each door.

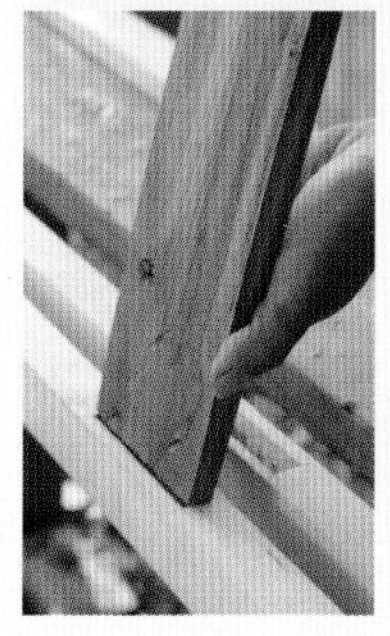

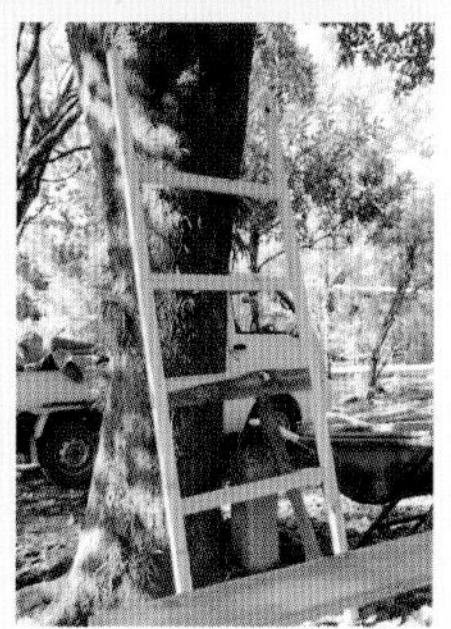

Step 20 Make hinges from 1⁄16-inch (0.2-mm)-thick sheet steel. In the doorframe insert a ½-inch (12-mm) strip of steel that has been folded in half and roll one end into a pipe. Take a 1½-inch (4-cm) length of metal and cut it into an "L" shape with an arrow head on the wider leg of the "L." Hammer it into the slot or drill a hole through the post and metal, and secure it with a screw. Hammer it into the slot or drill a hole through the post and metal and secure it with a screw. The loop on the doorframe side should fit loosely over this cut steel. Spray occasionally with oil to prevent rust.

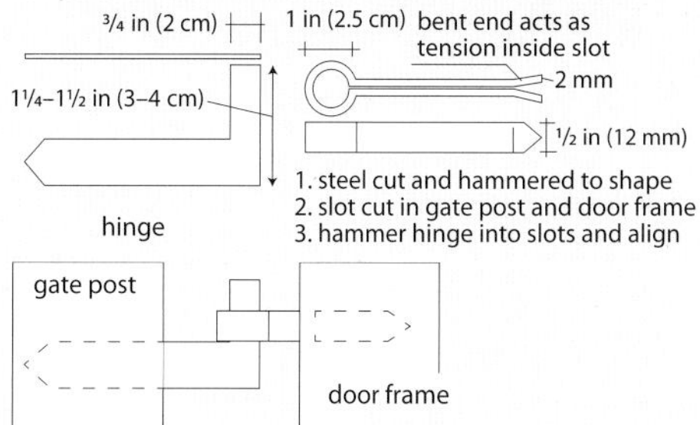

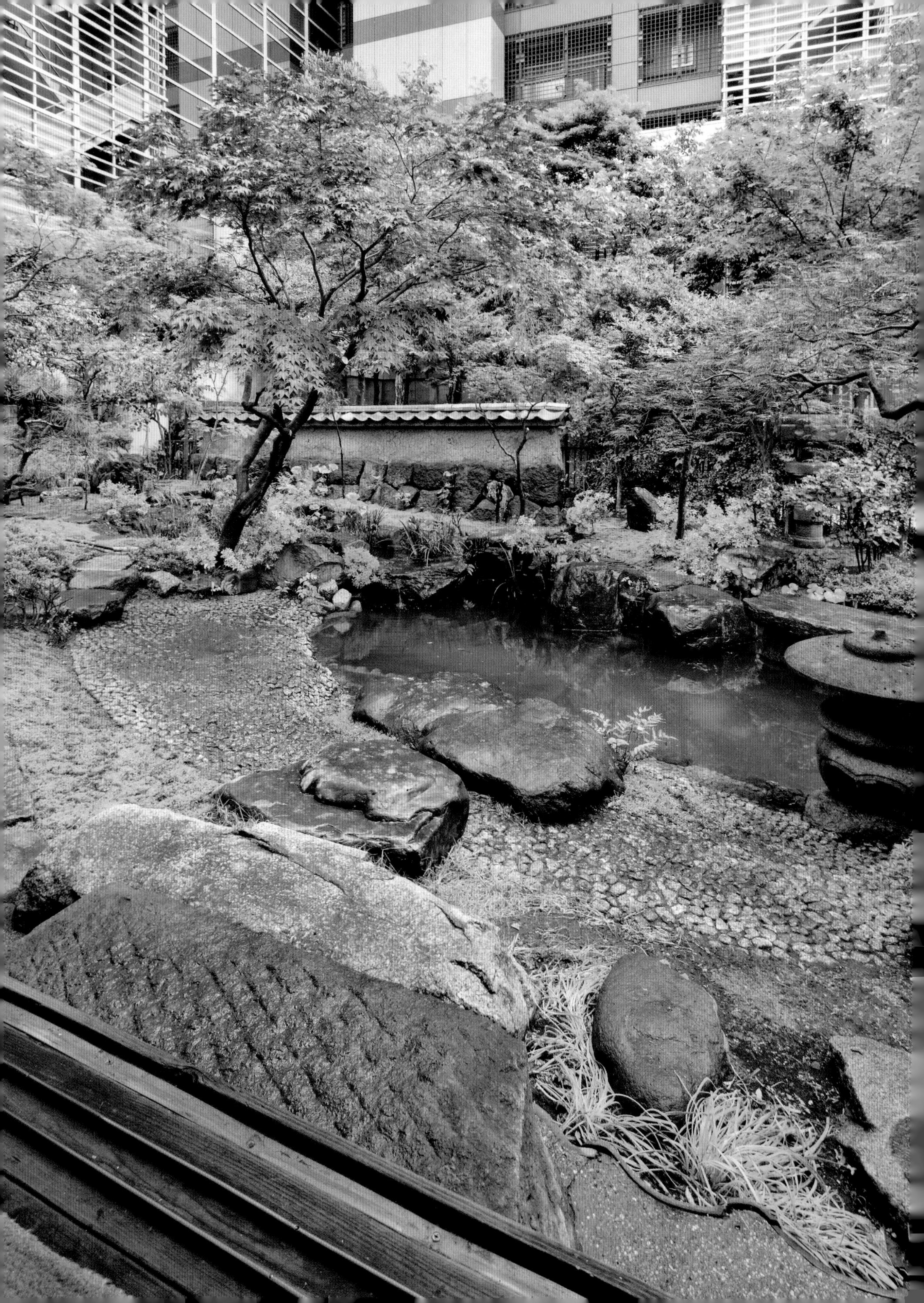

CHAPTER TWO

Backyards and Gardens of the Gods

Japan has no tradition of swimming pools and barbecues in backyards, but there is no reason why a Japanese garden cannot accommodate such uses. For example, Japanese homes often have a narrow, deck-like space called a *nure-en*. It is just wide enough to sit on and enjoy the garden while sipping a glass of tea or drinking a beer. Some homes have a deck large enough for a table and chairs while others may have a gazebo or even a teahouse. Some have expanses of open space which can be used for any purpose. Then there are those who prefer to enjoy viewing the garden from the comfort of their living room. A backyard is simply a private area of greenery behind the house. Each backyard is different and everyone has his or her own reasons for turning it into a garden.

Besides homes and businesses, I have been asked to make a number of gardens for Buddhist temples and Shinto shrines. The approach to making such a garden is no different than making a garden for a family's backyard. The difference is basically one of purpose. I include some examples of temple gardens so you can see there is no great difficulty to them, and to illustrate a few features not found in home gardens. Although there is much fascination in the West with dry gardens of stone-and-sand (*karesansui*), other than a verandah by one of my mentors you won't find any in this book. Though I have made karesansui gardens before, trees, moss, and flowing water are much closer to my heart."

In my years as a gardener, I have had the privilege to work for people from all walks of life. I'm happy to say that many have remained friends and customers. I have made gardens for restaurants, spas, and religious institutions, as well as private homes. One thing they all have in common is that the garden owner plays the most important role. That is because a garden requires care and maintenance over a long period of time, and only the garden owner can see to this. Whether you contract someone, or do your own maintenance, a garden must be cared for in order to mature well over the years.

Properly designed, built, and maintained, a garden will look better and better with age. I feel grateful that many of the gardens I created thirty or forty years ago are still cared for by the original owners. Some have become a little neglected but are easily revived. Of course, many no longer exist. An older generation, which valued beautiful gardens, is giving way to a younger generation with a different set of values. Large plots of land, which once contained a single house and a large garden, are sold to developers who build as many tiny houses as they can squeeze into the space. Whole neighborhoods are demolished to make way for massive apartment buildings and shopping centers. Zoning laws do not take into account that damage from extreme weather increases as areas of greenery in the cities decrease. No statistics are kept on how many acres of green disappear every year from this kind of overdevelopment. I wonder how many of the problems society faces could be solved by the simple act of building and maintaining a garden?

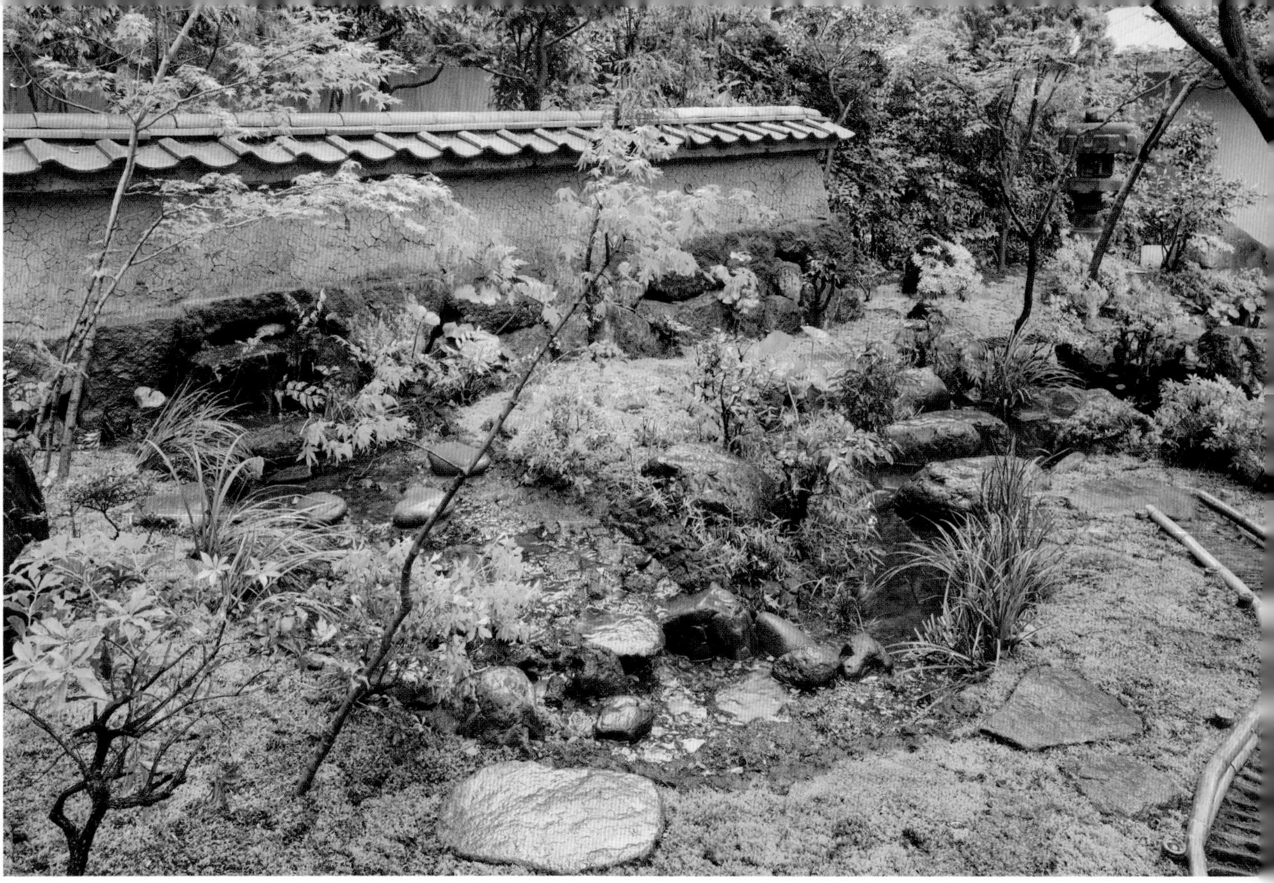

Paradise in an Urban Jungle

One of my customers, Hotaku Ishimori, was the principle of a junior high school in our town. Along with his sister, he also operated a private kindergarten in the Nishi-shinjuku district of Tokyo. Anyone familiar with Tokyo will know that Shinjuku is an urban center full of steel and glass skyscrapers. But he was one of the few small homeowners in the area. The kindergarten was next to his house and connected to it by the garden I made for him. It truly was a paradise in an urban jungle.

To begin, we dug a hole and made a pond. The garden is small but the pond creates a wonderful atmosphere. Naturally, when you make a pond, you need to make inlets and outlets for the water. These things, as well as the size of the fish, the recirculation system, and the overall shape, need to be decided before construction begins. The depth of

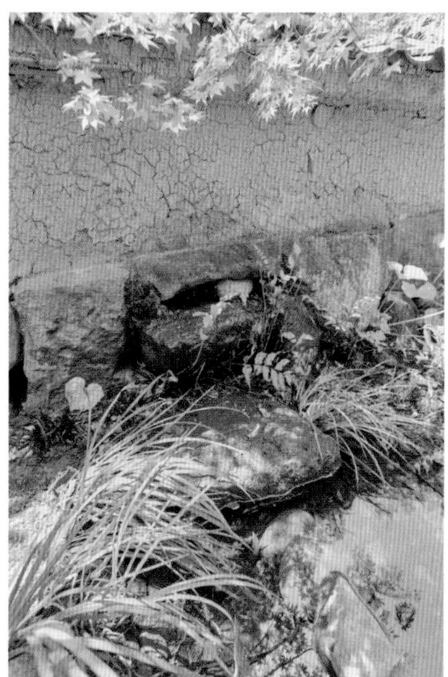

Above The water from the gutter meanders "naturally" until it falls again into the pond proper.

Left A small stone gutter in the stone base of a clay wall spills water into the pond.

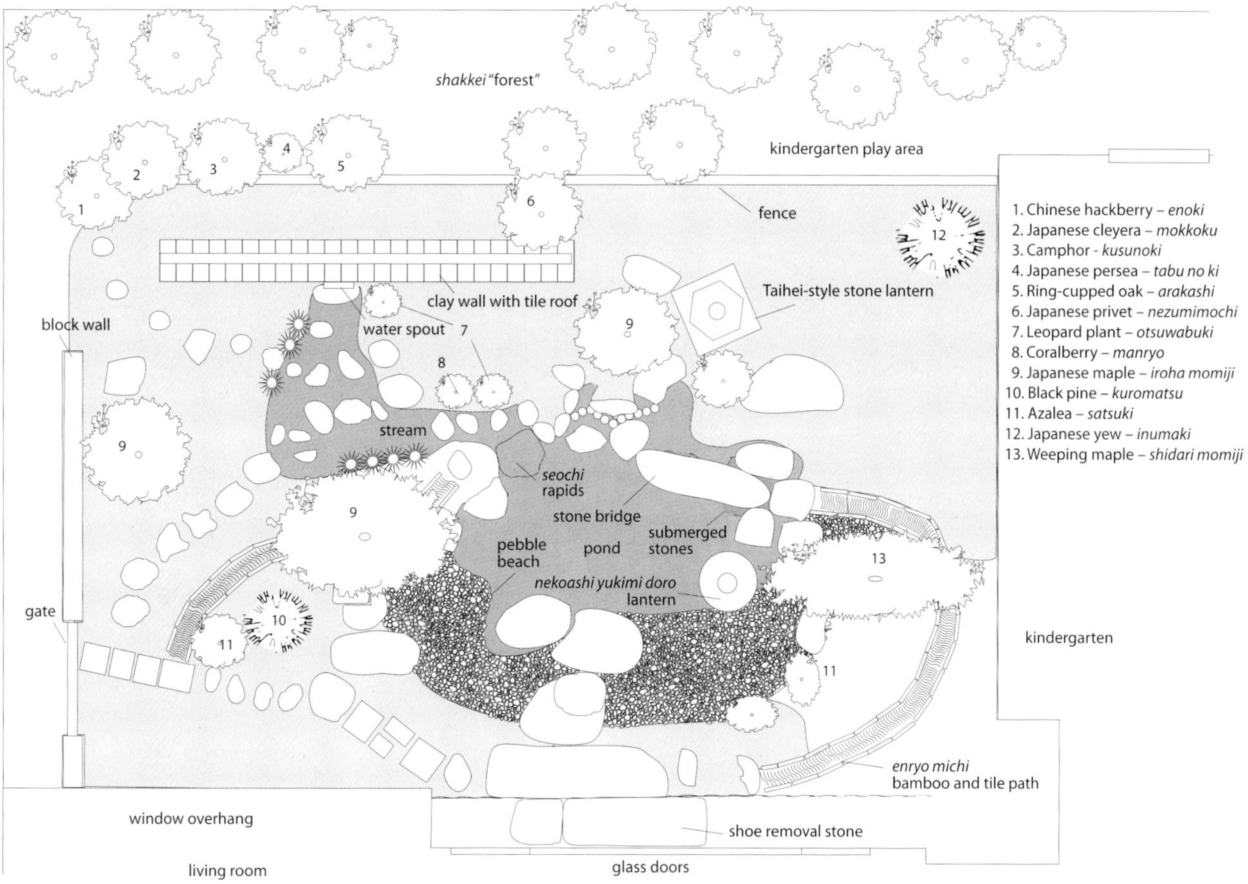

shakkei "forest"

kindergarten play area

fence

block wall

clay wall with tile roof

water spout

Taihei-style stone lantern

stream

seochi rapids

stone bridge

submerged stones

pebble beach

pond

nekoashi yukimi doro lantern

gate

kindergarten

enryo michi bamboo and tile path

window overhang

shoe removal stone

living room

glass doors

1. Chinese hackberry – *enoki*
2. Japanese cleyera – *mokkoku*
3. Camphor - *kusunoki*
4. Japanese persea – *tabu no ki*
5. Ring-cupped oak – *arakashi*
6. Japanese privet – *nezumimochi*
7. Leopard plant – *otsuwabuki*
8. Coralberry – *manryo*
9. Japanese maple – *iroha momiji*
10. Black pine – *kuromatsu*
11. Azalea – *satsuki*
12. Japanese yew – *inumaki*
13. Weeping maple – *shidari momiji*

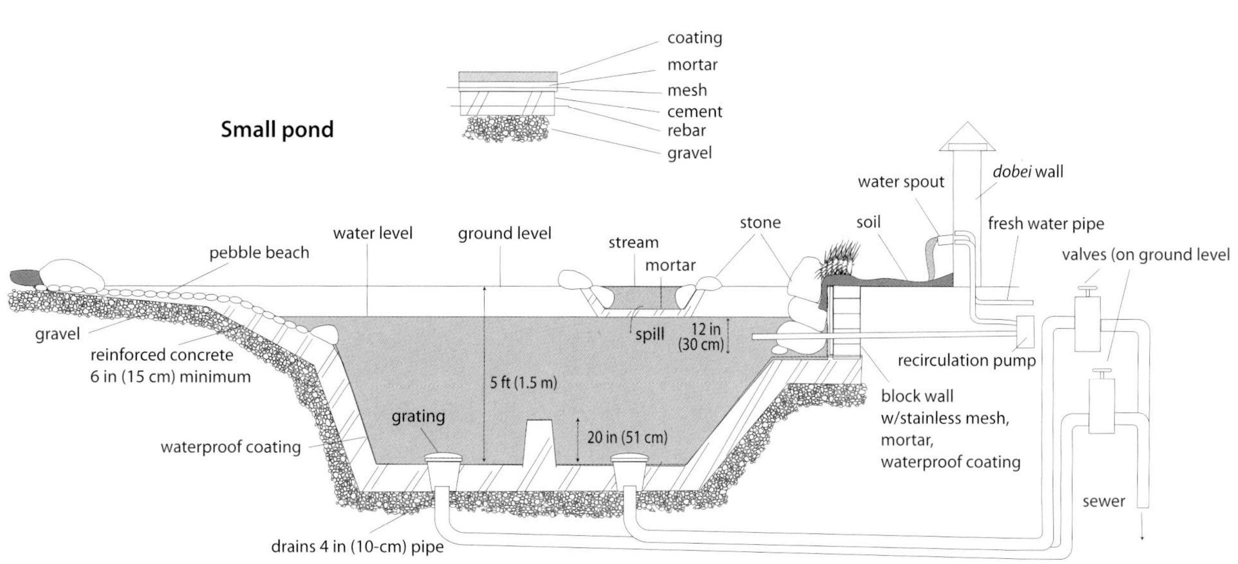

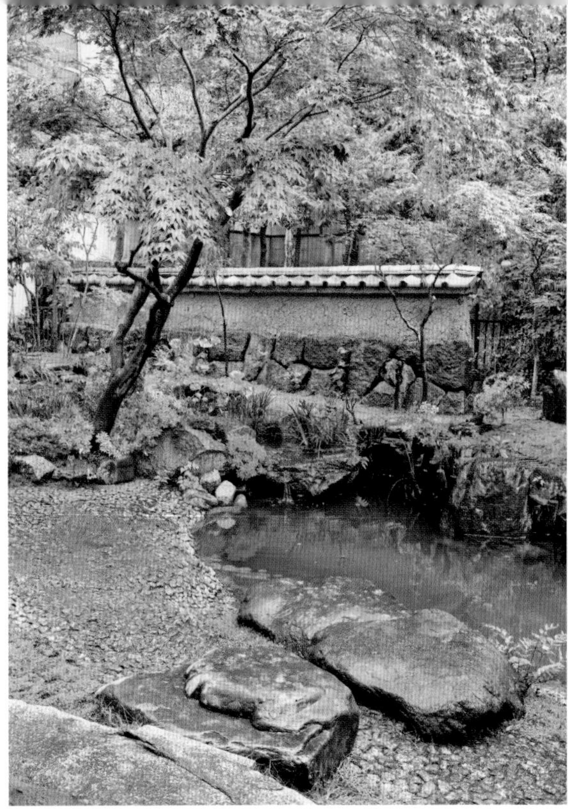

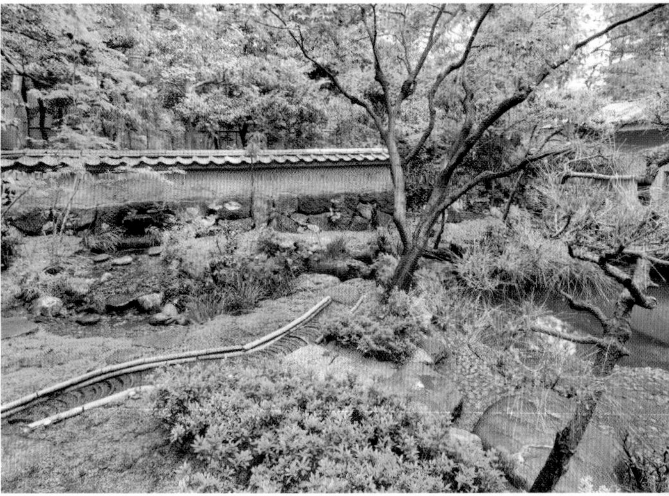

Left Large stepping stones make other objects seem distant by comparison.

Above The trees planted behind the wall create an artificial sense of depth..

Facing page Seemingly far removed from the city, the garden is an oasis of verdant nature in a barren metropolis of concrete and steel.

the pond relates to the size of the fish. In this case, carp of a maximum of about 32 inches (80 cm) needed a pond depth of about 5 feet (1.5 m). The outlets are two drains, which are separated by a 20-inch (51-cm) mound that runs along the center of the pond bottom. When the pond is cleaned, the side to be cleaned is completely drained and the fish shuttled to the other side. Depending on the conditions, ideally the pond should be cleaned once a month.

Inlets can be waterfalls, or gutters of stone or bamboo. PVC piping is used to connect to the municipal water supply. The water should be filtered. In this garden, the water is ducted to a stone gutter that peeks out from the stone base of the clay wall at the back of the garden. The recirculation pipe is also set here. Water from the upper 12 inches (30 cm) of the pond is recirculated through a pump. The incoming water forms a rivulet that encounters some stones, which turn it 90 degrees. We sloped the ground and created small rapids (*seochi*) where the water picks up speed. Then it falls over some large stones before tumbling into the pond, entrapping air as it goes. In this way, the pond not only provides a place to keep carp, but also creates sounds, reflections, and water evaporation that help keep the surrounding plants healthy. The tumbling action of the water helps entrap oxygen for the fish.

The pond, as I mentioned, begins with digging a hole. The soil and stone removed is used to create elevation changes—such as the slope. The soil at the bottom of the pond is mixed with gravel and pounded. A minimum of 6 inches (15 cm) of reinforced concrete covers the gravel. Where walls are needed for the pond, they can be constructed with cinder block covered with a stainless-steel mesh and mortar, on top of the concrete base. Stones are arranged in mortar around the edge of the pond and in other places. All concrete and mortar gets painted with a waterproof coating. On the side of the pond close to the house, we created a pebble beach composed of rounded stones called *ise jari.* These are 2 to 4 inches (5 to 10 cm) each, also embedded in mortar. The beach slopes gently and then drops steeply at the edge of the pond. The water covers 1 to 2 feet (30 to 60 cm) of the pebbles.

Two other things associated with ponds are bridges and lanterns. Here we have two lanterns, a tall Taihei-style lantern on the far side of the pond and a short cat's paw snow-viewing lantern (*nekoashi yukimi doro*) on the pebble beach. Although it is called "snow-viewing," this type of lantern with a large umbrella is usually used at the edge of a pond. The light reflected on the underside of the umbrella then reflects off the water. Towards the rear of the pond we built a stone bridge. The right side of the bridge is connected to land but the left side is open. A large stone sits just past the end and you step off the end of the bridge onto the stone to continue. It is safe to walk across the main bridge stone, which is flat and well anchored. The stones supporting the bridge are discards from the Imperial Palace in Tokyo. The stone is rugged but the bridge has a light feeling due to the open configuration.

The room facing the garden has floor-to-ceiling glass doors that slide open to give a fantastic view of the naturalistic landscape and the urban cityscape behind it. We also used some large stones near the living room on the front edge of the pond as stepping stones leading to the pond. The large stones in the front make other objects in the garden seem smaller and therefore more distant than they really are. To soften the appearance of the scene, we planted moss, azalea, coralberry, and other low shrubs around the pond. We planted a well-shaped weeping maple to the right and a large *iroha* maple to the left. In the background, we planted a number of tall trees such as Chinese hackberry, camphor, ring-cupped oak and others. The rugged naturalness of large stones, encompassed within leaves of many shapes and shades of green, contrast favorably with the strict geometry of the buildings outside.

The key here was to place a 5-foot (1.5-m)-tall tile-roofed clay and stone wall behind the pond. The wall is only about half the width of the garden but plays an important role. A steel fence separates the garden from the kindergarten play area next to it. The wall partially blocks the view of the fence and the children playing next door. More importantly, we planted many tall trees in the play area to create the effect of "borrowed scenery" (*shakkei*). By this I mean that because there is no view to "connect" the garden to, we created the impression that there is. The wall fools the eye into thinking that the garden ends there. The trees planted behind it present a strong impression of greater depth beyond. The eye is deceived into thinking there is a forest next door when in fact it is all part of the same garden. The total effect is to push the wall of tall buildings further into the distance. That and the intimacy of the small pond beneath the trees create a strong perception of a concealed, lush enclave.

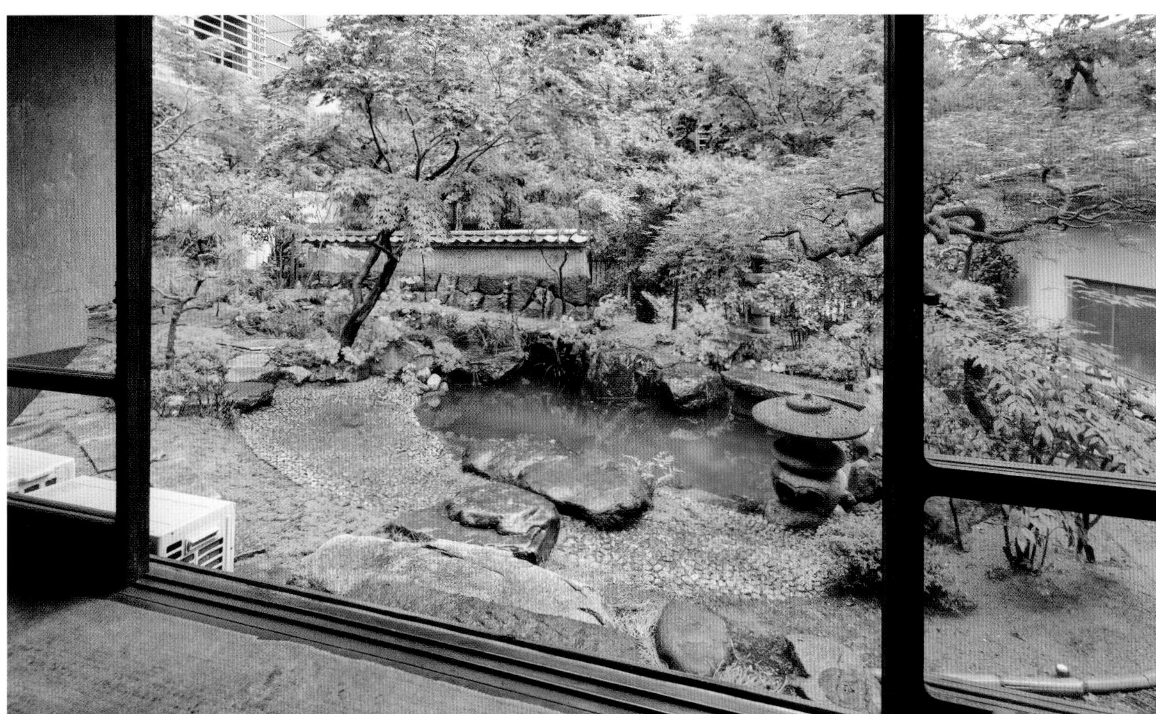

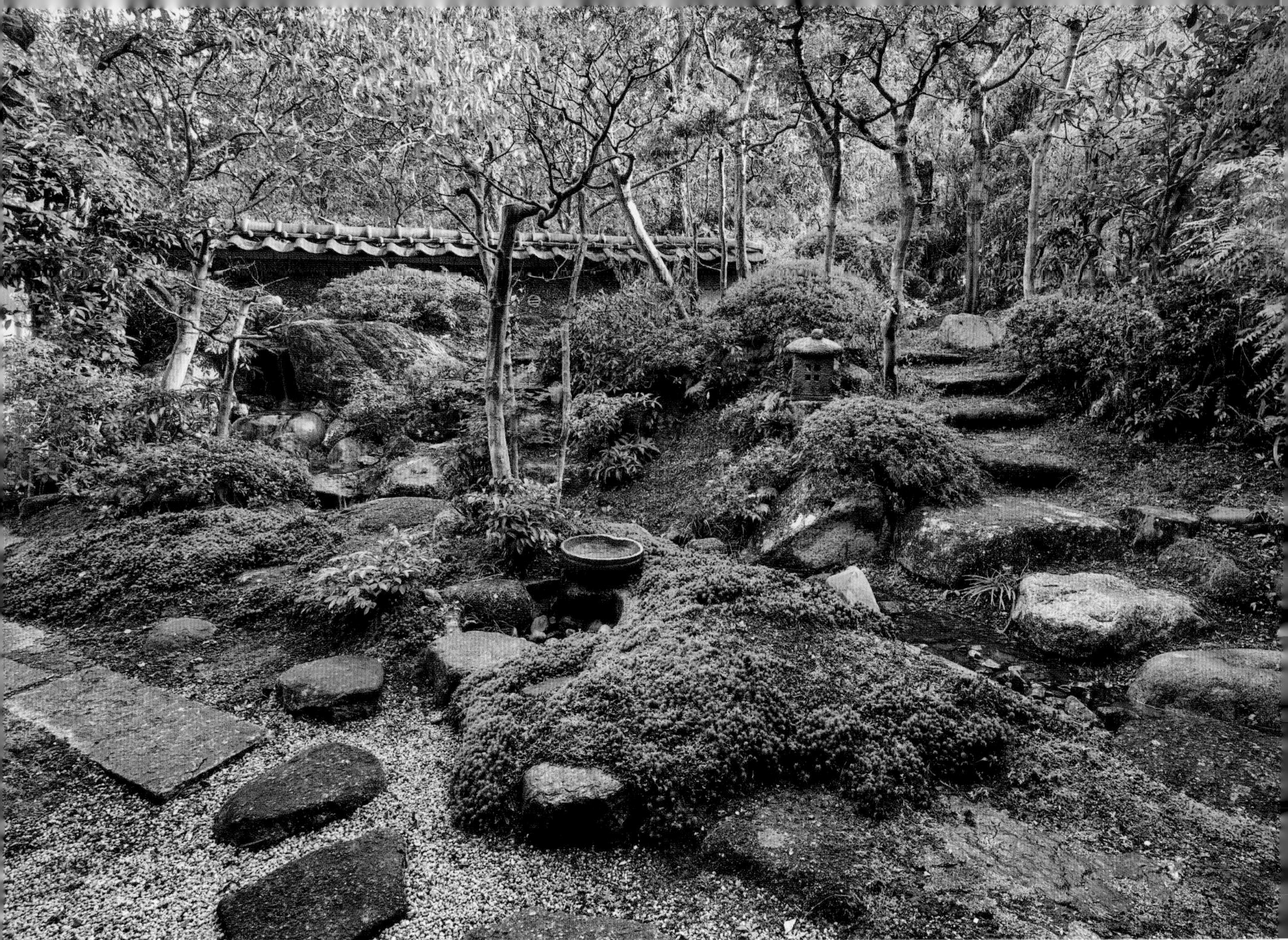

A Stairway up the Mountain

The backyard of Mr. and Mrs. Kobayashi is adjacent to a sizable chestnut tree nursery. The land has a 5-foot (1.5-m) upward slope from the back of the house to the back of the garden. I could have leveled it, but that would have required making a tall retaining wall and great cost. Instead, I kept the grade and built a stone stair up the right side of the garden. From the top of that stair there is a wonderful view of the chestnut-tree field next door. It's a great surprise because there is no hint of it when you are on the street in front of the house. Even after walking into the garden, except for the treetops, there is no hint of the view that lies beyond the stair.

The garden is only 16 feet (4.8 m) deep on the short side and 26 feet (8 m) on the long side but appears much larger. In order to enhance this effect, I made a low, tile-roofed clay wall (*dobei*) at the top of the slope along the back of the garden. At only 30 inches tall (76 cm) it's enough to hide the view beyond until you peek over it. More than that, it amplifies the connection of the garden to the landscape beyond by covering the middle ground, giving an illusion of continuity between the foreground and the distance—a technique that we call *shakkei*. The garden may also appear larger because the steep slope presents a larger "face" than a flat area would.

In this garden, because of the slope, you might think at first glance that everything is immediately visible. But as you look closer, you begin to discover interesting views that are "hidden." One secret of traditional Japanese gardens is that they are not as easy to see as you might think. A lot of techniques are used to carry the eye around and reveal things slowly. A good garden will continue to show you something new every time you look at it—just as nature does. The first hidden view, as I already mentioned, is the one over the wall from the top of the stair. The second is the stair itself, which is not only visually interesting but also hidden here and there, and can't be completely seen until you climb it. The roughness of the stair forces you to walk carefully to be sure of your footing. When you get to the top, you naturally look up to see the amazing view

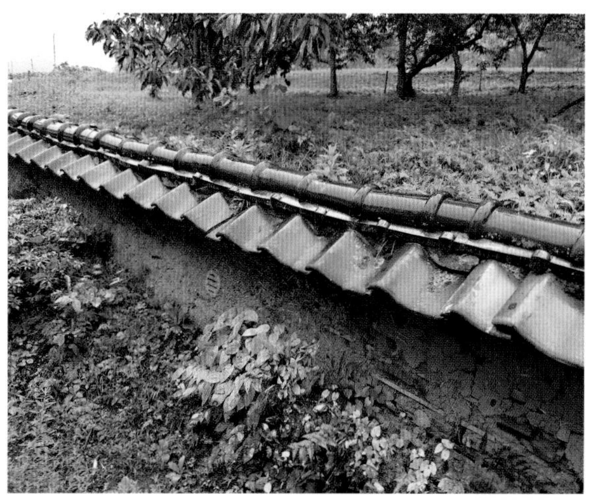

Facing page A rugged stone stairway seems to traverse the mountain and lead beyond.

Above In fact, the stair ends at a low wall that barely separates the garden from the chestnut nursery next door.

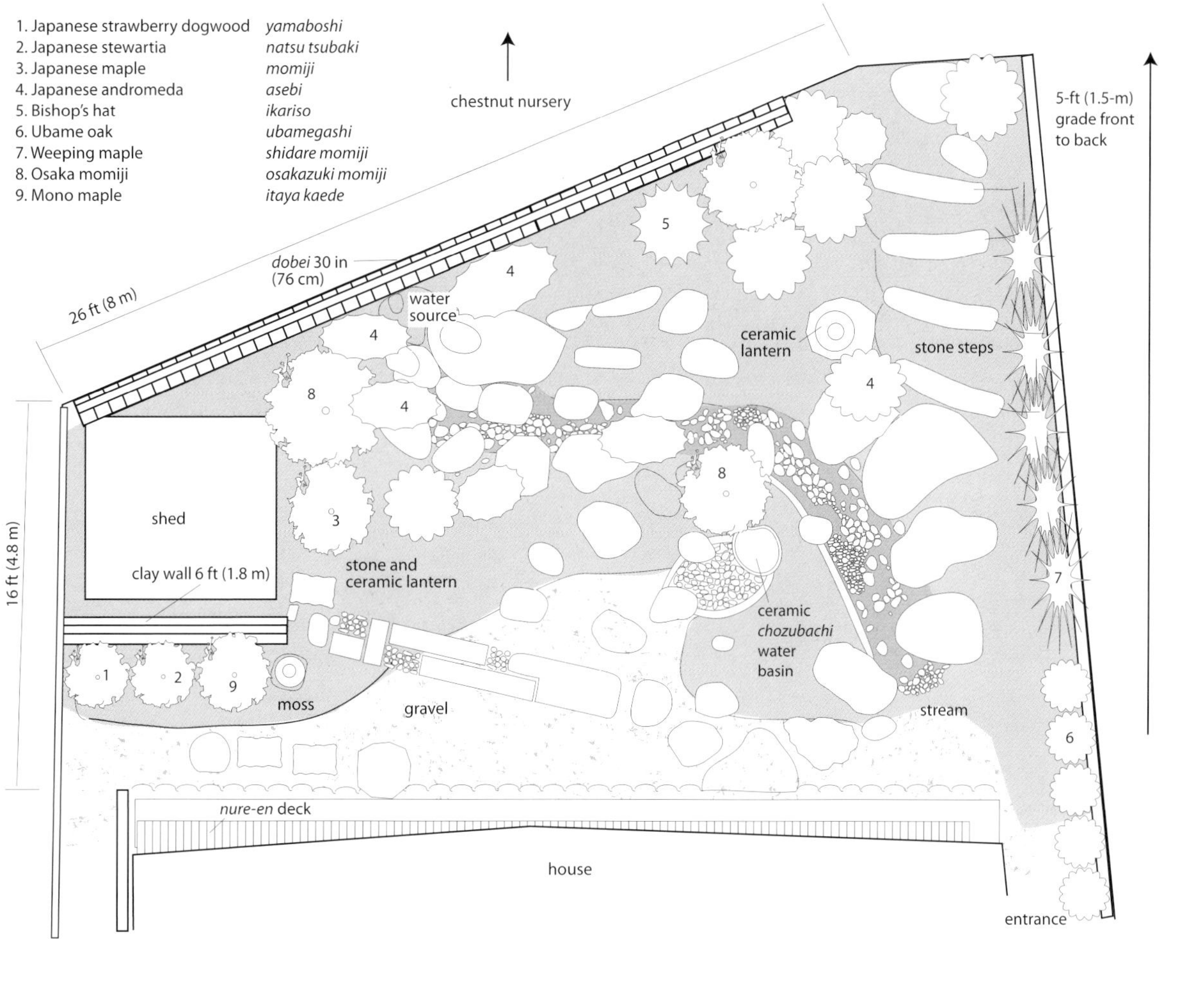

1. Japanese strawberry dogwood	*yamaboshi*
2. Japanese stewartia	*natsu tsubaki*
3. Japanese maple	*momiji*
4. Japanese andromeda	*asebi*
5. Bishop's hat	*ikariso*
6. Ubame oak	*ubamegashi*
7. Weeping maple	*shidare momiji*
8. Osaka momiji	*osakazuki momiji*
9. Mono maple	*itaya kaede*

chestnut nursery
5-ft (1.5-m) grade front to back
dobei 30 in (76 cm)
26 ft (8 m)
water source
ceramic lantern
stone steps
16 ft (4.8 m)
shed
clay wall 6 ft (1.8 m)
stone and ceramic lantern
ceramic *chozubachi* water basin
moss
gravel
stream
nure-en deck
house
entrance

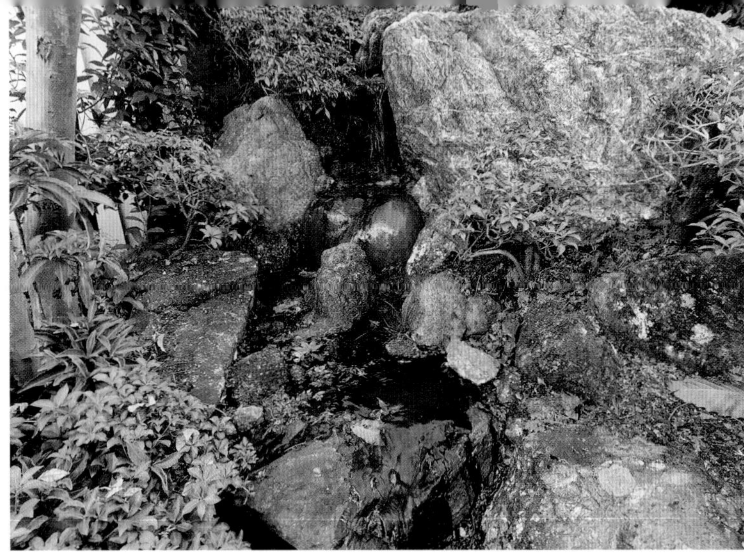

Left Water issues from an inconspicuous rock arrangement in the far corner of the garden.

Below The water is channeled into a stream that winds down the mountain.

Facing page An illusion of great depth is created by the sloping ground and the "borrowed scenery" from next door.

over the wall. This is another garden technique: controlling the viewpoint and pace of walking of the viewer by using stepping stones, walkways, stairs, and other features. Looking down at the garden from the top of the stairs presents a completely different view.

This is not a true stroll garden. It is too small and the view from the house is by far the main one. But even from the house many things are not so easy to see. Consider for example the waterfall at the left back side. This is the source of the stream (*nagare*) that curves from there to end alongside the stairs near the front of the garden. This stream and the waterfall are not completely visible because of variations in height, and obstacles such as stones and plants. There is a stepping-stone path that leads to a water basin (*chozubachi*) and then into the "mountain" on the left. It begins close to the base of the stairs but then diverges, taking a low road in the opposite direction. This serves the practical purpose of allowing access for maintenance. It also serves the visual purpose of widening the view and allowing the eye to wander along the stones in search of where they lead. The total effect is one of a studied naturalism that distinguishes the Japanese garden from any other in the world.

Again, we are talking about techniques—not rules. The purpose of those techniques is to produce a scene as natural as any you might come across walking through the woods or mountains. It is not a landscape that is untraveled. This is clear because of features like walls, lanterns (*toro*), chozubachi water

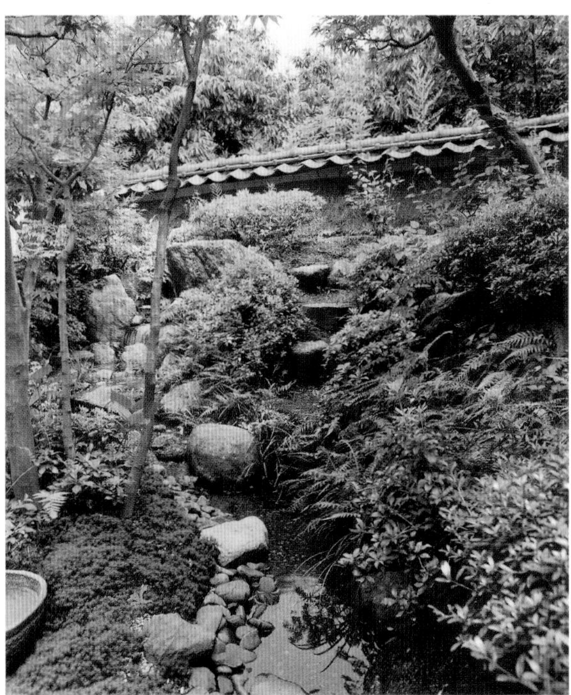

basins, and stepping stones. But it still feels like you discovered the place and each time you return and in any season, you discover it anew. Considering the small size of the garden, and the closeness of neighboring houses, it's amazing to create a space that allows you to completely forget that you are in the middle of a city. By the way, the usual stone lantern and water basin were replaced in this case with lovely ceramic ones made by Mrs. Kobayashi: a small but good way to personalize the garden.

Talking about techniques, one that somewhat

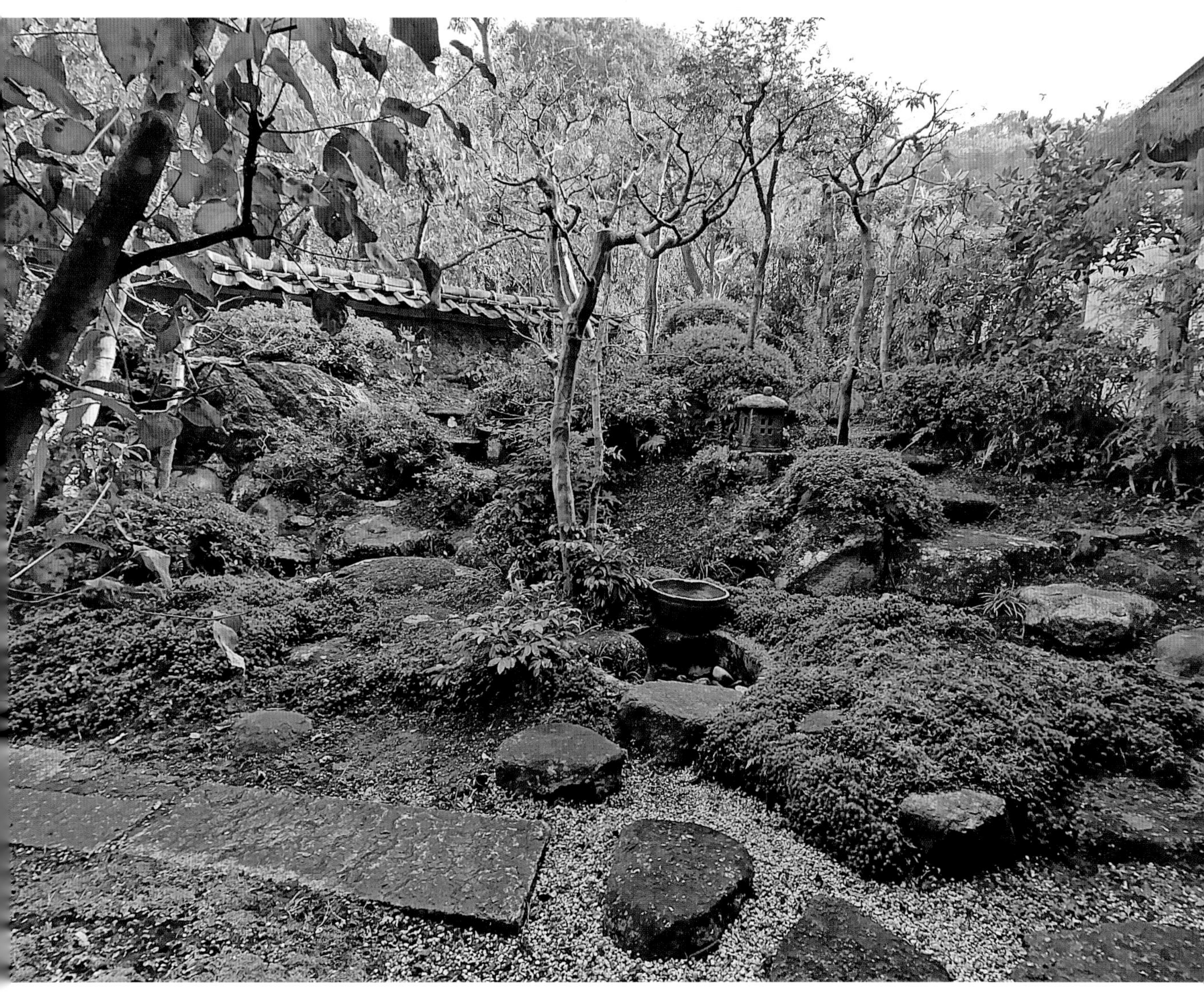

defines Japanese gardens is the planting of broadleaf evergreens. There are traditions about changing and unchanging features (see ***Permanent vs. transient***, page 13) and Japanese gardens clearly favor the latter. My gardens use both flowering and non-flowering broadleaf evergreens and a lot of stone, all of which can be considered unchanging features. But there is also a strong tradition of celebrating the change of seasons. In Asia, many countries have only a hot dry season and a hot rainy season, but Japan has been blessed with four distinct seasons. Much of our culture is related to anticipating and marking the change of these seasons. Flowering evergreens, such as camellia (*sasanka*), Japanese andromeda (*asebi*), and azalea (*satsuki*), keep their leaves while marking the season with a touch of color. Japanese maples, flowering cherry (*sakura*), and flowering plum (*ume*), Bishop's hat (*ikariso*), and Japanese strawberry dogwood (*yamaboshi*), which completely change appearance in winter and spring, play a more dramatic role in commemorating the seasons and the passage of time.

The Landslide That Became a Garden

The Holts are a Japanese and American couple. Mrs. Holt is a teacher of more than forty years and author of several cookbooks. They have a large property in Kamakura, a town famous for its statue of the Great Buddha, the Kamakura Daibutsu. The town hosts many old temples and shrines, and has an oceanside-resort atmosphere. It was the capital city of the first shogun, Minamoto no Yoritomo, and the era that began when the Minamoto clan came to power is known as the Kamakura period (1185–1333). It was said that the reason Yoritomo picked this spot was because mountains sheltered it on

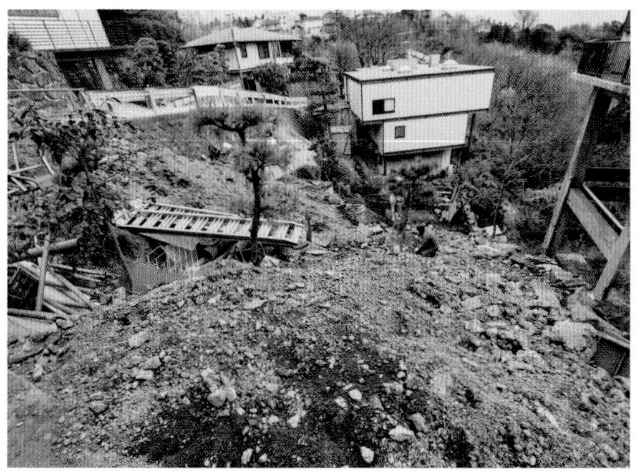

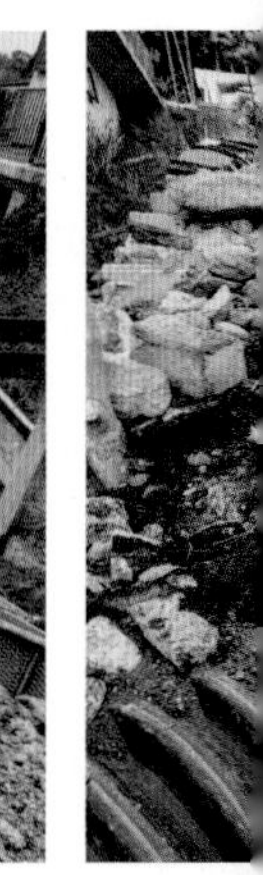

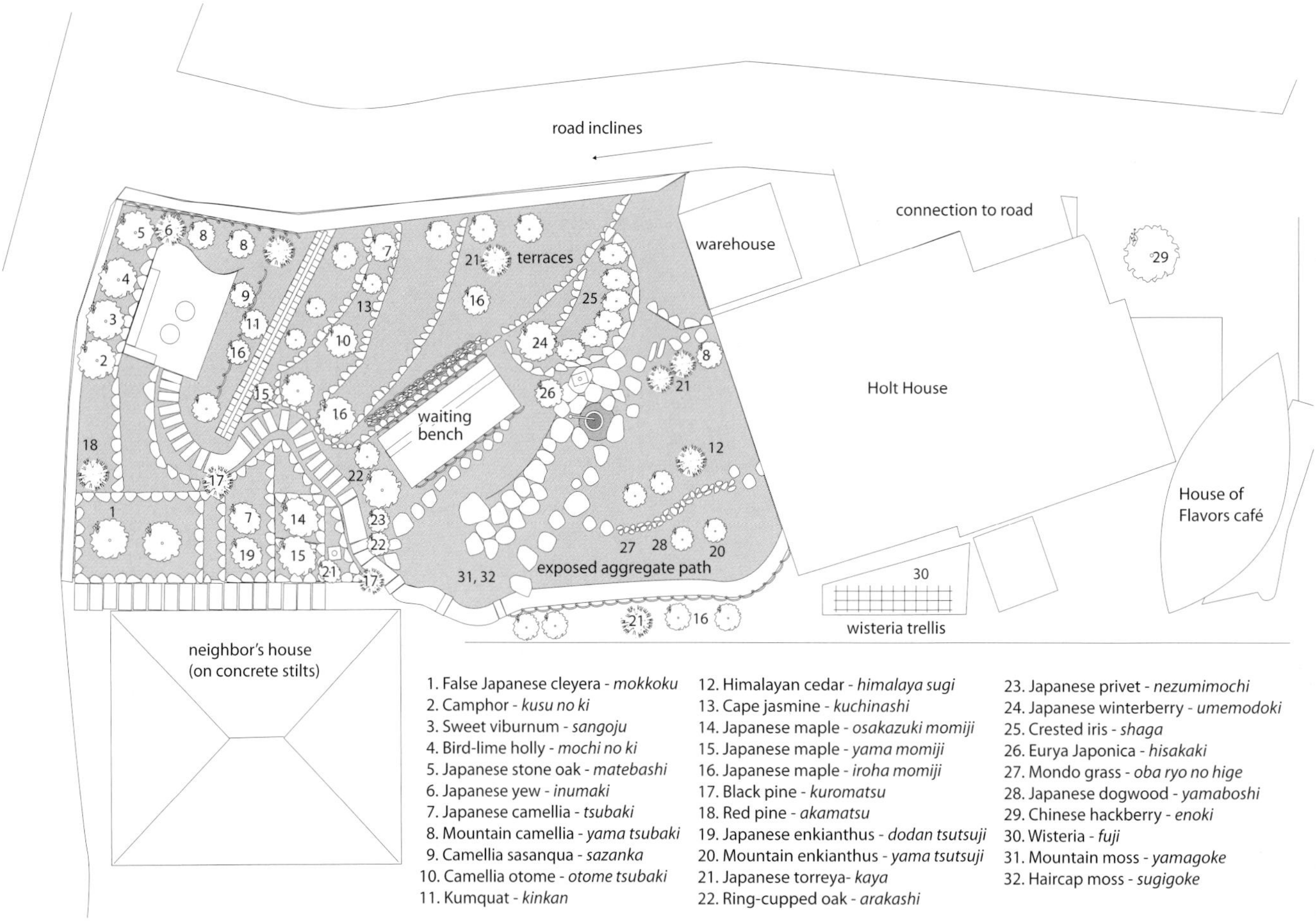

road inclines

connection to road

warehouse

terraces

waiting bench

Holt House

House of Flavors café

exposed aggregate path

wisteria trellis

neighbor's house (on concrete stilts)

1. False Japanese cleyera - *mokkoku*
2. Camphor - *kusu no ki*
3. Sweet viburnum - *sangoju*
4. Bird-lime holly - *mochi no ki*
5. Japanese stone oak - *matebashi*
6. Japanese yew - *inumaki*
7. Japanese camellia - *tsubaki*
8. Mountain camellia - *yama tsubaki*
9. Camellia sasanqua - *sazanka*
10. Camellia otome - *otome tsubaki*
11. Kumquat - *kinkan*
12. Himalayan cedar - *himalaya sugi*
13. Cape jasmine - *kuchinashi*
14. Japanese maple - *osakazuki momiji*
15. Japanese maple - *yama momiji*
16. Japanese maple - *iroha momiji*
17. Black pine - *kuromatsu*
18. Red pine - *akamatsu*
19. Japanese enkianthus - *dodan tsutsuji*
20. Mountain enkianthus - *yama tsutsuji*
21. Japanese torreya- *kaya*
22. Ring-cupped oak - *arakashi*
23. Japanese privet - *nezumimochi*
24. Japanese winterberry - *umemodoki*
25. Crested iris - *shaga*
26. Eurya Japonica - *hisakaki*
27. Mondo grass - *oba ryo no hige*
28. Japanese dogwood - *yamaboshi*
29. Chinese hackberry - *enoki*
30. Wisteria - *fuji*
31. Mountain moss - *yamagoke*
32. Haircap moss - *sugigoke*

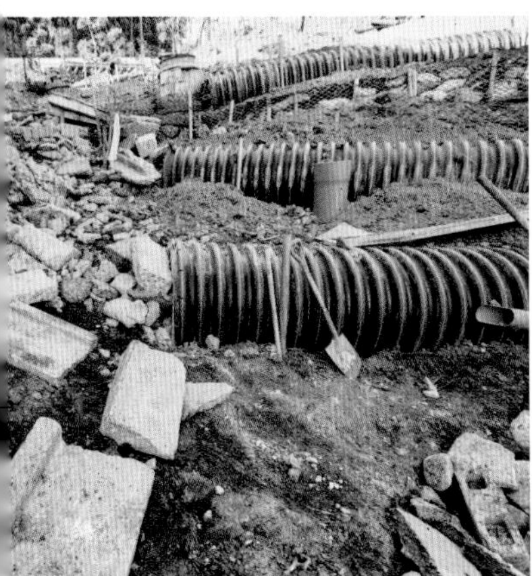

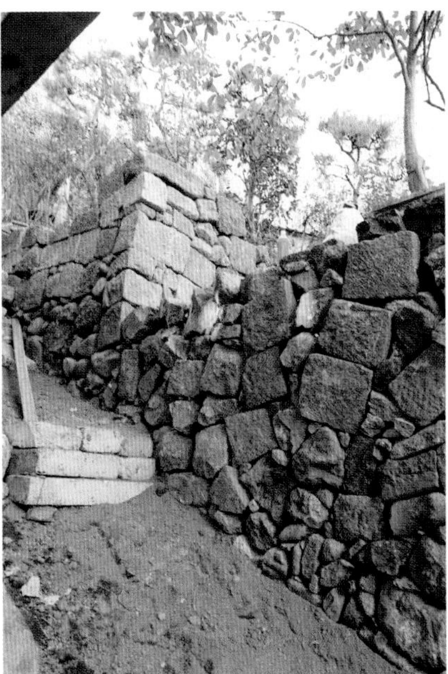

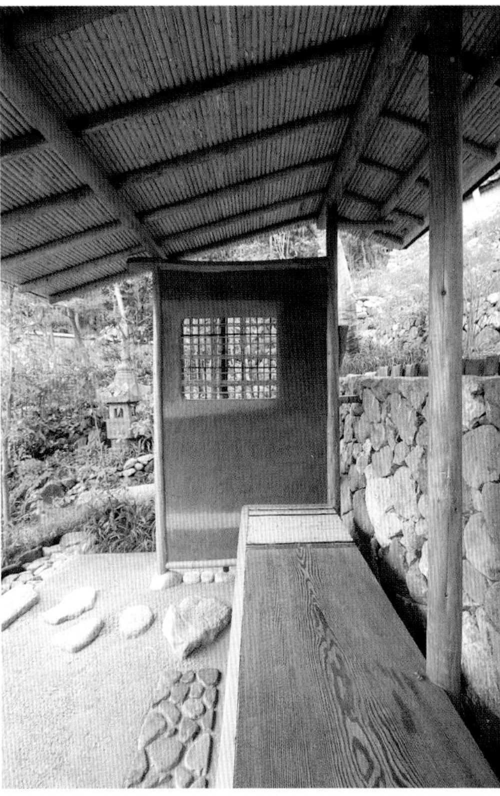

Facing page The garden begins as a total washout after a landslide.

Above The ground is roughly terraced. Polyethylene pipes will capture water.

Above A massive stone wall, backfilled with soil, supports terraces along the sloping property line.

Right Further along in the process, a covered waiting bench is constructed on one of the upper terraces.

three sides and the sea on the fourth. The entire town is composed of hills and valleys and precipitous climbs, making it difficult to attack.

The Holts' property is a sloping 9,500-square-foot (880-m^2) lot with a drop of about 32 feet (10 m) from top to bottom. The house is built on steel stilts such that the third floor of the three-story house is level with the surrounding road. This is not unusual for the Kamakura area or for much of mountainous Japan. Unfortunately, it is also not unusual to have landslides after heavy rains. This was the tragedy that struck the Holts and it was the reason I became involved. Basically, no one wanted to take on the work because it was dangerous and difficult. But we took it on with a team of only five. After six months of long hours and hard work, the landslide was well on its way to becoming a beautiful garden.

Our first task was to stop the land from sliding further, especially onto the neighbor's property. We cleared away soil and debris and piled up large stones and concrete curbs, which we got from a local construction site, along the property line. Then, we needed to ensure that a landslide would not reoccur by terracing the slope and providing for water runoff without the assistance of the municipal sewer system, whose capacities were fairly limited. In other words, any water that fell on the land needed to stay on the land without causing damage in the future. To handle this, we installed about twenty 13 to 16-foot (4 to 5-m) lengths of 32-inch (80-cm) polyethylene drainpipe. We didn't use these pipes to transport water but to capture it. About 4 tons of water can be stored in each pipe in the event of a long period of heavy rain. Stones were loaded into the pipes and each end was closed with metal grating to allow water to flow in and out slowly. More stones were pressed against the gratings to keep them shut. The polyethylene pipes

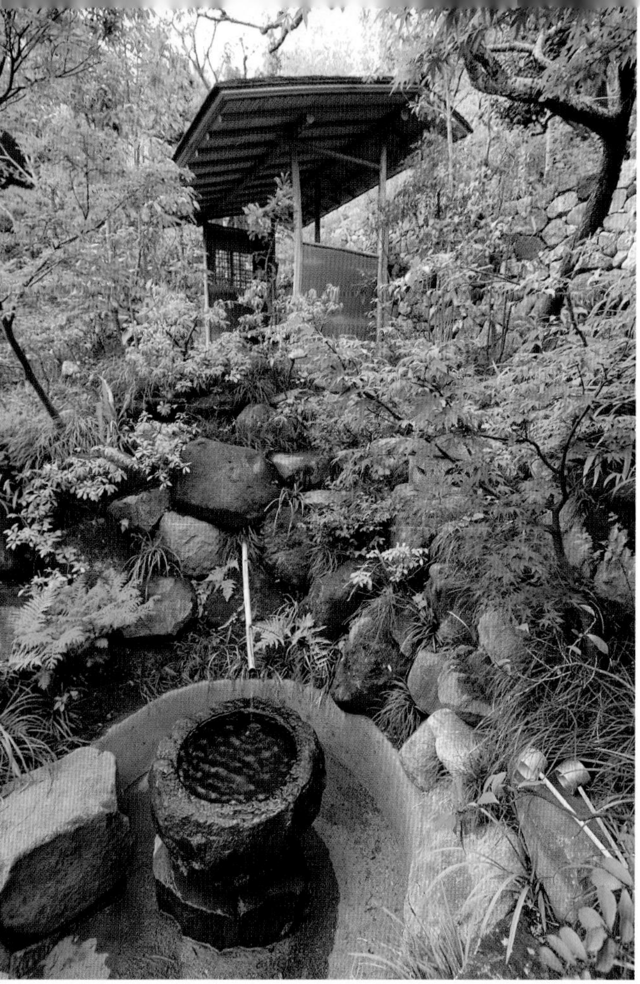

Left A *chozubachi* stone water basin on a lower terrace with a view to the covered waiting bench. Plantings soften the roughness of the stone.

Below Exposed aggregate *(araidashi)*, and quarried and natural stone create a beautiful means to access every level.

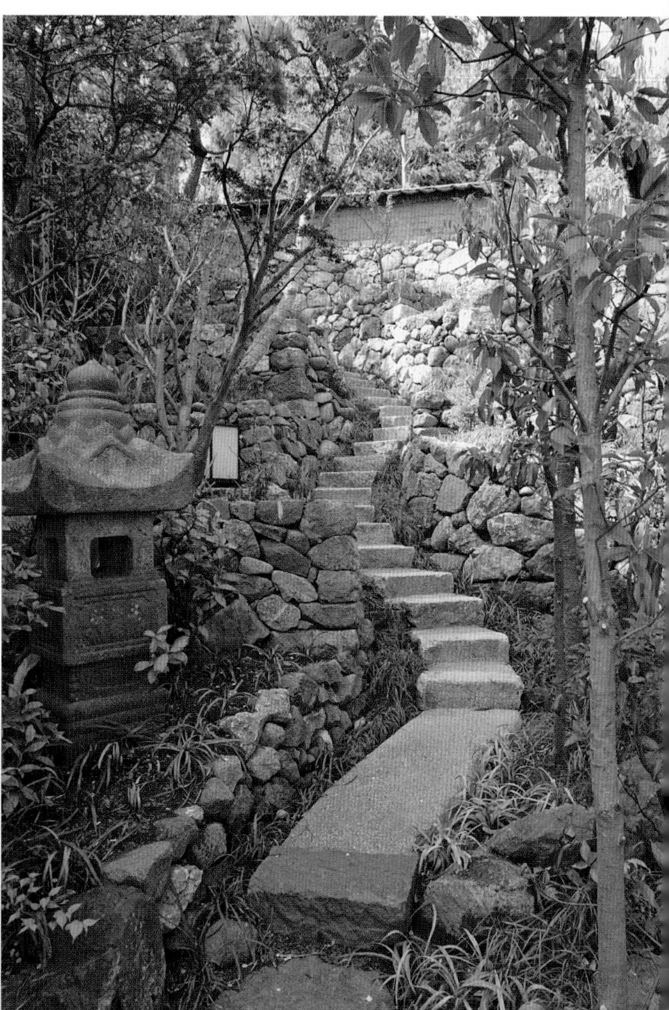

were held in place with metal pipes hammered into the ground.

This was not a conventional use of the pipe but it worked well for our purposes. We used a mini excavator to roughly terrace the ground and laid the pipes on these terraces. We also created fences of wire mesh and steel pipe along parts of the terrace. These were backfilled with sandbags, stones from the site, and concrete rubble. Our purpose was to capture excess water in the pipes but also allow rain to flow through the soil without washing it away. The mixture of stones and cement serves the purpose. This was the least expensive method of tackling the problem. We also utilized existing stone from the site for this ground preparation.

Terracing a steep slope is a typical way to stop mudslides but it is only the beginning. After the terraces were roughed out, we prepared the surface for planting, bringing in fresh soil—mostly volcanic loam (*akatsuchi*) and rice paddy soil (*hatake no tsuchi*)—and about fifty trees. First we reinforced the terraces by setting up steel planks with supporting pipes and backfilling with the new soil. In front of the steel we made low stone-and-mortar walls to create the finished terraces. On each terrace we planted trees, bushes, long grasses, and two types

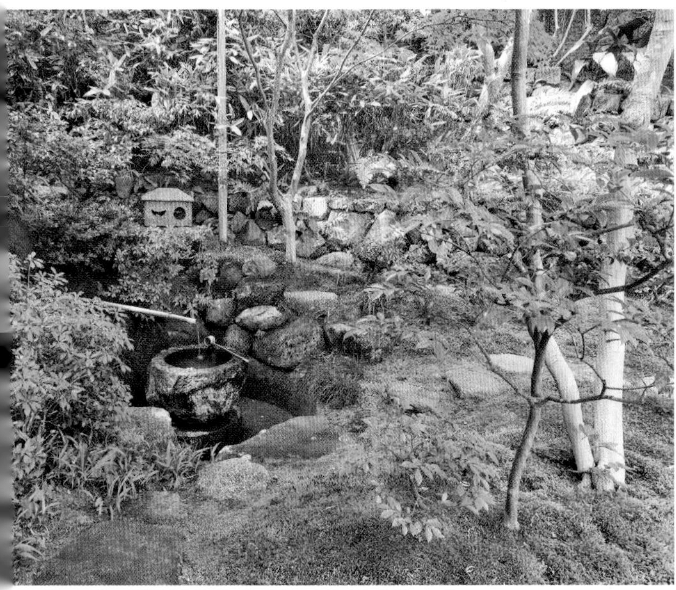

Left The water basin seen from another angle, in the midst of lush green moss, grasses and trees.

Below An exposed-aggregate (*araidashi*) path bordered with roof tile in a garden that belies its origins in disaster.

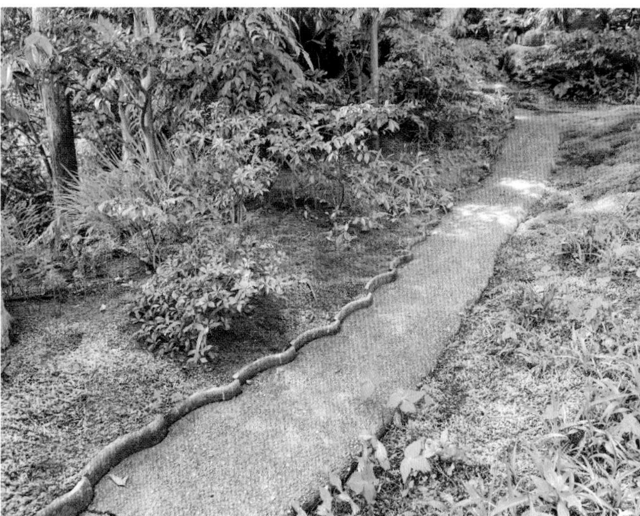

of moss: haircap (*sugigoke*) and mountain moss (*yamagoke*). The property has a distant view of Kamakura Bay so we situated some of the terraces to face that direction. On the top terrace we placed some stone tables and benches and created a small area for planting perennials. On a lower terrace we made an observation deck (*miharashi dai*) with a covered waiting bench (*koshikake machiai*).

The terraced garden also required stone stairs and exposed aggregate (*araidashi*) walkways. The longest one is bordered with ceramic roofing tiles and rounded river stones. The tiles have a decorative effect but are also a practical way of keeping adjacent soil from washing onto the walkway. The long walkway from the bottom of the stairs to the house has a 5 percent grade to keep rainwater from pooling. In areas of the stairway that allow for it, clay walkways are included to provide rest space and to allow easy connection to stepping stones or other pathways. Compared to stone, clay is easier to form into curves of any shape and length. The mix of 50 percent clay-rich soil (*arakida*) and 50 percent river sand (*kawazuna*) is laid on with a trowel to a thickness of 4 to 6 inches (10 to 15 cm). It hardens like cement and adds a softer feeling to the garden.

Stone, soil and clay aside, it is the roots of trees, bushes and ground cover that play the major role in holding and strengthening the land to prevent further landslides. Along with the numerous small steps of the terraces, the real key is the volume and mix of plantings. Other than the walkways and observation deck, not a patch of ground was left uncovered. The trees that were washed out (mostly small pines) were picked up and replanted in various places throughout the garden. In addition, we planted camphor (*kusunoki*), Japanese stone oak (*matebashi*), mountain camellia (*yama tsubaki*), among others. Now, after a number of years, the plants are well established and even after some record-breaking storms, the slope is stable and the garden grows more beautiful by the day.

HOW TO MAKE A KOSHIKAKE MACHIAI COVERED WAITING BENCH

Over time, Japanese gardens have settled on several typical forms: stroll garden (*kayushiki teien*); small courtyard garden (*tsuboniwa*); stone-and-sand garden (*karesansui*); hill-and-pond garden (*tsuki-yama*); tea garden (*chaniwa* or *roji*); and, in the modern age, deciduous-tree garden (*zokibayashi*). Each garden type has certain signature features. The covered waiting bench (*koshikake machiai*) is one indispensable feature of tea gardens.

Holt House is not a teahouse. It is a residence and a café, serving coffee, tea and great cheesecake. In this case we used some features of the tea garden to fit a new situation, in the spirit of *mitate*—to see old things in a new light—another concept associated with tea gardens. A typical waiting bench has a roof, sidewalls, and a back (our backless example is not typical). Even without a traditional teahouse, the waiting bench allows guests a moment of repose and reflection within the garden environment, before or after enjoying some refreshments in the café.

As with all the instructions in this book, please keep in mind that dimensions are approximate and should be checked and modified as needed.

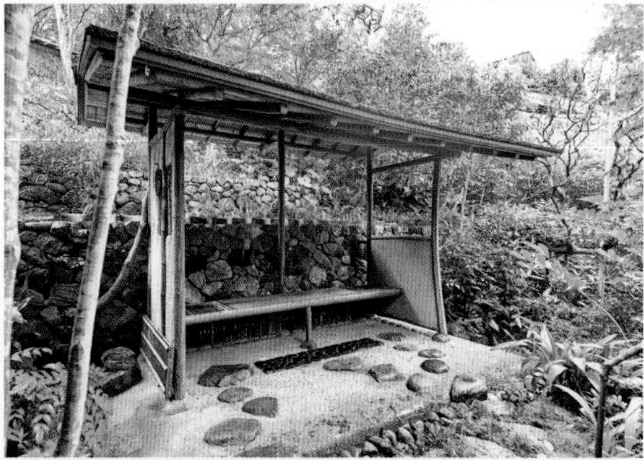

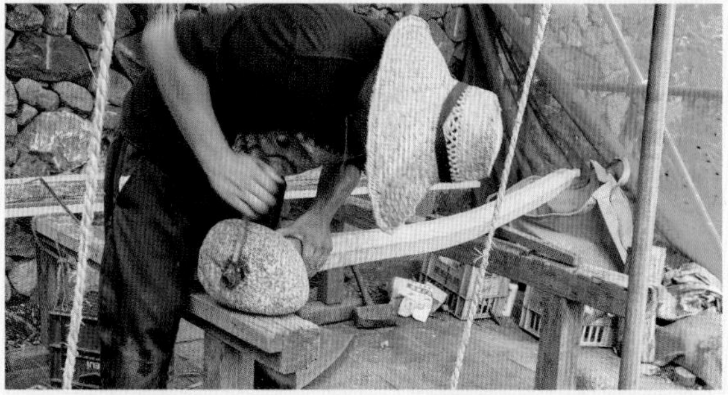

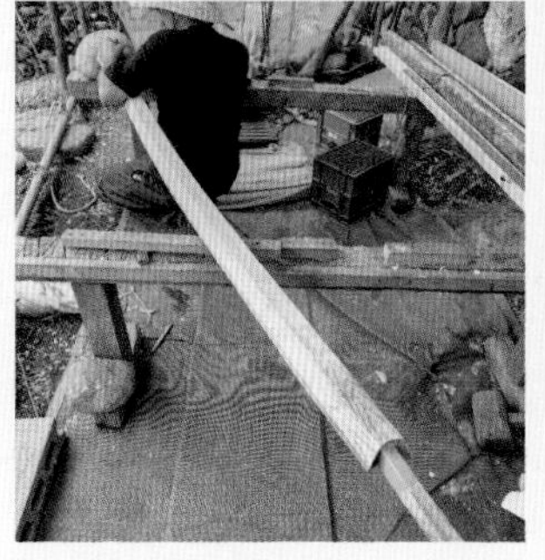

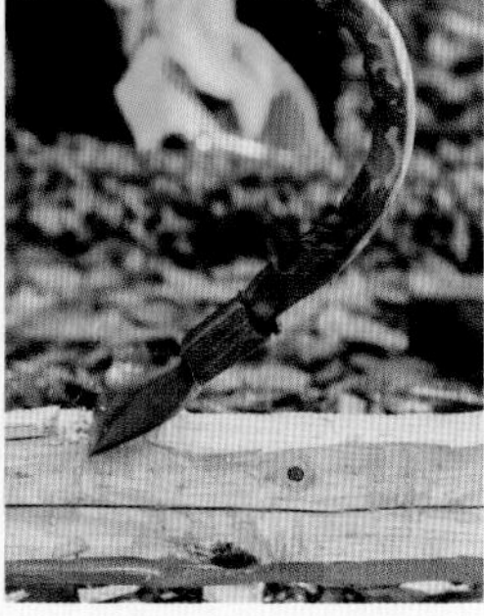

Step 1 We begin with rounded river stones about 8 inches (20 cm) diameter. Drill a 1¼-inch (3-cm) hole through each stone to insert bolts. The bottoms of the six stones need to be countersunk. Leave a minimum of 3 inches (8 cm) from the hole to the side of the stone. After the posts are prepared they will be connected to the stones with a spiral thread bolt (like a sleeper spike). This is the same procedure as for the *amigasa mon* "monk's hat" gate (page 42).

Step 2 Cut and shape five main posts and one bench leg. We will use 2⅜ to 2¾-inch (6 to 7-cm)-diameter poles, stripped of bark and given a light planing. We will shape one of the five with the adze into a six-sided figure. For this post, we selected a piece with an interesting natural bend. In general, where a round horizontal pole connects to a round vertical pole, drill a hole a third of the way into the vertical and insert the horizontal. For hexagonal poles, use mortise and tenon joints.

Step 3 Before connecting the post to the stone, drill a hole in the bottom of the post and shape the

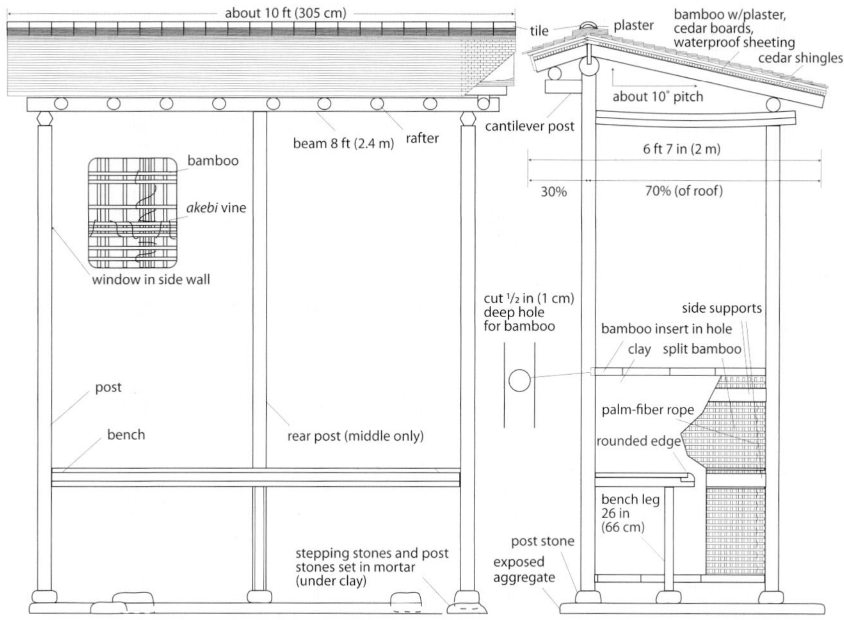

bottom to fit the stone. Support the post in position on the stone. Use a compass to transfer the profile of the stone to the wood. Use a chisel to cut a hollow in the bottom and shape the profile. Mark lines on the stone and wood to remember your alignment.

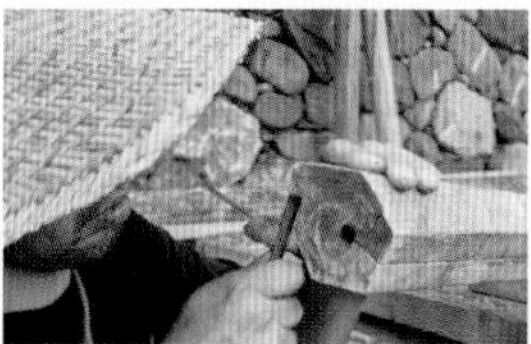

Step 4 Basically, we will be making a five-post rectangular frame with a bench and a roof. The three posts of the backside will be taller than the two front posts. This will determine the slope of the roof. The roof is asymmetric with a long front and short back side. The peak sits directly above the back posts.

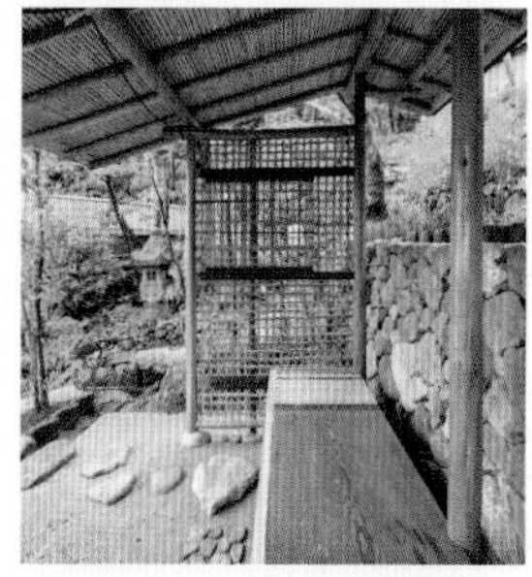

Step 5 Cut mortises in the front and rear poles (three on the window side, two on the opposite side) to insert the 4 x 7/8-inch (10 x 2-cm) side supports. Then cut holes to insert 2 7/8-inch (7-cm)-diameter bamboo poles. The poles and side supports should be 3 feet (90 cm) from post to post. The lower side supports are set to the same height as the bench (see the drawing above).

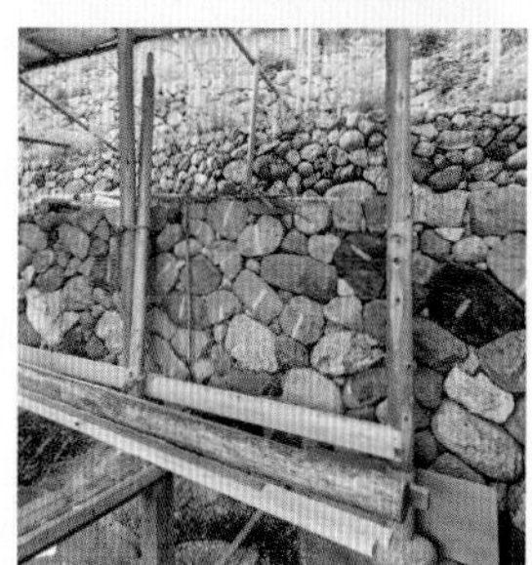

Step 6 Cut long tenons in the tops of the posts and mortises in the lintels. Cut the lower back support and three beams to the correct length. In our example, the length is 8 feet (2.4 m). Cut mortises in the front and center beams. Assemble and level the frame, including the stones, while supporting it with scaffolding. Adding a vertical bamboo pole on the exterior of the window side is optional.

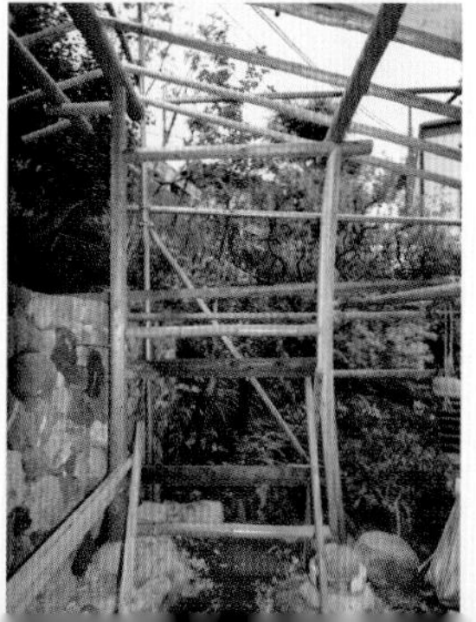

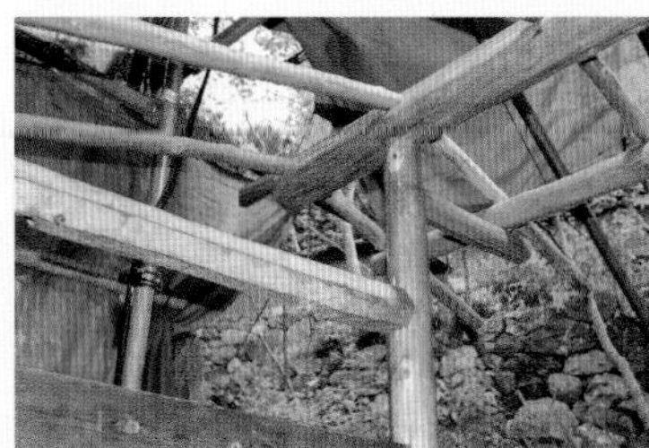

Step 7 Add three cantilevered roof supports to the back posts using mortise and tenon joints. Attach the third beam to these. Attach 3 x ⅞-inch (8 x 2-cm) boards to the top of the center beam with screws. The screws are driven at an angle, at a 16-inch (41-cm) pitch. Before attaching, cut ⅞ inch (2 cm) from the height of the board, beginning 12 inches (30 cm) from the edge. The board will overhang the beam by this amount. Use one or more boards to get the overall length.

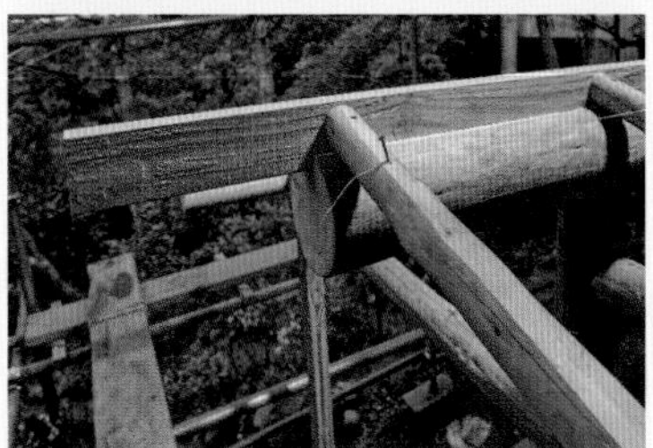

Step 8 Cut two sets of eleven poles, for rafters. The first set should be 5 feet 2 inches (1.6 m) long. The second set should be 16 inches (41 cm) long. The diameter of both sets of poles should be 2 inches (5 cm). Attach the longer rafters to the front of the board atop the center beam at a 16-inch (41-cm) pitch. Attach the first and last rafter before the others. Cut one board 1¼ inches (3 cm) thick by 3½ inches (9 cm) wide to a length of 8 feet (2.4 m). Attach it to the first and last rafter about 1½ inches (4 cm) from the edge. This will help to keep the rafters from moving. Continue attaching rafters at a 16-inch (41-cm) pitch.

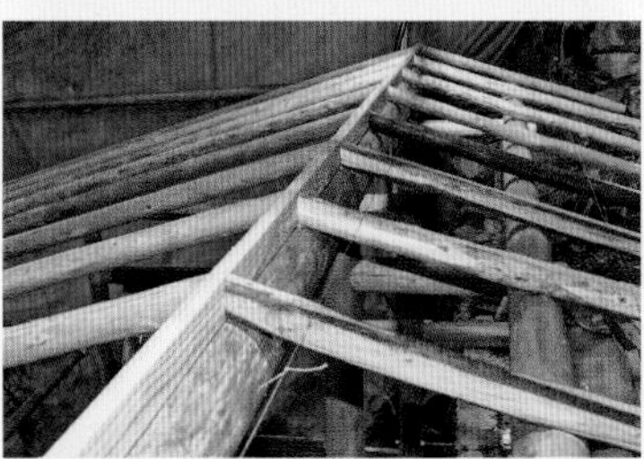

Step 9 Attach the 16-inch rafters to the back side of the top beam and the rear beam, in the same manner and at the same pitch. Cut 1¼-inch (3-cm) bamboo poles the full length of the roof and secure them to the rafters with screws. Drill holes for the screws or use an impact driver. If you can't find enough bamboo poles long enough, you can piece them together with the joints above the rafters. Start from the edge of the roof and fill to the peak.

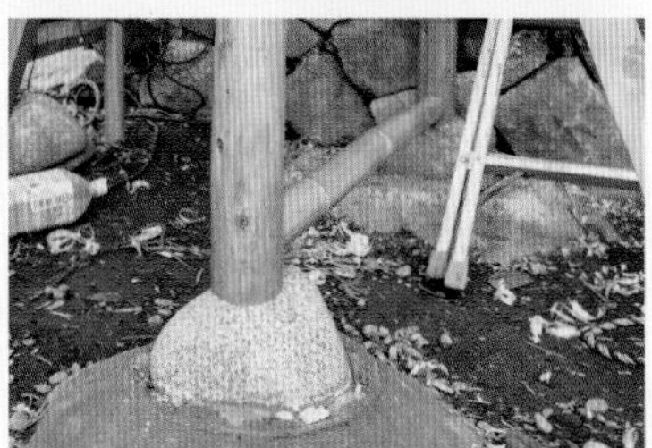

Step 10 When you have assembled the work and are satisfied up to this point, mix enough cement to set the stones. Keep the upper half of the stone clean because it will show above the exposed aggregate (*araidashi*) base that will form the floor under the bench. Keep checking the level of the frame and adjust until the cement is set.

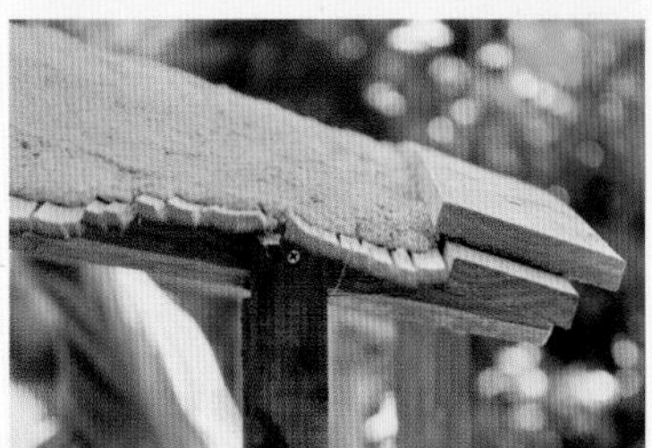

Step 11 Add powdered seaweed glue (*tsunomata*) mixed in water, or any starch-based glue to the plaster and spread over the bamboo about ½ inch (1 cm) thick. Add boards along the left and right roof edge and use them as a guide to fill in the plaster. When dry, cover the plaster with ¼–½ x 4-inch (1 x 10-cm) cedar boards secured with screws.

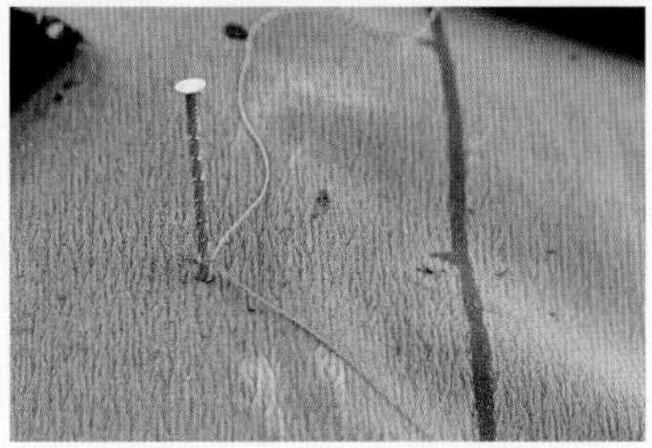

Step 12 Waterproof sheeting is secured with nails or staples over the boards. Finish the roof with cedar shingles about 8 inches (21 cm) square. First soak them in water to make them resistant to splitting when nailed. Lay them down, beginning at the roof edge and work to

the ridge. Trim the outside corners with pruning shears. The shingles should overlap each other by about 6 inches (15 cm).

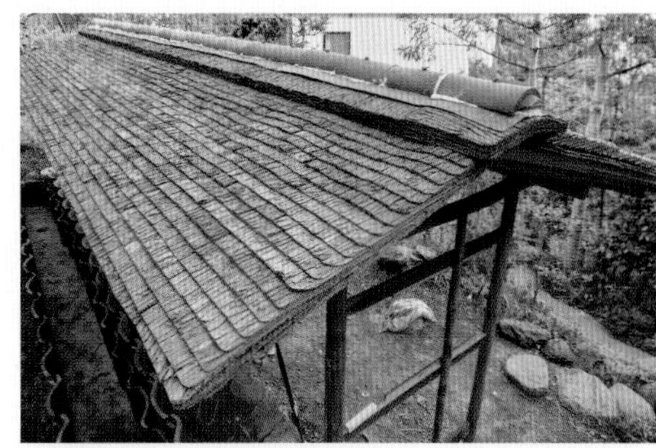

Step 13 Stack groups of four shingles and bend them over the ridge. Secure them with nails. Lay copper sheeting above this then use ceramic tiles, filled with plaster or clay and secured with wire, to finish the ridge. For a more informal look, you can use wide bamboo, cut in half, in place of the ceramic tile.

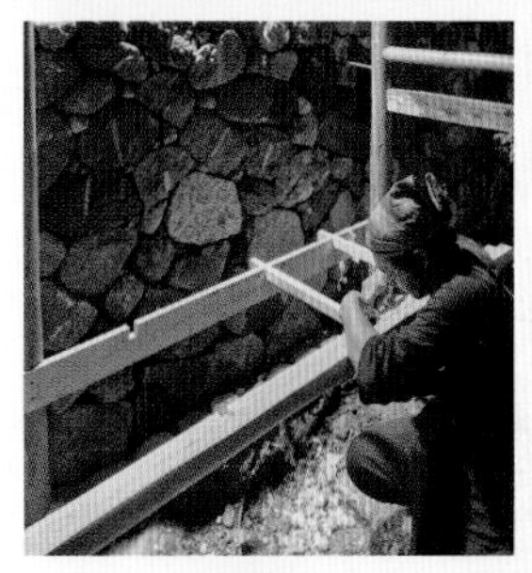

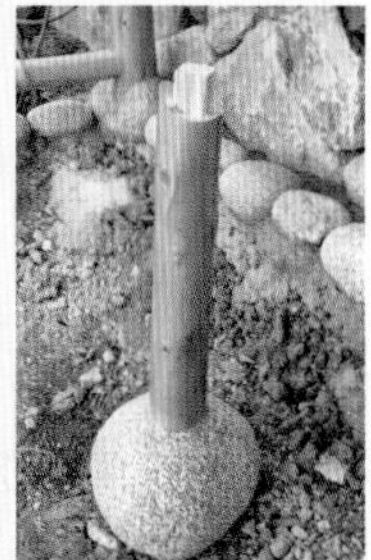

Step 14 Next, cut and fit the parts of the bench. First complete the frame, as pictured, and then attach the bench. In this case we used a wide cedar plank for about two-thirds of the bench, and bamboo for the rest. The length of the bench traditionally accommodates five people, which is typical for a tea ceremony (adjust the dimensions if a shorter bench is desired). Finally, attach the middle leg (made in Step 2) with a stone connected, as shown in the photo (right), and cement the stone in place.

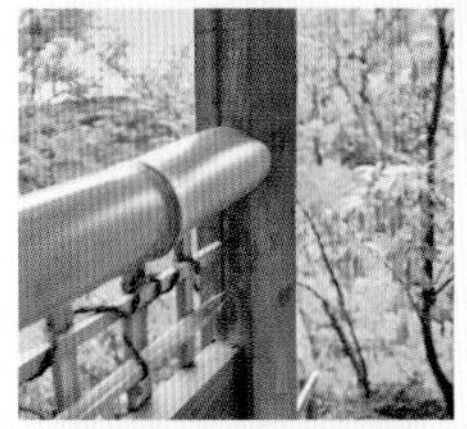

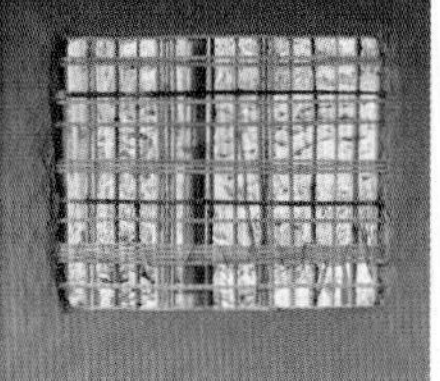

Step 15 To create a half wall on one side and a full wall on the other, begin with a framework of split bamboo, tied with chocolate vine (*akebi*) or palm-fiber rope (*shuronawa*). Not every joint needs to be tied, just enough to keep things in place. On the side with a full wall we will make a window called a *shitaji mado*, meaning an opening through which you can see the framework (*shitaji*) of the wall. The window allows the main guest to see when the host is coming. In this area we use whole bamboo of ¾ to 1¼ inches (2 to 3 cm) in diameter tied with akebi that has been soaked in water.

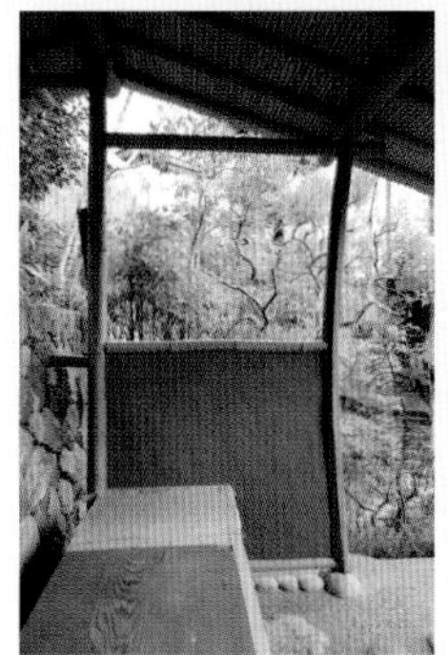

Step 16 On to this framework, trowel clay-rich soil such as volcanic loam (*akatsuchi*) mixed with 4 to 6-inch (10–15-cm) lengths of cut straw. The mixture should be kneaded and left covered for a day or two until it is sticky. Trowel it into both sides of the support to a thickness of about 1¾ inches (4.5 cm) and round off the corners and the edge around the window.

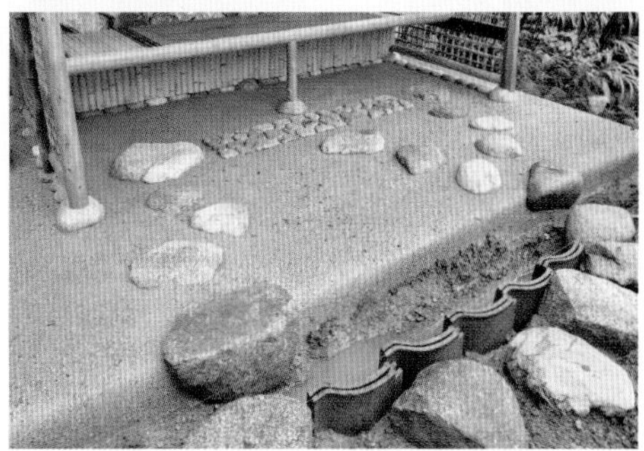

Step 17 Finally, mix enough soil—3 parts small rounded gravel less than ⅜ inch (1 cm), 2 parts clay, 1 part Portland cement—to make a floor of about 6 inches (15 cm) thick. The material is troweled on and leveled, and the corners rounded. When set and dry to the touch, rub the surface with a soft brush and water to expose the gravel. Clean any soil from the post stones and stepping stones. Leave it to dry a day or two before walking on it.

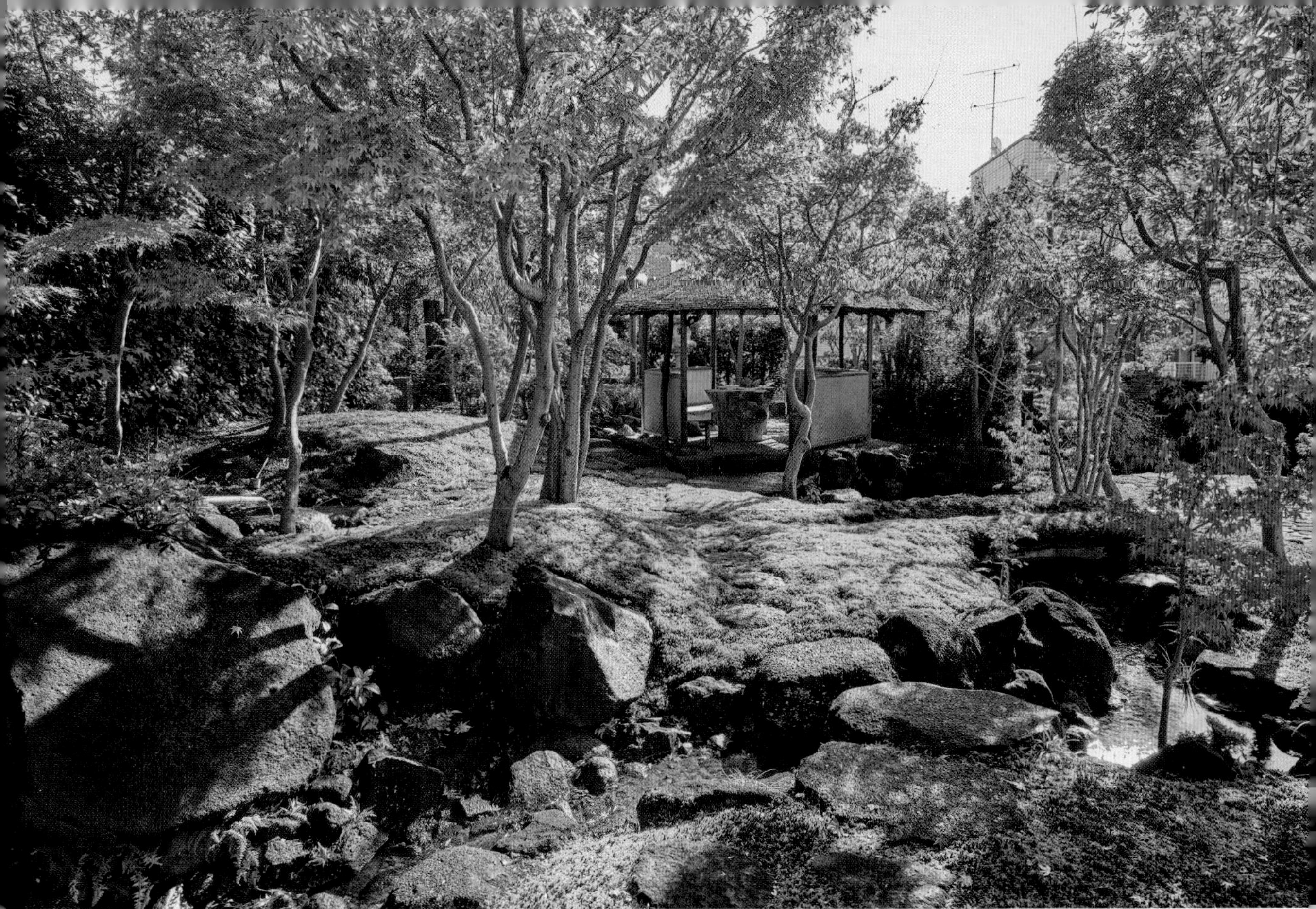

The Urban Farmer with a Backyard Stroll Garden

You might not know that in Japan all elementary schools have a kitchen and serve a hot lunch everyday. The Enomotos are urban farmers who have been growing potatoes and onions and selling them to Tokyo elementary schools for more than thirty years. Their house is located next to their field on a big lot in the southwest of the city. We made a lovely stroll garden (*kaiyushiki teien*) for them, which includes a gazebo (*azumaya*) where neighbors can meet and take some refreshments. Widely used in China, the gazebo is not a typical part of Japanese gardens, but the owner desired one and this garden is large enough to accommodate it.

The property occupies a corner of a large housing development in an area that was all farmland in the not too distant past. The 4,500-square-foot (420-m^2) backyard garden has four entrances: one each on the left and right side of the house, and two at the opposite end of the garden. The front entrance on the right connects the street in front of the house to the garden, and the one on the left connects the garden to the owner's field. The entrance across the garden and opposite the house connects directly to the driveway of a relative's property. It is the entrance closest to the gazebo and has only a simple *shiorido* hinged gate about 4 feet

(1.2 m) tall. Next to the relative's driveway, and facing the street at the side of the house, is the formal entrance to the garden and house. This entrance has a metal gate with an intercom.

The land has a 3-foot (1-m) grade from the back of the property to the front. First, we made a 6½-foot (2-m) wall of very large stones that runs along the left of the formal entrance and up the side of the street. It runs along the border to the front corner of the property and supports the rather soft ground. By the time it reaches the corner it is just over 3 feet tall. The large stones in this wall weigh between 3 and 7 tons. The formal entrance gate is at the tall end of the wall. From there we made a broad and powerful stone stair that curves to the left and rises about 6½ feet to enter the garden. The stone for the stair and wall is called *tsukuba ishi*, from an area north of Tokyo. The dark stone appears almost black

Facing page Beyond a rocky riverbank, a gazebo nestles in rolling hills of green moss and maples.

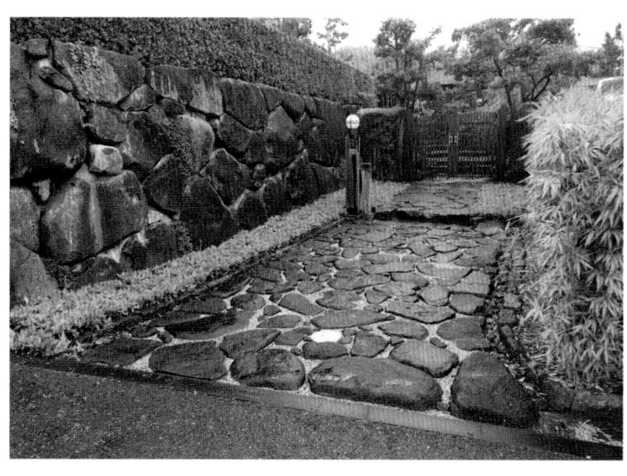

Below The formal entrance walkway of *tsukuba ishi* stone alongside a massive retaining wall of the same.

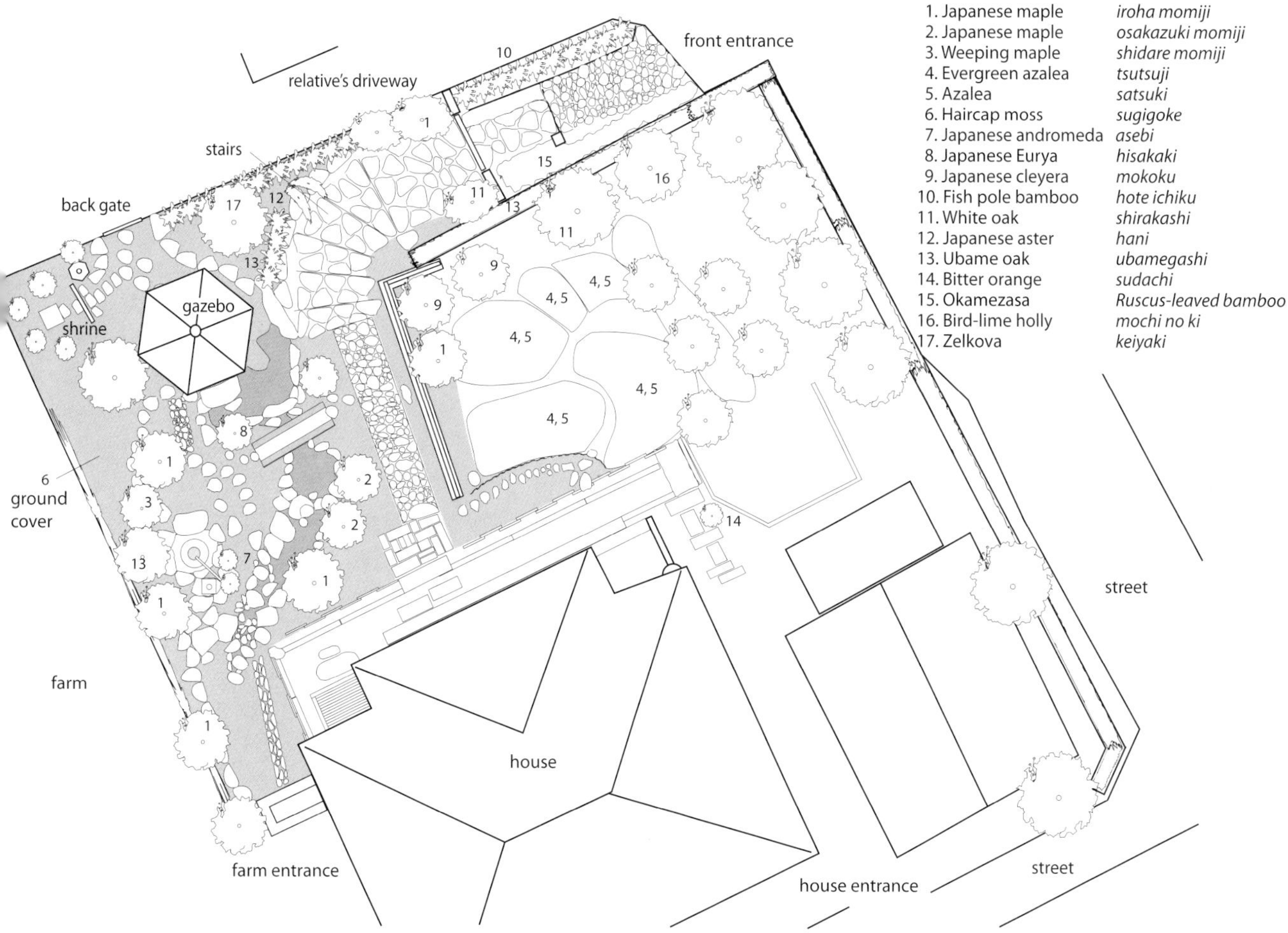

1. Japanese maple	*iroha momiji*
2. Japanese maple	*osakazuki momiji*
3. Weeping maple	*shidare momiji*
4. Evergreen azalea	*tsutsuji*
5. Azalea	*satsuki*
6. Haircap moss	*sugigoke*
7. Japanese andromeda	*asebi*
8. Japanese Eurya	*hisakaki*
9. Japanese cleyera	*mokoku*
10. Fish pole bamboo	*hote ichiku*
11. White oak	*shirakashi*
12. Japanese aster	*hani*
13. Ubame oak	*ubamegashi*
14. Bitter orange	*sudachi*
15. Okamezasa	*Ruscus-leaved bamboo*
16. Bird-lime holly	*mochi no ki*
17. Zelkova	*keiyaki*

in the rain. The top of the gazebo is glimpsed on the right as you climb the stair.

From the top of the stair we made a broad, informal-style *nobedan* stone walkway that runs straight to the back of the house. Along the left side is a brushwood fence (*shibagaki*). With its stone base and broad roof it is about 6½ feet (2 m) tall. It's made with Japanese aster (*hani*), which is also planted in the garden along the right side of the stair. The back side of the brushwood is a wall coated in clay. This fence hides the view of large hedges of azalea cut in the *fukiyose o-karikomi* style.

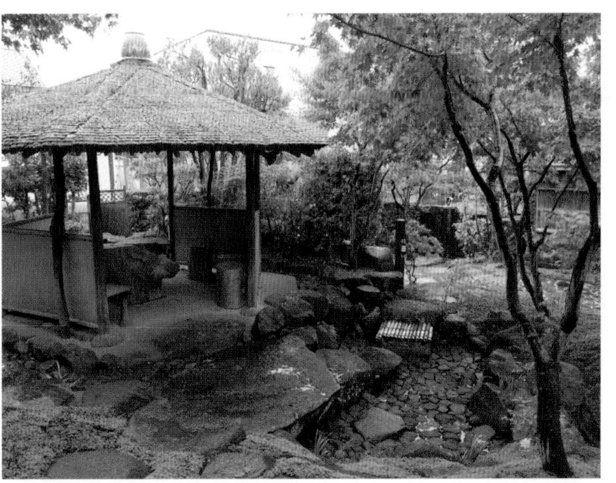

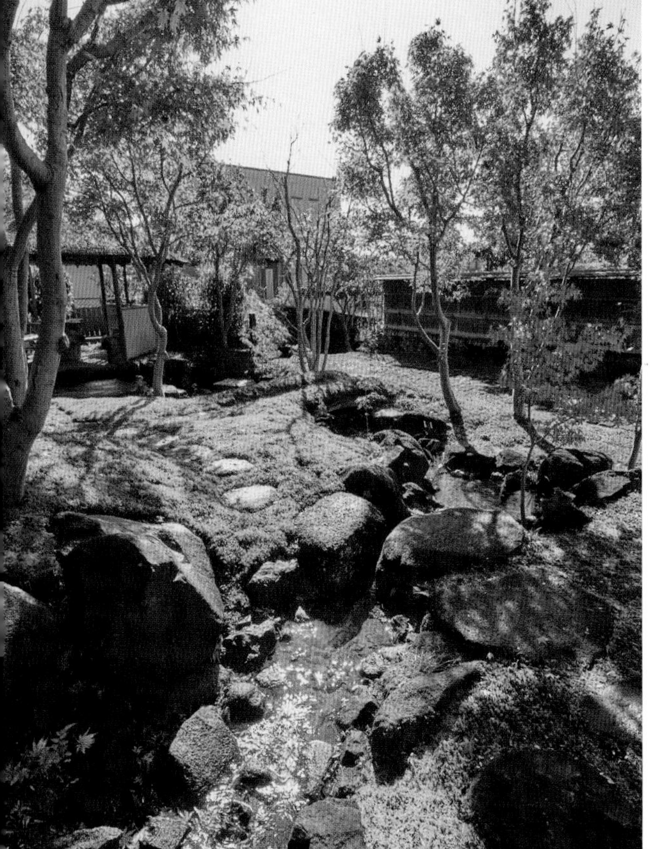

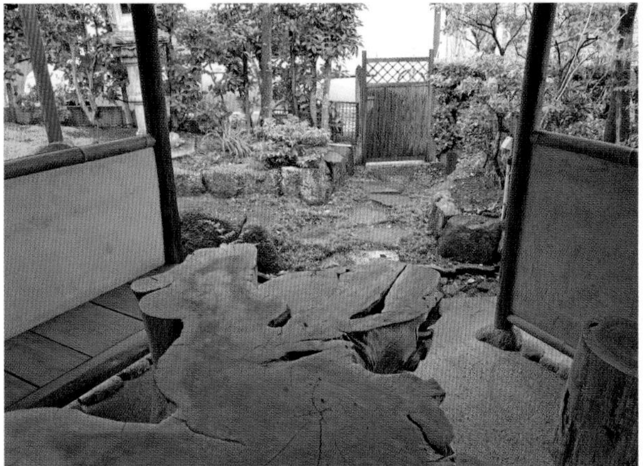

Enomoto-san cuts this hedge himself and he does an excellent job of keeping it pristine. The mass of evergreen azaleas looks beautiful when the leaf is bright green. When the flowers bloom in April the effect is dramatic. Next we created a water source and a stream. Finally, we built the gazebo, which is a six-sided structure with a half-wall (*koshikabe*) and a bench seat. The roof is made of round rafters, wide cedar boards, and cypress bark tiles.

This book is intended to aid with constructing a Japanese garden but I don't mean to suggest that this is a garden you could make on your own. The scale in terms of area and features is just too much for one person or even a small group of friends to handle. But there are many parts that could be tackled

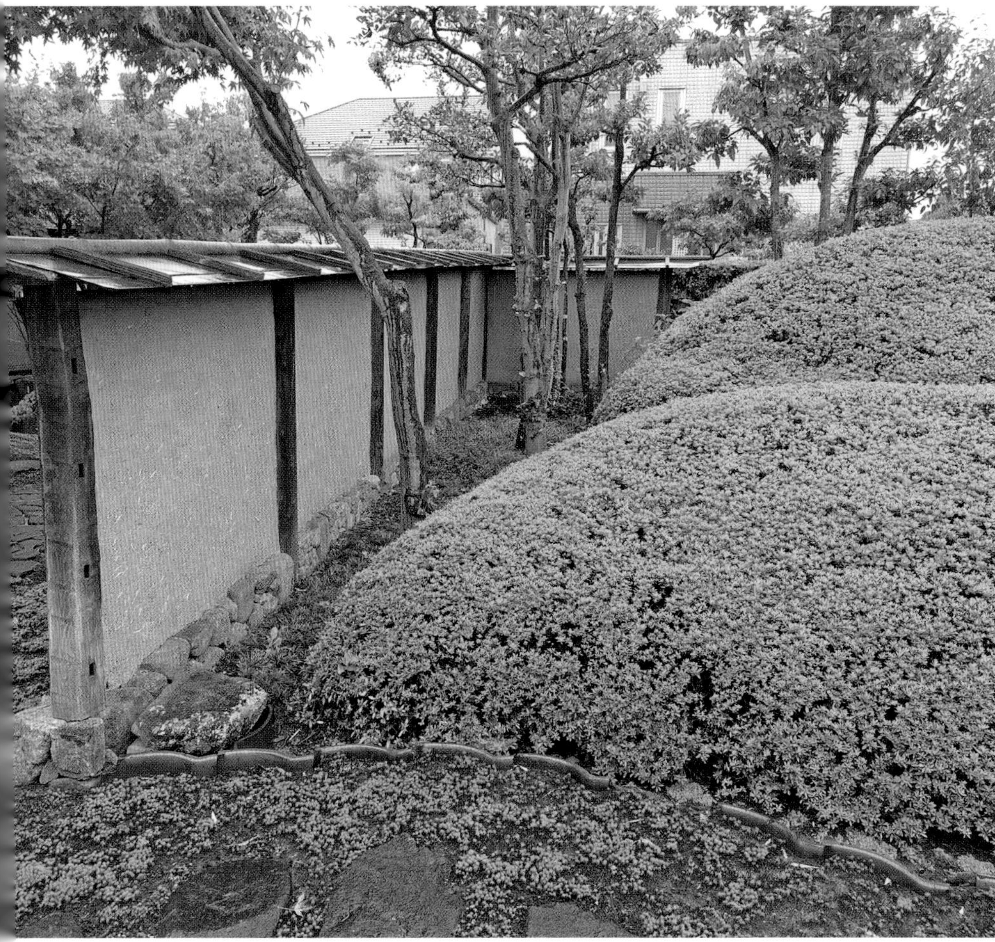

Facing page, bottom left A stream carries water under an earthen bridge to a pond.

Facing page, top right Looking like a hermit's hut on the edge of a cliff, the gazebo is set apart behind a small pond.

Facing page, bottom right A simple gate connects to a relative's house seen from the gazebo.

Left A wall of brushwood on one side and clay on the other separates the great sculpted hedge from the entrance walkway.

individually, especially if they are scaled-down. The gazebo, for example, could be made four-sided with half-walls on three sides and completed by two people in two or three days. All the woodworking projects in this book use the same basic tools and techniques. If you can manage one, you can manage them all. The same goes for projects that use clay or stone: making a small wall or walkway will give you a good feeling for what it takes to make a larger one.

For example, this garden has a small stream (*nagare*) that meanders along the right side of the nobedan and a small earthen bridge (*dobashira*) crosses it at about the halfway point. Compare this to the large bridge at Yushima Tenmangu Shrine on page 78. The difference between what can be made with two or three people in a day as opposed to six to ten people in a month becomes easy to understand. In this garden it's appropriate to have a small bridge for crossing a small stream. The stream narrows and widens and the water tumbles several times as it passes under the bridge and falls into a shallow pond (*mizutani*) at the foot of the gazebo. This bridge is easier to make than its larger cousin, which has a railing, a high elevation, and a much larger deck. The bridge in Enomoto-san's garden is small and lies at ground level. This makes it easy and quick to build and inconspicuous in the landscape. But the small bridge and pond are just enough to visually set the gazebo apart—as though one had come across a hermit's hut nestled in a distant valley.

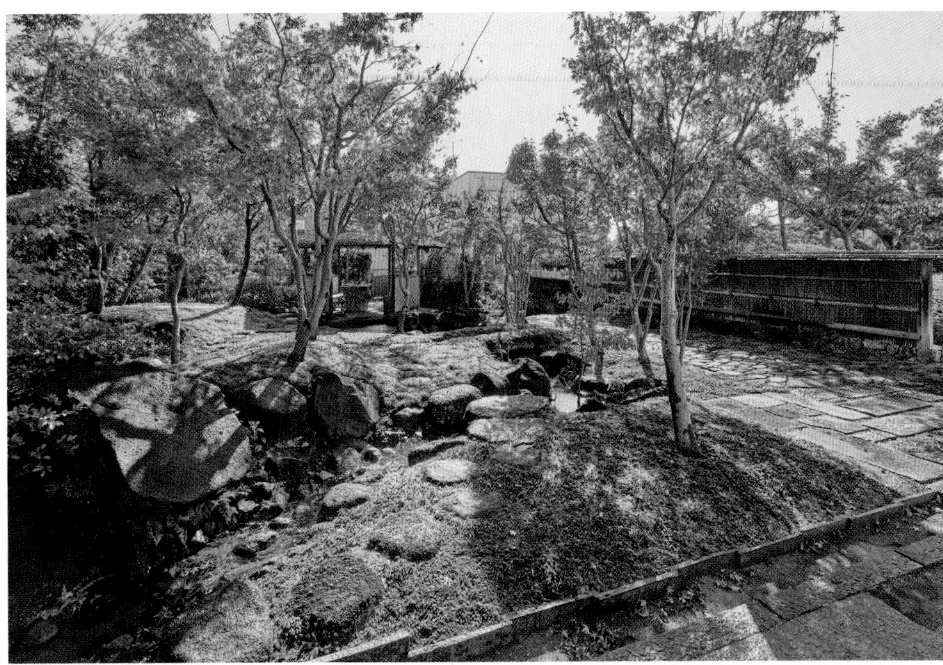

Left A stroll garden alternately hides and reveals the pleasant views in store for the rambler.

Behind the gazebo is a red *torii* gate. Several stone steps lead under the torii to a small *inari* shrine. Inari is the Shinto god of agriculture and such small shrines are common on private property. In Japan, agriculture equals commerce, so inari shrines are also found on the grounds of businesses.

Like any good stroll garden, this one accommodates many features and reveals different aspects of itself from different viewpoints. Passing through the formal entrance and climbing the stone stairs surrounded by massive stone walls, gives the feeling of scaling a mountain fortress. As you get to the top, the view opens to reveal the garden and house in front, and the gazebo and stream to the right. Sitting in the gazebo, drinking tea, admiring the view across the pond and garden filled with maples and moss, one feels far away from the city. On the other hand, from the house, the gazebo can be seen in the distance through the trees. At the same time, the azalea hedges appear behind the brushwood fence: a view of the garden that can only be seen from the house. A good stroll garden can be enjoyed from many viewpoints as one walks through, rests and ambles on again.

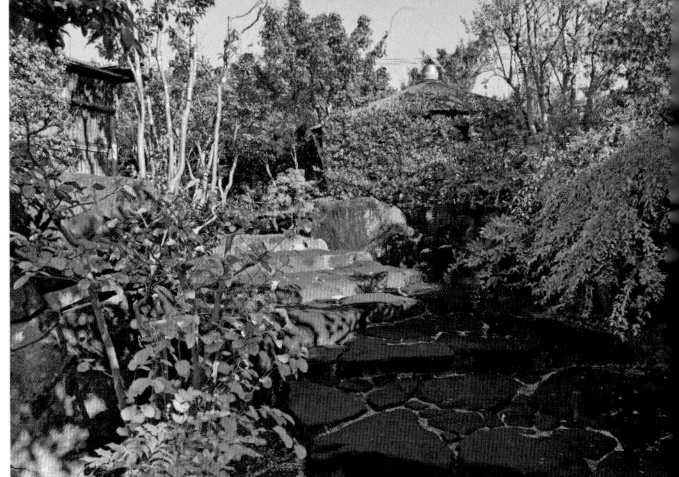

Above Broad stone steps lead from the main entrance at street level to the elevated garden.

HOW TO MAKE A SMALL DOBASHIRA EARTHEN BRIDGE

I mentioned the small earthen bridge in Enomoto-san's garden. Now I will show you how to make it. This bridge will be 5 feet (1.5 m) long and 2 feet (60 cm) wide. The bridge crosses the stream at a point where the water is only about 20 inches (51 cm) wide, and also extends over an area of rocky shore. The stream and shoreline are lined with stones and the bridge supports will also be stone.

Step 1 Use six logs of about 4 inches (10 cm) and trim them into hexagonal shapes. These will form the base of the deck. Use two 4 x 4-inch (10 x 10-cm), or 6 x 6-inch (16 x 16-cm) square support logs that will sit under the deck logs at both ends. The wood should be a rot-resistant type, such as chestnut, yew, etc., or treated wood. Check on the safety of chemicals used to treat the wood and avoid creosote or arsenic compounds.

Step 2 For the stone supports, use stone blocks with a flat top and set them deeply into the banks. It is best to use naturally squared or cut stones a little longer than the full width of the bridge. They should be packed into clay or mortar on the bank. Use natural stones to cover the square stone. If you use mortar in the joints don't let it show.

Step 3 Place a square support log on top of each stone support. Lay the deck logs side by side on top of this. There should be no gaps. Use some stones on the outside of the logs to keep them from slipping laterally. Then pack clay around the ends of the deck logs.

Step 4 Shape the area around the bridge with a clay-rich soil such as *arakida*. Also, mix it with a small amount of water and trowel it over the logs to make the deck surface. Starting at one end, pat it down with a block of wood until you have a flat build up of about 4 inches (10 cm) across the entire surface.

Step 5 Along both sides of the bridge, use a wet mix of clay-rich soil and water. Use a trowel to make soil berms an additional 4 inches (10 cm) above the deck of the bridge.

Step 6 Brush the deck with water and plant moss on the berms. Leave it a few days before walking on it. Check the stability of the bridge at every stage and before anyone walks across it.

Small earthen bridge

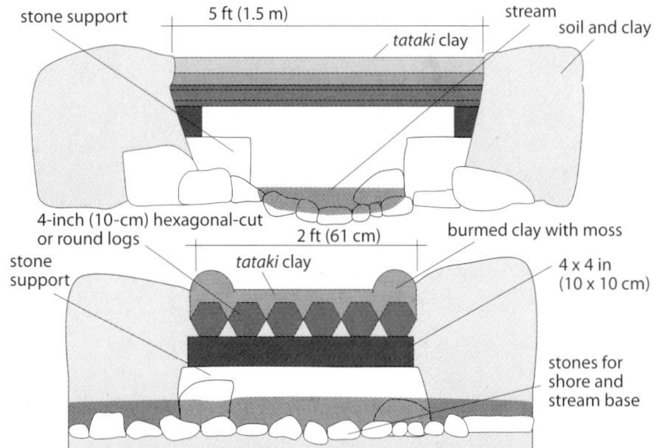

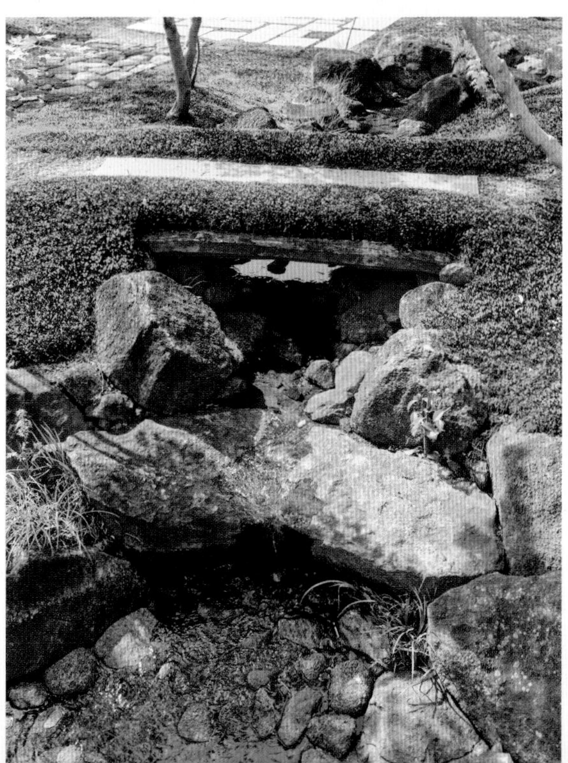

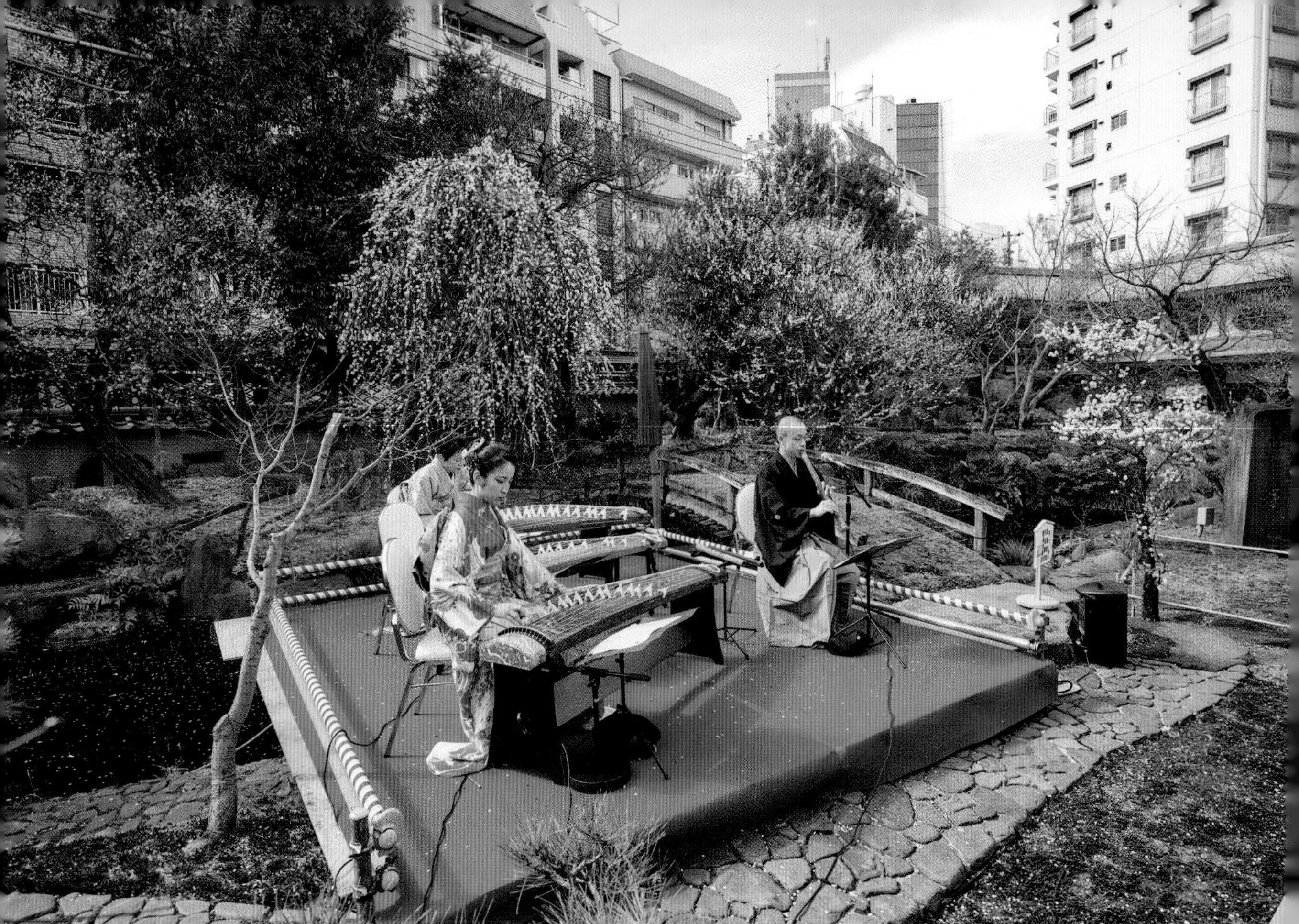

The Garden of Plum Blossoms and Students' Prayers

Yushima Tenmangu is a famous Shinto shrine in the heart of Tokyo. The soul of scholar, poet and politician Sugawara Michizane (845–903 AD) is enshrined here as the god Tenman-Tenjin (often shortened to Tenjin), considered the patron of scholars. Students flock to the shrine each year to pray for success in exams. Typically, these students purchase an *ema*, a small wooden plaque on which they write their aspirations and leave hanging in a location provided by the shrine.

Sugawara was a scholar of Chinese classics and his poetry is well known in Japan. In the ninth century, he was made a high government official, and that's when his troubles began. Jealous rivals falsely accused him of betraying the Emperor and he was exiled to the government outpost of Dazaifu in Kyushu. He soon died there, and in the following years a series of disasters and deaths that plagued his accusers were attributed to his angry spirit. To try and appease this spirit, Sugawara was posthumously elevated to a higher government position, and enshrined in Kyushu and Kyoto as the god Tenjin.

One of the many legends around Tenjin relates to his love of plum blossom. It was said that when he

1. Japanese maple - *iroha momiji*
2. Bamboo-leaf oak - *shirakashi*
3. Black pine - *kuromatsu*
4. Japanese maple - *yama momiji*
5. Weeping plum - *shidare ume*
6. Japanese sweet flag - *sekisho*
7. Camellia - *tsubaki*
8. Japanese cleyera - *sakaki*
9. Red plum - *kobai ume*
10. Evergreen camellia - *kan tsubaki*

All unmarked trees are plum

Features of the garden

- Stroll garden (*kayushiki teien*)
- 60 plum trees (Japanese flowering plum)
- large pond fed by a natural well, 300 feet (100 m) deep
- long earthen bridge (*dobashi*)
- "seesaw" cantilivered stone bridge 13 ft (4 m) x 6 in (15 cm)
- (1 ton stone slab and 4 ton counter weight)
- stepping-stone bridge (*sawatobi*)
- long "mountain road" in a semi-formal (*gyo*) style

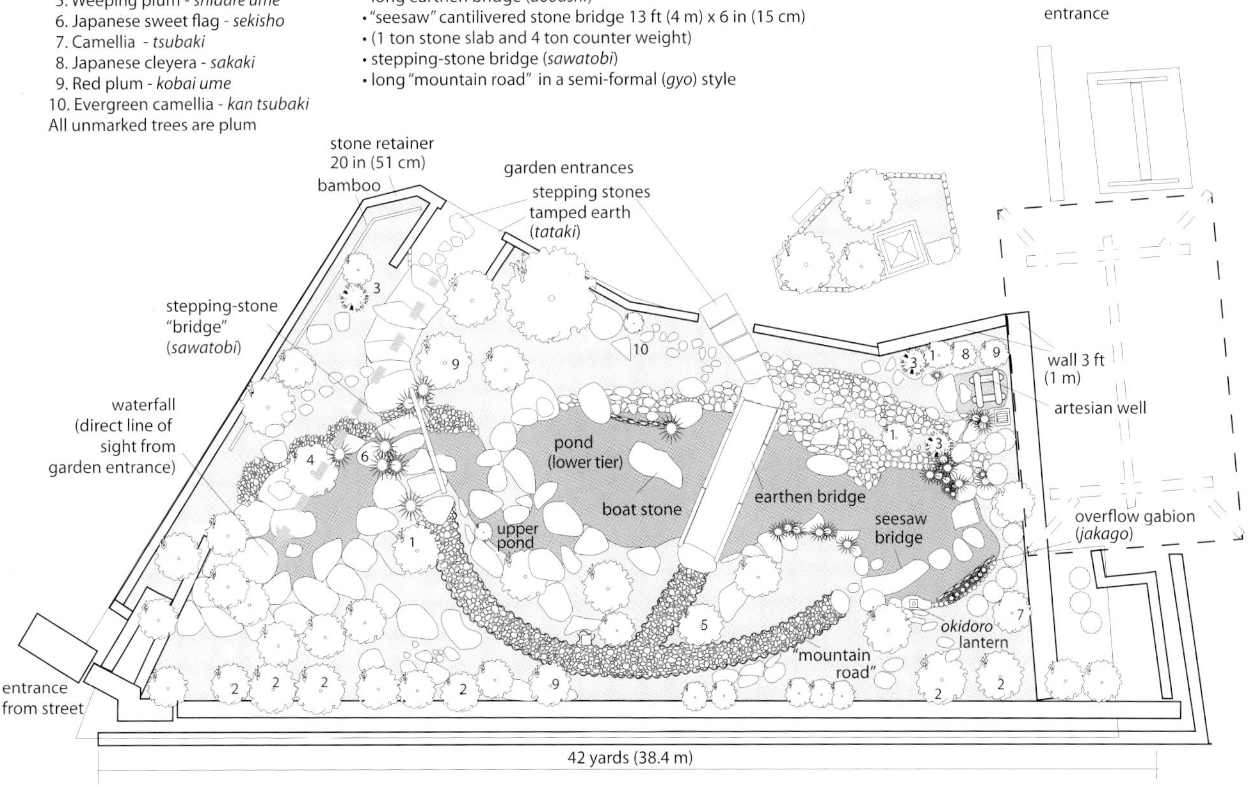

entrance

stone retainer
20 in (51 cm)

bamboo

garden entrances

stepping stones

tamped earth
(*tataki*)

stepping-stone
"bridge"
(*sawatobi*)

waterfall
(direct line of
sight from
garden entrance)

pond
(lower tier)

boat stone

upper
pond

earthen bridge

seesaw
bridge

wall 3 ft
(1 m)

artesian well

overflow gabion
(*jakago*)

okidoro
lantern

"mountain
road"

entrance
from street

42 yards (38.4 m)

died, his beloved plum tree flew from Kyoto to Kyushu where it still stands in front of Dazaifu Tenmangu Shrine. So the plum has always been a symbol of Tenjin, and when I was asked to make a new garden here, I expected that flowering plum trees would play an important part. They line the two famous sets of steps that lead to the shrine, the so-called "woman's slope" and "man's slope," and are planted in many other places.

We created a 5,600-square-foot (525-m^2) stroll garden with the feel of walking around a lake in the mountains. The garden occupies less than half of the total shrine grounds and the "lake" occupies about a third of the garden. We achieved the effect of a long journey, in a small space, by varying the ground level and by using the classic stroll-garden technique of hide-and-reveal (*miekakure*). To make the journey feel as long as possible, I made a path that enters from the front right of the garden and heads

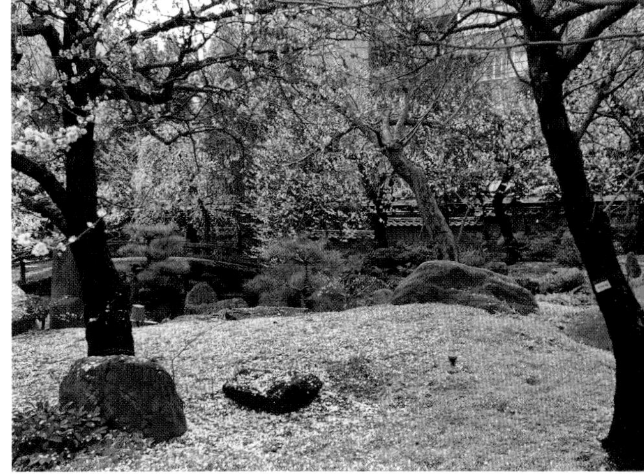

Facing page Musicians play *koto* and *shakuhachi* to welcome worshippers in the most auspicious season.

Above Plum blossoms, whether against nearly black bark or covering the ground like snow, make the gods smile.

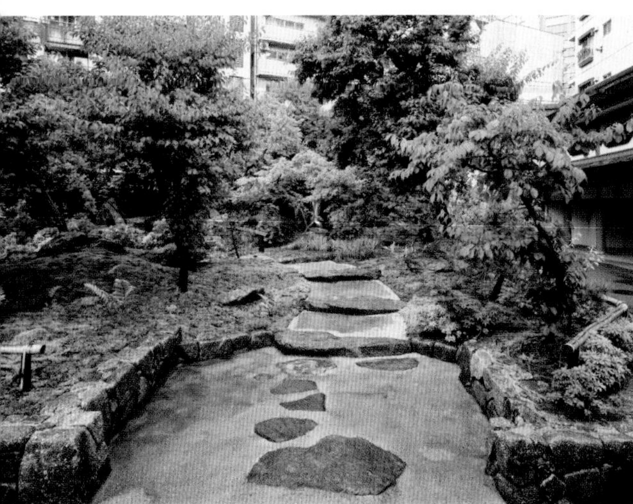

to the back side. Then it wraps around and returns to the front by two different routes: one across a large earthen bridge and the other across a stone bridge that extends the path to the deepest corner of the garden.

Walking along the path is truly like taking a hike in the mountains. First, you cross a stream by a massive stepping-stone bridge (*sawatobi*), which is slightly precarious, so you need to look down and watch your step. A wooden handrail is provided for safety. A curved and rising road of small river stones follows the stepping-stone bridge. Looking to the right, you pause to see a large waterfall through the trees. The waterfall is also visible from the entrance

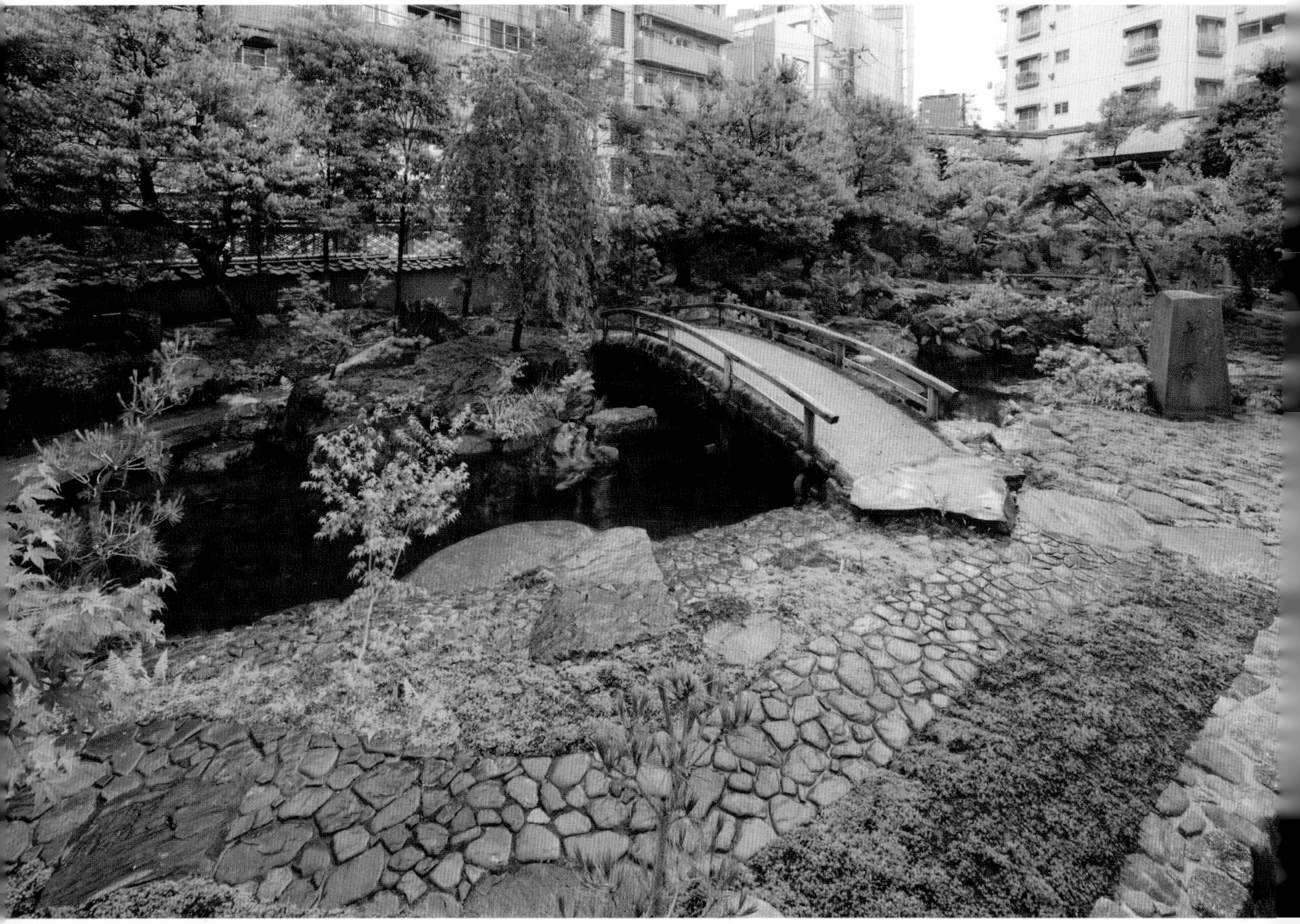

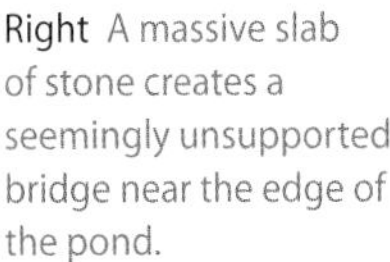

Right A massive slab of stone creates a seemingly unsupported bridge near the edge of the pond.

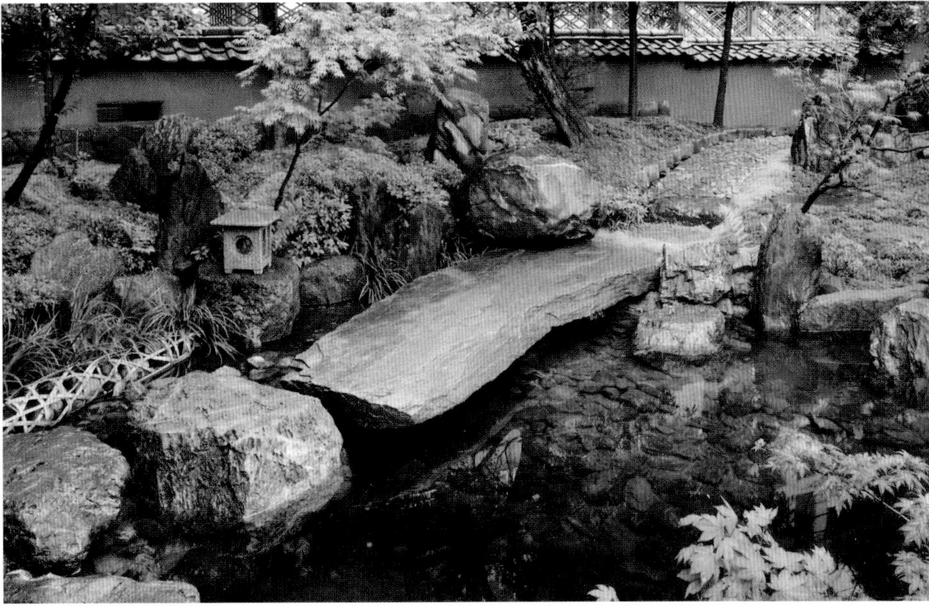

before entering the garden. Once you cross the boulders, you naturally raise your head and see the path rising as though climbing into the mountains. Looking left, you get an intimate view of the pond from under the trees. Passing by large stones along the rising road, you catch a glimpse of the pond below and feel the atmosphere of a mountain path.

There is an artesian well that feeds the pond from the left front side of the garden. The wellhead uses large, flattish stones, arranged in a shape that reflects the Chinese character for *ido* 井, which means "well." This is one traditional style for arranging a well. We had to drill over 300 feet (100 m) to hit the aquifer. The well water overflows from the wellhead into the pond. It is also pumped from the pond to cascade over the waterfall at the opposite end of the

Facing page, top An entrance of *tataki* tamped clay, and stone leads to the "mountain pass" behind the pond.

Facing page, bottom The arched earthen bridge crosses the pond to meet a broad stone step and a stone walkway on the way to a second entrance.

Right The informal *nobedan* path rises past a large stone on the beginning of a journey up the mountain.

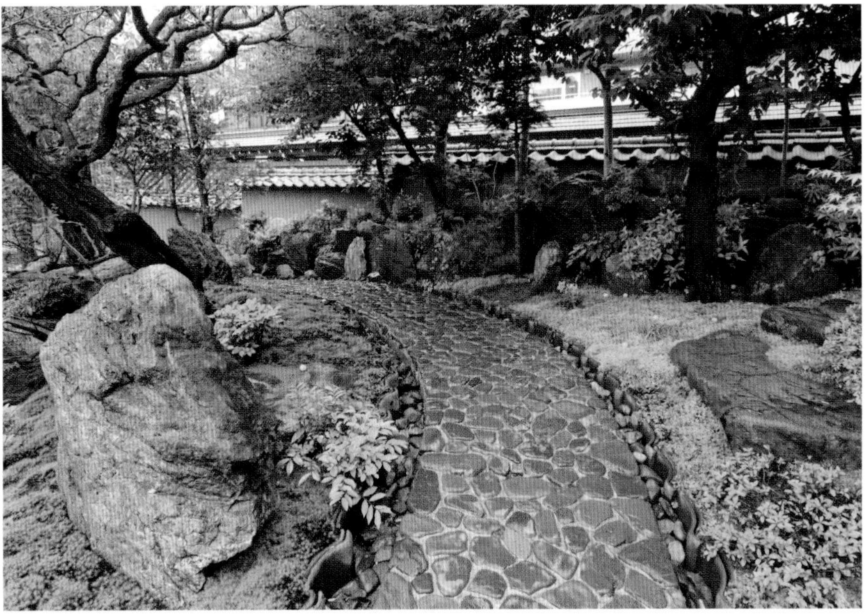

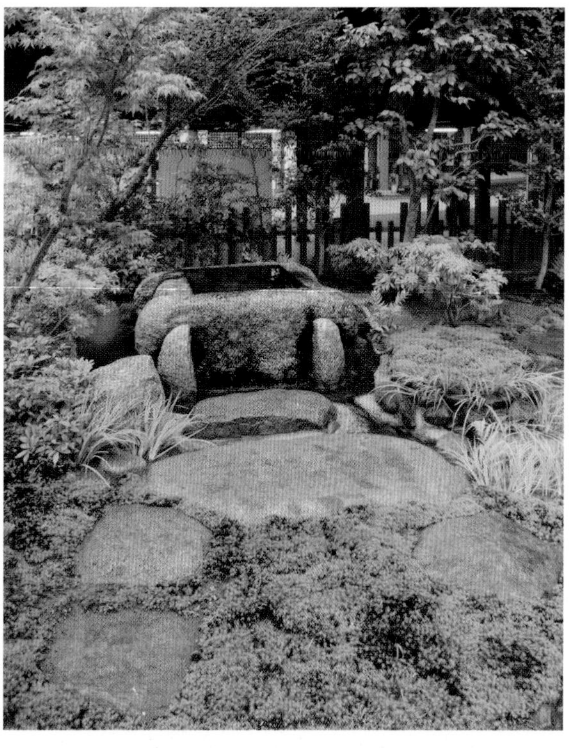

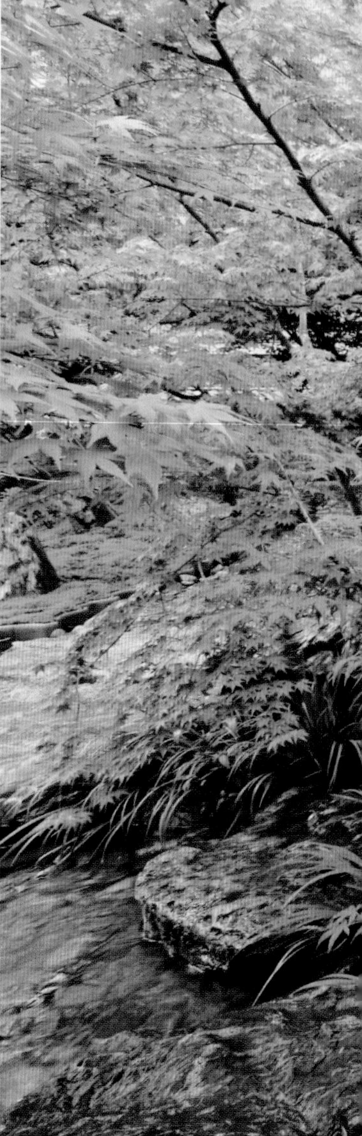

Left An artesian wellhead is defined by a traditional stone configuration that reflects the Chinese character for *ido* 井, meaning "well."

Right A waterfall like one you might expect to encounter along a mountain trail, crafted in stone for the pleasure of city dwellers.

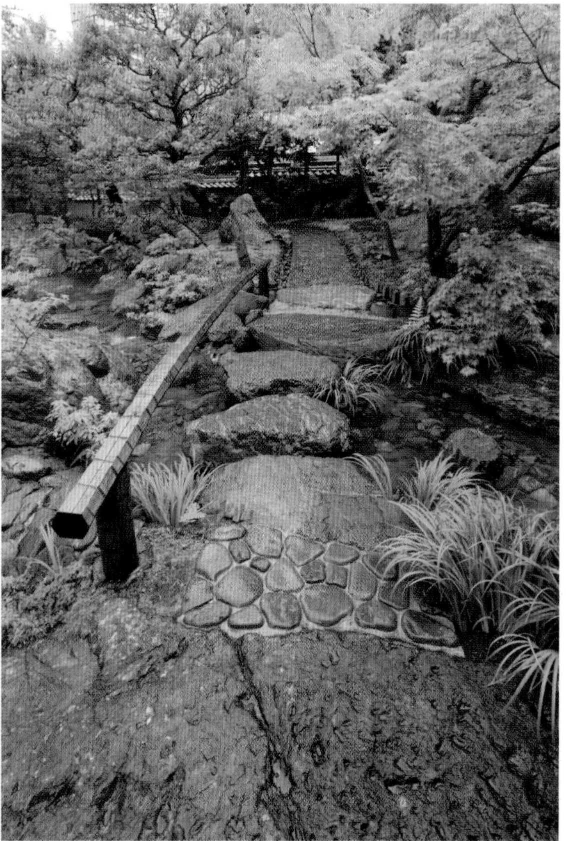

Left Crossing this rugged stone "bridge" requires watching your step. Hold the handrail; take a moment to rest; look to the right to enjoy the view of the waterfall.

garden. The idea of pure, flowing water has a spiritual dimension for a Shinto shrine. One of the core concepts of Shinto is the idea of purification by water (*misogi*).

Of course, along with an inlet, water needs outlets, and they must be regulated and balanced to maintain the correct level in the pond. This requires several drains, which are situated at various points around the pond, and a recirculation system. You will notice in the photo at the top of page 75 and the bottom of page 77 some long bamboo baskets full of stones. These are overflow gabions called snake baskets (*jakago*). They are both practical and attractive, and often used to supplement retaining walls around water features and other places. Here we used them to disguise the drains and to help retain the sweet flag planted along the edge.

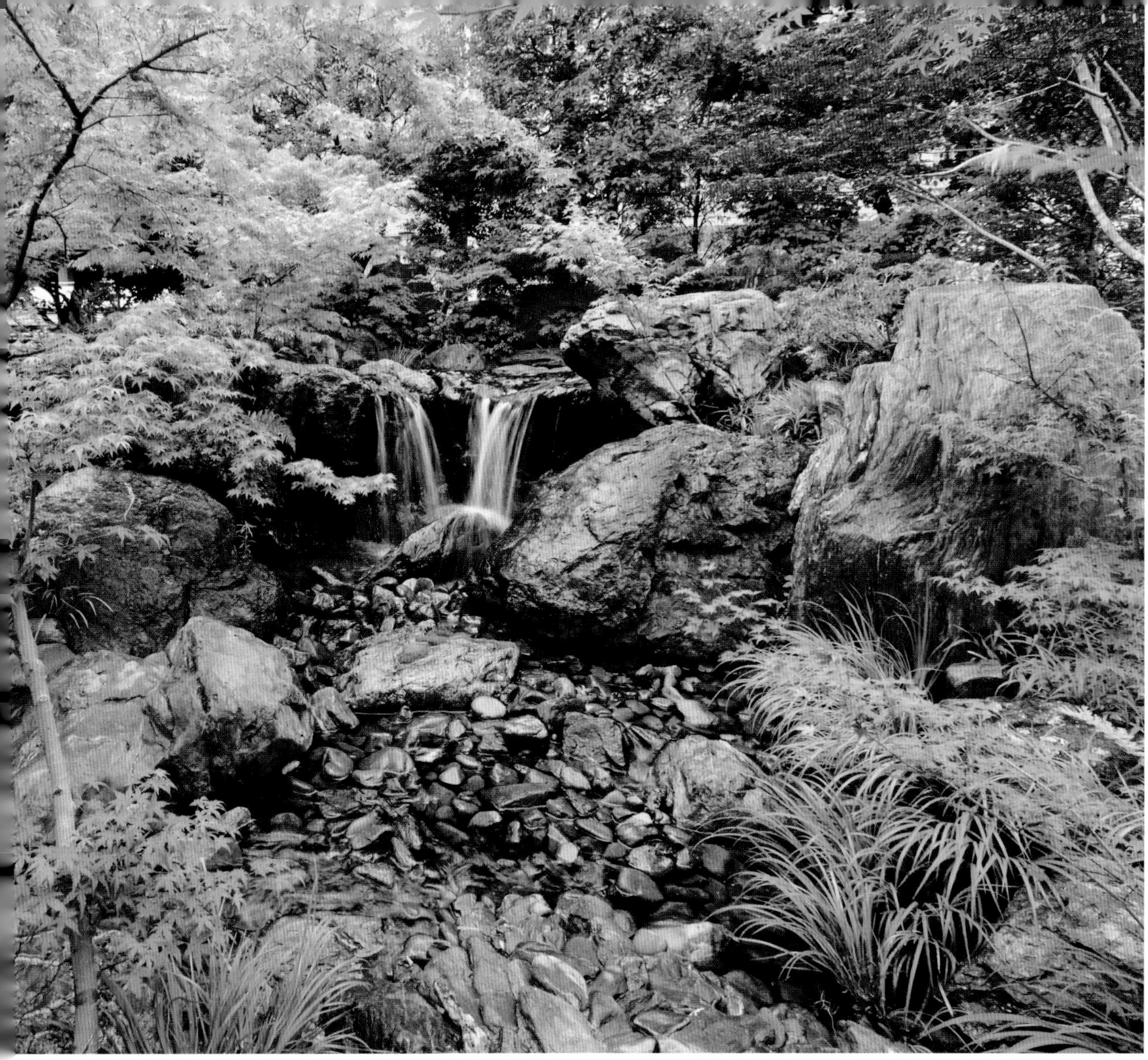

Besides the variety of plum trees, the garden is planted with tall, bamboo-leaf oak (*shirakashi*) along the side of the garden facing the street. These trees and the 5-foot (1.5-m) clay wall we made, help block the wind and interrupt the view of the tall buildings and the traffic outside. We also planted quite a few Japanese maples, especially around the waterfall and pond. The maples and plum are deciduous so the evergreen oaks play an important role keeping the garden green in the winter. Other year-round greenery includes black pine, camellia, ferns, moss, and a lot of sweet flag. Together they maintain a pleasant atmosphere until the plum returns.

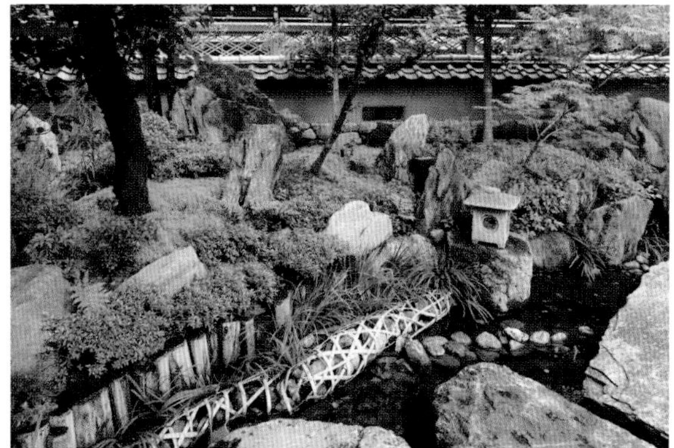

Above The "snake basket" is a traditional decorative method to disguise a drain or shore up an embankment.

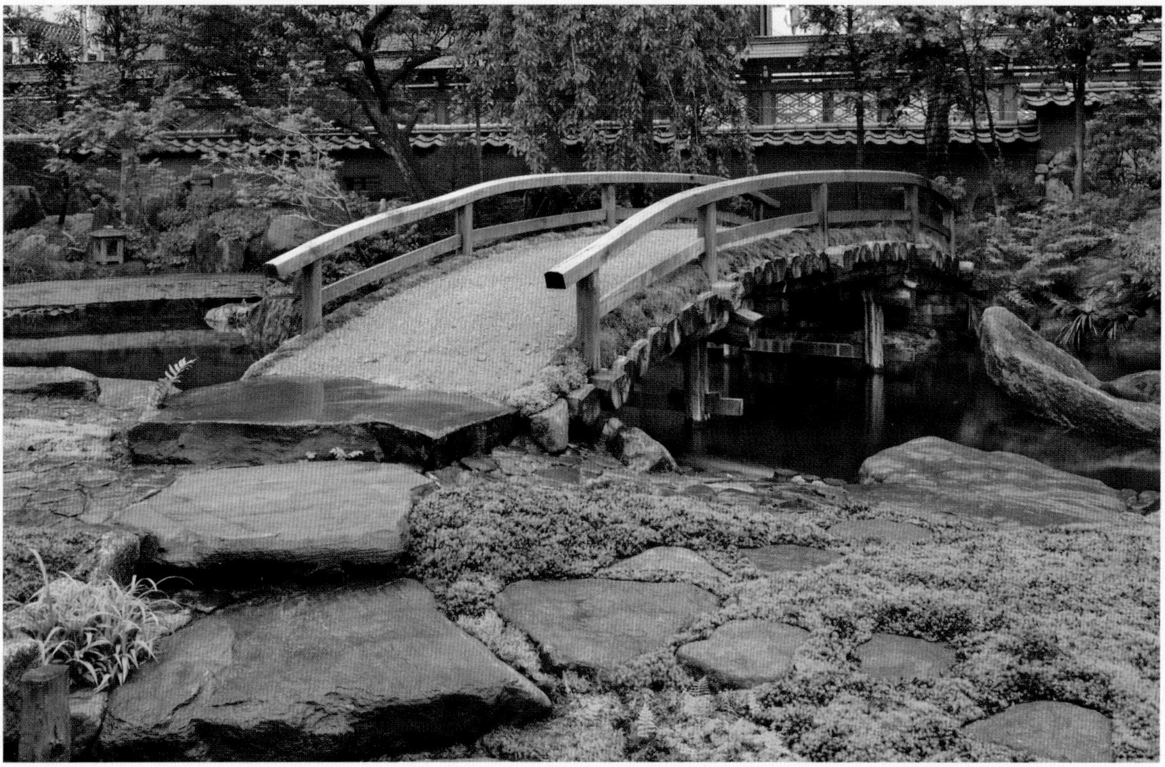

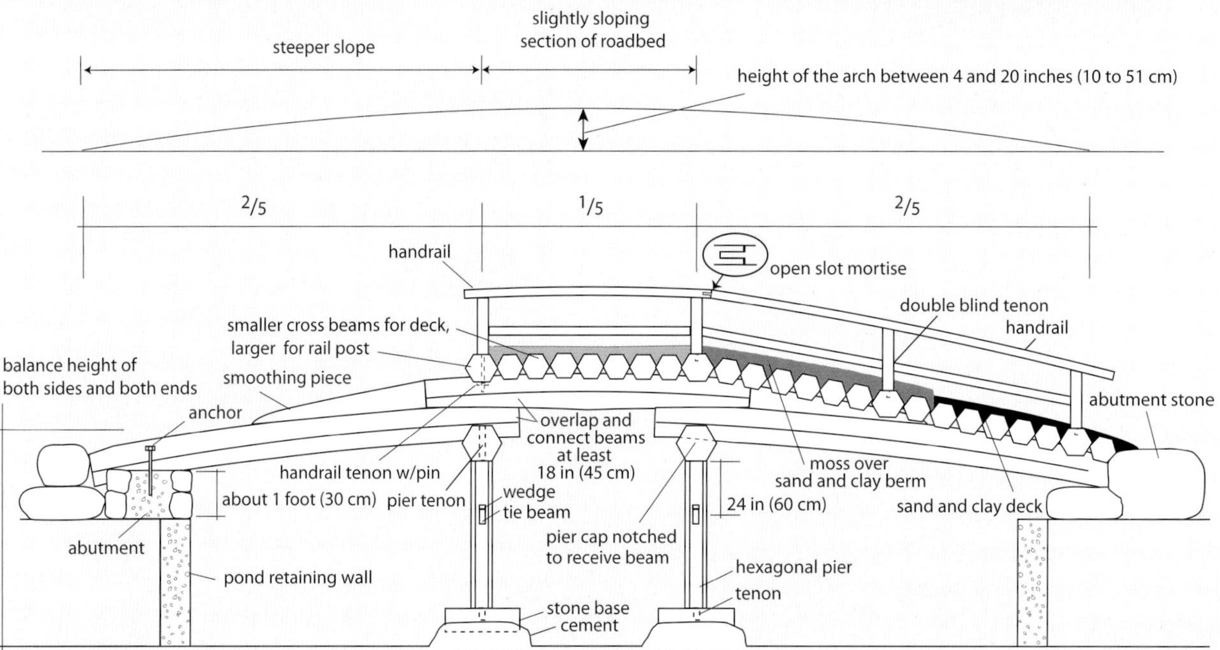
steeper slope
slightly sloping section of roadbed
height of the arch between 4 and 20 inches (10 to 51 cm)
2/5
1/5
2/5
handrail
open slot mortise
double blind tenon
handrail
smaller cross beams for deck, larger for rail post
balance height of both sides and both ends
smoothing piece
abutment stone
anchor
overlap and connect beams at least 18 in (45 cm)
handrail tenon w/pin
moss over sand and clay berm
about 1 foot (30 cm)
pier tenon
wedge
tie beam
24 in (60 cm)
sand and clay deck
abutment
pier cap notched to receive beam
pond retaining wall
hexagonal pier
tenon
stone base
cement

HOW TO MAKE A LARGE DOBASHIRA EARTHEN BRIDGE

The *dobashira*—earthen bridge—is a garden attribute we sometimes use with ponds and streams. As with most of the garden features I favor, the bridge blends well with the natural landscape. At 6 x 26 feet (1.8 x 8 m) it is the largest bridge we have ever constructed. Most of the woodwork was done by a veteran carpenter, assisted by one of my staff. Such a large bridge takes a total of five or six people to make and is not meant for the average home, but the methods outlined here can be applied to any size bridge. For example, the small earthen bridge (see page 71), can easily be completed by two people in several days. Although some may have the impression that every Japanese bridge is painted red, that is far from the truth. I suggest looking at pictures of the dobashira in the Kyoto Imperial Palace inner garden (*gonaitei*). Like this bridge, that one also has a handrail. The bridge in the garden of Katsura Imperial Villa, also in Kyoto, illustrates another type, without a handrail.

Step 1 We begin by building the superstructure with two sets of piers (bents), caps (*hashigeta*), and horizontal tie beams (*nuki*), and set them on flat stones. The stones are set in concrete on the bed of the river or pond. In our example, the distance from pier to pier is 6 feet (1.8 m). Each stone has a mortise cut to receive a tenon on the bottom of the pier. The weight of the bridge holds them in place. The caps are mortised to receive long tenons on the top of the piers. The tenons are cut off after assembly. The tie beams pass through the piers and are held in place with wedges (*kusabi*) hammered in from both sides.

Step 2 Build abutments at one or both ends of the bridge to support the ends of the longitudinal beams (girders). In this case, we used stones and cement to build a 3 x 6-foot (1 x 1.8-m) retaining wall on one end, and set large stones at the other end. Stainless-steel anchors are cemented into the abutment for connecting to the beams. The height of the abutment is flexible but should be no less than 1 foot (30 cm) and lower than the height of the pier caps to allow the bridge to arch gently. The slightly arched beams will slope upward from the embankment. The center section of the bridge must be level (but also slightly curved).

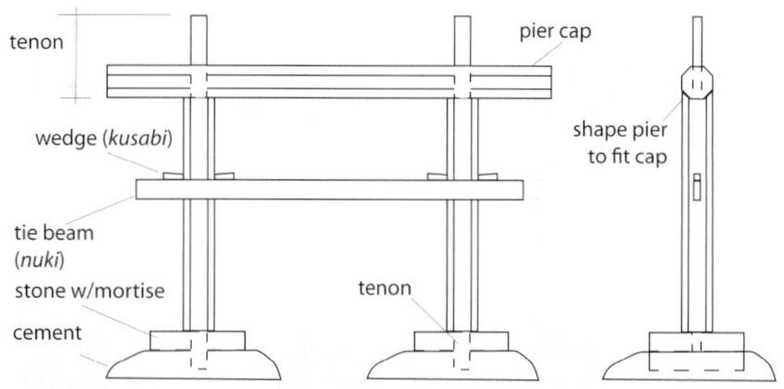

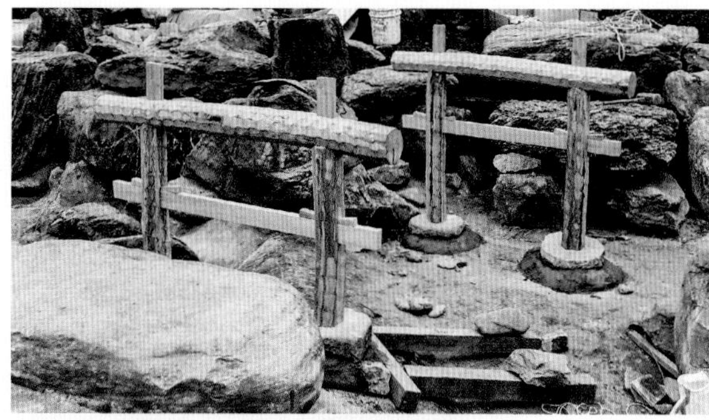

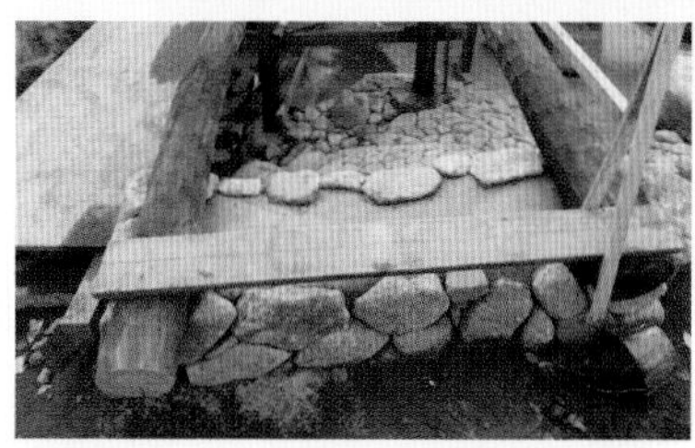

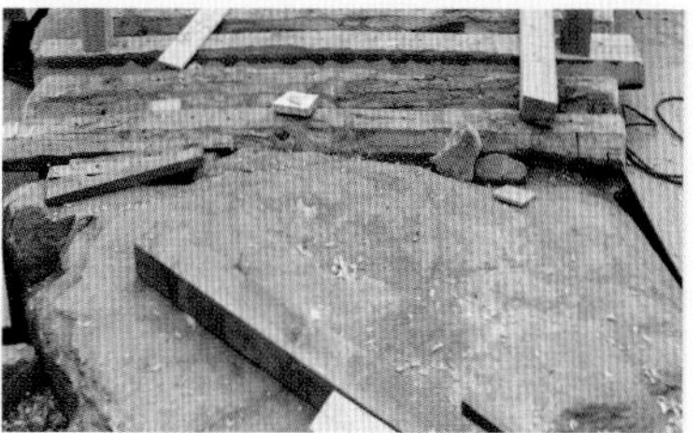

Step 3 Set up the beams above the pier caps, beginning with the section that rests on the pier and the retaining wall. The caps are notched to receive the beams. Bolts are used to hold the beams to the piers. In case of a very wide or long bridge, a third beam is used in the middle section. In order to balance the right and left sides and produce the desired arch, the height of the beams can be adjusted by trimming and layering. Finally, all these parts receive a waterproof coating to prevent erosion by water and insects.

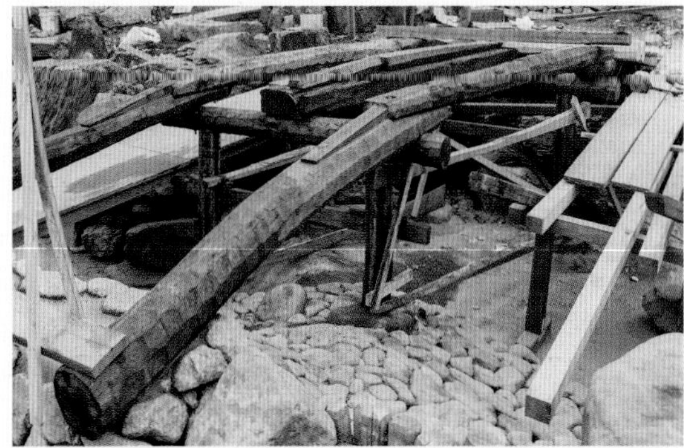

Step 4 Prepare the crossbeams (*keta*). In this bridge the crossbeams are side by side and also form the deck. They are cut in a six-sided figure and set up with the flat sides top and bottom and the corners touching the adjacent beam. The crossbeams are also notched on the underside to help secure them to the girders. Slightly longer and wider crossbeams are used where the handrail posts will be attached. These longer crossbeams are bolted to the main (longitudinal) beams.

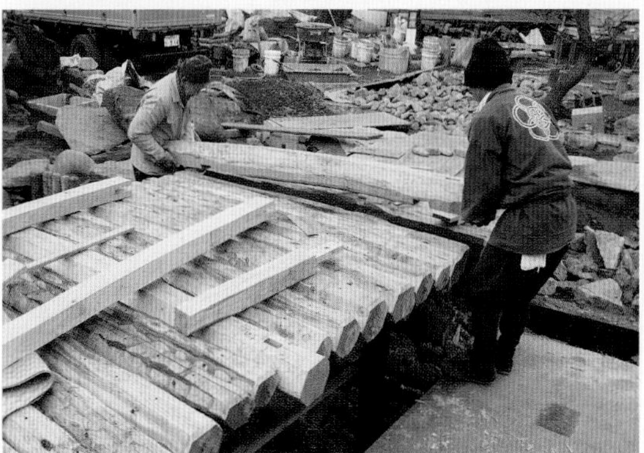

Step 5 Prepare the handrail. The rail is cut in a six-sided figure, wider than tall, with a flat bottom. A hand-held belt sander will be used to rough out the shape and then it will be finished with a plane. In our example, the rail is quite long and pieced together from three lengths. We used open slot mortises (*sammai-gumi*) to join them, along with wood epoxy. The undersides of the left and right handrails are mortised in five places to receive five posts each.

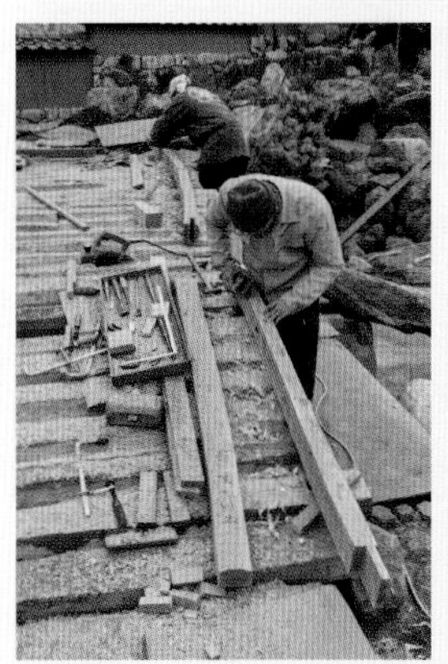

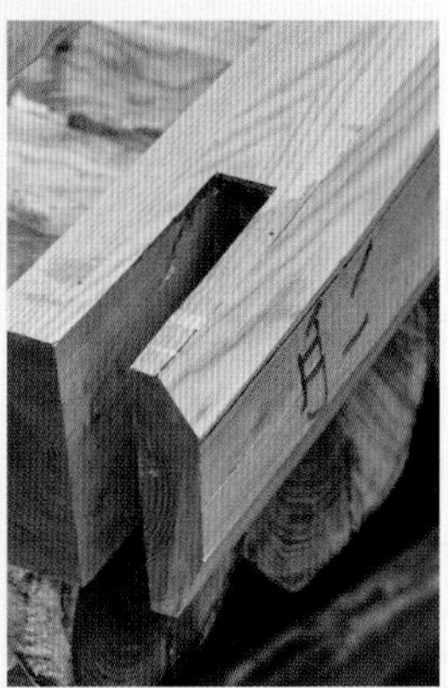

Step 6 Before you assemble the rail, prepare the square handrail posts. A long tenon is cut on the bottom, to fit the mortise on the crossbeam. A slot is cut in the tenon at the point that it will penetrate the crossbeam. This will receive a square pin (*komisen*) to secure the post during assembly. The bottom of the post will also be shaped to conform to the curve of the bridge. A much shorter tenon is cut on top to fit the handrail (90 degrees to the crossbeam). Cut mortises halfway down the post to receive the tie beams. These are not true tie beams but double blind tenons.

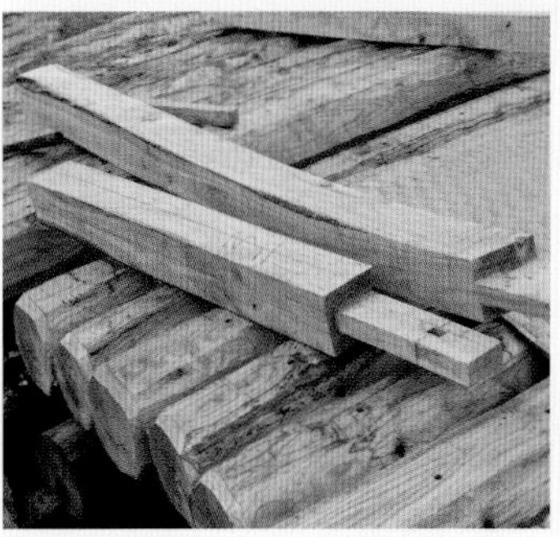

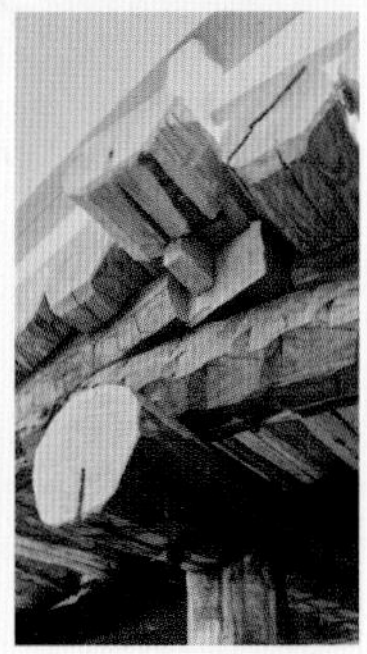

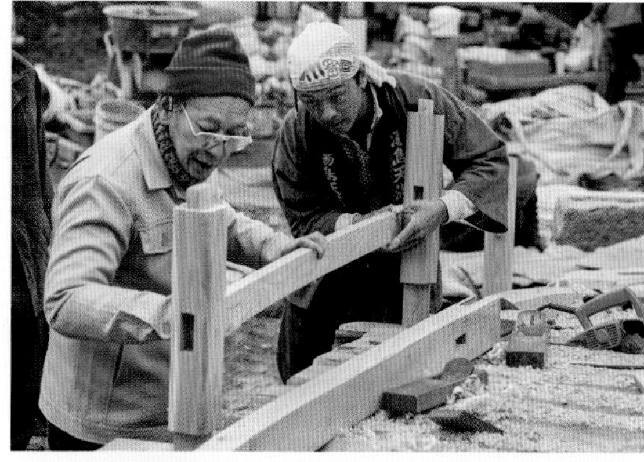

Step 7 The handrail is attached to the crossbeams by inserting one set of posts and horizontal tie beams at a time. When finished, assemble the handrail on the posts and cement the joints. Finish the joint with a belt sander. You might want to cover the finished rail with plastic or paper to keep it clean before the next steps.

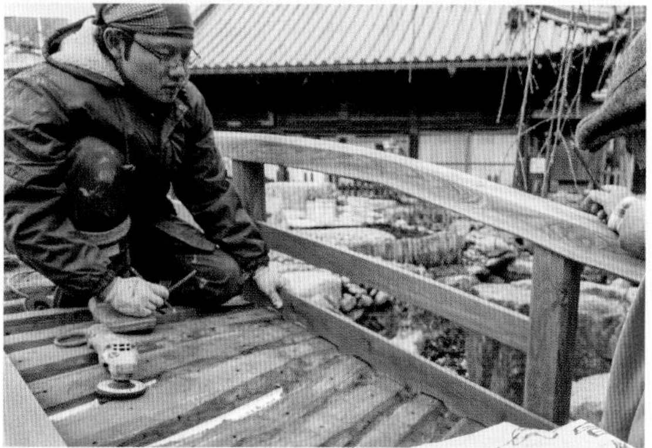

Step 8 Use a board 4 inches x ½ inch x 6 feet (10 cm x 1 cm x 1.8 m) as a buffer edge for the clay mixture that will form the surface of the deck. The board is cut to conform to the shape of the crossbeams. It is held in place, away from the rail posts, with blocks nailed to the crossbeams. After the buffer is set along the full length of the bridge, the cracks between the crossbeams will be filled with clay.

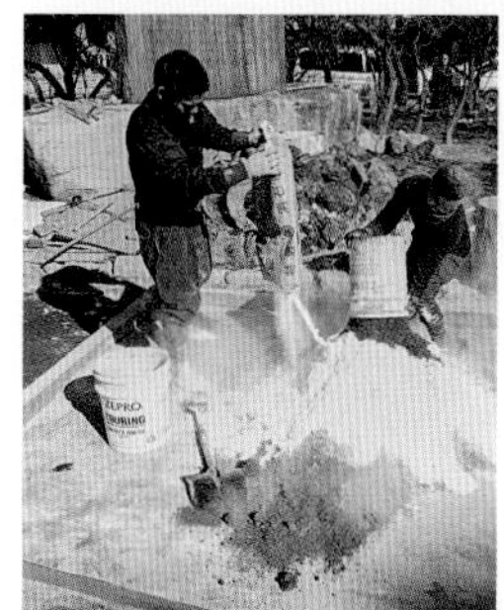

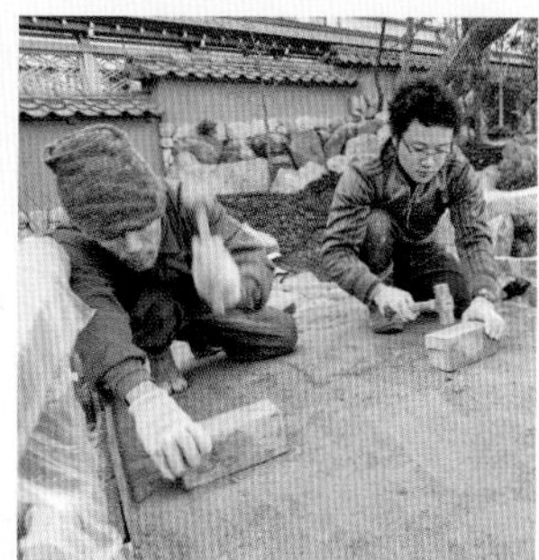

Step 9 Mix your soil. Set up an area large enough to handle all the material at once. Mix 1 part limestone (*sekkai*), 1⁄10 part magnesium chloride (*nigari*), and 1 part soil made up of decomposed granite (*masatsuchi*) and volcanic loam (*akatsuchi*) in equal parts. Mix well while sprinkling lightly with water. Pour out the mixture on the crossbeams and tamp down with wood posts or blocks. Keep tamping until you have a flat and even build about 4 inches (10 cm) thick. When finished, brush down the surface with water.

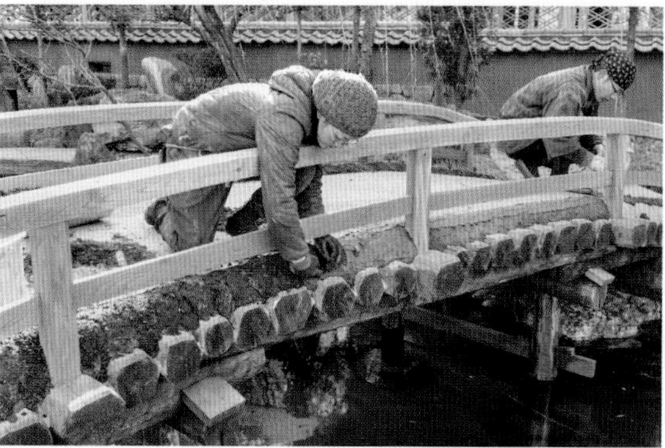

Step 10 Make a berm along the edge using the same mix as in Step 9, and pile it up several inches above the road bed. When dry, pile up another inch or two so that it protrudes past the rail posts. Set moss to cover the entire berm while the clay is still wet.

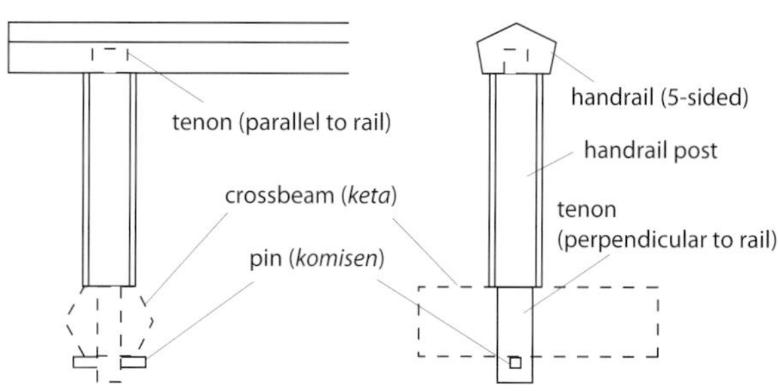

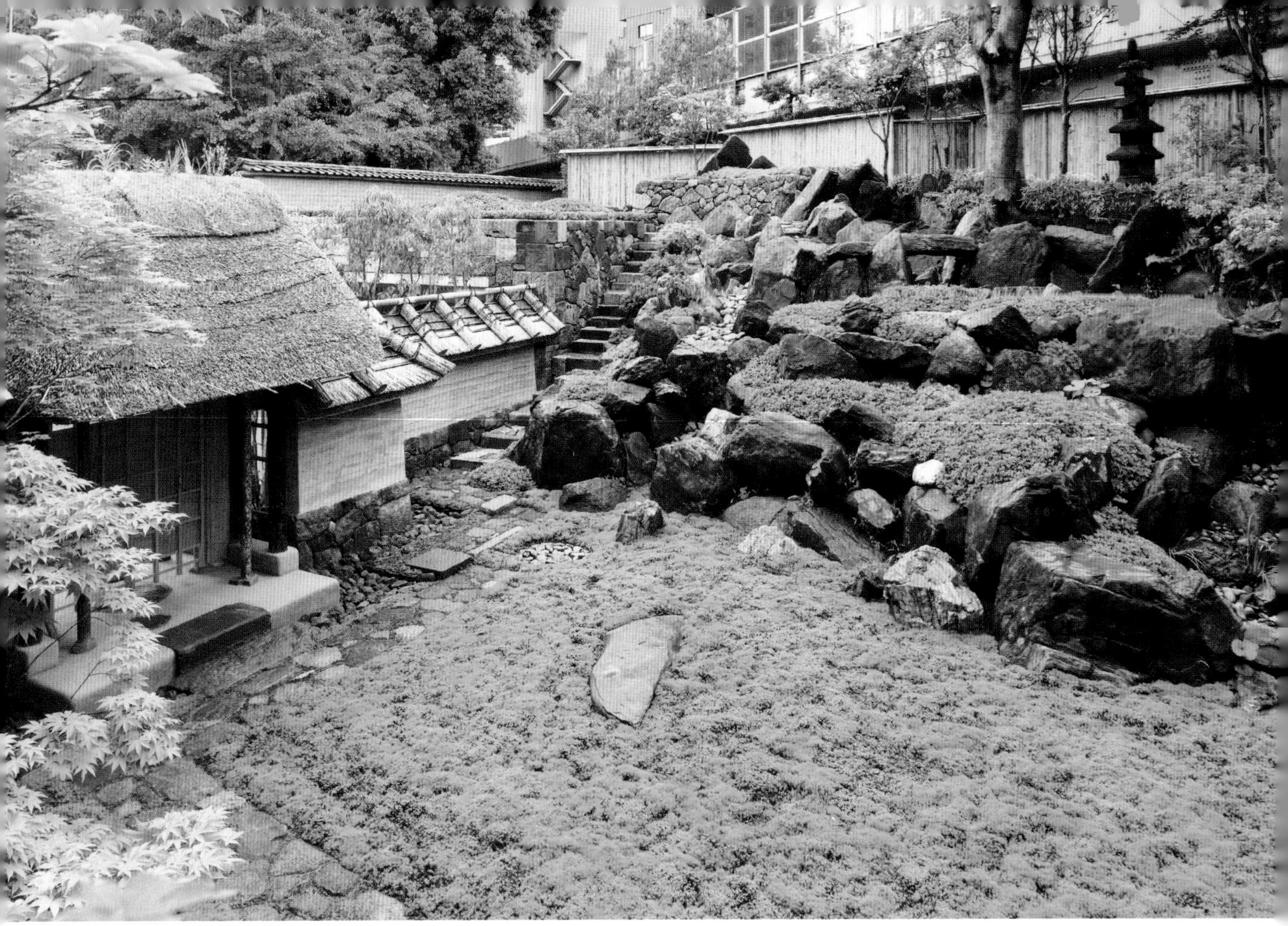

Buddha's Mountain Retreat of Moss and Stone

Above Inside the gate a sea of fluffy moss evaporates into clouds that envelop a symbolic mountain of stone.

Myojo-in Temple is a branch of nearby Zojoji Temple. It was founded in 1763 by the ninth Tokugawa shogun, Ieshige, and now belongs to the Jodo Shinshu sect. Myojo-in has undergone many physical changes since its beginning. It was destroyed by firebombing in World War II, and it was completely boxed in by the Metropolitan Expressway and Route 319. However, it has survived and flourished as a venerable Tokyo landmark. We made a garden for this temple around the time of the first Tokyo Olympics in 1964. We remade it in 2005 when the temple was again reconstructed.

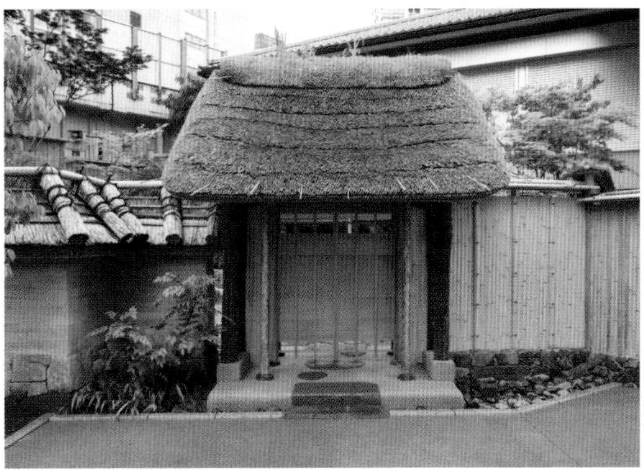

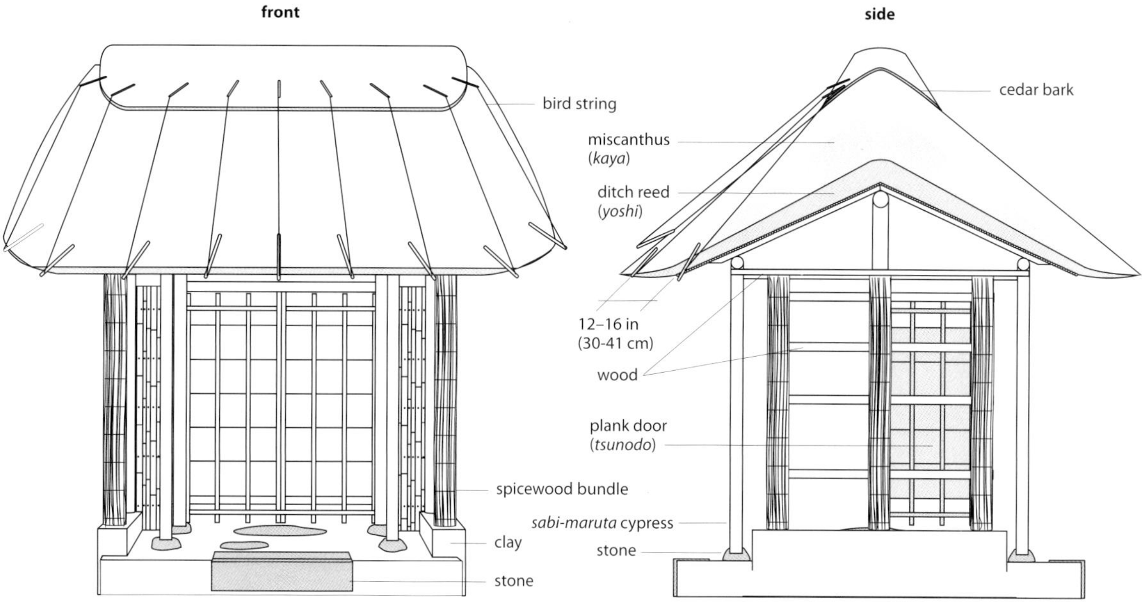

Located in an urban area near Tokyo Tower, the front of the temple is pressed against a major road and the side is pressed against a highway. This situation meant that the area for the garden was limited to the back of the temple. The original garden was completely enclosed by a wall, but this time an entrance through the garden was desired. The entrance is intended to accommodate large groups of worshipers. In this garden I attempted to express two aspects of Buddhism: gentleness, and an immovable spirit.

Although the entrance is at the back of the temple, it has become the main access for automobiles. That is why an entrance and a path through the garden was needed. There is a large garage at the rear of the driveway space, against the highway side of the plot. We surfaced the 13-foot (4-m)-tall garage with rough granite blocks. We built a 6½-foot (2-m)-tall rammed-earth wall (*hanchiku*) extending 90 degrees from the front of the garage. Because the clay is rammed into a wooden form, the surface is smooth. The wall is topped with a straw roof and forms one side of the entrance to the garden. On the other side of the entrance gate, a 6½-foot-tall, 10-foot-long (2 x 3-m) fence made of vertical split-bamboo (*tokusazuke*) completes the front wall

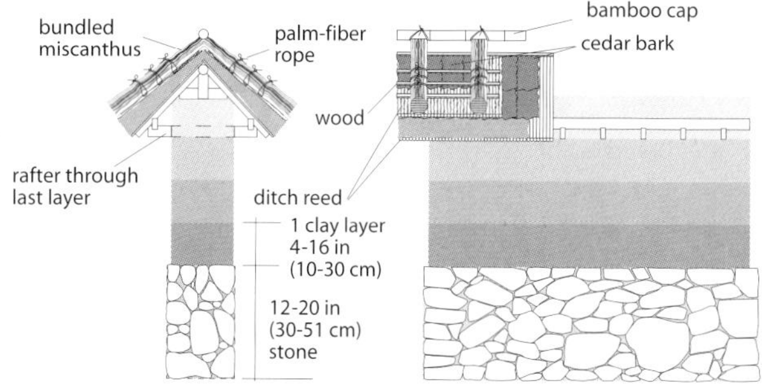

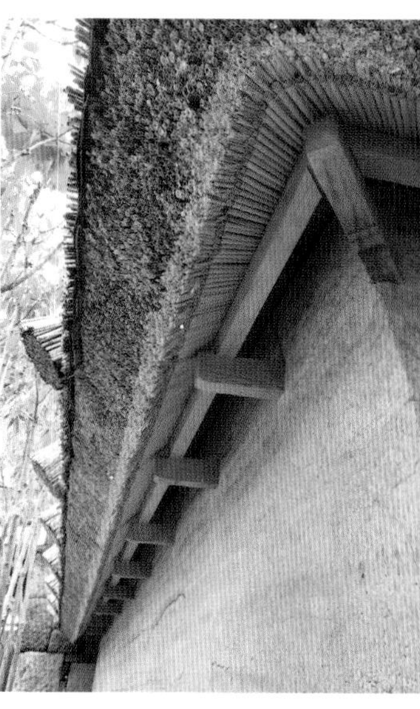

Facing page bottom, and this page My interpretation of the Emperor's entrance, Miyukimon, uses a rammed earth wall to create a formal appearance.

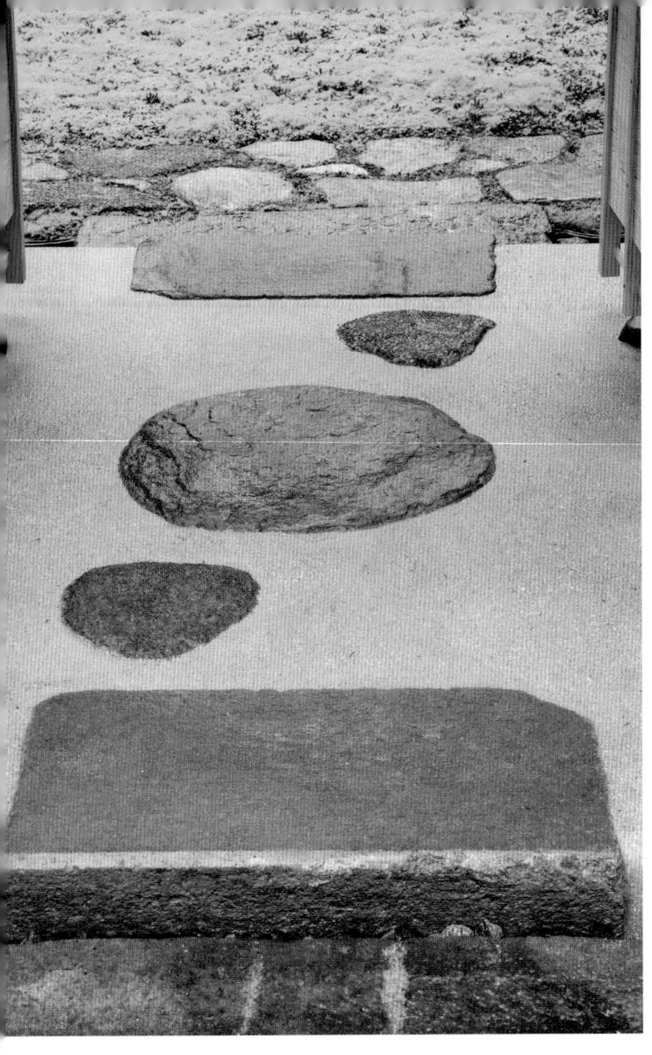

Left Exposed aggregate (*araidashi*) and natural stone used in a manner that enhances their dignified character.

Below A towering bay laurel atop a stone mountain is not only symbolic, it has the practical purpose of disguising the ugly highway.

them an even more formal appearance. Three of the pillars on each side of the gate are made from tight bundles of spicebush wrapped around steel poles. Three more are made of *sabi-maruta* cypress wood, usually used for *tokonoma* alcoves and in teahouses. The original Miyukimon is much more rustic in appearance, using gate posts made from a cork tree (*abemaki*) with the bark intact.

The gate doors are made of horizontal boards and vertical slats. This type of gate is called a *tsunodo* or *sarudo*. When closed, it blocks the view of the garden. Inside the garden, the view is unobstructed. A broad green lawn of haircap moss (*sugigoke*) greets visitors first. Looking to the left, one is surprised by a massive, terraced mountain of granite boulders. This reflects the immovable and rugged spirit of Buddhism. Most of the stone was

of the garden. Extending 90 degrees from the end of this fence, we made a slightly taller brushwood fence from spicebush (*kuromoji*) branches, with a wood-plank and bamboo roof.

The entrance gate is my interpretation of the Miyukimon Gate of Katsura Imperial Villa in Kyoto created in the seventeenth century. That is a gate through which retired emperors and dignitaries passed into the villa grounds. Our gate is topped with a tall straw roof reminiscent of a farmhouse (*minka*) or a hut in the mountains. Materials like clay, bamboo, tree branches, and straw can appear rustic but in this case they were made to look quite formal. All the materials and the way I used them give off a soft and dignified air. The exposed-aggregate (*araidashi*) base under the gate includes sand and cement, which gives a fine surface texture. The *kurama ishi* stepping stones are basically flat and smooth and some have been squared off, giving

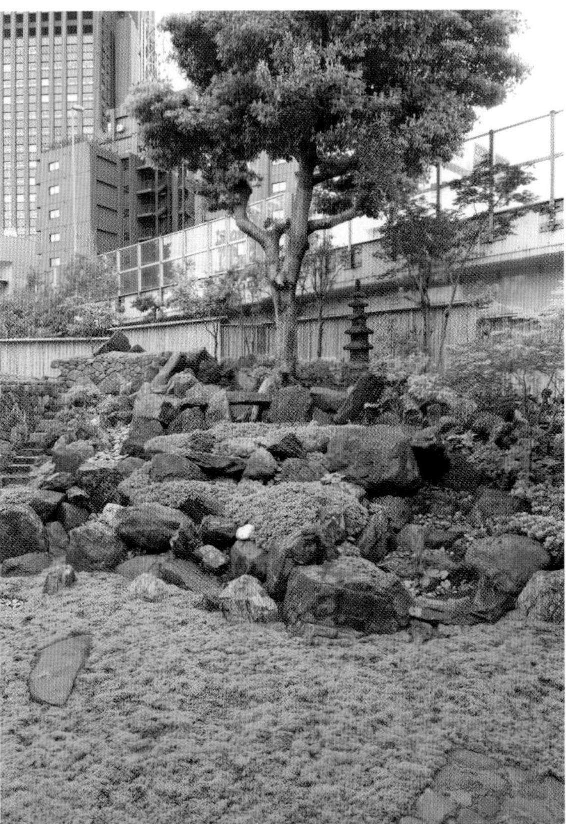

reused from the previous garden. Interspersed with the boulders, we planted moss, Japanese sweet flag, azalea and others, giving a soft and gentle cloud-like appearance. Near the top of this mountain is a large bay laurel (*tabu no ki*) near which we placed a stone pagoda (*gojunoto*) which is symbolic of an actual five-tiered temple. Bay laurel bark is also the basic material of incense. The mountain is reminiscent of Mt. Sumeru, the mythical sacred mountain at the center of the Buddhist universe, where the Four Heavenly Kings (*shitenno*) live. In gardens, the

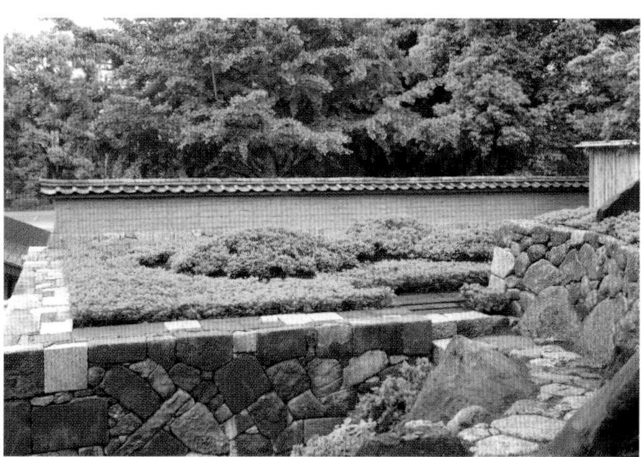

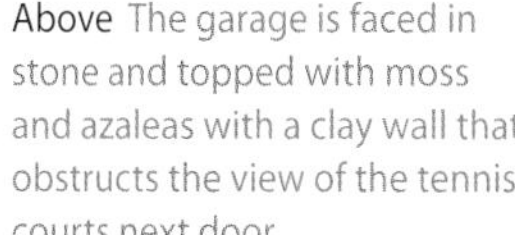

Above The garage is faced in stone and topped with moss and azaleas with a clay wall that obstructs the view of the tennis courts next door.

Left and below Two sets of steps, one along the garage and one up the mountainside, lead to the summit of the mountain, where a group of Buddhist triad stones (*sanzonseki*) overlooks the garden.

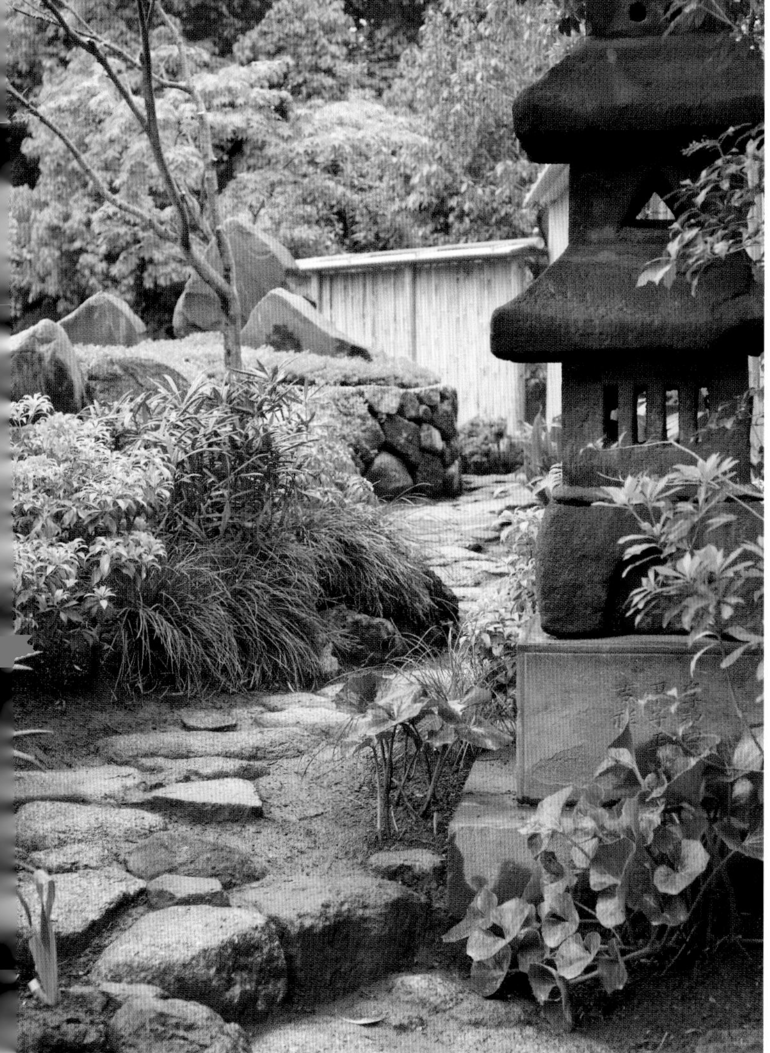

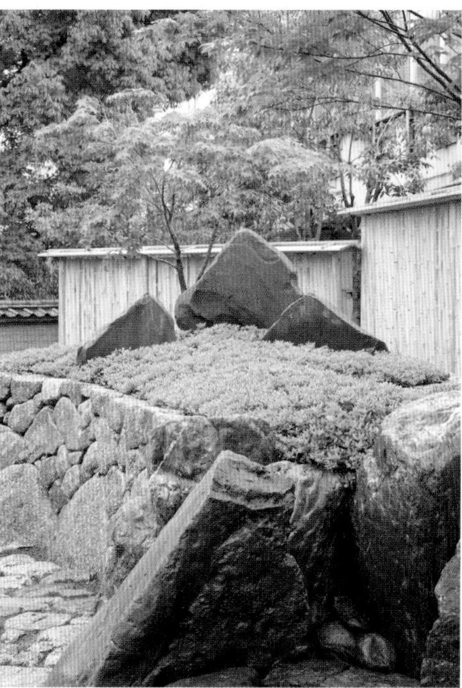

symbolic depiction of this concept, called *shumisen-shiki iwagumi,* was introduced to Japan in the sixth century. I employed this image of great strength and, in the process, disguised the section of the highway that abuts the temple. The large tree is also significant as a link between heaven and earth, and it is said that the Buddha achieved enlightenment while sitting under the Bodhi tree.

Stone stairs left and right of the mountain lead to the peak where a *sanzonseki* three-stone arrangement, symbolizing the Buddha flanked by two bodhisattvas (*bosatsu*), sits above the garage on a bed of azaleas. The image is implicit not explicit. This stone grouping is often used in Japanese gardens and here it occupies the highest position. We also created a waterfall in the style of "Dragon's Gate" falls (*ryumonbaku*) from where gravel "water" trickles down the mountainside. Behind this is a 5-foot (1.5-m) *teppogaki* bamboo fence, covered by a

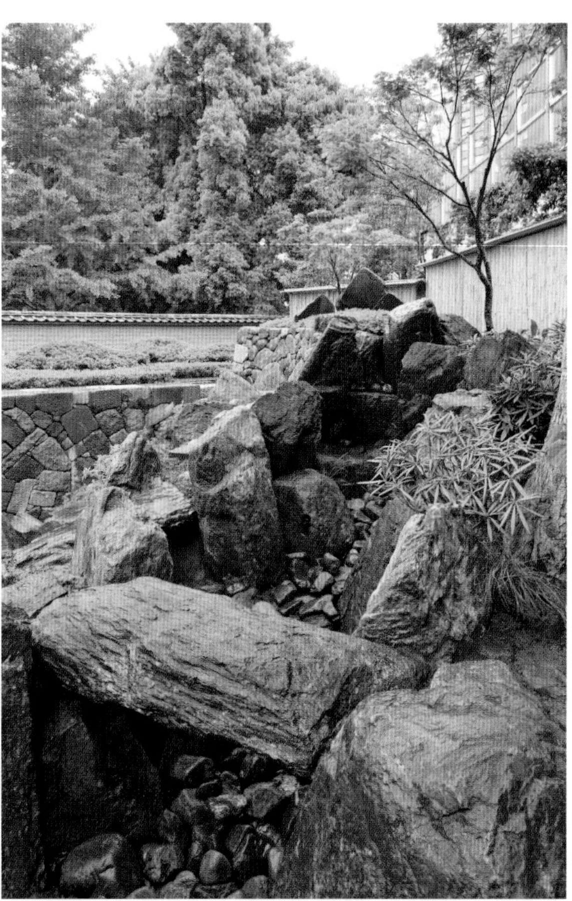

Below The narrow walkway leads to a large shoe-removal stone and a spacious modern-style room with a panoramic view of the garden.

Right A stone bridge crosses a river that flows from the spiritual and physical heart of the mountain.

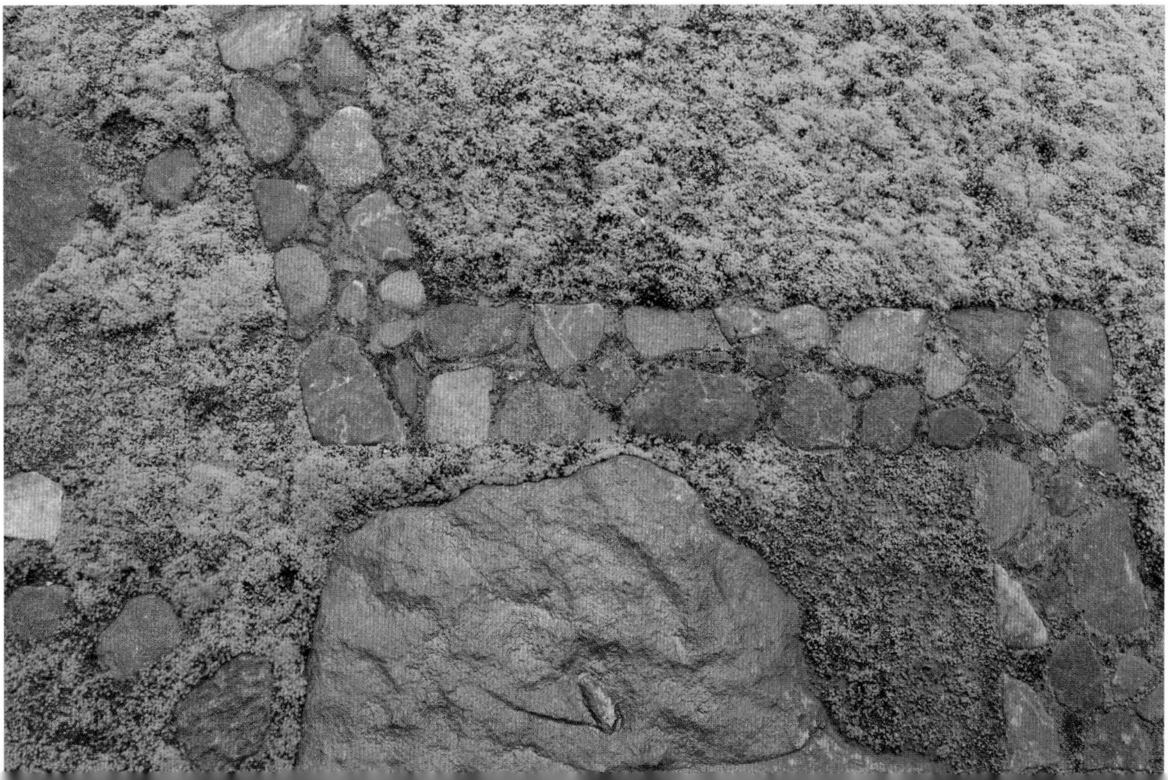

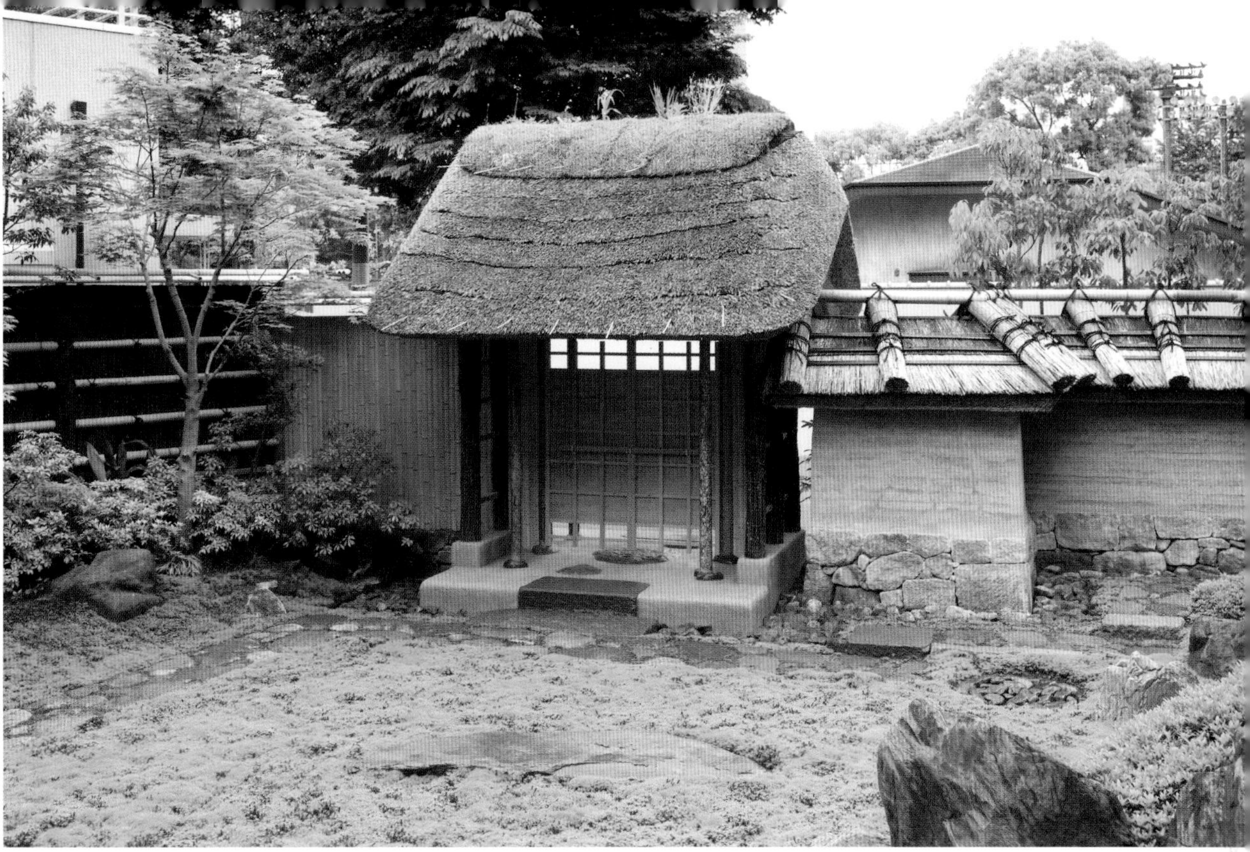

wooden-board roof. Japanese maples and other trees are planted to peek up over this fence. Along the left side of the garage roof is a 3-foot (1-m)-tall clay wall, topped with ceramic tile.

This garden is a good example of using moss (*koke*) instead of grass. We rarely use lawn grass in traditional Japanese gardens. If we do it is usually Korean grass (*zoysia*), which, like moss, does not need mowing, but it turns brown during the winter. Moss has the merits of a bright green color and a soft appearance. In many ways it is a good substitute for grass if you want to reduce mowing time. The negative point is that, like grass, it can be damaged and may turn brown in cold and dry conditions or if subjected to strong sunlight for extended periods. It will usually resuscitate with consistent watering. When it dies it must be replanted. Like grass, it is sold in square mats that are planted whole or broken into pieces of the size needed. There are hundreds of varieties but we usually use haircap moss (*sugigoke*). Here we use an automatic sprinkler system just as one would for a grass lawn. The irregular length and soft appearance makes moss a perfect combination with stone walkways and stepping stones.

Above and below A stately entrance to a contemplative world beyond the chaos of the city, and a well to draw purifying water.

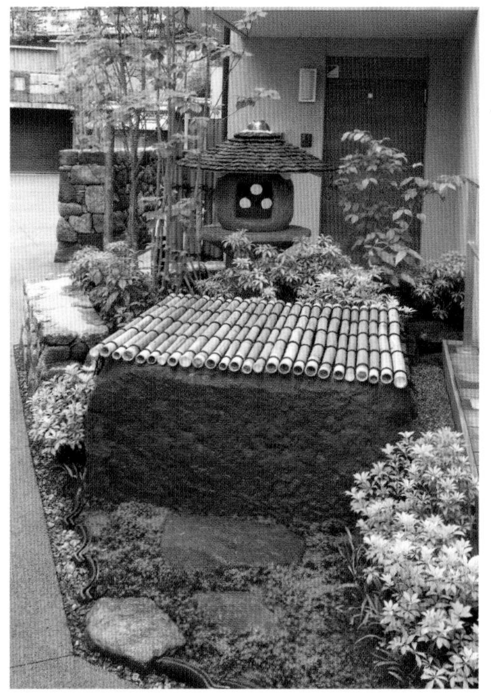

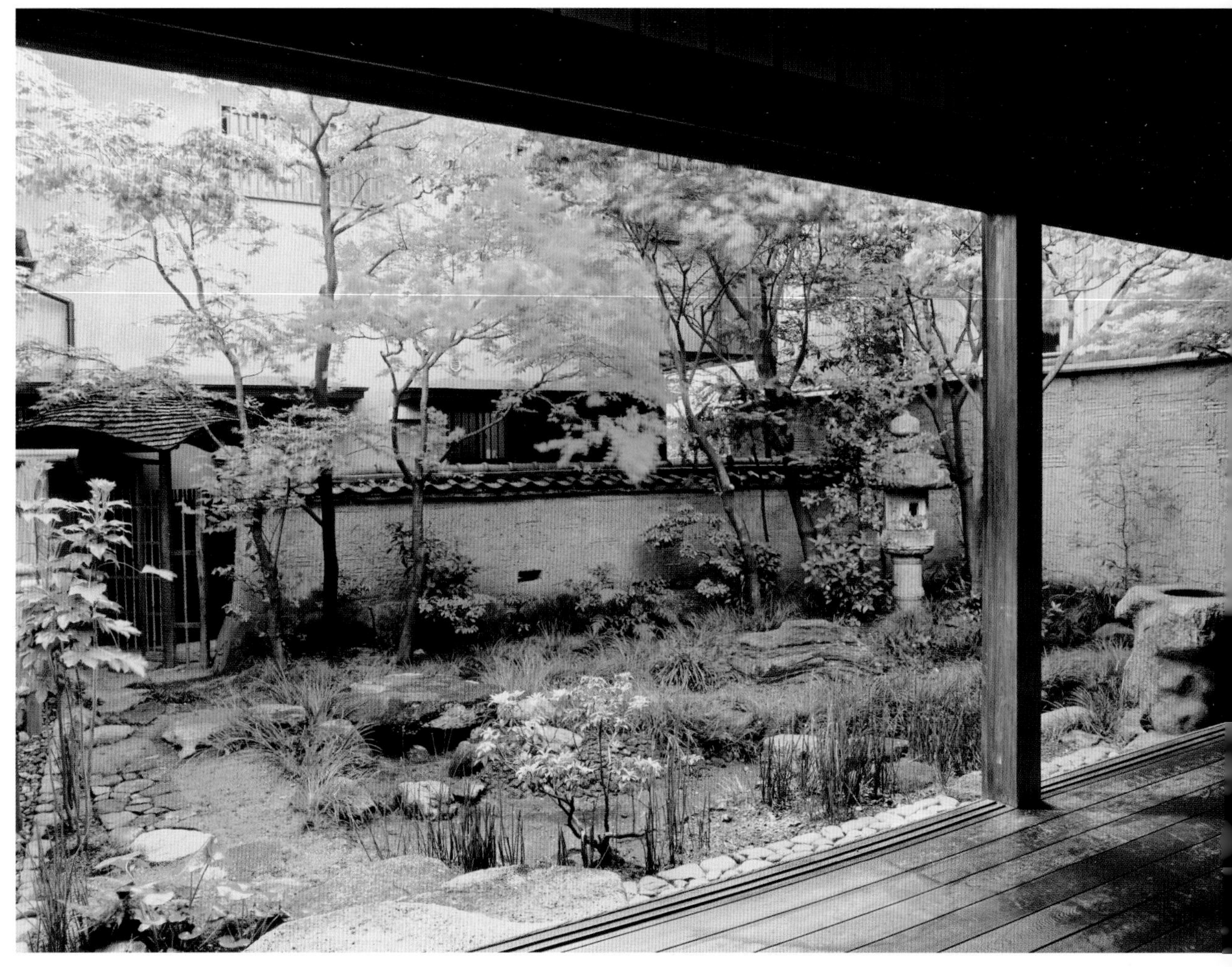

The Tatsutagawa River Garden

In what is considered to be the first collection of Japanese poetry, the *Kokin Wakashu* of 905, there are some poems about the Tatsutagawa River in Nara. One attributed to Ariwara no Narihira reads:

Unheard of
Even in the age
Of the mighty gods—
These deep crimson splashes
Dyed in Tatsuta's waters

In the eighteenth century, artist brothers Korin and Kenzan Ogata again picked up the theme of maple leaves floating on the Tatsutagawa. The brothers' paintings, ceramics and other works left a strong mark on Japan's arts. I also picked up the theme for a garden I made for Tenyo-in, a sub-temple of nearby Zozoji Temple, one of Tokyo's most famous. Tenyo-in's small "hidden" garden, located in a very metropolitan area of Tokyo, sits at the back of the temple facing a long, interior corridor (*engawa*).

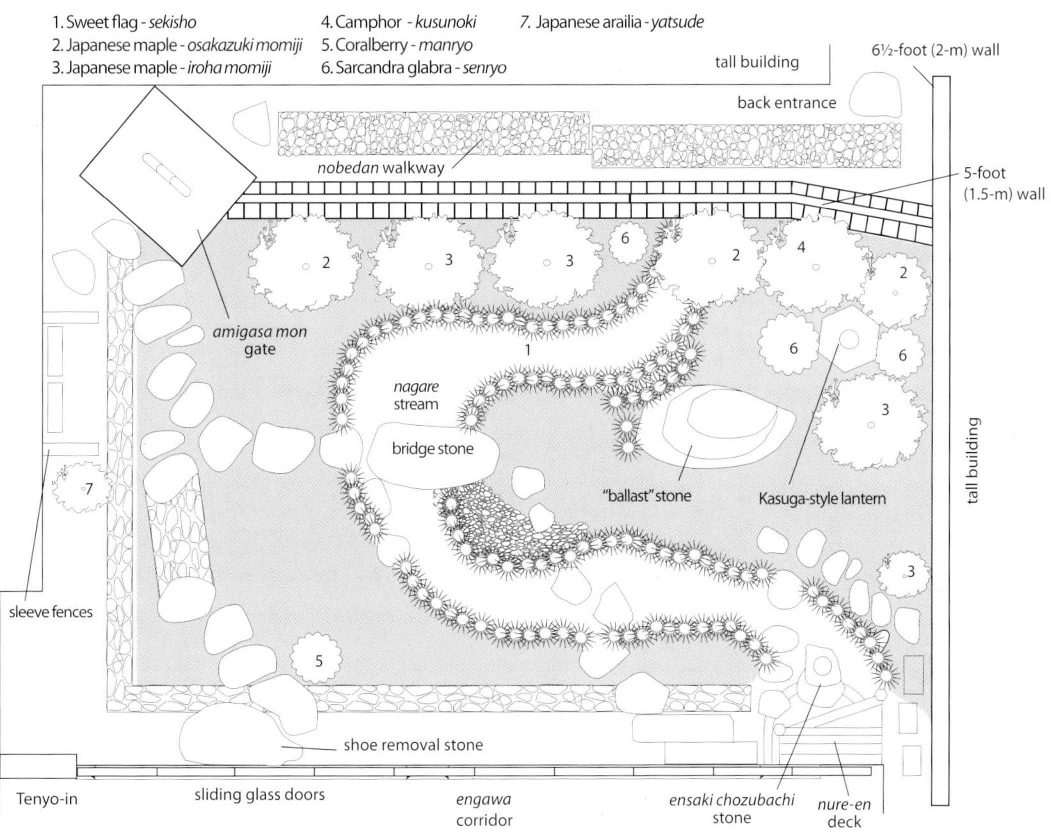

The main physical features of the garden are the winding stream and the many Japanese maples. First of all, we built a 6½-foot (2-m) clay wall (*dobei*) along the side of the property, running between the temple and the tall buildings next door. Then we made a 5-foot (1.5-m) wall at 90 degrees to that. The lower wall runs along the back of the garden and creates an entrance corridor behind it. At the end of the corridor we made an entrance gate.

The water for the shallow winding stream flows from an opening in the clay wall and snakes through the garden. It represents the idea of a river that ebbs and flows, bringing water from the mountains to the sea, and returning again when the rain falls, in an eternal cycle—in other words, the flow of life (*jinsei no nagare*). Another theme is the Edo period (1603–1868). This was a long period of peace when the Tokugawa shogun forcefully unified the country. It was during this period that Zojoji and its many

Facing page The view from the *engawa* corridor with the sliding doors removed. A hidden garden and an eternal cycle of life.

Below An interesting old ballast stone from the Edo period alludes to the history of the temple.

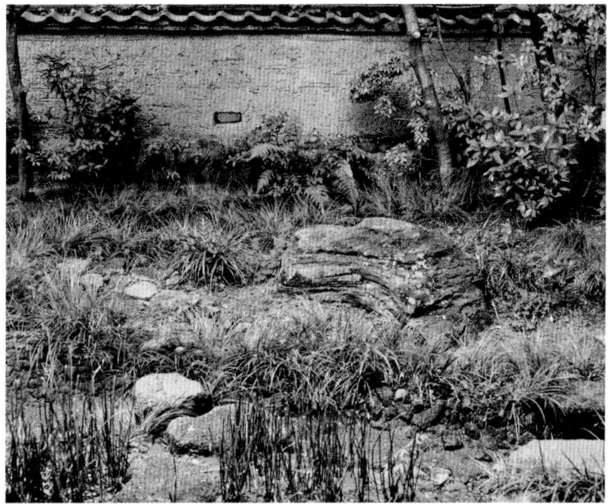

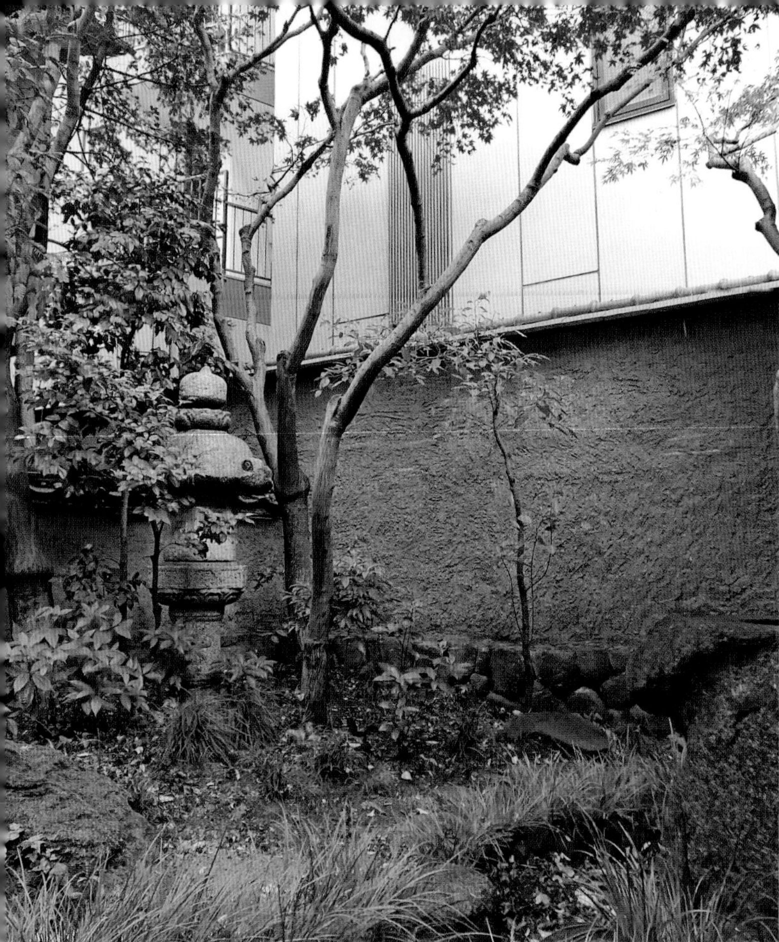
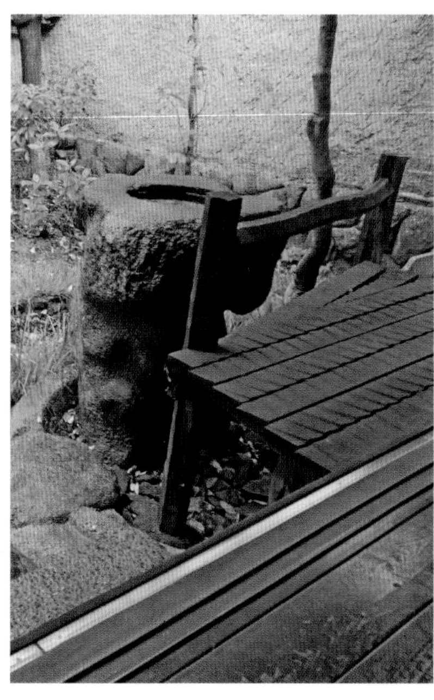

sub-temples were first established in what was then the small fishing village of Edo.

The massive Zojoji Temple, located just up the street, next to Tokyo Tower, came to be one of the most important temples of the Jodo sect of Buddhism. It is also the final resting place of six of the twelve Tokugawa shoguns. Today it is a Tokyo landmark. Established here in the same year as Tenyo-in, Zozoji has been rebuilt many times but its huge gate has survived fires, earthquakes and wars since 1622. Even though the total area has shrunk, and it no longer has forty-eight sub-temples, Zojoji is still one of the two most famous Tokyo temples—the other being Sensoji in Asakusa.

In Japan, most families are associated with a temple for the purpose of conducting prayers and burials. This has been the case since a registration system intended to stop the spread of Christianity and root out any hidden Christians was introduced in 1638. Every citizen had to register at the local temple and obtain a *terauke* certificate (*tera* means "temple" and *uke* means "certificate"). Administrative temples, Tenyo-in among them, were charged with various administrative functions related to the massive job of certifying each citizen.

The Edo period was peaceful and prosperous. The *sankin kotai* system meant that daimyo feudal lords from all over the country and their retinues had to reside in Edo every other year. Their families had to reside in the city throughout the year as hostages. Daimyo from wealthy domains had huge estates in the city, and they all had large gardens. Upkeep required goods and services that cost a lot of money. It was during this time that ships from all over Japan brought products to the shogun's capital. Those wooden boats used large stones as ballast and then sold them for use in gardens. Many of these gardens became public parks when the Edo period came to an end, and this is how some of the famous gardens of Tokyo acquired these large stones. It happened by chance that several such stones were available when we made this garden.

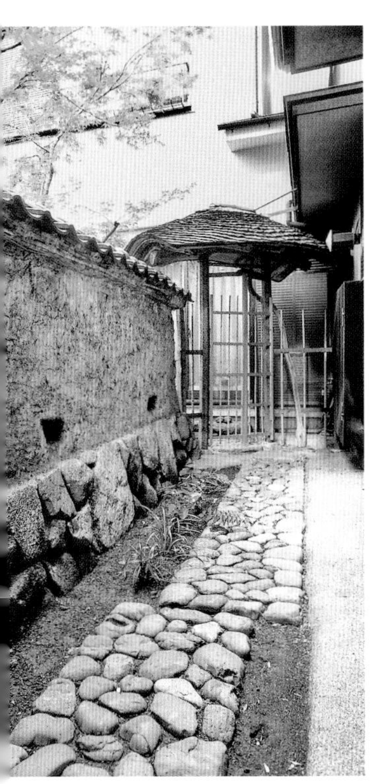

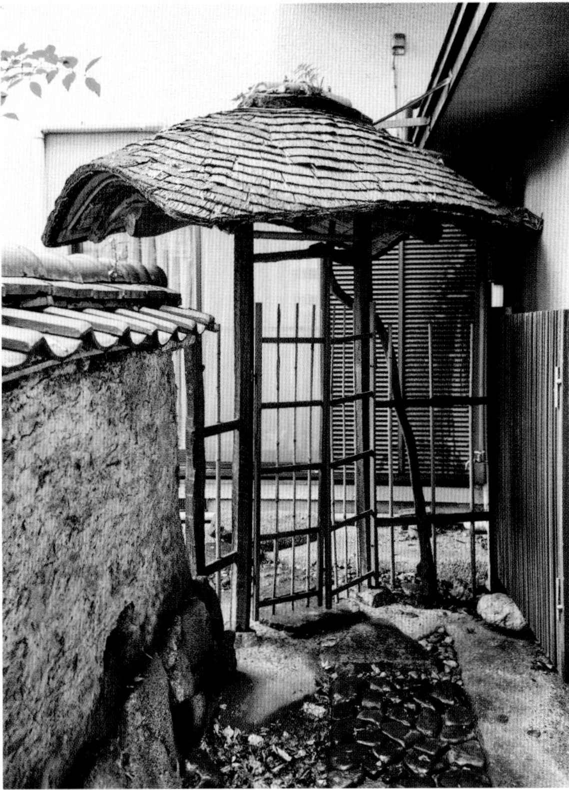

Left to right The base of a Kasuga-style lantern is removed to reduce its height. A tall water basin stands beside a wooden deck at the service of the resident monk. A stone walkway leads behind the garden wall to an *amigasa mon* "monk's hat" entrance gate.

As the garden is small, we didn't use tall stones except the water basin stone (*ensaki chozubachi*) that we placed close to the temple. Before the days of running water, the occupants used tall water basins within reach of the house to wash their face and hands, filled daily from a well by a servant. We made a small platform onto which the monk of the temple could walk outside to wash his hands without setting foot in the garden. These days the water basin is mostly symbolic, used on special occasions.

Again, for reasons of size and scale, I took the unusual step of removing the base of the existing stone lantern and burying the pedestal in the ground. That is usually done with Oribe-style lanterns, which have no pedestal to begin with. In this case I wanted to keep the beautiful Kasuga-style lantern, but tailor it to the small garden size. At its full height it would have looked awkward and cast its light over the rear wall.

Several large "ballast" stones are used in the garden: a bridge stone, and one that has the appearance of a small mountain, but none more than 24 inches (60 cm) tall. The garden is basically a flat *hiraniwa* style with no waterfall or mounded soil. This was partly because of the small size and partly because access was needed from the front and back of the garden. There are small stones along the winding stream and we planted a lot of Japanese sweet flag (*sekisho*), which gives the feeling of a wetlands stream and clean flowing water.

Another feature is the *amigasa mon* entrance gate (see pages 42–47). The roof of this gate is based on the shape of a Buddhist monk's hat. Monks were often seen going to funeral services or begging for alms wearing such a hat. The first use of this gate is unknown but like so many other features—such as the stone lantern (*ishidoro*)—this gate was adopted for use in the tea garden. Sixteenth-century architect, tea master, and garden designer Kobori Enshu was probably responsible for the design. The amigasa mon here is quite small but it lends an air of dignity to this simple, unassuming garden.

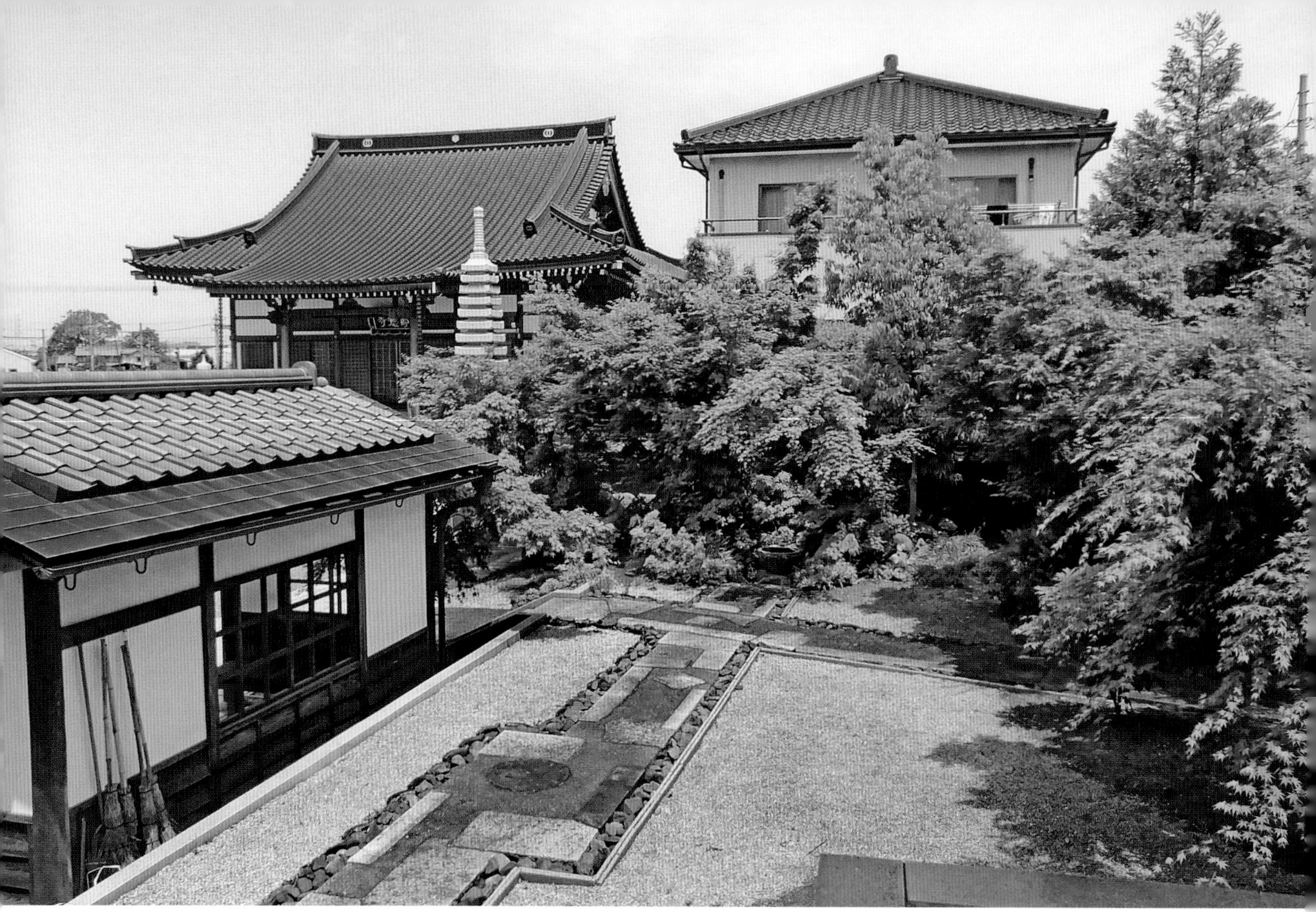

Garden of the Bell Tower

Jutokuji is a Shingon sect temple in Saitama Prefecture near Tokyo, connected with the famous Hasedera Temple of Nara founded in 686. It is a temple which maintains a graveyard, as most temples in Japan do. A number of years ago they built a new bell tower. A large bell, which is struck on the outside by a suspended wooden beam, is a feature of every Buddhist temple. It is used to call monks to prayers and on other occasions. Originally, these bells were struck three times a day (dawn, noon, and dusk) to mark the time. During the Edo period, it became an hourly strike. At the New Year, the bell is rung 108 times in a ritual intended to overcome the "108 earthly temptations" that keep our souls from being released from the endless cycle of death and rebirth.

I was asked to make a small garden around the bell tower one year after its completion. The small, 225-foot-square (21-m^2) space lies between the temple of Jutokuji, its graveyard, and the monks' living quarters. It sits next to the "water house" (*mizuya*) where pails of water and brushes are available for cleaning the gravestones and for refilling the vases of fresh flowers that are placed on graves. I tried to make a simple garden that would lighten people's hearts as they set about the task of honoring their departed loved ones.

When the bell tower was built, the sloped ground

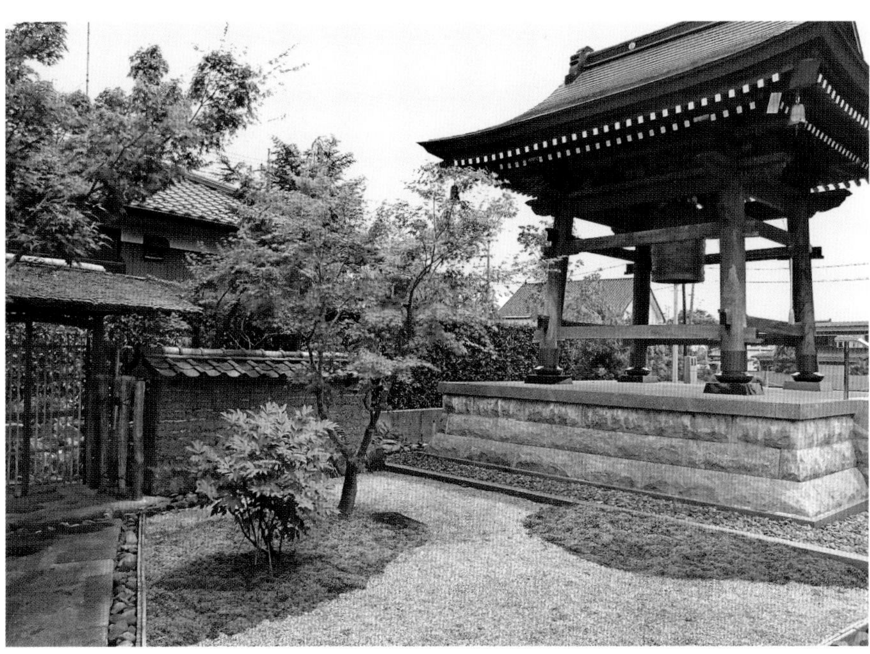

Facing page The view from the bell tower with Jutokuji Temple in the background.

Left The new bell tower was the impetus for constructing the simple garden.

Below Looking at the garden from the monks' quarters, which are separated from the garden by a clay wall and a *sukiyamon* gate. This is similar to an *amigasa mon* gate but without a curved roof.

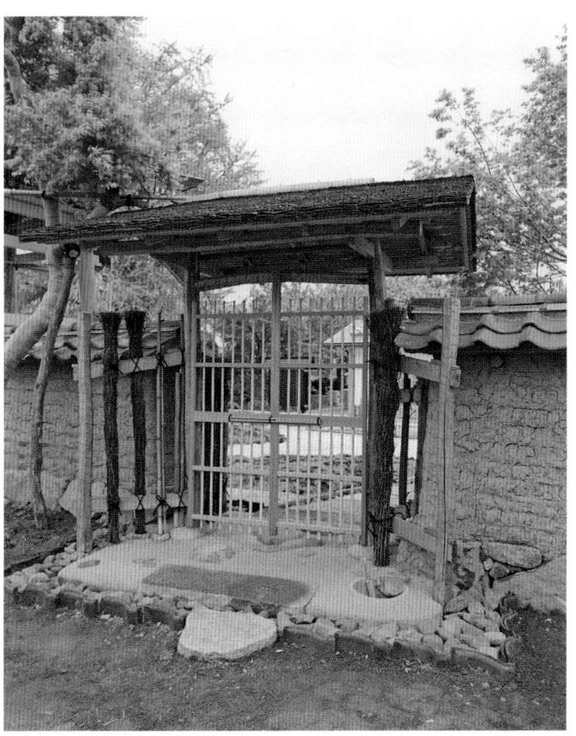

was leveled and a 2-foot (60-cm) granite retaining wall with stairs was created. The stair side is open to the plaza area and the temple. The opposite side is level with the monks' quarters, an elevation of about 3 feet 3 inches (1 m). We began by making a 5-foot (1.5-m) clay wall (*dobei*) along this side and another at 90 degrees—an "L" shape bordering two sides. The rough warmth of the dobei lends a comforting air to the otherwise cool surroundings. We opened an entrance in one wall and inserted a simple, covered gate (*sukiyamon*). It has similarities with the amigasa mon (pages 42–47) but the construction is easier and the roof line straighter and more modest.

Then we made several walkways (*nobedan*) to cross the space. They are of the Kobori Enshu style, mixing flat "label stones" (*tanzaku ishi*) with exposed aggregate (*araidashi*). Enshu, a sixteenth century garden designer and tea master, developed a style known as *kirei-sabi* that was pioneered by tea master Furuta Oribe. *Sabi* relates to the patina of aging, and *kirei* means beautiful or clear. It is a difficult idea to grasp without viewing many examples, but it was a step toward the clean, simple geometry that is sometimes considered a bridge between Japanese design and modernism. It is said that both men were deeply influenced by the culture of the West and that Enshu introduced straight lines into the garden.

The nobedan walkways are bordered by ceramic roofing tiles backfilled with black river stones. One stretches from the covered gate of the monks' quarters to the plaza between the temple and the graveyard. It ends at one of the sets of granite steps. The other crosses the first and leads to the bell tower and another set of steps. At the other end lies a water-basin arrangement (*tsukubai*). The water basin allows people to wash their hands and mouth before or after visiting a grave. It contains a water harp (*suikinkutsu*) which gives off a soothing sound when falling water overflows the basin to run through the stones beneath.

We used some polished granite in the nobedan walkways. This is the same material used in the base

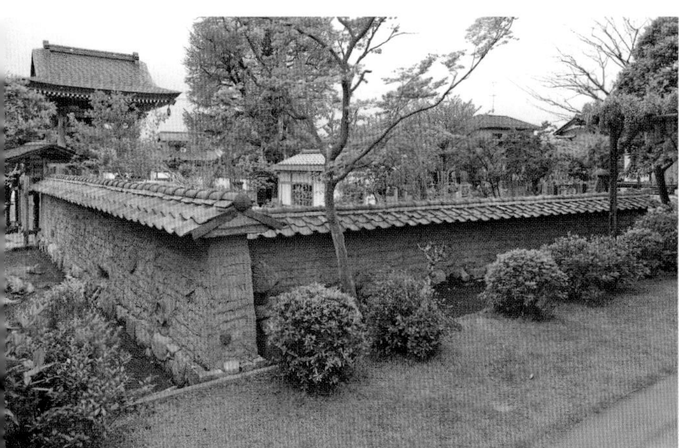

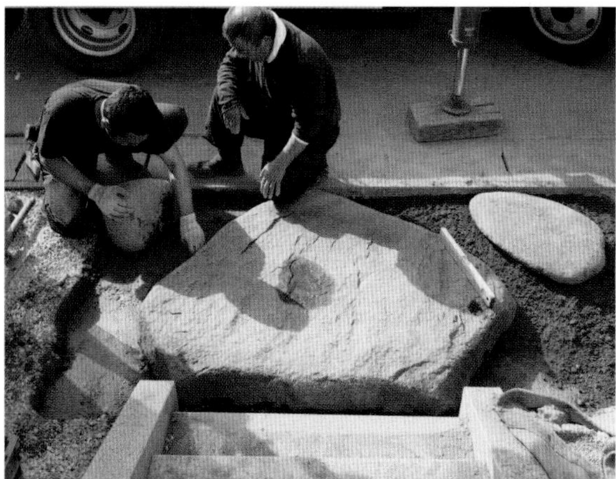

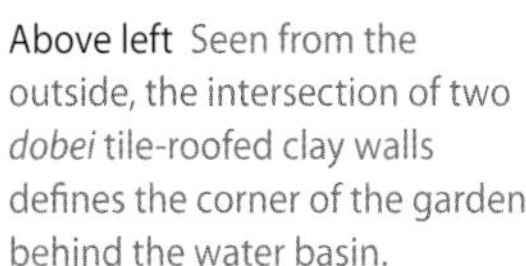

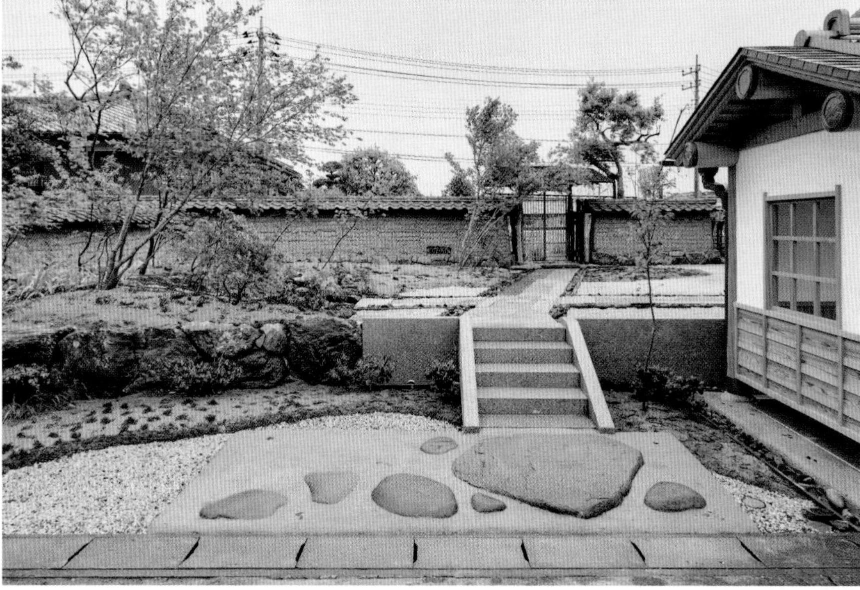

Above left Seen from the outside, the intersection of two *dobei* tile-roofed clay walls defines the corner of the garden behind the water basin.

Above right, and left Working with one of my crew to set a huge stone at the base of the stairs. The final result (left), set in exposed aggregate (*araidashi*), with other stepping stones.

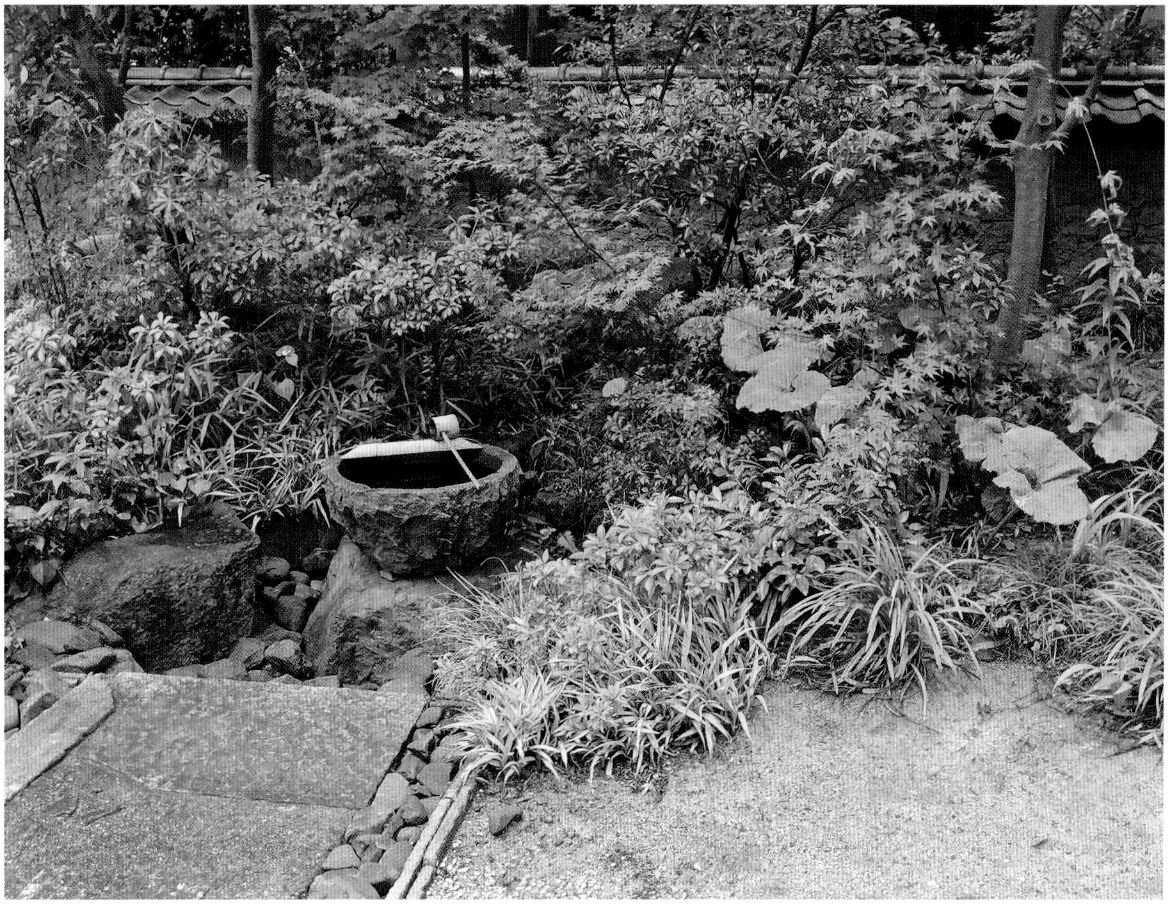

A *tsukubai* water-basin setting, enveloped in green, to comfort and refresh visitors paying respects at the graves of loved ones.

of the bell tower and stairs. It adds continuity and a slight formality. We filled the flat areas between the walkways with white gravel. Behind the tsukubai, extending from the corner made by the meeting of the two dobei walls, we mounded soil and covered it with haircap moss (*sugigoke*). The irregular-shaped mound extends across the nobedan and creates an island on the other side, where it meets another island in a sea of white gravel. The soft, fluffy character of moss can be exaggerated by mounding the soil underneath it. This also contributes to good drainage. We used the soil dug from this site to build the dobei because it is very rich in clay. For the same reason it was not suitable for planting. For the moss mounds and for tree planting we brought in a mixture of black soil (*kurotsuchi*), volcanic loam (*akatsuchi*), and leaf mulch (*fuyodo*).

Into the mounds we planted Japanese maple (*iroha momiji*), stone oak (*matebashi*), ubame oak (*ubamegashi*), Japanese cleyera (*sakaki*), Japanese andromeda (*asebi*), leopard plant (*otsuwabuki*), and azalea (*satsuki*) shrubs. Generally speaking, taller trees are planted around the edge of the garden to act as a windbreak and a backdrop. Smaller shrubs form low borders or settings with stones, especially around the water basin. Flowering shrubs are placed in mixed settings with non-flowering shrubs. Japanese gardens do not make a show of one type of tree or flower but instead aim for a mix that appears natural and appealing all year round.

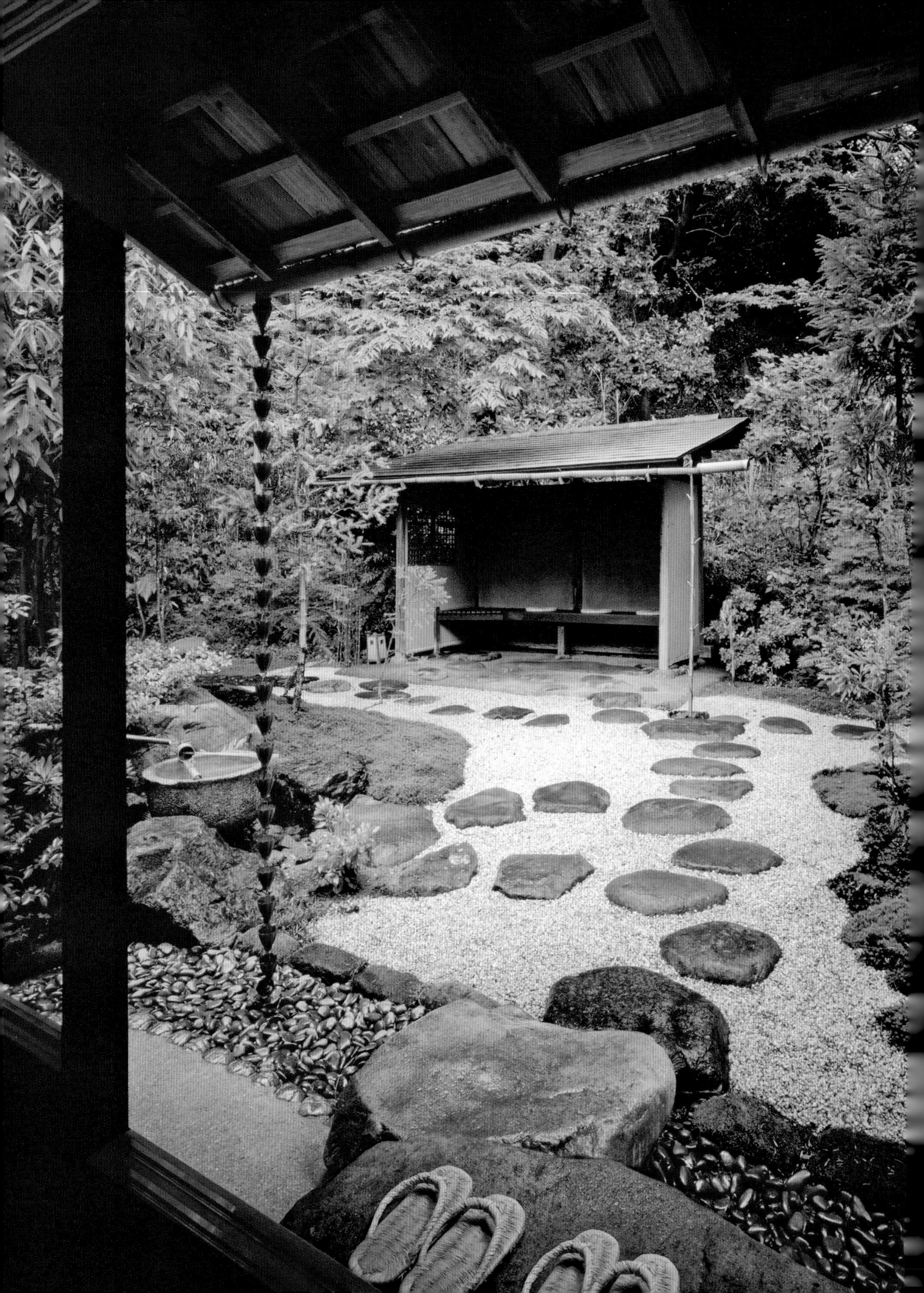

CHAPTER THREE

Small Sanctuaries and Gardens for Refreshment

To give some idea of the meaning of "small" in the title of this chapter, the largest garden in this book is approximately 9,500 square feet (880 m^2). By contrast, the smallest garden in this chapter, the *tsuboniwa* for the Nagaokas on page 108, is about 26 square feet (2.4 m^2). Such small gardens are usually referred to as *tsuboniwa*. The word *tsubo* can denote an area measurement of 35.5 square feet (3.3 m^2). But the term has other uses and connotations. For example, a style of architecture that was prominent among the aristocracy from about the ninth century is called *shinden zukuri*. Without going into too much detail, this type of structure had distributed rooms connected by covered corridors. The distribution created a number of small courtyards within the confines of the building. These small spaces were also called tsubo and were often filled with one type of plant, such as wisteria (*fuji*).

So the nuance of small size and enclosure have always been part of this garden type but the room for interpretation is great. One other important aspect is the intimacy of such gardens. That most of these gardens were not even known to exist by anyone other than the occupant of the house highlights their private nature. However, intimacy does not always equal privacy. Instead, it implies a scale and a level of detail that requires close contact with the viewer. In the "Getting Started" section of this book (page 14, top left) there is a photo of a stone-and-sand garden (*karesansui*) designed by one of my teachers, Katsuo Saito. It is actually in the veranda of the third floor of a three-story house. It can also be considered a tsuboniwa. In fact, this is not uncommon, especially in an age of high-rise buildings and apartment houses. Even rooftops have become places to create small gardens and I have made tsuboniwa for restaurants, spas, and hotels as well.

The "refreshment" in the title refers primarily to the culture of tea. Teahouses and tea gardens occupy a broad and deep position in Japanese culture. Even today, "the way of tea" is an accepted method of learning courtesy and etiquette. Many of the features found in all types of Japanese gardens began in the *roji*—meaning tea garden. For example, stone lanterns (*ishidoro*), are now a common fixture in every type of garden. But originally they were absorbed from temples into the tea garden before gaining wider acceptance. A true tea garden is built according to certain conventions, some of which depend on the style of tea. Many conventions can be traced to tea-ceremony master Sen no Rikyu (1522–91). Many more started with those who came before and after him. In this chapter I present a number of gardens that represent interpretations of the genre. Whether you drink tea or find some other reason to gather in a garden to enjoy the company of friends, I hope you will find something here that suits your taste.

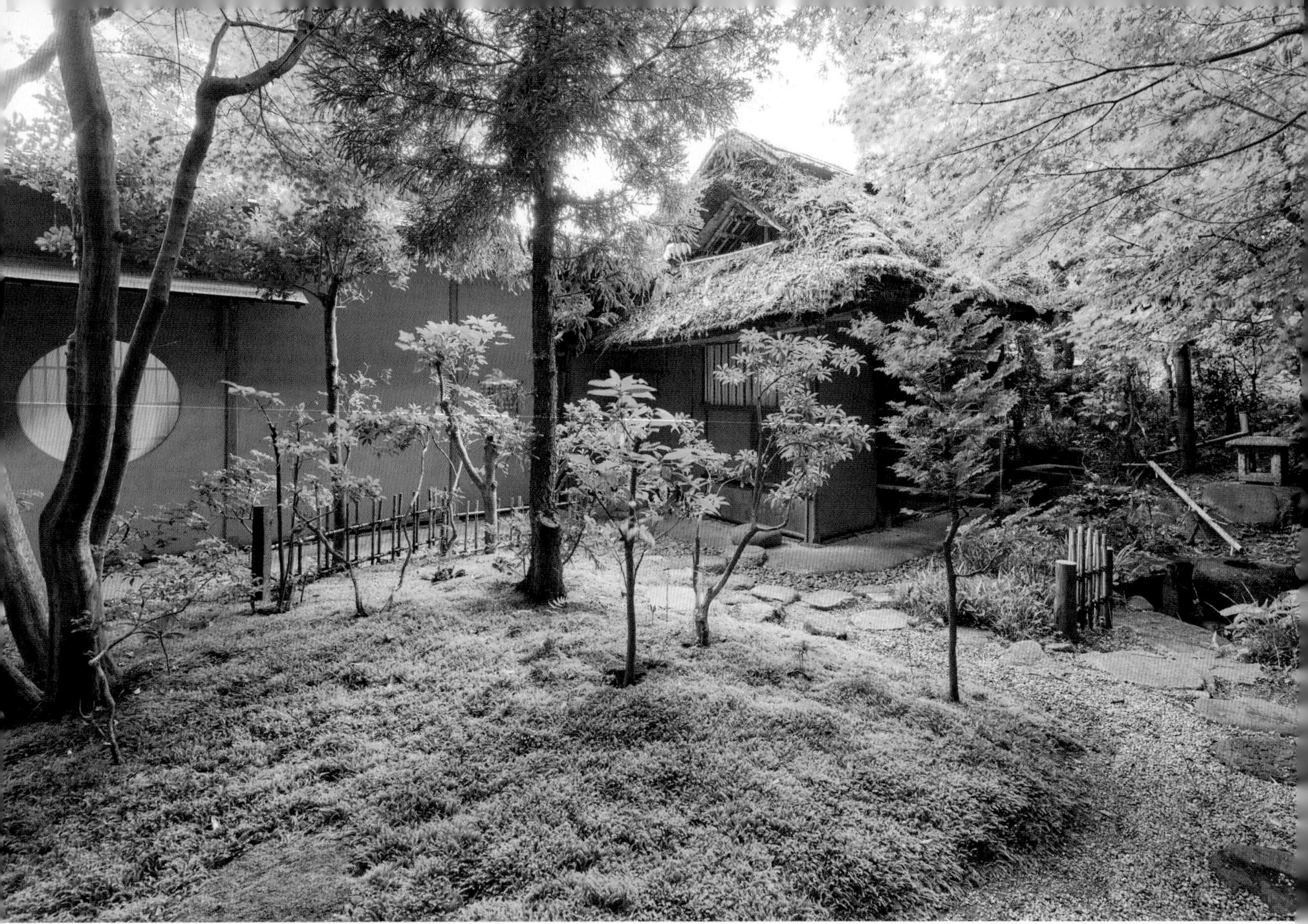

Garden for a Tea Get-together

Kokonotsuido is a group of tearooms serving *kaiseki ryori*, Japanese-style, full-course meals. The owner, Chiomaro Shibuya, began by opening a soba noodle restaurant in 1968. That restaurant is now a complex of cottages that dot a small hill. Beside the restaurant and tearooms, Shibuya-san has created a school and studios for ceramics and glass, as well as a large gallery in a restored merchant's house (*machiya*) relocated from Kamakura. All his businesses are involved in promoting and supporting traditional Japanese culture.

A kaiseki meal may have five or six courses or as many as fifteen. More than the number of courses, the aim is to present the finest of traditional Japanese cuisine. The dishes vary by season and region. Food is carefully prepared, artfully presented and can be equated with Western haute cuisine. A course is arranged by certain time-honored principles such as the inclusion of vegetables, fish, and rice, and various preparation methods including steaming, boiling, pickling, fermenting and raw. *Cha-kaiseki* is traditionally a meal served before tea or with the tea ceremony. It is simpler than the full-course kaiseki and often served in an elegant bento lunch box.

Both types of kaiseki have their roots in the Buddhist prohibition against taking a life, which meant no meat or fish could be eaten. This prohibition, and the practice of drinking tea, are said to have started with the return to Japan of the Rinzai Zen monk Eisai (1141–1215), after his studies in

The 4½-tatami-mat teahouse in the tea garden of Kokonotsuido exudes the spirit of the thatched hut (*soan*).

China. Thus Buddhist temple food (*shojin ryori*) was developed within cloistered temples by the priesthood. From the monks, the practice spread to the aristocracy. In the fourteenth century, teahouses (*chaya*) started popping up around temples. Samurai gathered to drink tea and contests to guess where a particular tea came from, called *tocha*, began. In the fifteenth and sixteenth centuries, the growth of a wealthy and educated commercial class gave rise to a more sophisticated and ritualized tea ceremony. This is the age of the original "tea masters": Murata Juko, Takeno Joo, and Sen no Rikyu. These men were greatly influenced in their tastes and practices by the painter and poet Noami and the Zen monk Ikkyu of Daitokuji Temple in Kyoto. Noami preferred the genteel use of fine Chinese ceramics and drawing rooms (*shoin zukuri*) for drinking tea. Ikkyu influenced tea in the direction of the natural and rustic. Ikkyu's disciple, Juko, took tea from the larger shoin to the tiny, thatched hut (*soan*) and from Chinese to native, unglazed ceramics. This eventually became the ideal known as *wabi cha*.

Takeno Joo popularized this style among wealthy merchant friends, going so far as to construct a rustic 4½-tatami-mat hut behind his home for the purpose of serving tea. He also served a light meal before tea, which is sometimes said to be too strong to drink on an empty stomach. This meal was limited to soup and three dishes and is considered the origin of cha-kaiseki (*cha* means tea). The food was influenced by shojin ryori, and the tea—as it had been since its introduction—was in powdered form. Enter another tradition from the monk Ingen and the Obaku branch of Zen.

Ingen came to Nagasaki in Japan from China in 1654 and eventually found his way to Kyoto where

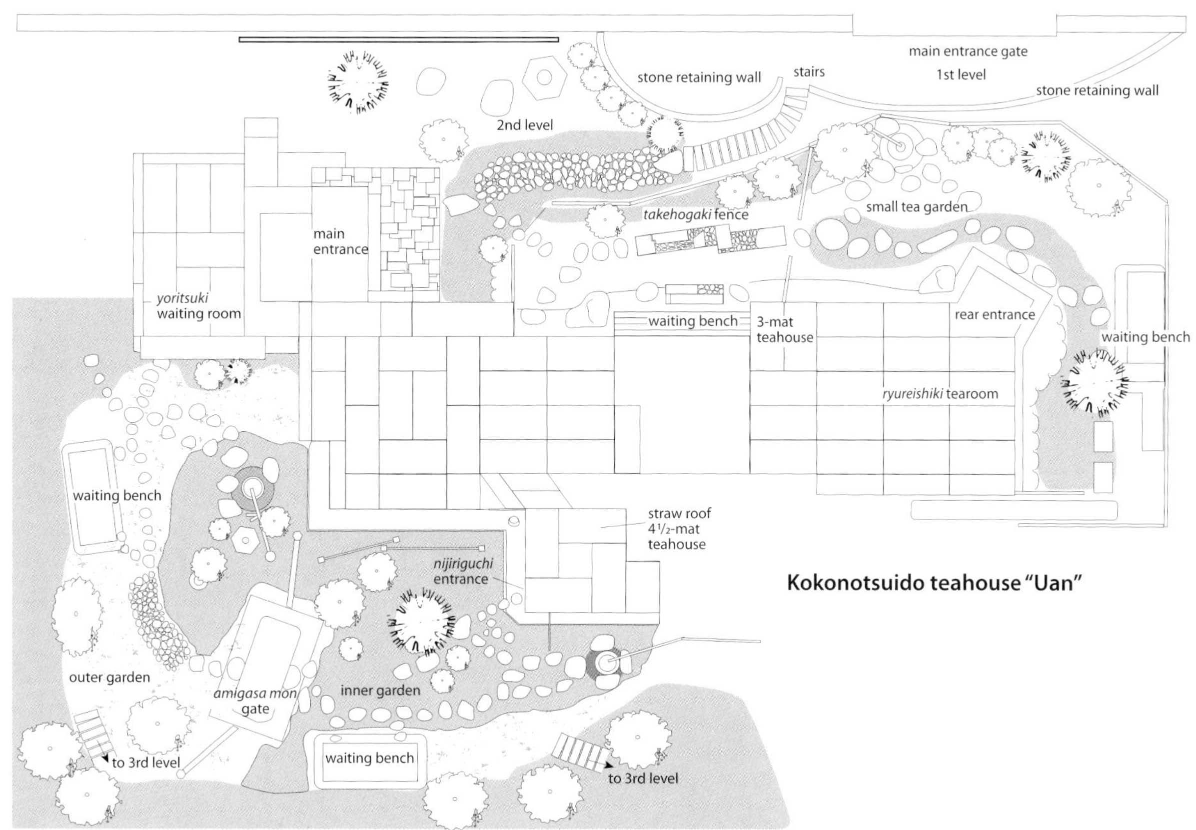

Kokonotsuido teahouse "Uan"

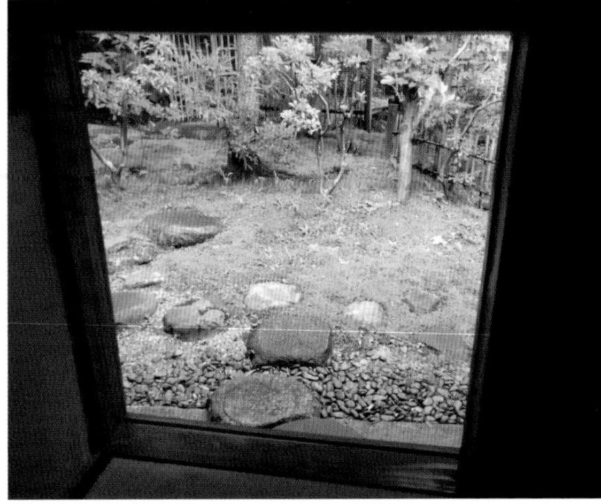

Stepping stones lead to the *nijiriguchi* entrance seen from inside the teahouse.

he founded the temple Manpukuji. Here, the tradition of drinking whole-leaf tea (*sencha*) with *fucha ryori* was practiced. Fucha ryori consists of two soups and six vegetable dishes and uses five colors, five methods, five flavors and five senses as the basis for food preparation. This is now part of standard Japanese cooking. While kaiseki is served in stages to each individual, in fucha, the food is served on a communal table and everyone picks up their food and places it on their own plate. The food also uses more oil and starch and is therefore more filling. Modern kaiseki draws on all these traditions as well as the elaborate *honzen ryori* cuisine of the fourteenth century, established by the samurai class. These days, a meal may also include meat and alcohol depending on the needs of the guests.

Kokonotsuido is located in the town of Ofuna, south of Yokohama on the way to Kamakura. They serve both kaiseki and cha-kaiseki. Passing through the entrance, guests climb the stone stairs on the right. This leads to the main level where we made a 6-foot (1.8 m) tall bamboo-branch fence (*takehoga-ki*). The tall fence protects waiting guests from wind and dust. Behind the fence there is a waiting bench against the wall of the *ryureishiki* (lit., "standing bow"), a large room where tea is served at tables with stools. We made a small garden here with a *tsukubai* water-basin setting. The head of the Urasenke school of tea ceremony, known as Gen-gensai, initiated the practice of serving tea at tables in 1873, when he convinced the Meiji Emperor to allow him to perform the tea ceremony at the Vienna International Exposition. It was already well known that Europeans were uncomfortable sitting on the floor.

From the top of the stairs we made an informal *nobedan* walkway along the outside of the fence. From there a guest can turn left into the exterior

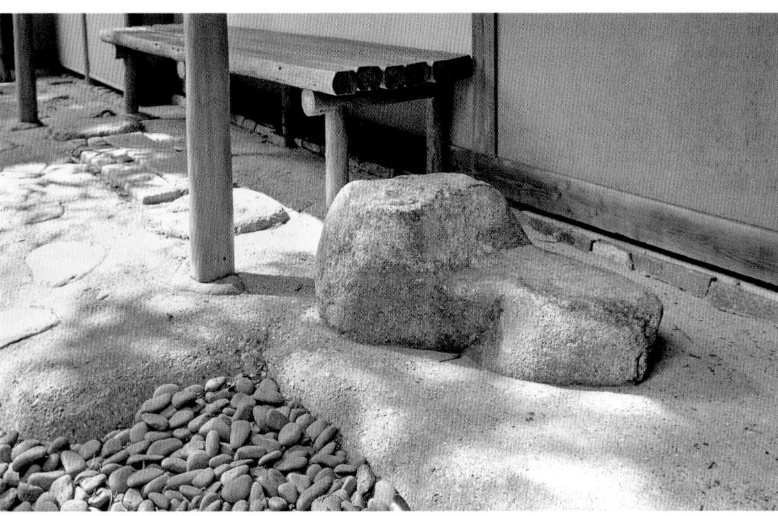

The tradition of a sword-hanging stone next to the teahouse reminds guests to leave animosity outside.

Below The main teahouses and garden are on the second level, accessed by a stone stair.

Right The waiting area to enter the complex is a small garden behind a tall *takehogaki* bamboo-branch fence.

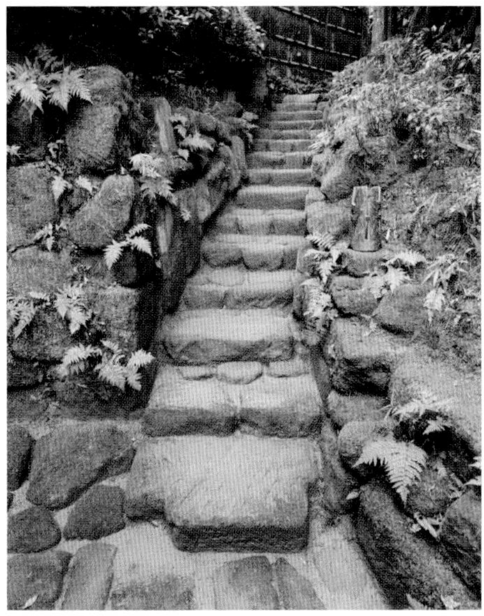

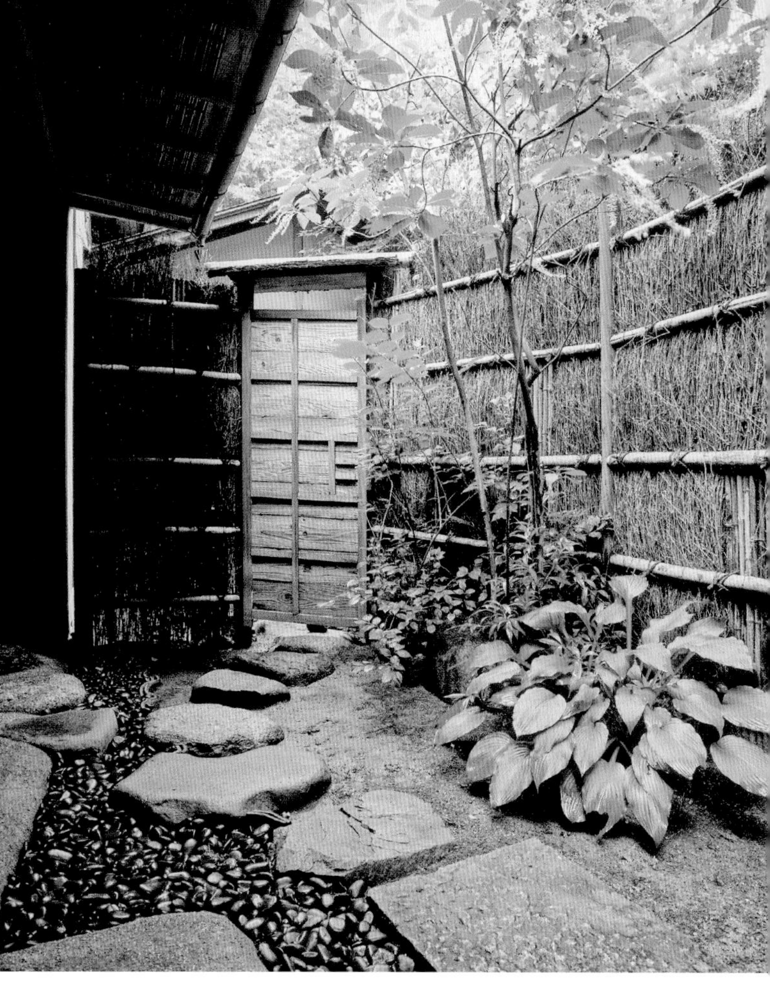

waiting area or go straight into the main entrance. The complex, named "Uan" ("universe"), has five or six large and small tearooms. The large grounds are covered in old cedar trees that provide a wonderful mountain atmosphere. From the main level, another stair leads to the ceramics workshop and exhibition space at the highest point of the hill. Guests who are attending a ceremony in the 4½-tatami-mat straw-roof teahouse pass through the main entrance to an inside waiting area (*yoritsuki*) and then outside to the tea garden. First they will enter the outer garden (*soto roji*) where a waiting bench (*koshikake machi-ai*) is located. The outer and inner tea garden, where the second waiting bench is located, are separated by a *yotsumegaki* fence (see picture, page 148) with an *amigasa mon* "monk's hat" gate (see picture, page 43). This fence and gate are not meant to keep people out, but rather boundary markers that divide here and there without being clearly open or closed. This kind of ambiguous space division may be uniquely Japanese. At the least, it allows for a view of the garden as a whole, while building anticipation for the next stage in the sequence from outer to inner garden to teahouse. The teahouse appears all the more rustic thanks to its straw roof with a lower pent roof on the gable side.

In the main building, guests can reserve an entire room or a single table. Tea and a sweet can be tried inexpensively, but only a licensed tea master may reserve the teahouse. Because tea masters of any school may use the teahouse and garden, it is tailored more generally to accommodate any style. We planted many maples and Japanese andromeda in the garden, and covered the ground with moss. I think the atmosphere is just as the old tea masters must have imagined it. The teahouse and garden are at their busiest in November when the *kuchikiri* ceremony for unsealing the new tea of the year takes place. In the world of tea, this time is equivalent to New Years.

ARRANGING STONES FOR THE KOSHIKAKE MACHIAI COVERED WAITING BENCH

As the tea ceremony gained acceptance with the warrior and the growing merchant class alike, it evolved into one of Japan's highest art forms. It also developed many supporting physical and philosophic structures. The *koshikake machiai* covered waiting bench embodies both.

The tea ceremony developed many unique structures such as the tea garden (*roji*), teahouse (*chashitsu*), and the koshikake machiai. Each of these structures is shaped by the philosophy that animates the tea ceremony. One aspect of this is courtesy. Another is the importance of hierarchies. This aspect of the culture is expressed in the order and procedure of ceremony.

For example, the tea garden always includes a water-basin arrangement (*tsukubai*), which embodies the courtesy of cleansing the body before engaging with others. The brief walk through the garden represents a hierarchal passage from the profane to the sacred world. The small, rustic form of the teahouse represents an environment of simplicity and humility within which the tea master

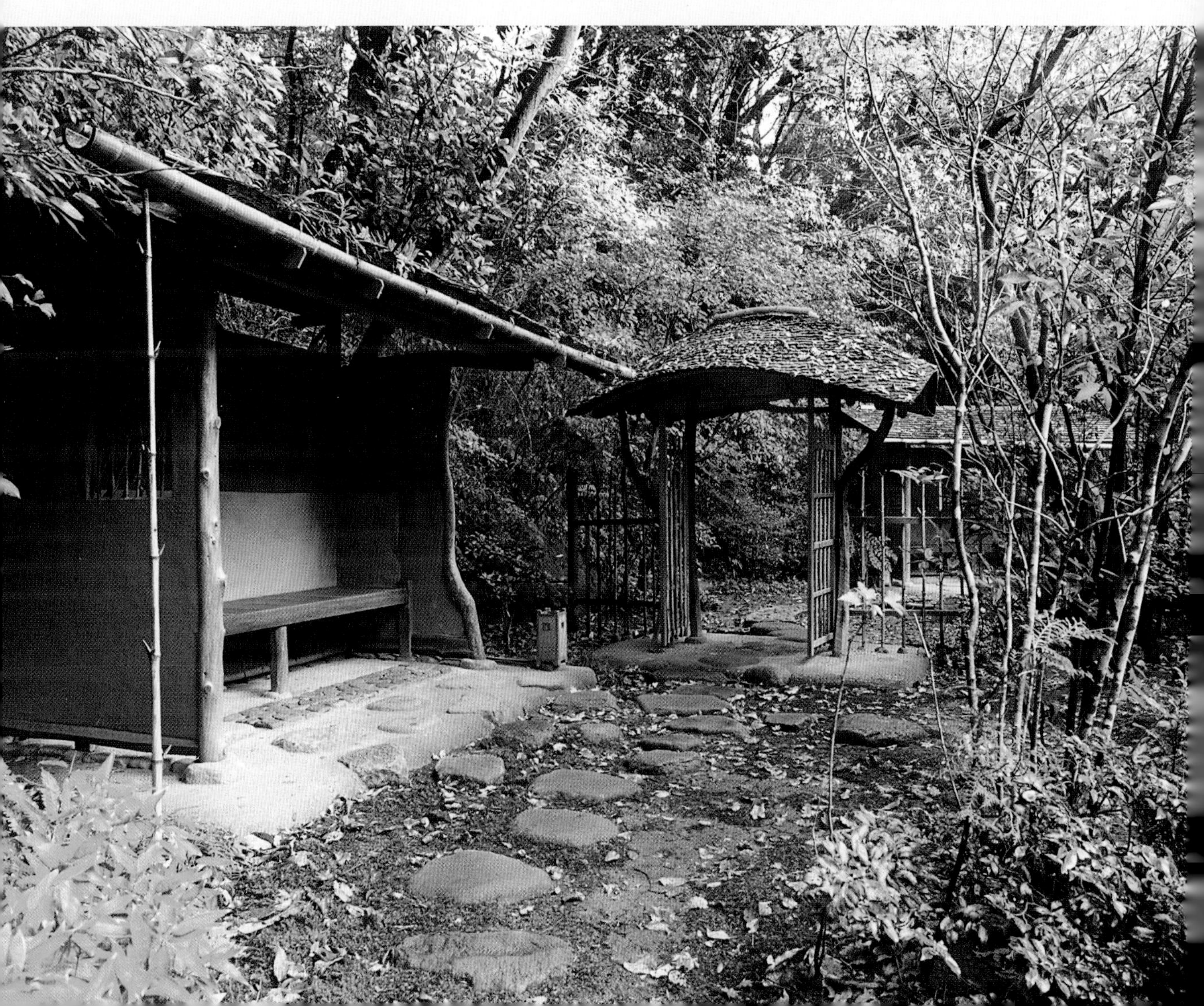

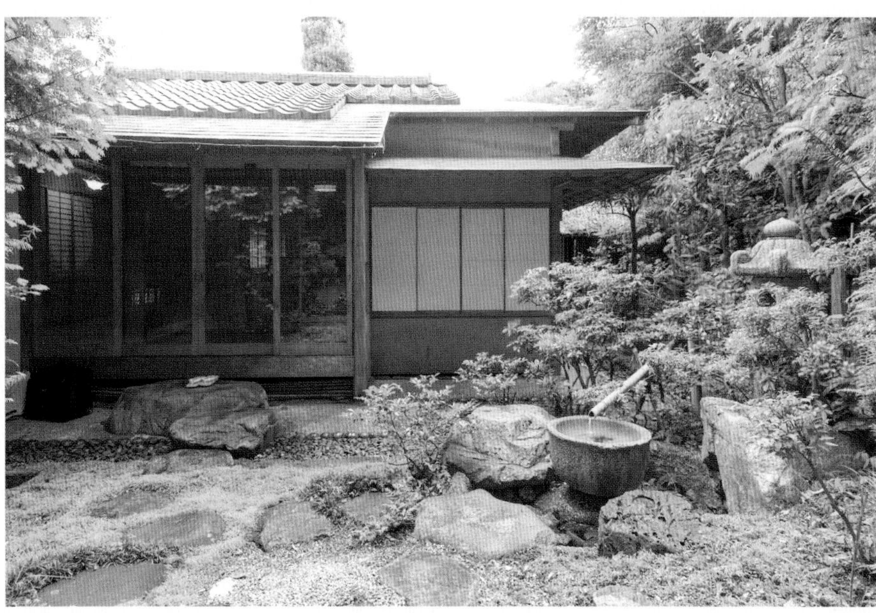

Facing page Looking from inner to outer tea garden. Both gardens have their own waiting benches, and are separated by an *amigasa mon* "monk's hat" gate.

Left Guests enter the outer garden from the *yoritsuki* indoor waiting area.

may display exquisite utensils, hanging scrolls, and flower arrangements. The contrast encourages guests to rethink hierarchy and embrace the coexistence of the humble and the splendid.

The koshikake machiai reflects a hierarchy in the importance of the guests. It generally seats four or five people. The primary guest (*shokyaku* or *jokyaku*) is the first to be greeted by the host (*teishu*). This guest, responsible for communicating with the host and the other guests, enters the garden first and sits first. The last guest is called the *tsume*. Stones on the ground mark the seating positions and reflect the hierarchy. A large single stone (*kinin ishi*) marks the seat of the primary guest. Next to this is a long stone or a *nobedan* pavement to mark the position of the other guests. Finally, a small stone marks the position of the last guest, who has to ensure the koshikake machiai is tidy before setting out for the teahouse. The first and last guests are both key to the success of the ceremony. They have met with the teishu in advance and discussed the purpose of the gathering and the teishu's vision for it.

The stepping stones (*tobi ishi*) lead guests from the entrance to the waiting bench to the tsukubai to the teahouse and back again.

Koshikake machiai (top view)

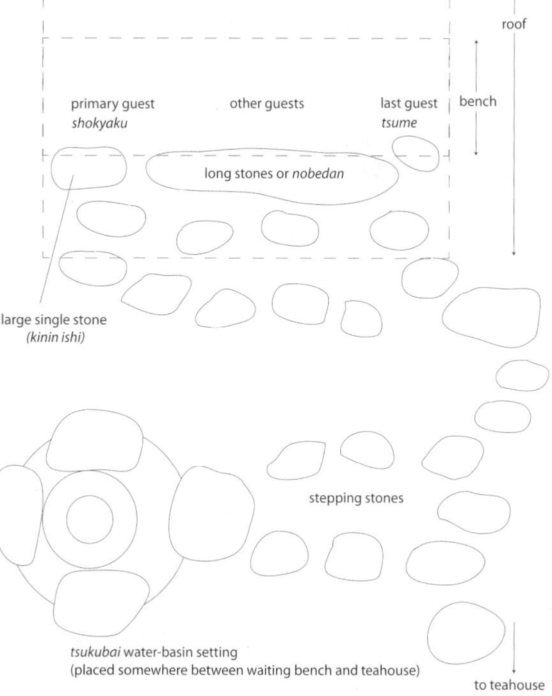

A Tea Garden for an Urban Farmhouse

Traveling through Tokyo's Setagaya district, you might wonder if you've made a wrong turn and ended up in the countryside if you see the Edo-period farmhouse (*minka*) of Fumiko Miyazaki, a painter married to Akira Miyazaki, a diplomat in the postwar period and Japanese ambassador to Holland, Ireland, and Turkey. Due to Ambassador Miyazaki's position, they often entertained foreign guests. Fumiko was also versed in the culture of tea and practiced *nodate chakai* (outdoor tea ceremony) in the garden of their home, which is preserved in splendid condition. The house is usually rented out and a previous tenant commissioned me to make a new garden. Thinking about the atmosphere of the farmhouse and the family history, we proceeded to make an elegant tea garden.

The land is elevated about 3 feet (1 m) above street level. The 12 x 57-foot (3.6 x 17.4-m) garden is on the long side of the house, with the entrance on the narrow side. Between the minka and the other house on the same property, where the owner now lives, a few steps lead from the street to a shared entrance with covered gate and sliding door (*hikido*). To increase privacy of tenant and owner, we made a brushwood fence (*shibagaki*) of spicebush (*kuromoji*) and pear wood (*nashi*) branches, with a wood-plank and bamboo roof. A single row of large stones completes the base. This type of fence, made since the eighth century, is often used in tea gardens.

There was a garden between the two houses and many of the existing trees needed to be preserved. Several are outside or just inside the gate, including

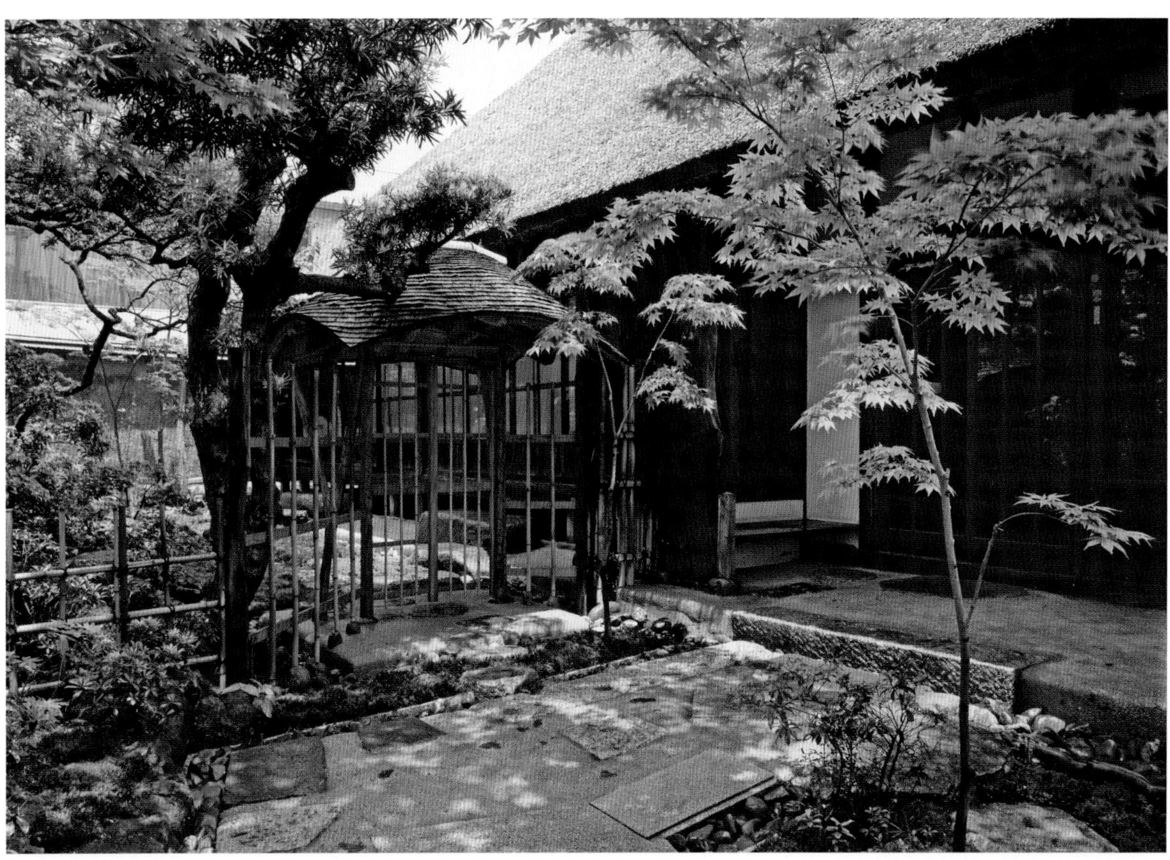

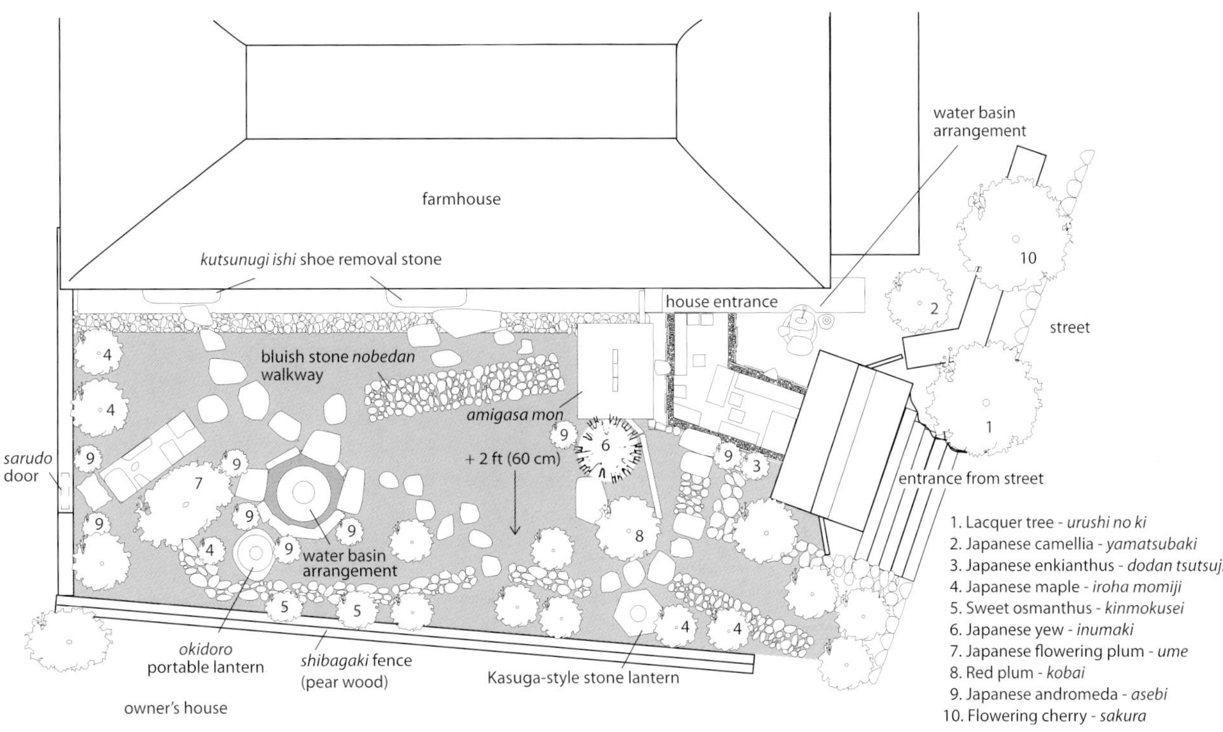

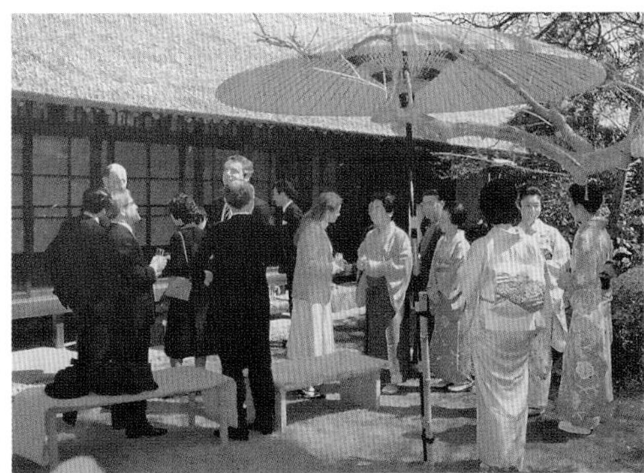

Facing page Drenched in dappled light, the *amigasa mon* "monk's hat" entrance to the garden and the *minka* farmhouse on the right.

Left After the war, the Miyazakis often had tea gatherings in the garden (*nodate chakai*) for foreign guests.

Below, left and right The entrance to the elevated property and the entrance walkway.

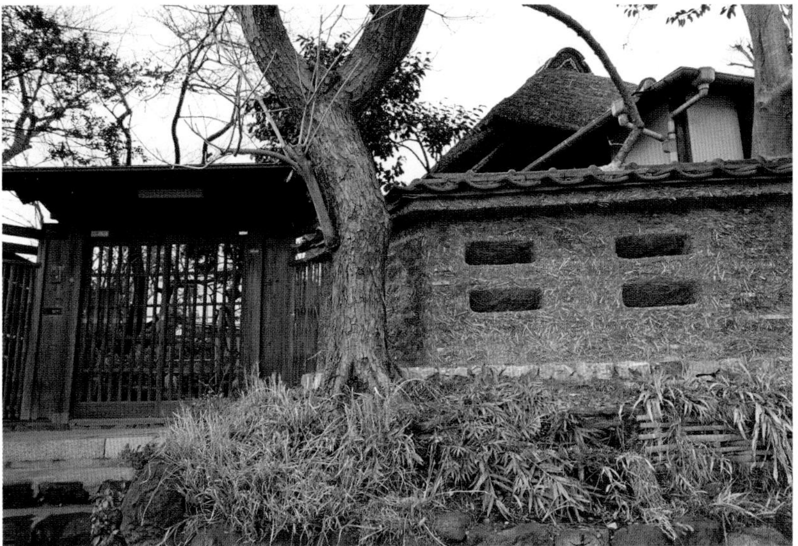

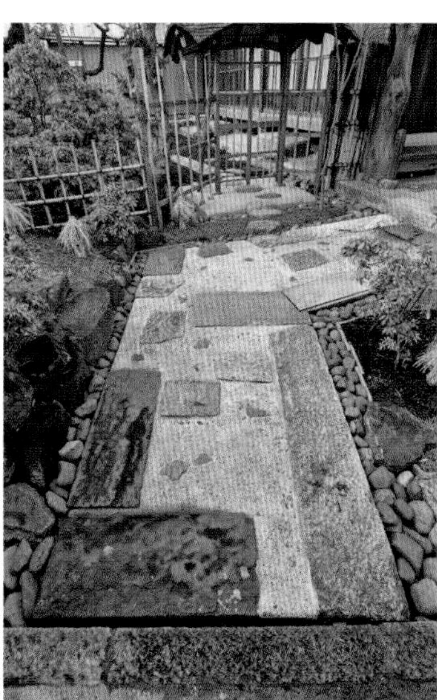

a 13-foot (4-m) lacquer tree (*urushi no ki*) by the stairs, a mountain camellia (*yama tsubaki*), and a flowering cherry (*sakura*) the same size as the lacquer tree. To separate the garden from the street we made a 5-foot (1.5-m)-tall clay wall (*dobei*), full of long straw. With the bamboo frame peeking out of the surface and the roughness of the straw, this wall has a unique appearance that harmonizes perfectly with the straw roof of the minka farmhouse. Minka usually have a thatch roof and a single-room structure, subdivided in various ways. Some have very steep roofs and the garret may constitute a second or even third floor.

From the entrance gate, we made a wide *nobedan* walkway that goes straight for 10 feet (3 m), then turns right to the door of the house where it meets a broad and deep step with a waiting bench (*tomomachi*) on the left. This is where a driver or servant of a high-ranking guest would wait. It also acts as a covered waiting bench for the garden. To the right of the door is a water basin for visitors to refresh themselves. On the left side of the wide nobedan we made a 2-foot (60-cm) retaining wall of stone. Through a gap in the wall we made three steps, leading to two casual walkways branching right and left. The left leads to the end of the brushwood fence and accesses the owner's house. The right leads to the back side of the garden along the side of the fence. The 2-foot slope from the front to the rear of the garden necessitated the retaining wall and steps.

Beyond the nobedan, before it turns toward the house, stepping stones lead to an *amigasa mon* "monk's hat" gate at the tea-garden entrance, fitting well with the atmosphere of the house. The entrance walkway is made of large, rectangular stones and clay dug from the site. The floor under the amigasa mon is also made of clay, but smoother and finer with stepping stones across it. The walkway leading from the entrance to the house receives general traffic and greater wear. The floor under the amigasa mon is for garden guests and so is less used and more refined.

Passing through the amigasa mon you enter the garden. A bluish stone (*makuro ishi*) nobedan leads to stepping stones and the water-basin arrangement (*tsukubai*). This is the tea garden proper. Looking towards the house you see two long shoe-removal stones (*kutsunugi ishi*). The shoe-removal stones are particularly long because of the many guests that

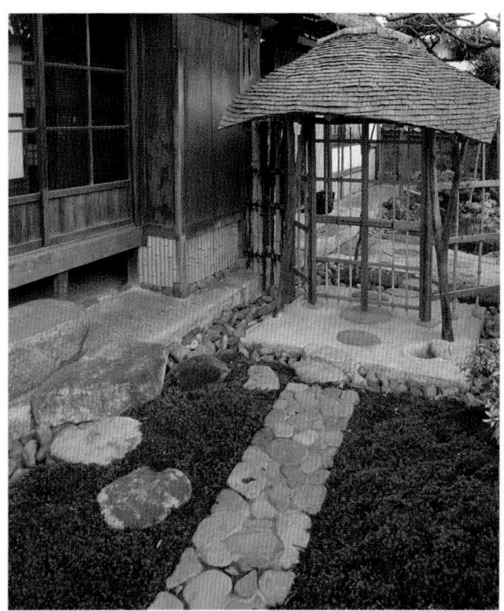

Left An informal walkway of bluish stone and stepping stones leading to one of the large *kutsunugi ishi* shoe-removal stones.

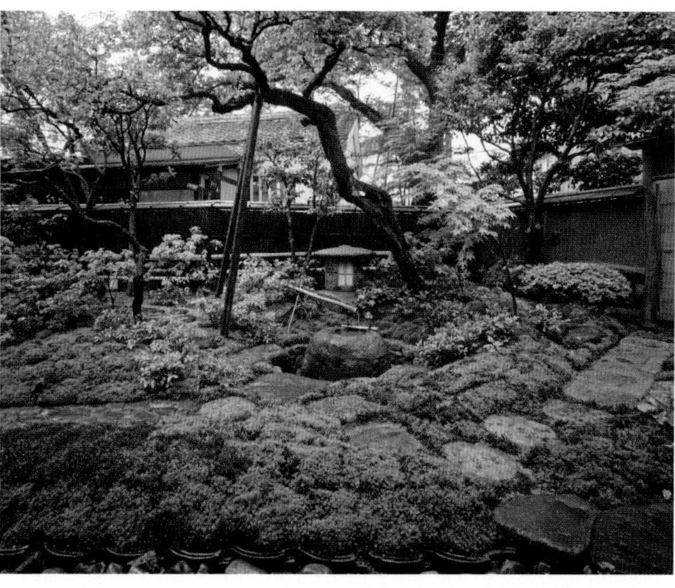

Right The *tsukubai* water-basin setting in the midst of moss and stone under an old plum tree.

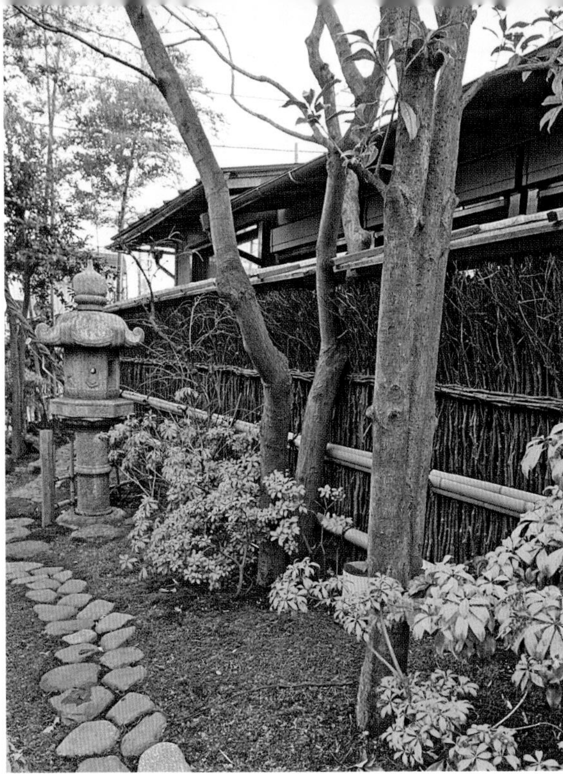

Left In front of the spicebush fence is a tall Kasuga-style lantern where the path branches left and right.

Below A slightly short *kugurido* door reminds those who use this rear entrance that this is a tea garden.

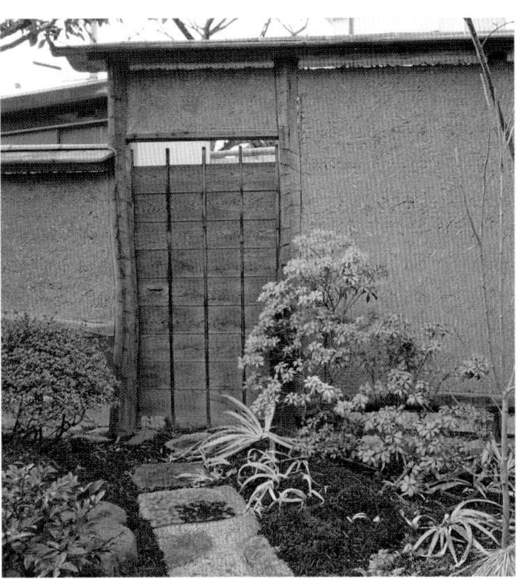

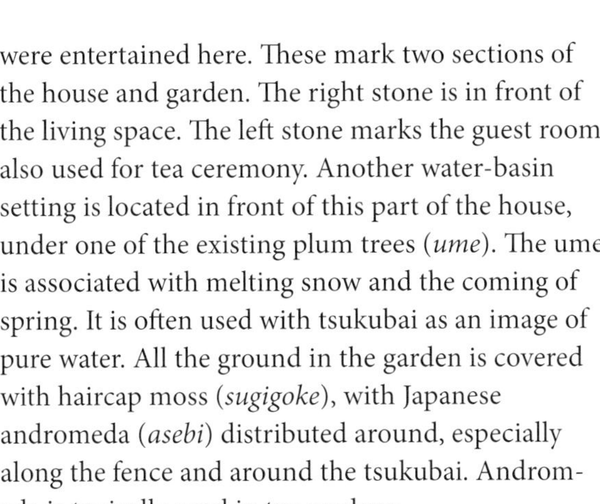

were entertained here. These mark two sections of the house and garden. The right stone is in front of the living space. The left stone marks the guest room also used for tea ceremony. Another water-basin setting is located in front of this part of the house, under one of the existing plum trees (*ume*). The ume is associated with melting snow and the coming of spring. It is often used with tsukubai as an image of pure water. All the ground in the garden is covered with haircap moss (*sugigoke*), with Japanese andromeda (*asebi*) distributed around, especially along the fence and around the tsukubai. Andromeda is typically used in tea gardens.

Stone lanterns are used extensively in Japanese gardens. Even when they are not actually used for illumination, they should be placed as if they were still serving that function. I placed a tall Kasuga-style stone lantern at the junction of the branching walkways at the top of the three steps leading from the entrance nobedan. A second portable lantern (*okidoro*) is set to the rear left of the water basin. It sits on a stone at a height such that the light would fall on the hands of the person washing there. A *teshoku ishi* stone, where a candle or small lantern can be placed, is always part of a tsukubai grouping. Other than the places where we used the lanterns, usual locations include along footpaths, at the foot or head of stairs or alongside a pond.

There are two more points about this garden. One is the wall and door at the end of the garden furthest from the entrance. This type of clay wall (*tsubashira kabe*) has a wood frame on the bottom and sides but none on top. It is topped with a wood and bamboo roof, supported on the posts that also support the clay and bamboo lath. The roof is separated from the wall by several inches. The wall has a wood plank door (*tsunodo* or *sarudo*) that is a little shorter than a normal door. This short door is called a *kugurido*. It causes a person to bow the head to pass through. It is not so small as the typical *nijiriguchi* entrance, which forces guests to enter the teahouse on their knees, but it reminds anyone coming in from this side that they have entered a tea garden. The other point is the small, decorative straw snow covers (*yukigakoi*) covering the peonies near the garden entrances and in other spots. The yukigakoi protect the flowers in winter and add to the atmosphere of a farmhouse tea garden.

View of a Tsuboniwa from the Couch

The garden of the Nagaoka family is featured in Chapter 1 of this book (page 28). Here I want to talk about one part of it that constitutes a separate garden in its own right. Next to the entrance of the house and viewed from the living room through a floor-to-ceiling pane of glass, I made a small garden, 48 x 81 inches (120 x 206 cm), which can be considered a *tsuboniwa*—usually described as a small courtyard garden. As with other small gardens I have made, it is an interpretation of the genre. It can be viewed from only three sides and it is on the exterior. Still, the history of Japanese gardens is one of loose interpretation of standards developed in China and Korea and reinterpreted in Japan as early as the eleventh-century treatise called the *Sakuteiki*, the oldest published text on garden-making. In time, standards came to be based on famous gardens, like that of Kyoto's seventeenth-century Katsura Imperial Villa. Much of the scenery in that garden is based on depictions in the eleventh-century literary classic, *The Tale of Genji*. In fact, a lot of Japan's original garden imagery is based on literary images. Ancient poetry collections, such as the eighth-century *Manyoshu*, are odes to various flowers and plants,

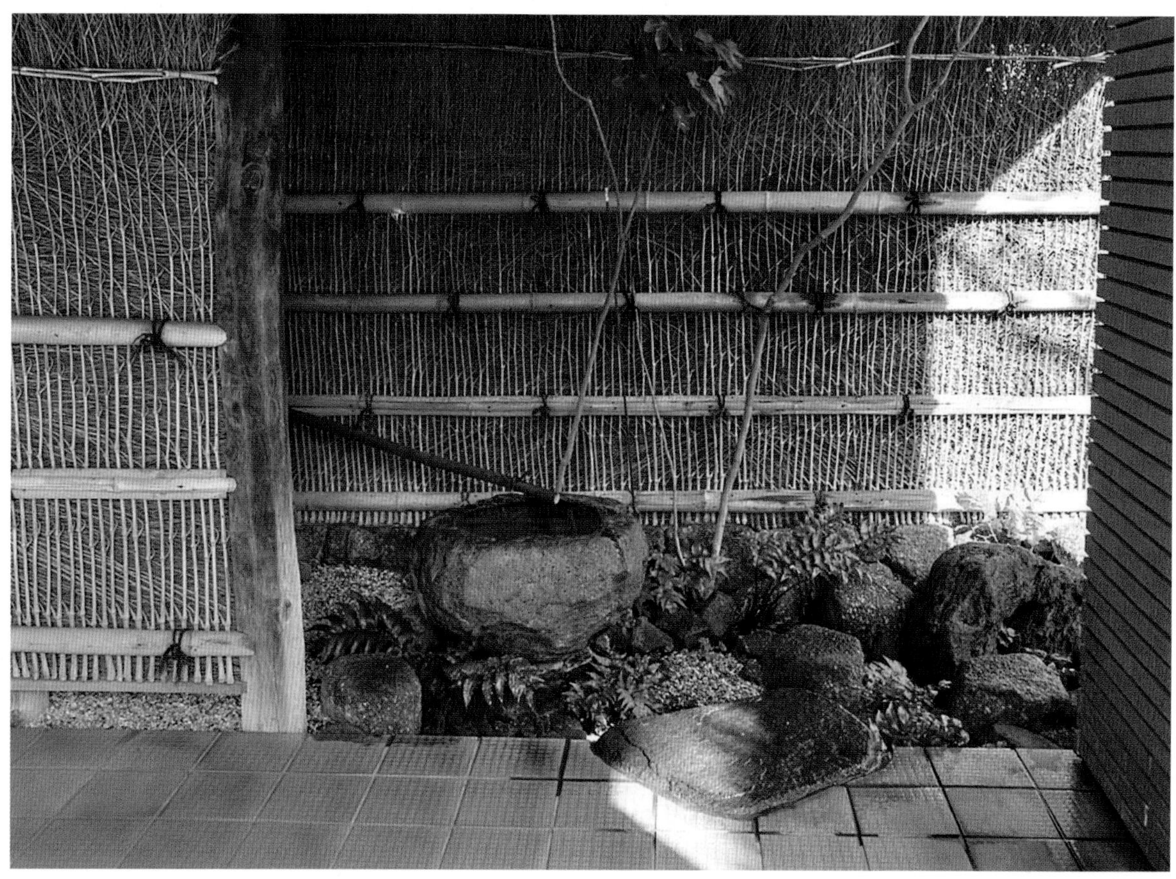

Facing page This *tsuboniwa* courtyard garden can be viewed from three sides. This is the view from the house entrance.

Right The view from inside the garden, looking toward the floor-to-ceiling window of the living room.

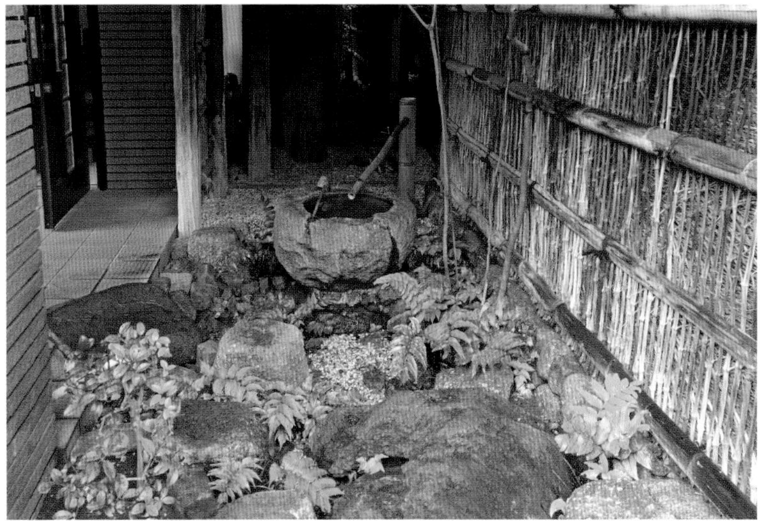

and associate them with seasons and emotions. This formed a basic reference for creating gardens: a case of life imitating art. Also, Buddhist monks and government officials returned from abroad with stories of famous places they had seen. Some tried to recreate those scenes and others soon imitated their efforts: art imitating life. Later, the idea of recreating famous scenes from different parts of the country in a stroll garden became an early Japanese version of an amusement park.

The point is that all of these gardens called for interpretations of visual or literary imagery. It is safe to say that most of the famous places being interpreted were never actually seen by the people creating the gardens nor their audience. Many rules were passed down on how gardens should be made, and this accounts for the continuity of styles from long ago. But rules are a means to an end, and the end lies far beyond the rules. While I am imparting some rules for you to interpret in your own gardens, remember that more than anything a tsuboniwa should invoke feelings of privacy and intimacy.

Some of the rules I mention elsewhere, such as designing the garden to be seen from multiple viewpoints (see A Tsuboniwa for Visvim, pages 118–121, for example). Generally, small plants should be used but tall and slender plants, such as bamboo or tree ivy (*kakuremino*), which like the wet and shaded area of the Nagaoka's garden, are also appropriate. Narrow bamboo that does not grow tall—such as black bamboo (*kurochiku*) and arrow bamboo (*yadake*)—is also used in very small gardens. Typically a tsuboniwa includes a stone lantern (*ishidoro*) and a water basin (*chozubachi*), relating to the need for light and water in the interior spaces where the gardens were usually found. In the case of Kyoto town houses, the roof above the internal "courtyard" is often open, allowing light and rain to enter freely. But even so, light is needed at sundown. For an exterior garden, rules can be adapted to the situation.

For this tsuboniwa, we "married" a combination of *kurama ishi* stone from Kyoto and *tsukuba ishi* stone from north of Tokyo with only a few plants: Japanese andromeda, tree ivy, and Japanese holly fern. To isolate the garden from the red-tile wall behind it, I made a tall *katsuragaki* bamboo fence to cover it. I also made a sleeve fence (*sodegaki*) in the same style, on the left front side. This shields the view of the living room from the entrance area. Finally, we made a *suikinkutsu* water harp under the water basin. Guests entering the house can hear its melodic sounds and, if one listens carefully, it can even be heard from the living room couch.

Climb the Stairs to a Private Gem

The landscape outside the garden is often as important as the garden itself. In China and Japan this fact was realized at an early date and lead to the concept of *shakkei*, which can be defined as "borrowed scenery" (see page 12). When I made this garden for the Konno family, about forty years ago, I made it to incorporate the beautiful view of trees and mountains that could be seen from this small, second floor garden. Fast-forward to today, the beautiful scene is gone, replaced by a view of the surrounding houses. These are accompanied by numerous telephone and electric poles, and the attendant wires that now blight every view in Japan.

The home on the left side existed from the beginning, so first we built a 6-foot (1.8-m)-tall *katsuragaki* fence along that side to create some privacy. But as I mentioned, the view directly in front of the house was of trees and mountains. To create shakkei it is not enough to just have a view. The garden, which is the foreground, must be linked with the background by means of a middle ground. Since we can only manipulate what happens in the foreground we use various techniques to create the illusion of a link. Here, we accomplished this by making a 5-foot (1.5-m) clay wall (*dobei*), with a ceramic-tile roof that runs along half the length of the garden. On the garden side of the wall I planted Japanese maples and black pine trees which lean over the top.

The low wall interrupts the view of the actual

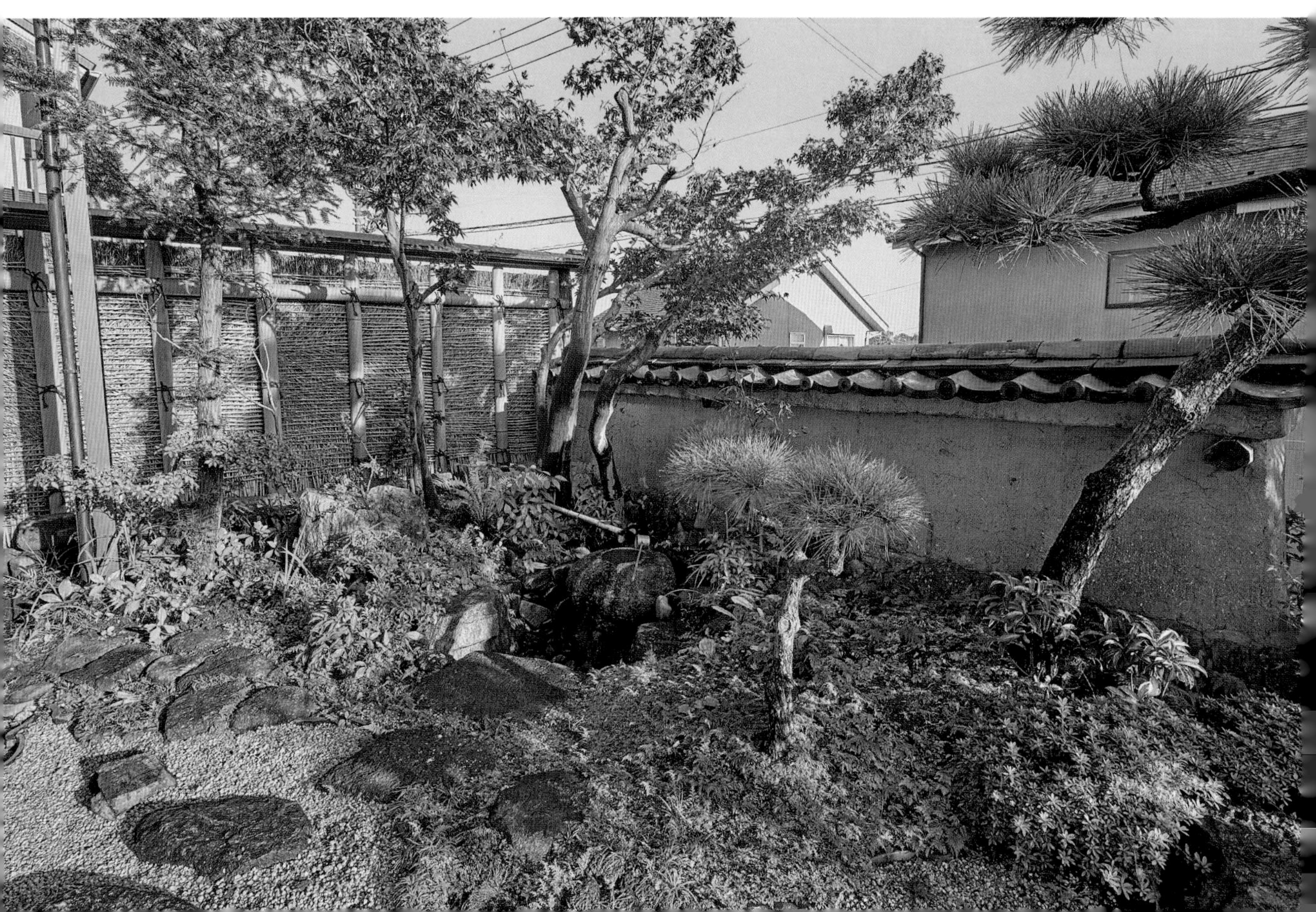

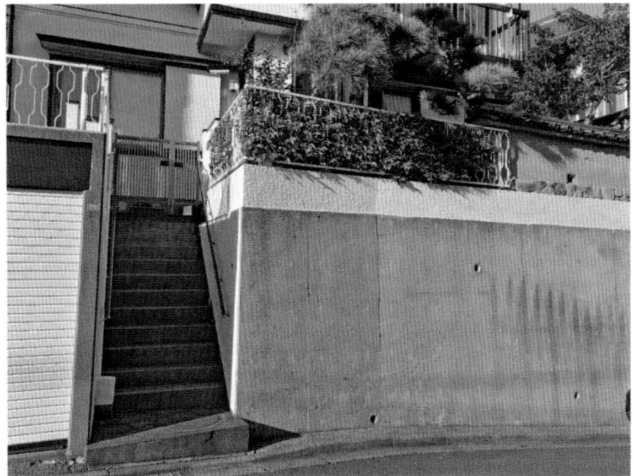

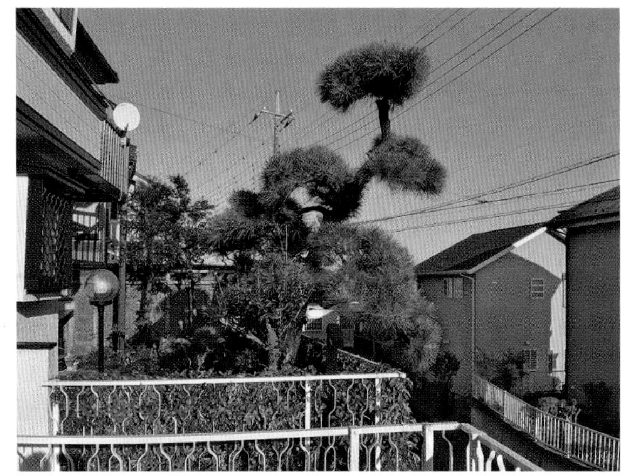

Facing page A tall *katsuragaki* fence was built to block the neighbor's building from view.

Above, left and right In this hilly area, the second story is actually the first floor. The garden is glimpsed from street level and from the top of the stairs.

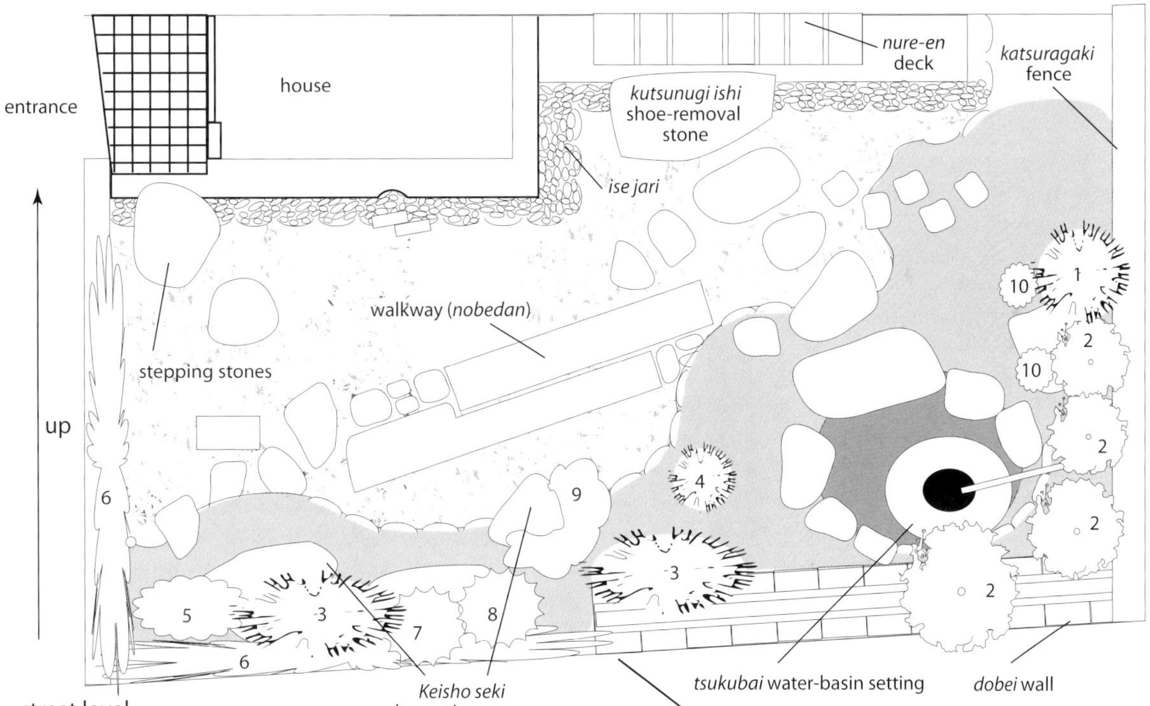

entrance

house

nure-en deck

katsuragaki fence

kutsunugi ishi shoe-removal stone

ise jari

walkway (*nobedan*)

stepping stones

up

street level

Keisho seki decorative stones

tsukubai water-basin setting

dobei wall

2nd floor garden area

1. Japanese yew	*kaya*
2. Japanese maple	*momji*
3. Black pine	*kuromatsu*
4. Red pine	*akamatsu*
5. Japanese camellia	*tsubaki*
6. Ubame oak	*ubamegashi*
7. Sarcandra glabra	*senryo*
8. Coral berry	*manryo*
9. Azalea	*satsuki*
10. Japanese andromeda	*asebi*

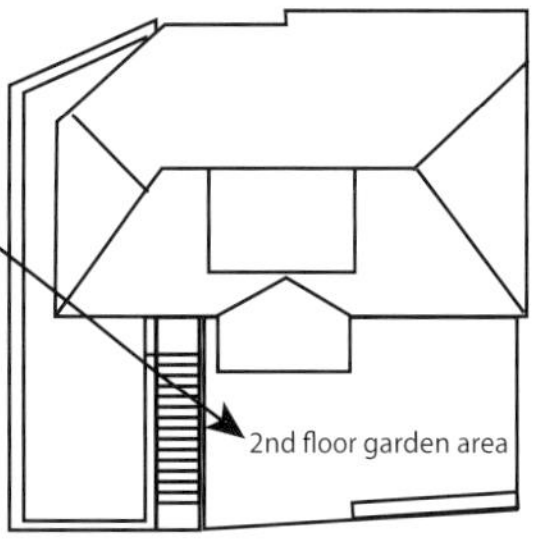

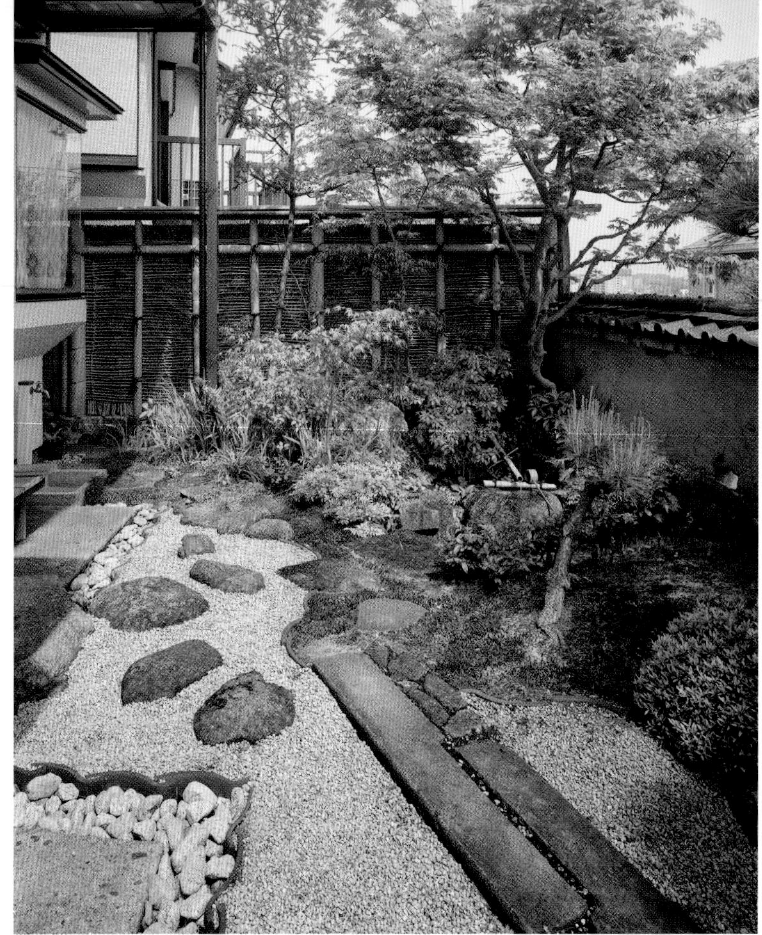

middle ground, and gives the gardener the opportunity to create an apparent middle ground—one that forms a strong link to the more distant view. The maples and pines served this purpose, reaching out to the distant view. The wall tapers slightly towards the right, which subtly increases the perspective (*enkinkan*) and helps lead the eye to the distance. The low wall also serves the purpose of keeping the garden private. As I mentioned, the wall is not the full length of the garden. The remainder of the garden border is planted with ubame oak that is kept about the same height as the wall. This kind of hedge (*ikegaki*) creates an ambiguous edge that links with tree growth outside the garden.

The owners enjoy tea ceremony, kimono, and photography. The garden is quite picturesque and has a water-basin arrangement (*tsukubai*) with a *suikinkutsu*, which is basically a ceramic vessel, buried under the water basin in such a way that water dripping into it makes a melodic sound. The vessel may be 3 feet (1 m) deep or more. Mrs. Konno still talks about how surprised she was to come out of her house and see nothing but my head sticking out of a deep hole in the ground. I should mention that the first floor of the house is the second floor compared to street level. The area around here is hilly and the houses are all built on high, concrete foundations to level them. They also have steps from the street level to the first floor. The concrete base is filled with soil with a depth of about 10 feet (3 m) so I had plenty of space to dig. The sound of the dripping water is loud enough to be heard in the dining room, which faces the garden.

Although at 200 feet square (18.5 m^2) this is not quite a *tsuboniwa* courtyard garden, it is a very small garden and a very private gem. A *tsubo* is a measurement of area equal to 35.5 square feet (3.3 m^2). This does not apply strictly, but implies a very small garden. Another meaning of *tsubo*, written with different characters, is "ceramic vessel." This adds to the sense of the garden being not only small, but also enclosed within a space. Some of the most famous tsuboniwa are within the small courtyards of Kyoto townhouses. But tsuboniwa principles of simplicity, and arranging the garden to be seen from multiple viewpoints, were also applied here. The garden has an entrance and viewpoint from the top of the stairs. It has another entrance and viewpoint from the dining room.

A small *nure-en* porch in front of the dining room allows for enjoying the garden while sitting outdoors. A large shoe-removal stone and stepping stones lead to the water basin on the left. Another set of stones leads right where they join a small *nobedan* walkway and continue to the entrance gate and stairs. The stones cross an area of white gravel, which I placed there to give an impression of a large

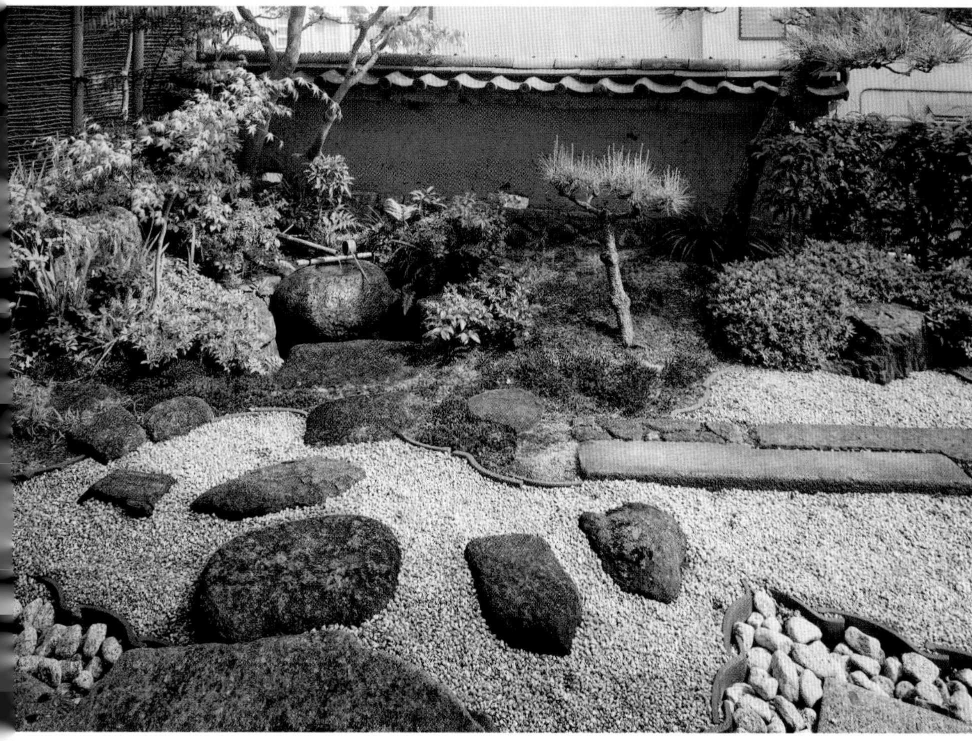

Left and far left Originally the garden was built to incorporate the beautiful landscape. Now, the low, tile-roofed *dobei* clay wall helps retain some distance from the encroaching city.

expanse, as if crossing an ocean. This is another method of manipulating the viewer's perspective, in this case, within the garden. The largest decorative stones (*keishoseki*) are on the other side of this ocean of sand, enveloped in low bushes of Japanese andromeda and azalea.

Finally, returning to the *shakkei* "borrowed scenery," the question may arise—when the view over the wall became so poor why not make a taller wall to shut it out? It's a valid question that you may have to wrestle with at some point in the life of your own garden. As I have said, the garden is small, and enclosing it with a wall would have made it feel even smaller. There is also the question of decreased light in the garden and problems with wind. The *katsuragaki* on the left side had to be reinforced with steel embedded in concrete to adequately secure it. Then there is the problem of neighbors, some of who will wonder aloud what you are hiding behind those tall walls. For these reasons, in this case the answer was to leave well enough alone.

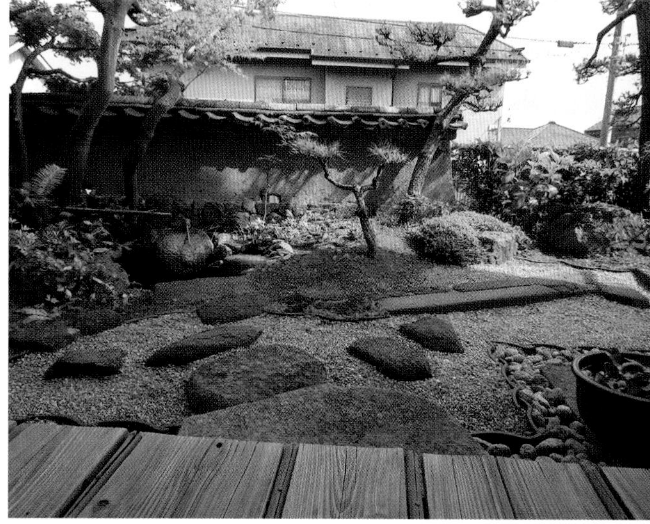

A *nure-en* exterior deck allows a place to sit outside and a low-angle view of the garden.

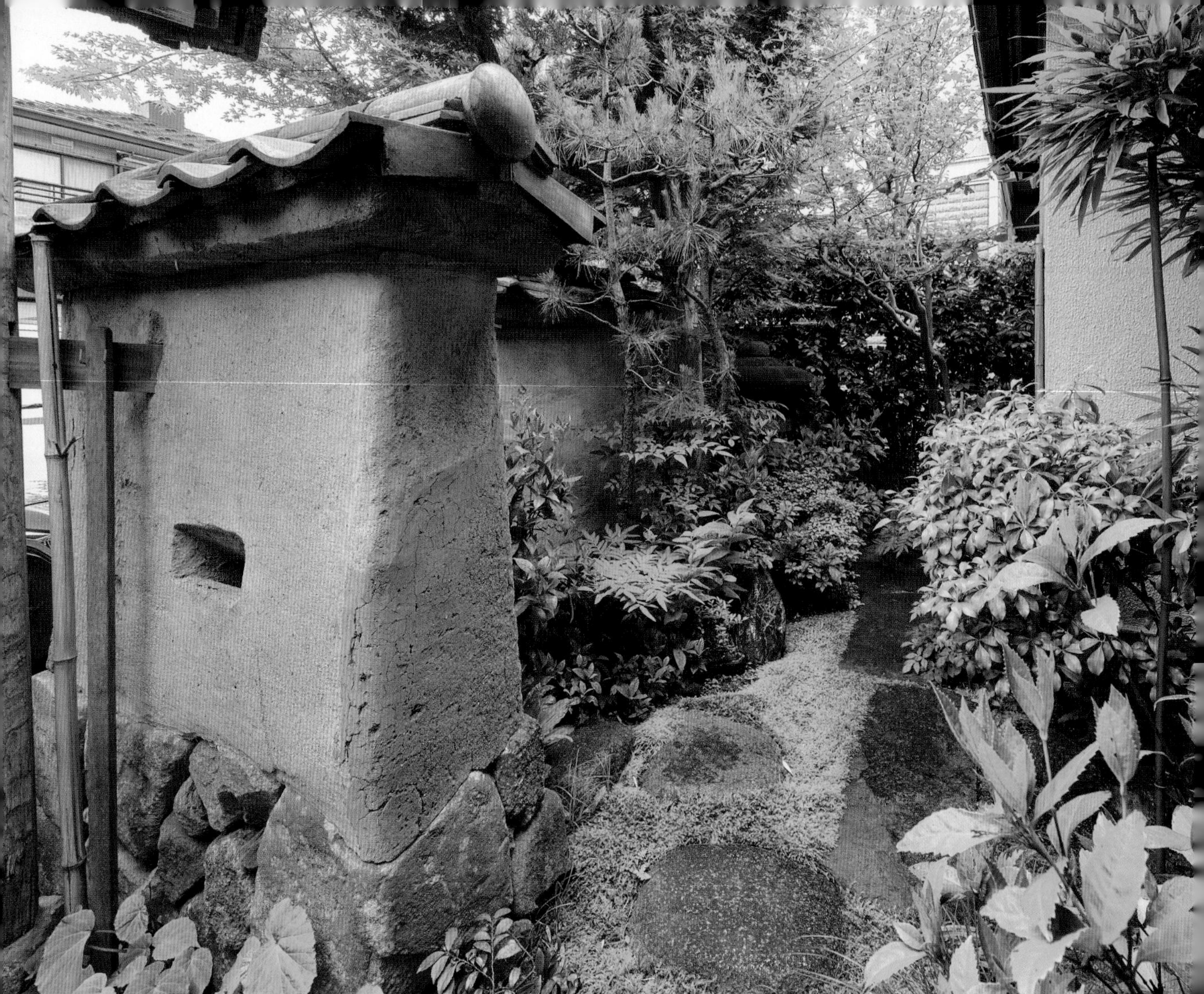

A Small Garden Made by the Birds

Sawaii-san has been a teacher of tea ceremony in the Urasenke style for over fifty years. Her house is on a cul de sac near where I live in southern Tokyo. It is a small property, high on a hill. From the back of the house there's a 360-degree outlook that includes a view of Mt. Fuji. The house has several tearooms and many years ago we made modest outer and inner tea gardens (*soto roji* and *naka roji*), and a *tsuboniwa* courtyard garden in front of the house—or maybe I should say—the birds made it.

Strictly speaking, we made the garden and the birds contributed. Sawaii-san did not want a formal garden. The tea garden behind the house already served that purpose. We planted Sarcandra glabra (*senryo*), marlberry (*yabukoji*), and coralberry (*manryo*). These bushes of the ardisia genus are considered auspicious and the potted plants are usually displayed at the New Year. They produce bright red and yellow berries that are eaten by the birds. The birds excrete the seeds and the number of

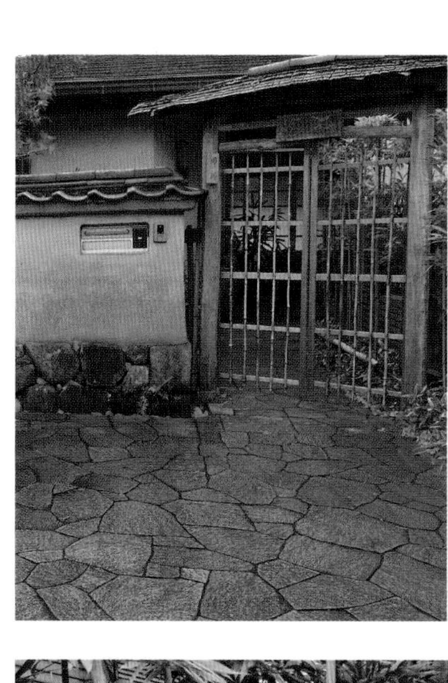

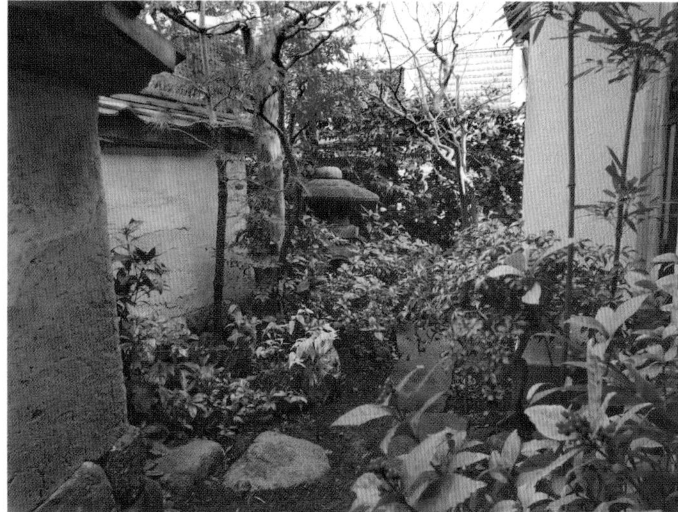

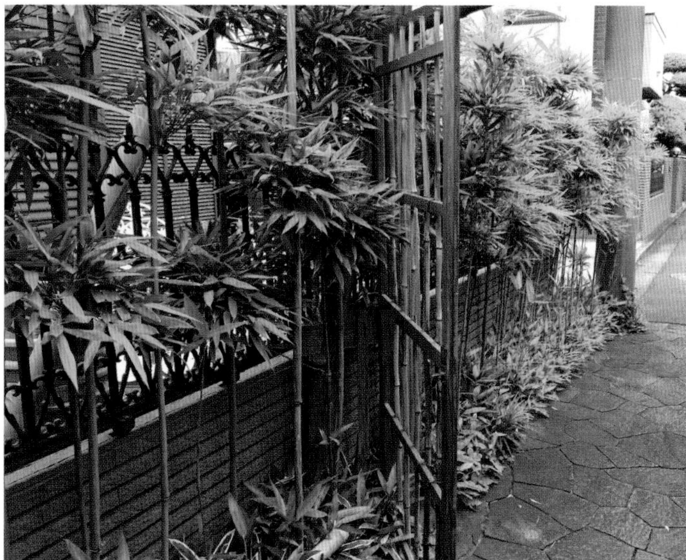

Facing page Past the gate and on the way to the entrance, a small *tsuboniwa* garden grows unfettered.

Above, left The house sits on a cul-de-sac with a Kiso stone pavement.

Above, right The fruit of the *senryo* bushes are a beautiful sight and a treat for the birds.

Left One side of the entrance is lined with bamboo and bamboo grass (*sasa*). Grouped with plum and pine they are a symbol of good fortune.

plants increases. A red pine (*akamatsu*) also appeared without having been planted. Normally, in a garden this size—about 6 by 20 feet (1.8 x 6 m)—such wild plants would be removed. But as mentioned, this garden was never intended to be formal.

Still, thinking about the many students who come here to learn something about Japanese culture, we could not ignore the symbolism connected with plants. Along the entrance we planted bamboo and in the garden we planted black pine and flowering plum. In Japan, there is the expression *sho, chiku, bai* (pine, bamboo, plum). These "three friends of winter" are drawn from Chinese culture and so called because all three are strong in the winter months. They are also considered symbols of good fortune. To add to the color we planted osaka maple, which turns a brilliant red in winter.

We made a 6-foot (1.8-m) clay wall (*dobei*) with

a covered gate to separate the garden and entrance from the street. As this is the last house on a cul de sac, the area in front of the wall is a parking space, which we paved with stone from the Kiso region of Japan in a pattern called *ishidatami*. The gate is set at an angle to reduce the symmetry. The name of the teahouse "Ju-an" (meaning something like "tree hermitage") is carved on a plaque attached to the gate. Passing through the gate, the entrance to the tsuboniwa is on the left. Some stepping stones and long *tanzaku ishi* "label stones," surrounded by moss, lead deeper into the garden. Near the end, the dobei wall steps back to create a wider space, where we placed a large *yukimi* stone lantern. Sawaii-san was surprised that I used this large lantern in such a small space. But I felt that the prominence of the lantern added a touch of structure to an otherwise unstructured garden. The top of the lantern can be seen from the entrance. We set up a scale progression from horizontal stepping stones, to an attractive standing stone, to the tall lantern. Both the wall and house side are lined with the ardisia shrubs, cinammon fern, camellia, kuma grass, and the ground is covered in haircap moss. Although stepping stones allow entry into the garden, most visitors will only view it from the entrance. The bamboo we used is *daimyo chiku*, whose leaves grow in clumps on the upper third of the culm.

At the far end of the tsuboniwa, a stone path leads around the side of the house to the tea garden at the rear. The main access to the tea garden is through the house from the front entrance. This leads directly to the garden in the back and also serves as a waiting area for tearooms on the left and right. The floor is covered with the same Kiso stone as the driveway and entrance. In this floor, toward the end facing the garden, we made a *tsukubai* water-basin arrangement. The rooms on both sides have an elevation of about 1 foot (30 cm). Sitting on the wood ledge of the elevated floor is equivalent to sitting on a covered waiting bench. The main

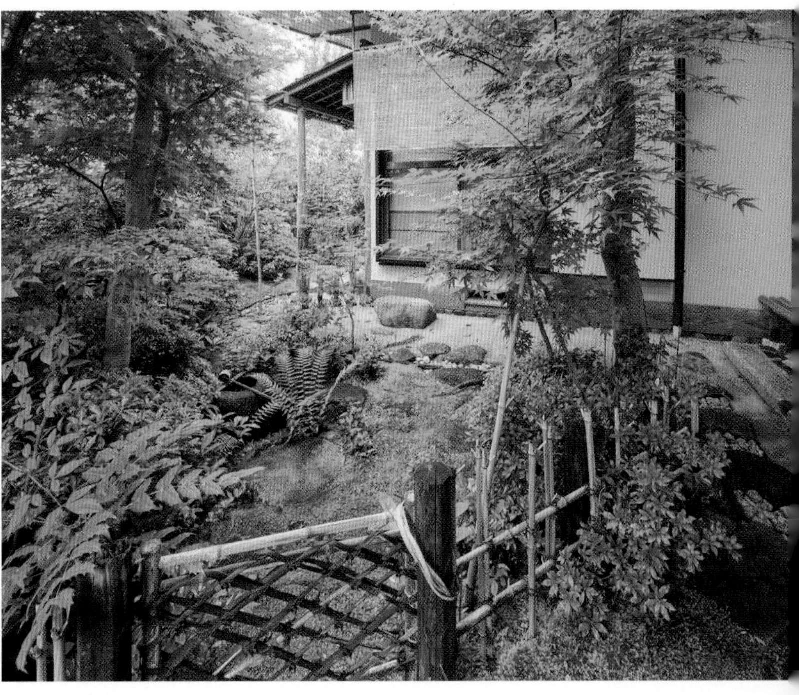

Above A water basin sits between the teahouse and waiting area The floor is the same Kiso stone as the entrance and shoes are worn here.

Right The entrance to the inner garden teahouse after passing through the waiting area. The garden overlooks the city below.

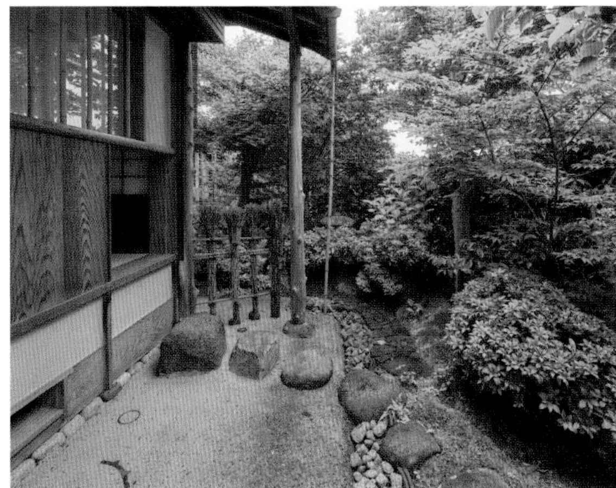

Left and below The *nijiriguchi* entrance to the teahouse from outside and in.

Bottom The bright green of summer gives way to the brilliant red of *osakazuki* maples in winter.

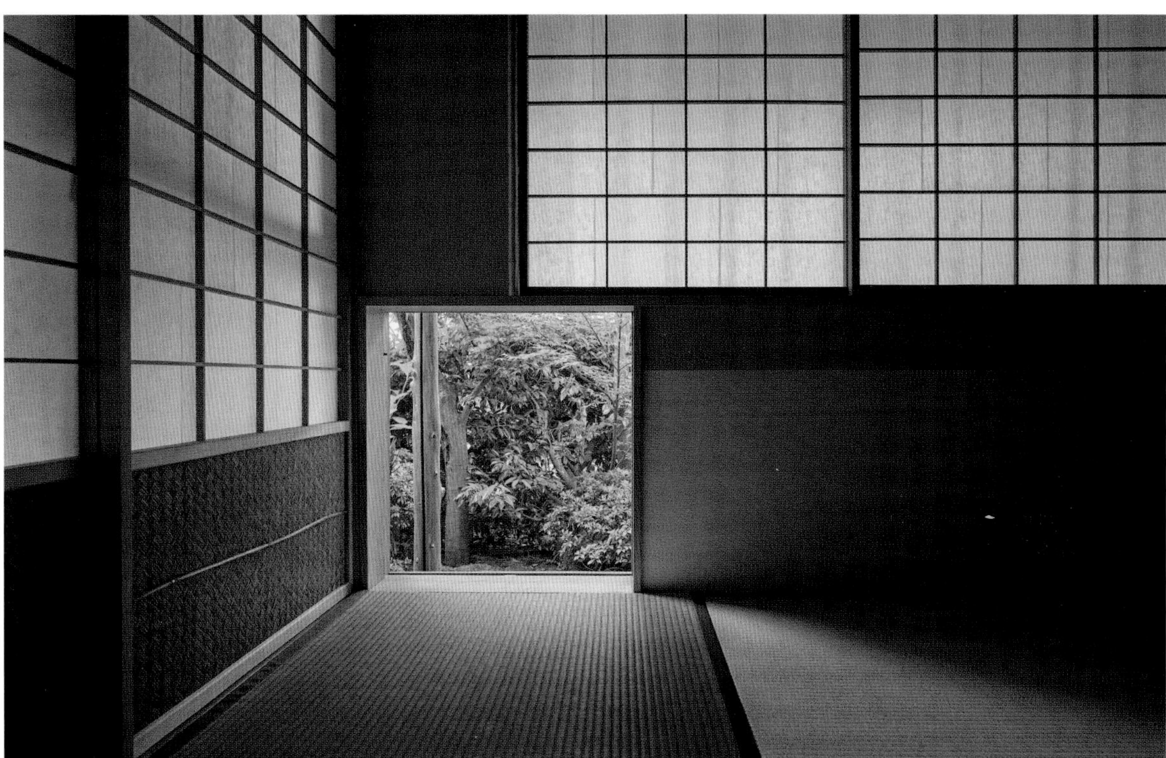

teahouse is connected to the back of the house on the right but the access is through the tea garden. All combined, the tsuboniwa and tea garden contain about thirty Japanese maple and fifty camellia trees. The maples closer to the house have had their leaves cut to eye level to allow a better view of the garden. We also planted another red berry–bearing tree, linden arrow wood, which is a medium size bush. So in early winter the predominant color of the garden shifts from green to red.

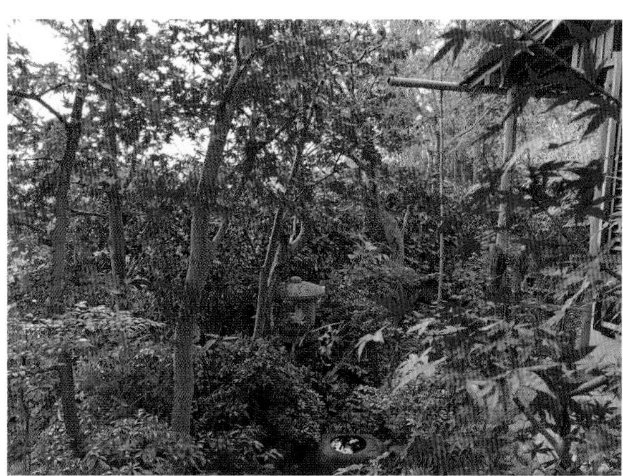

A Tsuboniwa for Visvim

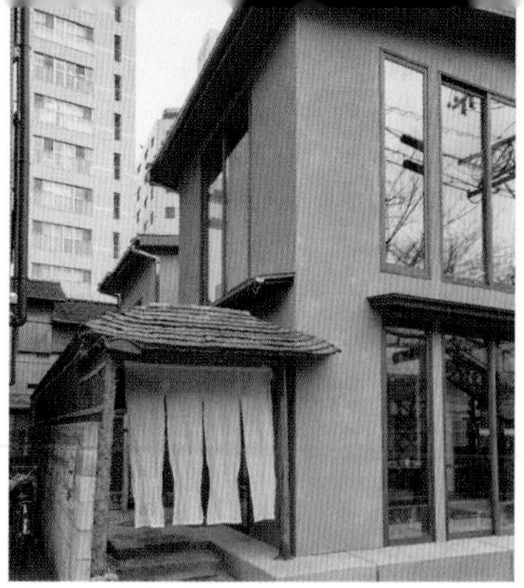

The Meguro River in Tokyo is famous for the cherry trees that line both sides. From about the end of March to the beginning of April tens of thousands of people wander under the trees, especially on weekends, taking photos, meeting friends, eating and drinking. Probably because it attracts so many people at that time of year, it now has many trendy clothing shops and eateries.

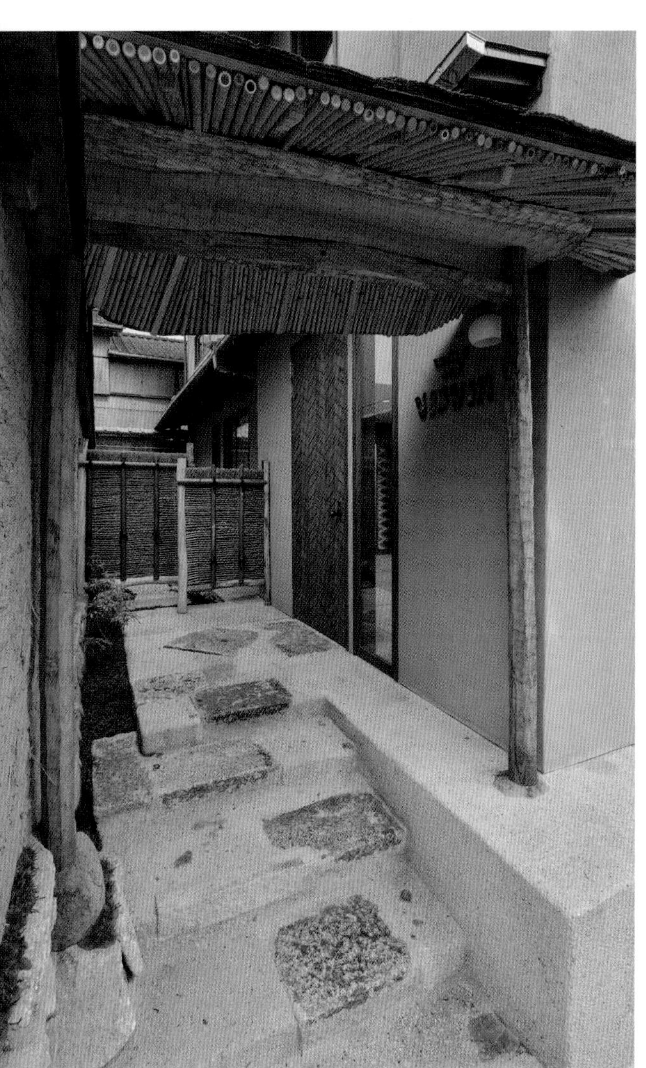

On page 104, I talk about the garden I created for an urban farmhouse in Tokyo. I mentioned that for many years past the house has been leased to various tenants. It was when one of the previous tenants was occupying the house that I created the garden. Hiroki Nakamura, the designer behind the clothing brands Visvim, WMV, and Indigo Camping Trailer, currently occupies the house. Nakamura-san enjoys my garden and asked me to do something for his newest shop along the Meguro River.

The shop is in a light and airy earth-colored building with high ceilings and floor-to-ceiling windows. I made an exposed-aggregate (*araidashi*) floor for the shop and a small courtyard garden (*tsuboniwa*) at the side. An acquaintance of mine came to the site after the floor was done but before the rest of the shop and garden were completed. When he came back later he said he was surprised. Because of the floor, he expected the shop to be Japanese style but it was actually closer to Santa Fe style. What surprised him was the perfect match between the two. I don't know about that but I think it must have been Nakamura-san's vision. Having lived in California for many years, I guess he saw the connection.

The entrance is on the left side of the shop and this is where I made the garden. The shop elevation is about 2 feet (60 cm) above street level. I made a stair of exposed aggregate and flat stones. The exterior floor connects seamlessly to the interior and to a 36-inch (90-cm) walkway along the length of the shop. Over the stair I made a covered gate with a cedar-bark roof. The underside of the roof is made of ¾ to 1-inch (20–30 mm)-diameter bamboo poles—a little larger than normal. The wood of the gate is roughly cut with

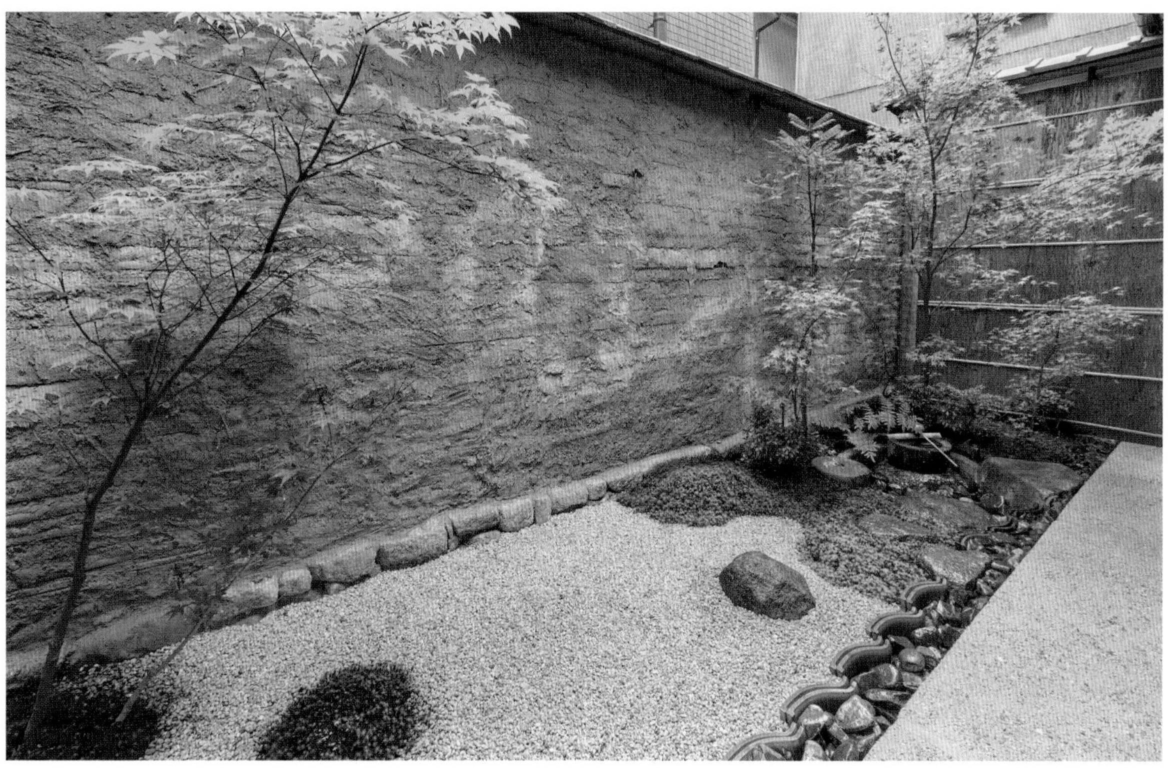

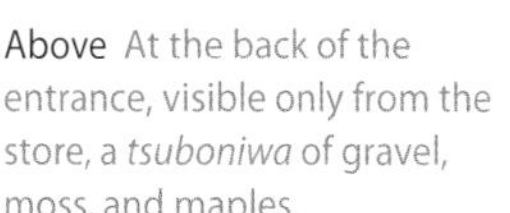

Above At the back of the entrance, visible only from the store, a *tsuboniwa* of gravel, moss, and maples.

Below The store is located in Tokyo along the Meguro River, a crowded cherry-blossom viewing spot in spring.

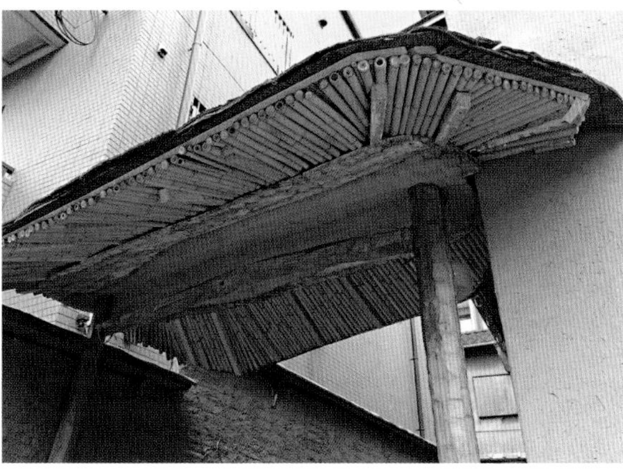

Facing page, top and bottom The two-story shop and the entrance of exposed aggregate (*araidashi*), which also covers the shop floor.

Above Roughly cut wood, cypress bark, bamboo, and a mud wall might look as much at home in Santa Fe as Tokyo.

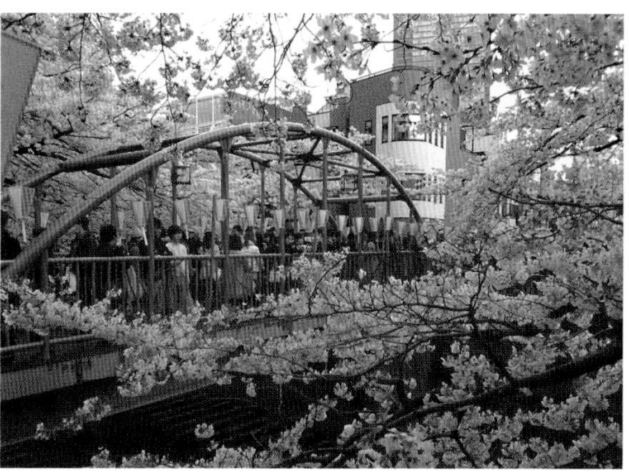

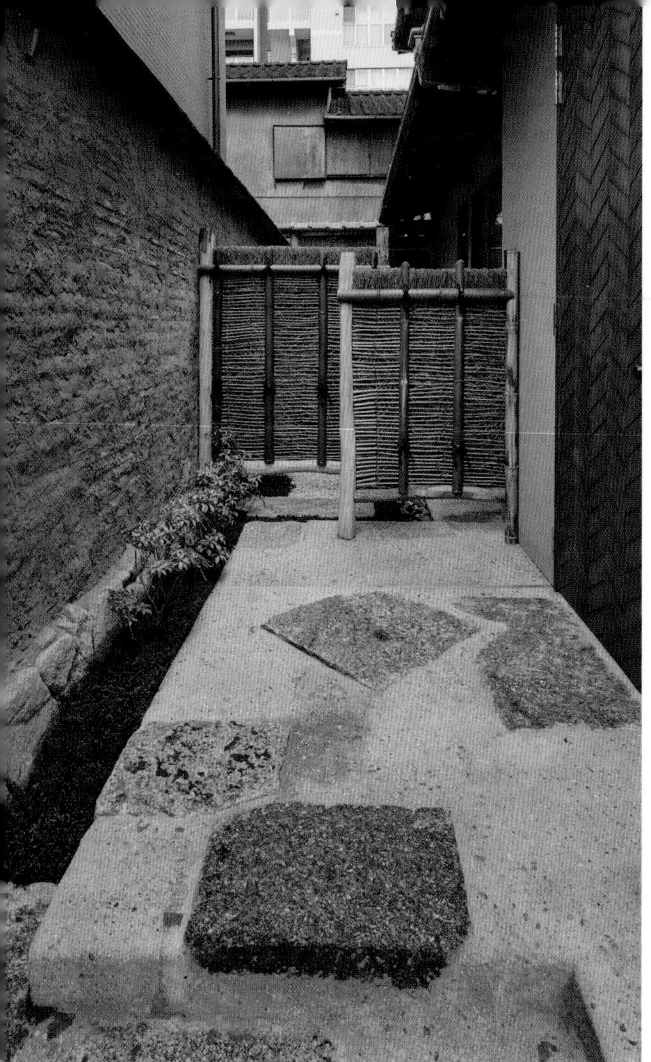

Above A split and staggered *katsuragaki* bamboo-branch fence conceals the entrance between as well as the garden beyond.

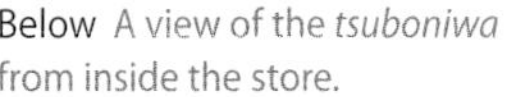

Below A view of the *tsuboniwa* from inside the store.

Right The *tsuboniwa* as viewed from the very end of the garden.

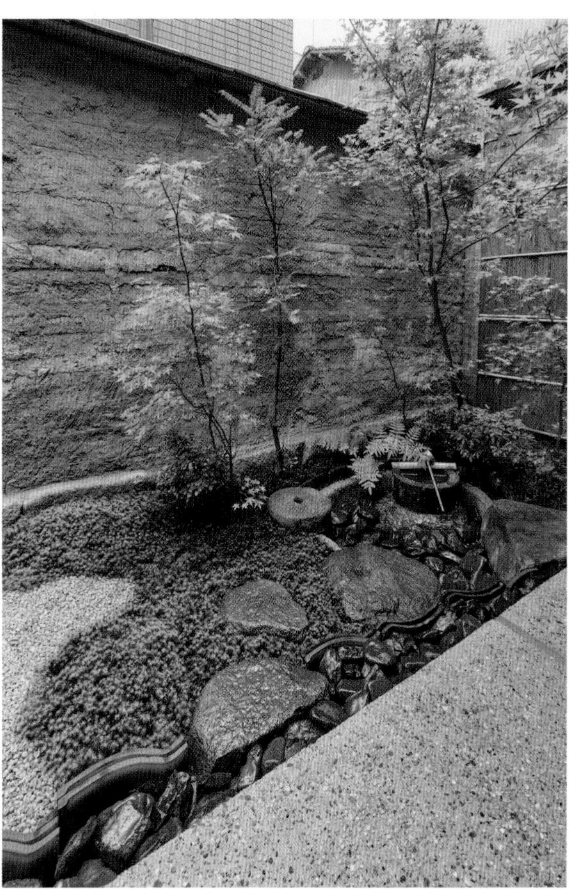

an adze and the roof has only a shallow curve. These subtle details create a flavor that might be considered as much Mexican as Japanese.

Along the left side of the entrance I made a clay wall with a stone base. This wall separates the garden from the neighboring building. The split-bamboo framework of the wall shows through the clay, which adds to the rustic appearance. If you walk up the stair and go straight past the shop entrance, you could enter the garden directly. But the tsuboniwa is for the pleasure of the shoppers so a staggered *katsuragaki* bamboo fence, a little above eye-level, conceals it from the street. The staggered fence allows for a way to move in and out of the garden without revealing an entrance.

The back side of the fence is made with wide sections of cedar bark, arranged vertically. This matches the wall at the opposite end of the garden.

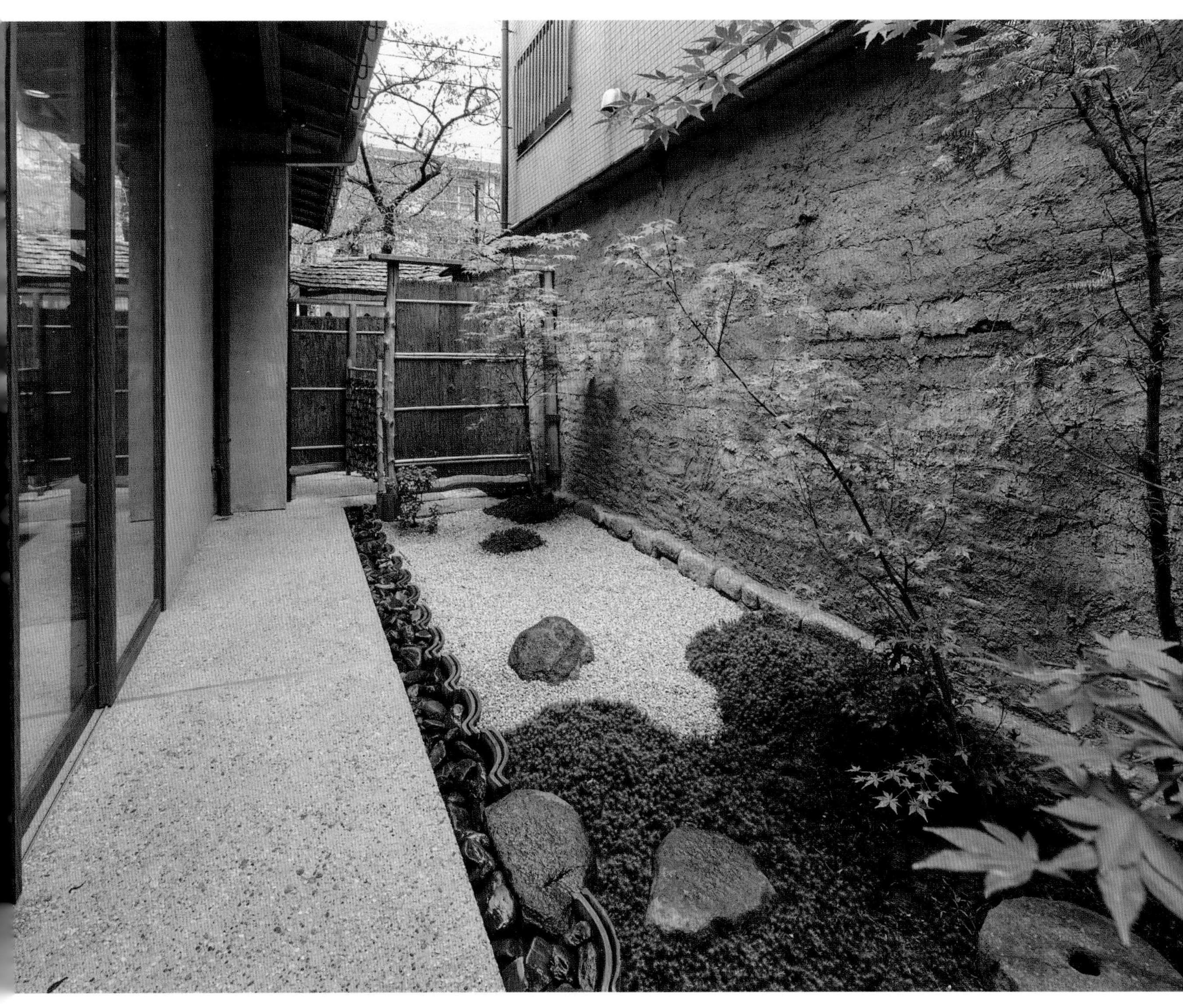

The garden itself is viewed from the side when standing inside the shop. When the glass doors are slid open the garden can be entered along the walkway. The garden proper is about 4 feet (1.2 m) wide and 16 feet (5 m) long. The front side of the garden (viewed from the street) is white gravel with a single stone and a small mound of moss. The image is of an island in the sea. A slender Japanese maple is planted inside the fence and peeks over the top. At the opposite end of the garden I made a *tsukubai* water-basin setting on a bed of haircap moss. The plantings are few: several slender maples, some Japanese andromeda, Japanese eurya (*hisakaki*), and a single Japanese torreya (*kaya*).

This garden, made at the beginning of 2020, will take several years to mature. I hope the shop's returning customers will enjoy the growth and change for many years to come.

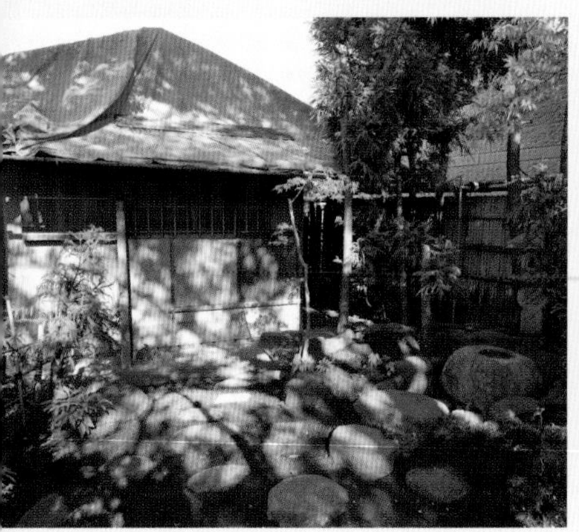

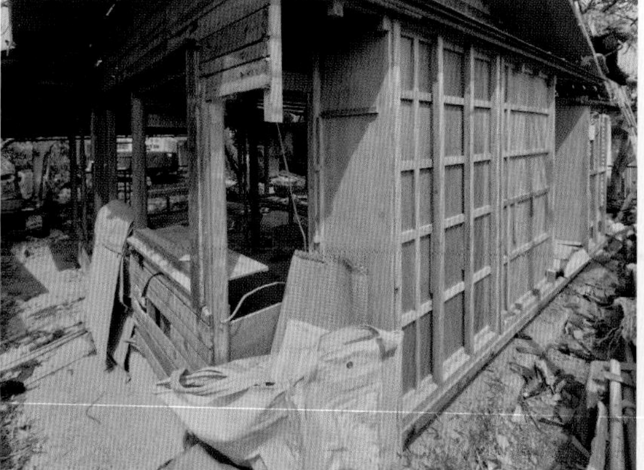

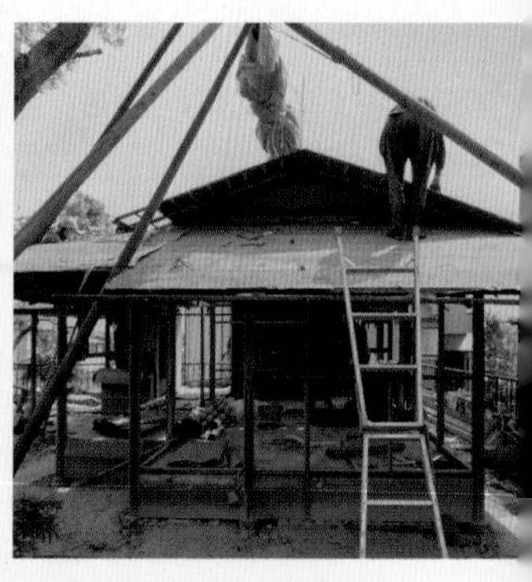

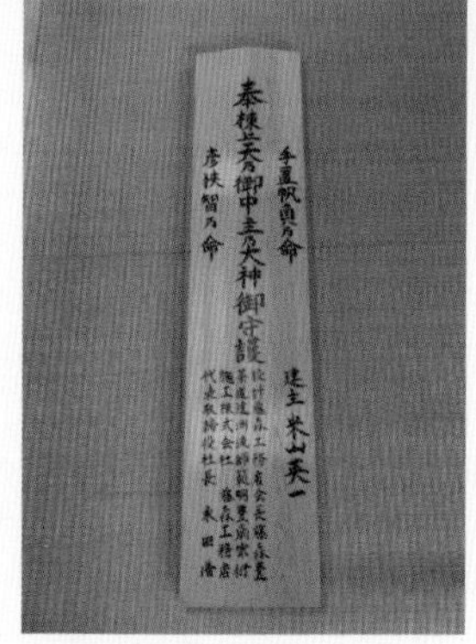

RECONSTRUCTING AN OLD TEAHOUSE

The gardener can extend his skills in several directions: planting and cultivating plants; making walls, gates, and fences; making ponds, waterfalls, and other water features; and making structures like arbors and teahouses. Of course, in terms of woodworking, the scope of a gardener is not the same as a carpenter, but they share certain skills and knowledge. The ability to handle basic tools and knowing how to manipulate materials is common to both crafts. It may seem that carpenters only work with wood but the fact is they usually know how to use cement, stone, and carry out plaster and clay work too. This also applies to the gardener. The more you know about aspects of the job that touch on the garden, the better equipped you are to make the garden as well.

In Japan, gardeners were often called on to make teahouses. These days, we usually ask a *sukiya daiku* to do the work. *Daiku* means carpenter; *sukiya* is difficult to define but initially, around the sixteenth century, it was synonymous with tearoom. Originally, part of a large room with a tatami-mat floor, was enclosed with sliding paper doors (*fusuma*). This area was called by several names (*zashiki*, *kakoi*, *koma*, etc.) and served as the tearoom (*chashitsu*) until, eventually, a separate building was constructed for the purpose. That building was also called a *chashitsu* even though *shitsu* means "room" or just "space."

The tea garden (*chaniwa*) was originally no more than stepping stones (*tobi ishi*) leading to the tearoom. Sen no Rikyu (1522–1591) was not the originator of the tea ceremony nor of the use of stepping stones, but he was one of the greatest practitioners and theorists of tea. Rikyu added a modest fence to demarcate the garden, a low water-basin arrangement (*tsukubai*) for washing the hands and mouth, a stone lantern to provide light, the *katanakake* sword-removal rack, the *nijiriguchi* entrance and some small plantings. He was instrumental in turning the tea ceremony into a spiritual exercise. He took to calling the garden a *roji*, a term taken from a Buddhist sutra describing a place where souls are reborn. A Zen monk named Nambo Sokei recorded the teachings and secret writings of Rikyu and other tea masters in the book *Nanporoku*

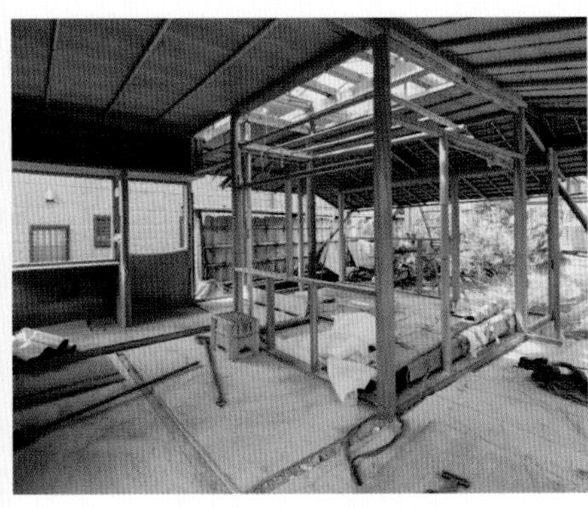

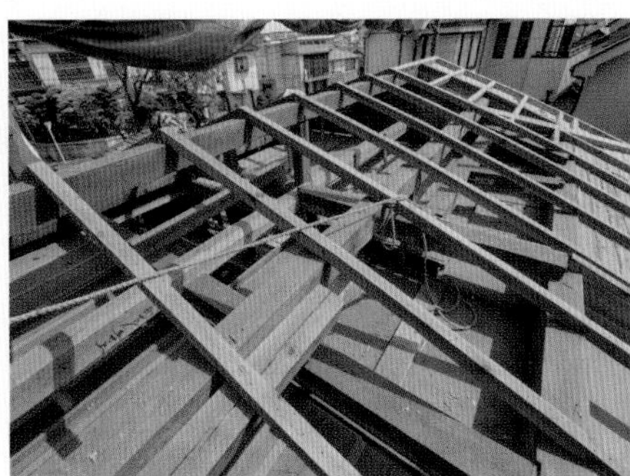

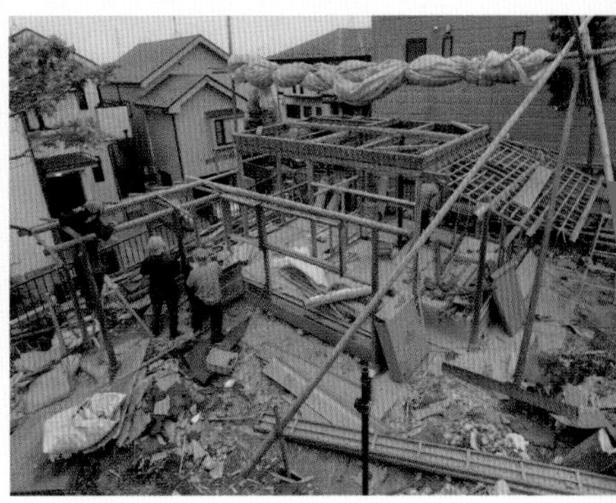

Facing page The *munafuda* ridge plaque (left), removed from the ridge pole inside the roof of the original teahouse, is preserved. It bears the name of Meihosai Fujimori, who built it.

Above The teahouse is carefully disassembled. The structural pieces will be numbered and transported for reassembly in combination with new materials.

Below The finished teahouse and garden on the grounds of Ryodenji Temple, founded in 1690.

(1690). In it, Rikyu implies that the main purpose of the tea ceremony is to "attain salvation through Buddhism."

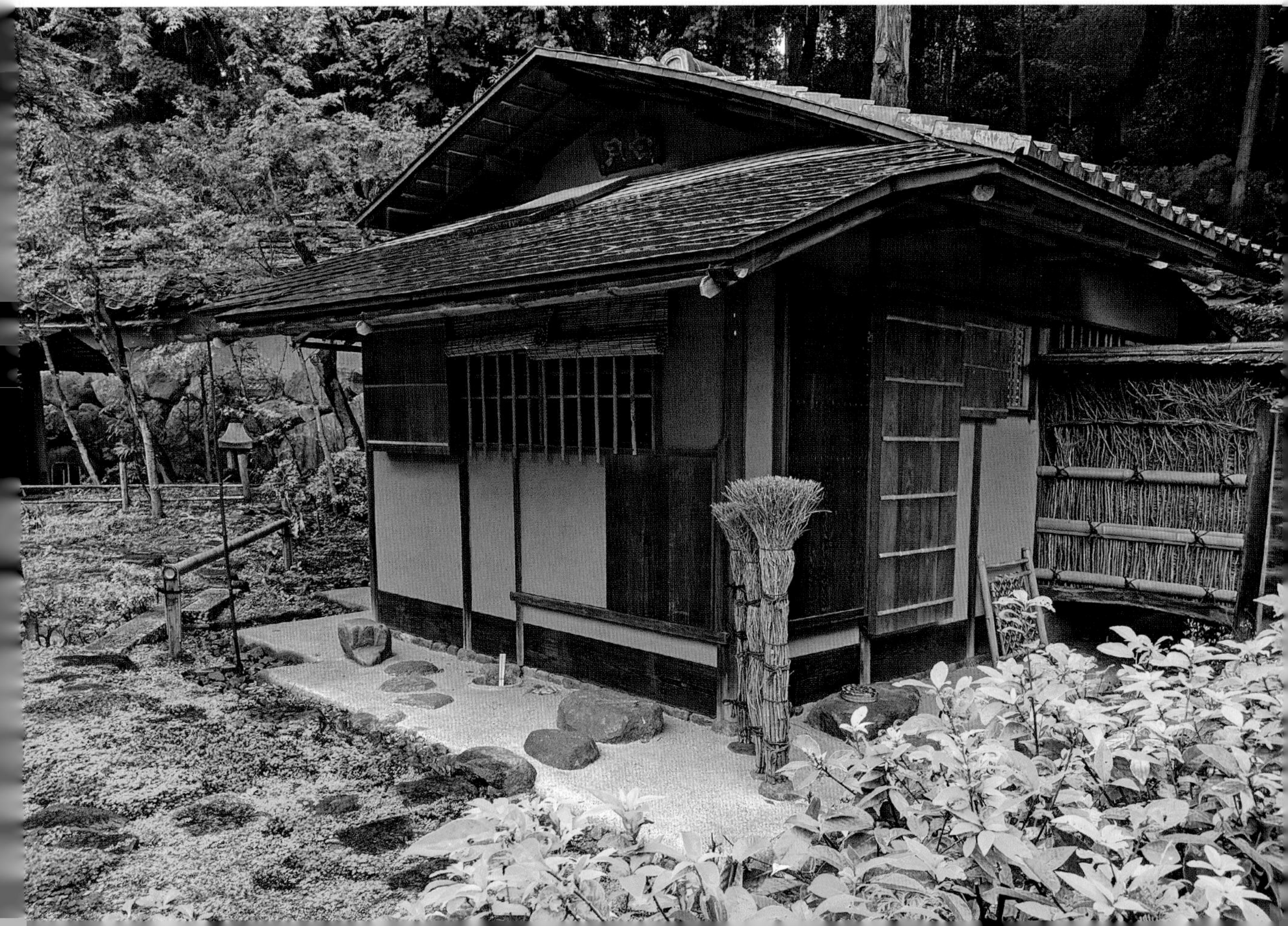

Rikyu also recorded details of proportions for the tearoom, and descriptions of shelves and tea utensils with many illustrations. This secret text was eventually copied, both with and without permission. The Sen family and famous disciples developed standards and elaborations that others followed. Three of Rikyu's great-grandchildren inherited the

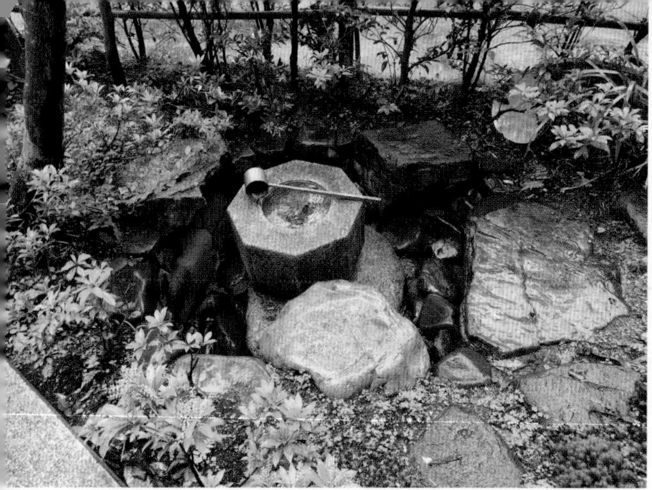

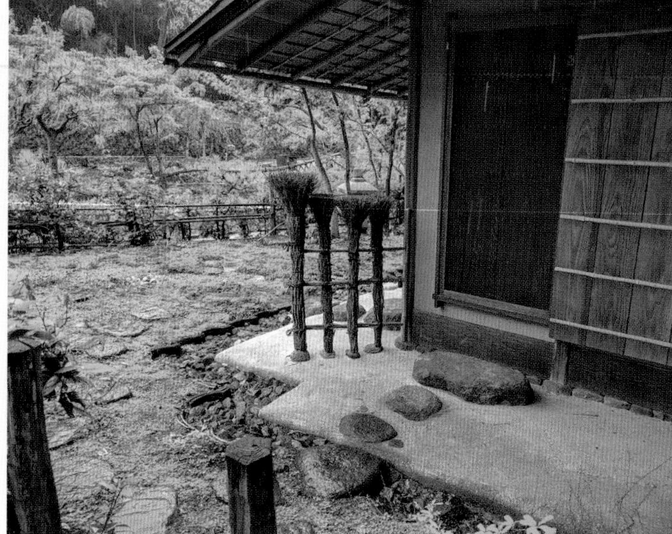

right to begin their own school of tea. This is how the Omotesenke, Urasenke and Mushanokojisenke schools of tea—each with their own characteristics—began. Then in 1608, Masanobu Heinouchi wrote the *Shomei,* a compilation of standards and building techniques for gates, shrines, temples, castles and others. He inherited this knowledge from his father, Yoshimasa Heinouchi, who was the first of a long line of craftsmen that became the official builders for the Tokugawa shoguns. Many of those standards were also applied to the teahouse.

Also at this time, the term *sukiya* came to be defined as an intimate style of architecture, which paid special attention to details and the use of materials that expressed the rustic and natural, for example, the use of clay and paper for walls, the use of wood with the bark intact, and the use of natural wood shapes fitted into a geometric frame. Such specialized material handling and aesthetics became the purview of the sukiya daiku. The different styles of the various tea masters, coupled with the secrecy surrounding building techniques and rules, lead to different schools of thought. One such was the school of master builder, designer, and tea master, Kobori Enshu (1579–1647). This leads us to the teahouse of Ryodenji, originally designed and constructed by a disciple of the Enshu School, Meihosai Fujimori.

This teahouse was constructed in the postwar period and resided on the grounds of Tamagawa Gakuen University in Tokyo. It was sold to Ryodenji Temple and we were involved in the demolition, relocation, and reconstruction. Only about one-third of the original teahouse is used in the new one. It requires study and coordination with a sukiya daiku to know what material to save and what to discard. We also prepared the new site and arranged for transporting old and new materials. If you want

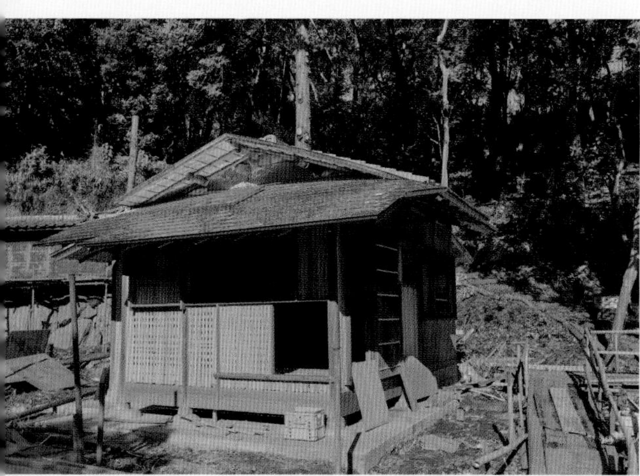

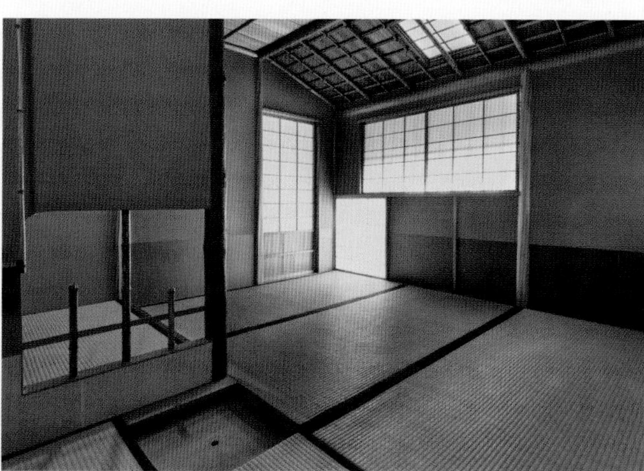

Facing page, top left and right A new *tsukubai* water-basin setting is constructed at the entrance to the tea garden. A cement foundation is covered with exposed aggregate (*araidashi*).

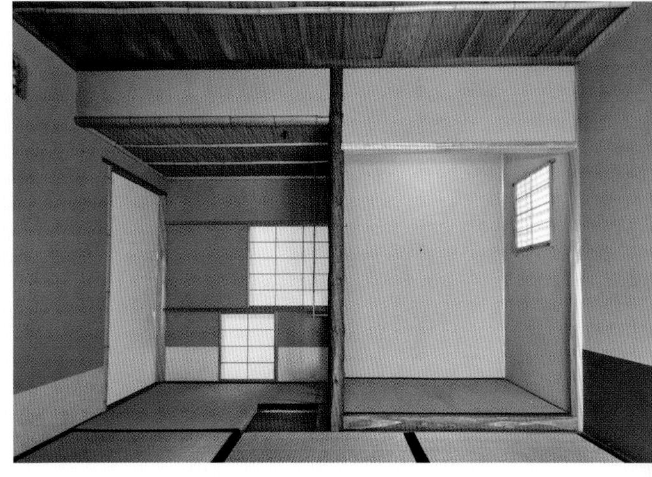

Right Inside the reconstructed teahouse, the *tokonoma* alcove faces the entrance. The wall, floor, and ceiling coverings are all new.

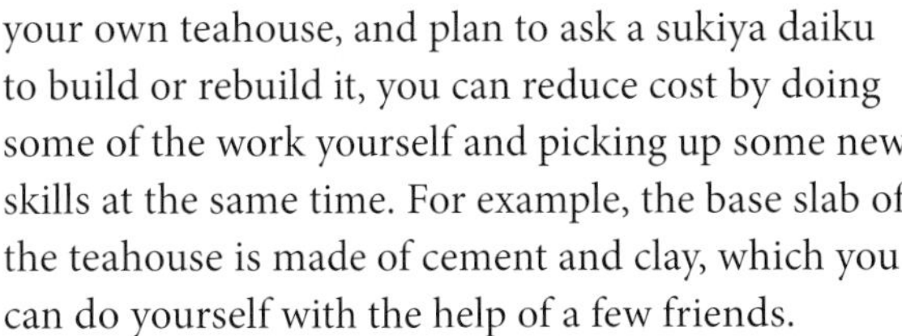

your own teahouse, and plan to ask a sukiya daiku to build or rebuild it, you can reduce cost by doing some of the work yourself and picking up some new skills at the same time. For example, the base slab of the teahouse is made of cement and clay, which you can do yourself with the help of a few friends.

Extensive details about building a teahouse are beyond the scope of this book. I hope the photos of the process give you some idea of the construction and finishing. As gardeners, our work usually begins when building construction ends. But the gardener must have input into the placement of doors and windows, water supply, and other aspects of the work. This is the best way to create the necessary harmony of house and garden.

When the teahouse was reconstructed, we completed the finishing work. We covered the visible parts of the concrete foundation with exposed aggregate (*araidashi*), added additional stepping stones, a sword-hanging stone (*katanakake ishi*), and a shoe-removal stone (*kutsunugi ishi*). Along the bottom of the board that conceals the crawl space, we added a border of small stone. Around the slab we added a line of ceramic roof tiles backfilled with small stones to catch rainwater. Finally we added some fences. The fence at the corner of the teahouse is called a torch fence (*taimatsugaki*). It is made of bush clover (*hagi*) and the tradition of this fence is that one of the bundles is removed and used as a torch to provide light in the garden at night. We also relocated and reconstructed the *koshikake machiai* waiting bench which was an original part of the teahouse made by Fujimori-san.

Left to right A new roof and exterior walls. The finished interior with a paper-covered wainscot (*haritsuke*), skylight (*tsuikage mado*), and polished bamboo fixtures.

Below Looking every bit the hut in the woods, the teahouse sits against an undulating clay wall at the foot of Higashimukai mountain.

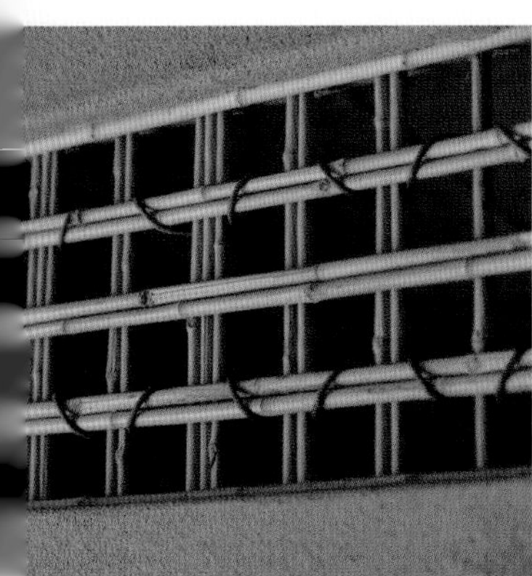

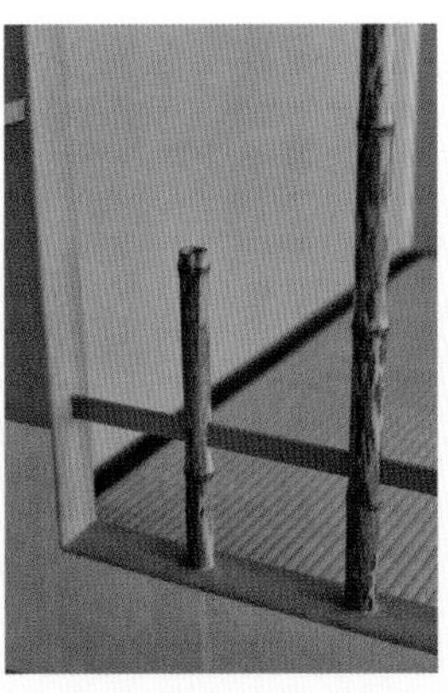

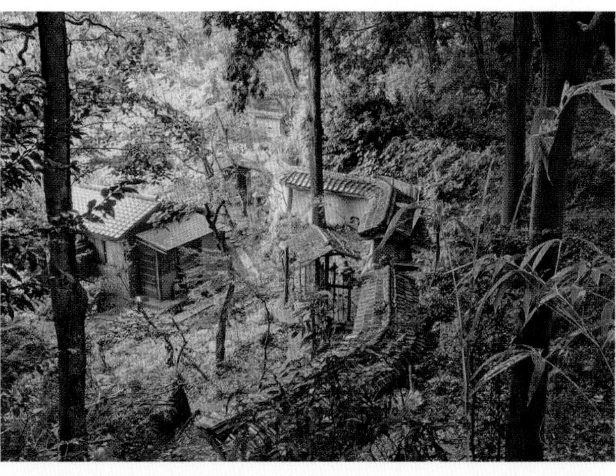

CHAPTER FOUR

Some Other Things You Should Know (1)

Handling Stone and Making a Japanese-style Stone Wall

In Japan, stone walls are everywhere and from every period of history. In my time, I have made more than I can possibly count. Most visitors are greatly impressed by the massive *ishigaki* castle walls of the sixteenth and seventeenth centuries. Unfortunately, most of the castles themselves are gone: first, the Tokugawa shogun limited castles to one per lord, and then many were destroyed by the modernizing Meiji government (1868–1912), fearing a resurgence of feudalism. But many of the stone walls that formed the bases of the castles still exist today. The obvious message: stone endures.

Besides the size of these massive stone walls, the reason they are so impressive is the careful crafting and fitting that went into their creation. Such walls use no concrete but have endured five hundred years in an earthquake-prone country. Osaka Castle, which burned down and is now reconstructed in reinforced concrete, sports several stones over 100 tons and many more over 50 tons. Most stones are much smaller than this but their cut (long and wedge shaped) and their fitting (set at an incline with the higher end making up the wall surface) keep them amazingly stable and strong. To put it in more technical terms, most of the stones in the wall are header stones.

The stone walls of castles are usually quite deep but usually not freestanding. They are usually built around mounded dirt, or backfilled with dirt and large gravel. These walls use both cut and natural stone. Cut stones in particular are used to make the dramatic sloping corners that give castles such a distinctive look. They are also sometimes used in an interlocking pattern, somewhat like a brick wall, called *nunozumi*. In this case, the roughly squared stone is aligned along the top and bottom. The width of the stone varies but the vertical joints are staggered. All exterior steps are made of cut stone. We rarely use straight-cut stone in the garden (with the possible exception of walkways). Instead, we create beautiful and durable walls from naturally weathered stone. I will talk about several ways to do this.

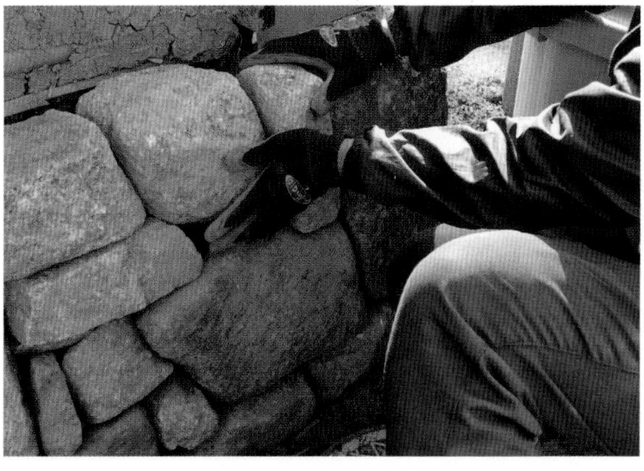

Fitting natural stone into a wall is a time-consuming puzzle. Unlike a brick wall, the mortar stays in the background.

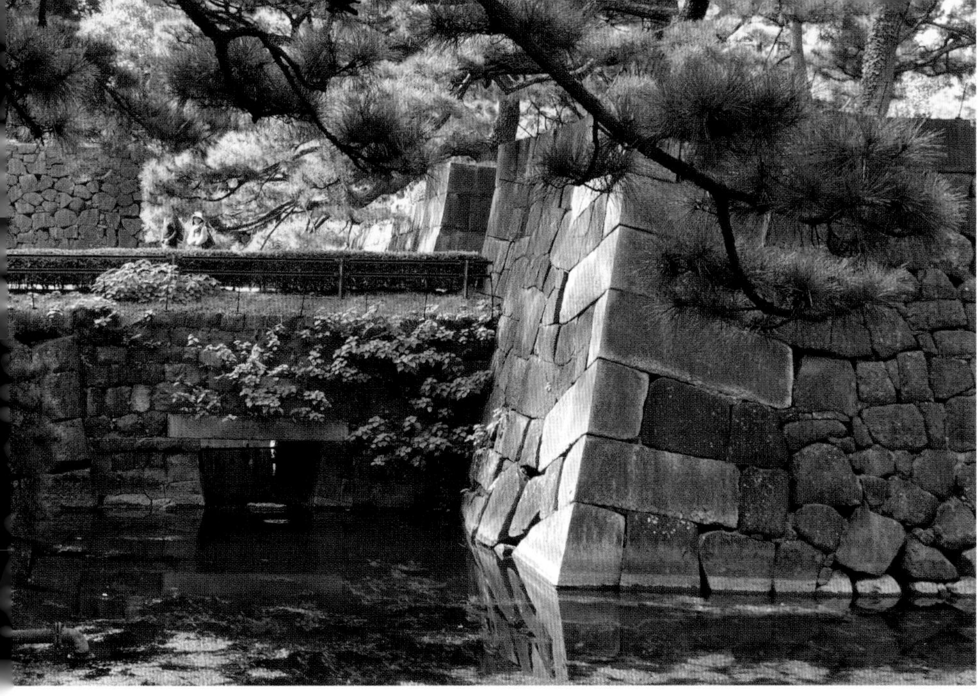

Left The remains of the former Edo Castle, now on the grounds of the Imperial Palace in central Tokyo. Even here, cut stone is only used for the dramatic sloping corners.

Below Our "crumbling" stone walls are made to look haphazard but they will withstand earthquakes and floods.

General terms

With such a long history of using stone, there are enough methods and terms to fill an encyclopedia. I have already mentioned a few. The type of wall we most often construct is a *nozurazumi* or *kuzurezumi*. This basically means a "crumbling" wall, which refers to the fact that the stone is rough and there are no straight lines other than the outside edges. This wall uses mortar to hold the stone together but the mortar is kept well back from the surface. In this way, it looks like only stone piled upon stone. There is another method, which doesn't use mortar, called *karatsumi*. We don't usually use this method due to the risks of earthquakes shaking the stones lose and the need for such walls to be wider and backfilled.

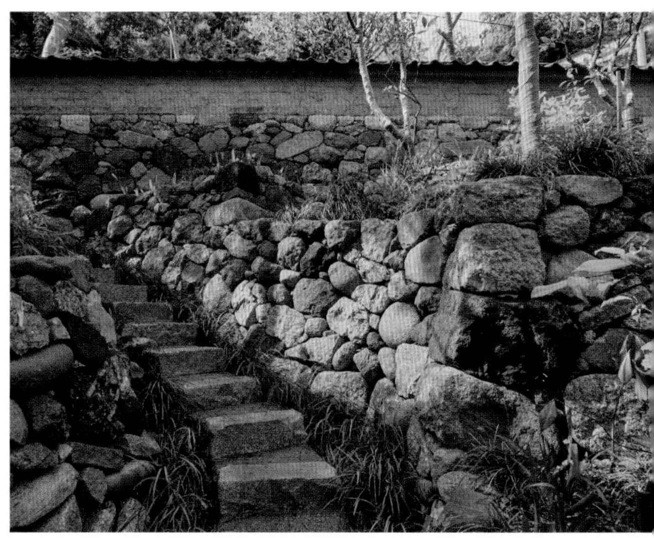

Side view, double-sided wall stone, clay, mortar

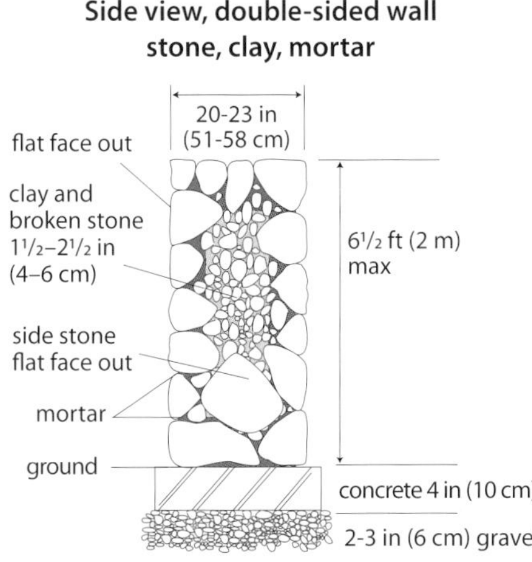

Leveling the stone wall

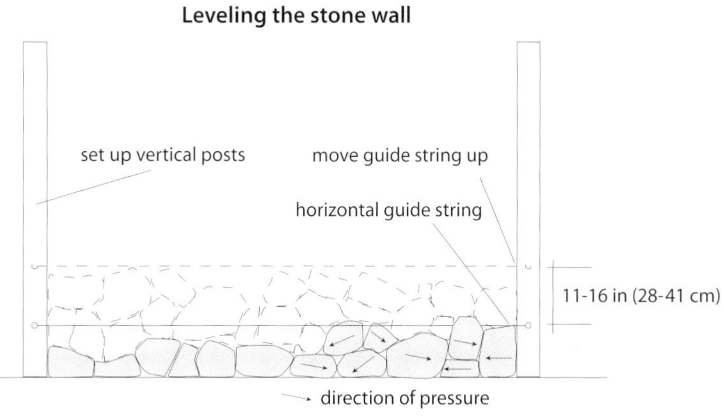

Double-sided stone walls

No matter what type of wall you decide to make, you need to start with a foundation. First dig a ditch several inches to 1 foot (15 to 30 cm) deep and a little longer and wider than your wall will be. This should be filled with ¼ to 1 inch (0.6 to 1 cm) gravel to a depth of 2–3 inches (6 cm) and tamped down. Above this, pour 4 inches (10 cm) of concrete. If you want a clean and straight edge to the concrete, you can make a wood frame and pour it into that. If not, just dig the trench deep enough to accommodate the gravel and concrete. Smooth the surface and get ready to build the wall.

We will use uncut granite stones of a maximum 88 pounds (40 kg) or whatever one or two people feel comfortable lifting. Start by ordering a range of 4 to 16-inch (10 to 41-cm) stones, about 50 to 60 percent more than you will need for the size of the wall. This is to ensure you have enough sizes and shapes to fit your purpose. You need about twice as much large stone as small. Set up some wood posts just outside the foundation. Run a length of string 11 to 16 inches (28 to 41 cm) above the ground level and secure it to the posts. This will be your level guide. Mix some mortar and start laying stone from the corner. Pick a stone with relatively square sides and be sure these sides face the surface of the wall. Slap some mortar onto the foundation and embed the first stone. The foundation should be slightly lower than the ground level (unless you have some reason to make it visible). You want to keep enough space to cover the foundation and the first 1 or 2 inches (2.5 or 5 cm) of stone with soil.

Choose your second stone and set it in mortar next to the first. Use a length of wood to check the straightness of the face of the wall. Keep in mind that the second stone should align with the front of the first stone, but not the top. We want to stagger the heights and avoid straight lines or "rivers." Continue on the opposite side until your first line of stones is in place.

Move the string up the post to the next level. It's a good idea to mark the posts with all your levels from the beginning. The second level is more difficult to place than the first. You need to find stones that will fit on top of the first ones. It may help to use a length of bent wire to approximate the size of the opening. Select the next stone using the wire as a guide. As you gain experience, you can do away with the wire. Slap some mortar on the lower

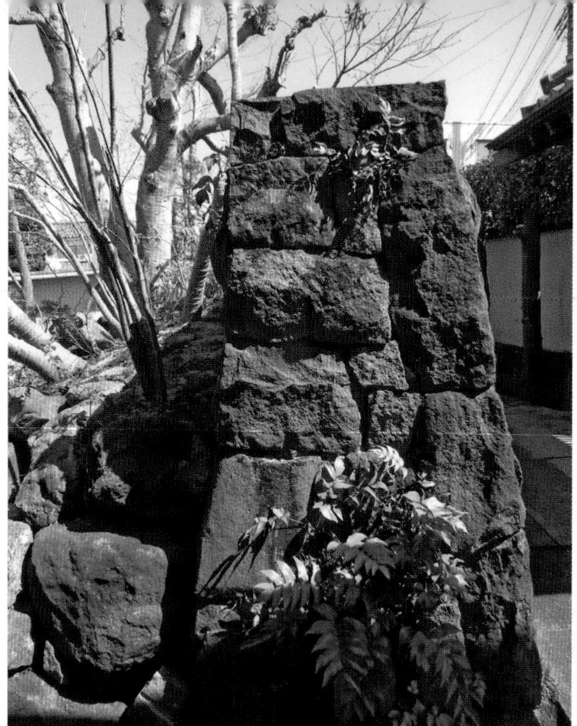

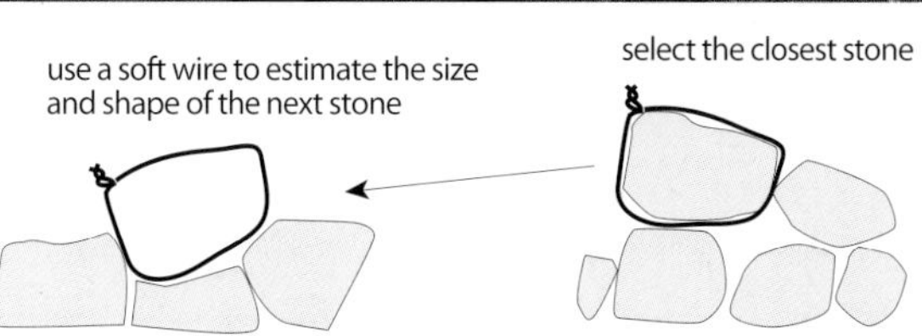

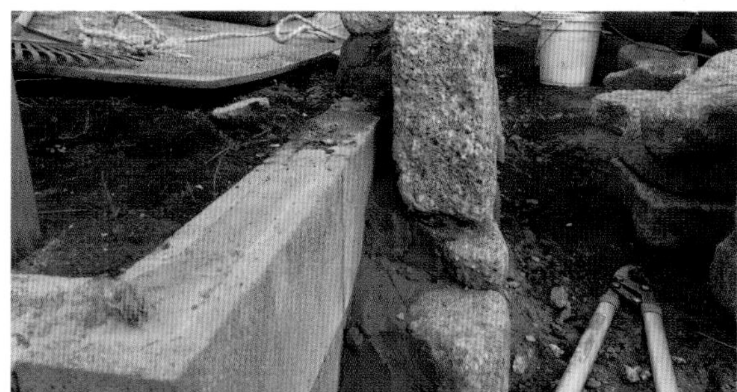

Top This tall double-sided wall is sloped toward the top to guarantee stability.

Above and facing page Fitting stone Is the same for single or double-sided walls. Having enough stone to choose from is essential.

Side view, tall wall

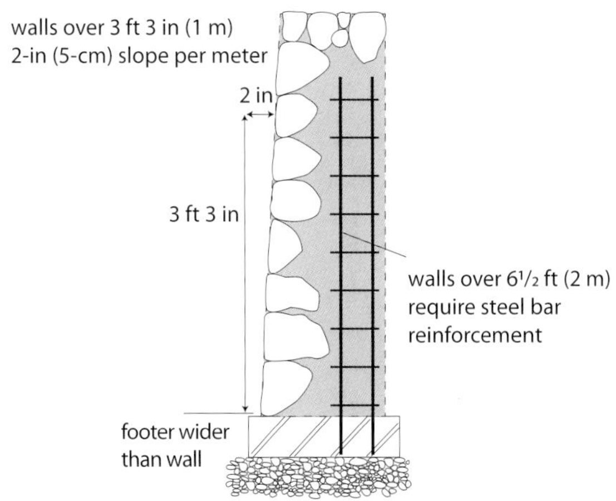

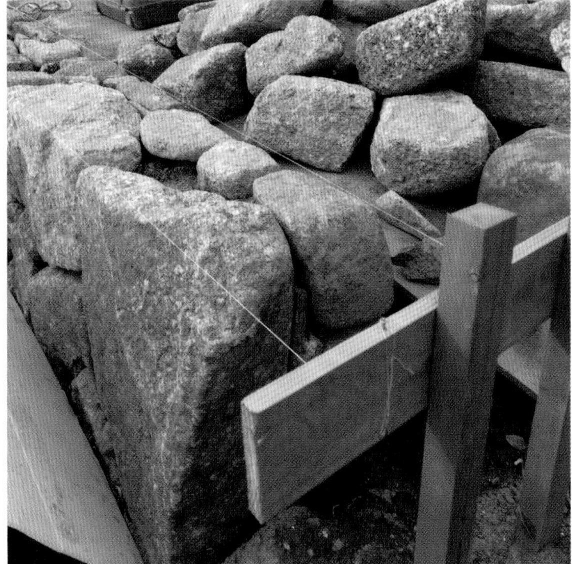

stone and fit your stone into this. Try not to get mortar on the front of the stone or let it show between the stones. Unlike a brick wall, we don't want to see the mortar when the wall is finished.

Continue on the opposite side of the wall and the sides. After three or more levels, and after constantly checking the alignment, you can begin to backfill with a mix of mortar or clay and gravel or broken stone in sizes of 1½ to 2⅜ inches (4 to 6 cm). If the wall is only two stones deep, only mortar is needed.

Continue stacking stone until you reach the intended height. The top row will use stones that are flat on more than one side. Before putting on the top row, allow the backfill to dry enough that the top stones don't sag. Check alignment by using a level, a square, a length of straight wood, or other instrument. Even on the top level, the mortar should be kept well back from the surface.

This wall can be made to just about any width and a height of up to 6½ feet (2 m). That height also depends on the width—a narrow wall should be shorter. Taller walls will require reinforcing with steel rebar. The horizontal and vertical bars form a cage held together with twisted wire. The vertical bars are embedded in the foundation. Rebar comes in diameters of ¼ inch (6 mm) to 2 inches (5 cm) or more. You should check regulations in your area for building walls that border a public space. Even within your garden, take every precaution to build a wall that will not topple over. If you want to be on the safe side, anchor some rebar in the foundation, no matter the height of the wall.

Side view, combination wall

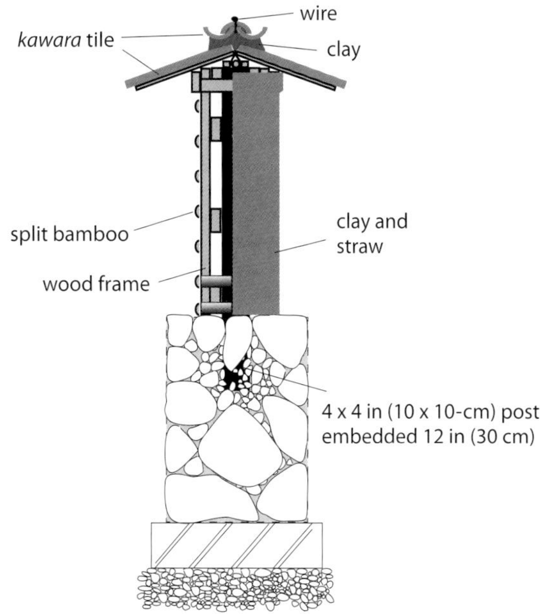

Single-sided walls

Handle the stone for single-sided walls in the same way as for double-sided ones. The difference is that the stone is used as a facing over some other structure, such as a cinder block wall. Naturally, such a substructure must be sound and capable of supporting the stone. Avoid trying to attach the mortar and stone to a rusting or painted surface, or to a cracked wall. Clear away the ground in front of the wall and check the limit of the existing foundation. You may need to extend it enough to support the new stone. Lay the mortar above and below the stone but also fill the gap between the stone and the supporting wall. Where large gaps exist between stone, leave the mortar recessed, then later fill with smaller stone backed with mortar. Be sure the stones do not lean toward the face of the wall.

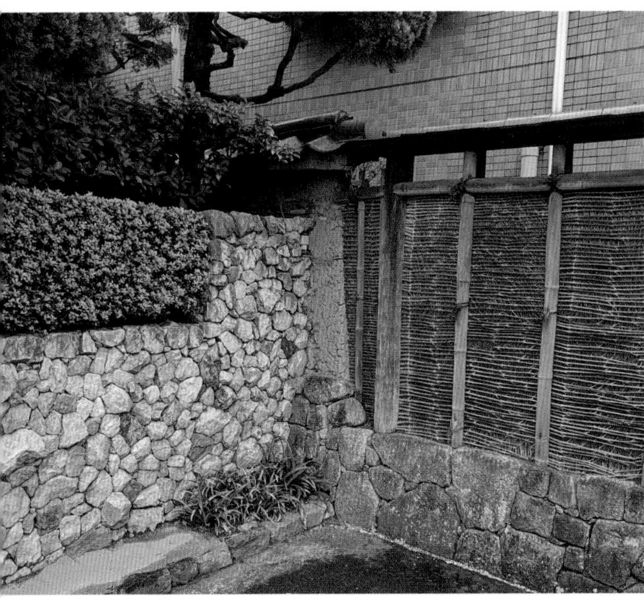

Above A limestone wall, a granite base under a bamboo fence, and a clay wall with a tile roof shows the diverse skills used by the gardener.

Right The hammer-like *koyasuke* is held against the stone and rapped with a small *setto* sledgehammer to split and shape the stone.

Tall walls

Whether single or double-sided, the taller the wall is the more the possibility of it falling. As I mentioned before, tall walls may need to be reinforced with rebar. In Japan, where earthquakes are a common event, we slope taller walls back toward the top. That slope is roughly 2 inches (5 cm) for every 3 feet (1 m) of height. This can be done with single or double-sided walls. Calculate the approximate foundation width needed to achieve the height you want. If you start with a base that is too narrow, you may not be able to achieve the desired slope.

Combination walls

Another place where we often use stone is the base of other walls, such as bamboo, brushwood, wood, or clay. Besides the beautiful appearance and strength that stone lends to these walls, it protects the other materials against damage from standing water. A stone base extends the life of any other wall type by many years. If the wall is one-sided, with a substrate of cinder block or some other material, the strength of the wall above the stone depends on the substrate. In that case, the stone at the base is handled the same as for a single-sided stone wall.

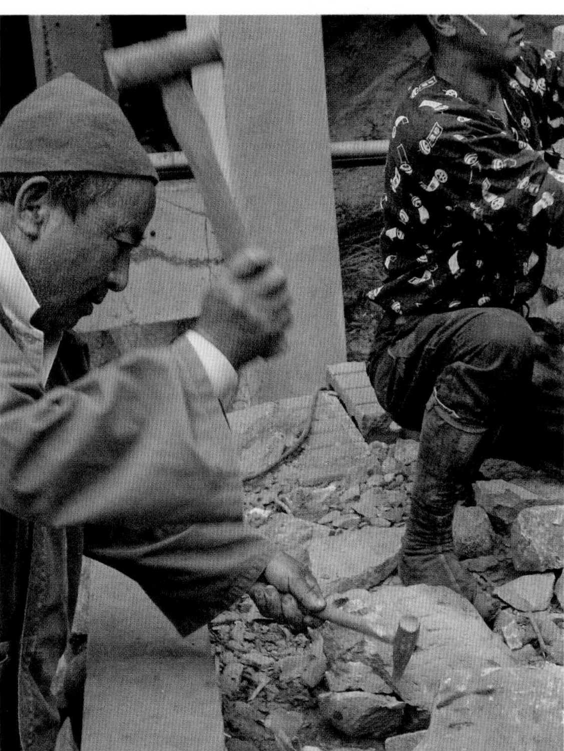

Placement patterns, front view

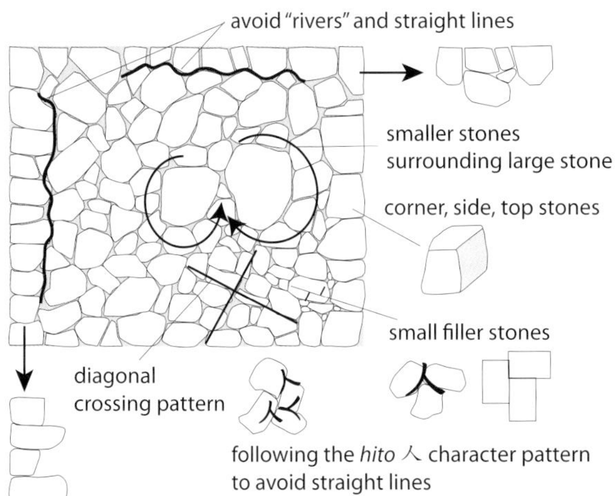

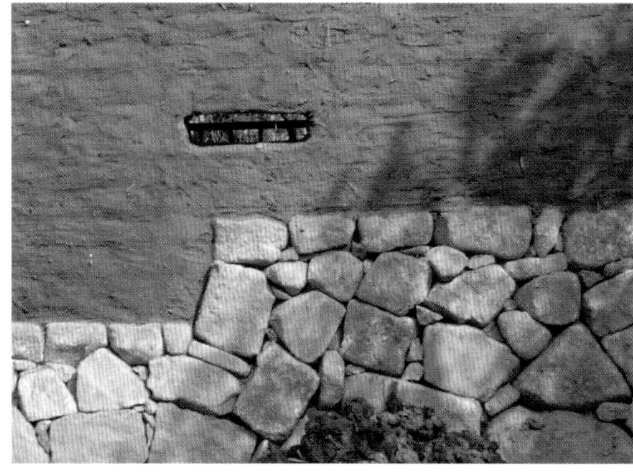

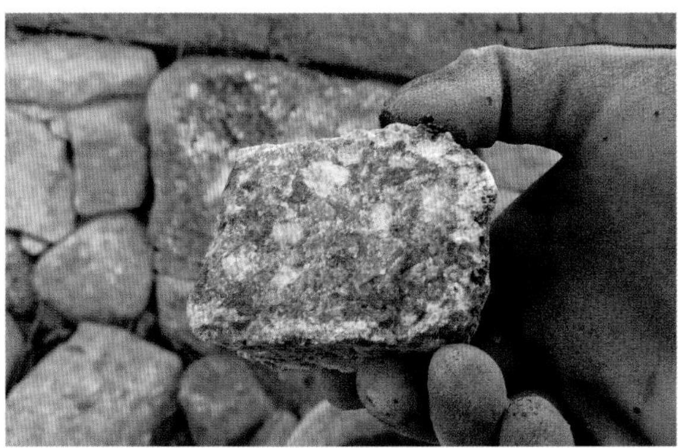

Left The split granite will reveal a different color. This face is turned toward the inside of the wall, never toward the surface.

Above Bamboo, clay or wooden walls are durable except in standing water. A stone base makes a beautiful and durable wall.

If the wall is freestanding, the stone base will need to support the upper wall. In that case, a double-sided stone wall is filled with mortar, and vertical studs are embedded. The studs are held in place with the mortar and stone but you need a depth of at least 12 inches (30 cm) to embed 4 x 4-inch (10 x 10-cm) studs. Temporarily hold the studs in place with cross ties so they don't move while the mortar is setting. If the stone wall is less than 12 inches (for example just a single stone height), you need to embed the studs in the foundation under the wall.

I said above that we don't use straight-cut stone in the garden, but when fitting stone you may need to chip it into the desired shape. As long as the cut side is not on the surface, there's no problem. When granite is cut or chipped, the color inside the stone is different than the surface. To chip the stone we use a small sledgehammer called a *setto*, and a *koyasuke*, a tool with a kind of hammer on one end and a blunt chisel with a carbide edge on the other. Hold the chisel edge against the stone and hit the back of the koyasuke with the setto until the stone cracks. For larger stones and slabs, scoring the stone with an angle grinder first makes it easier to break. It is also necessary to use small stones to balance larger stones and fill gaps. These pieces may be natural or chipped from larger ones. Remember to use protective eyewear when chipping stone.

When fitting the stone, on large or small walls, keep some rules in mind. First, try to avoid straight lines and "rivers." We stagger the sizes of adjacent stones and try not to create regular patterns. Keep in mind several methods shown in the illustration at the top of this page. Diagonal layouts are better than vertical and horizontal. Smaller stones surrounding larger ones is another method to avoid regularity. When staggering stones, try to keep edges from aligning. In other words, the edge of one stone should align with the middle of the next one—similar to a brick wall but not as regular. In Japan, we think of the Chinese character *hito* 人 (person) when arranging the stones.

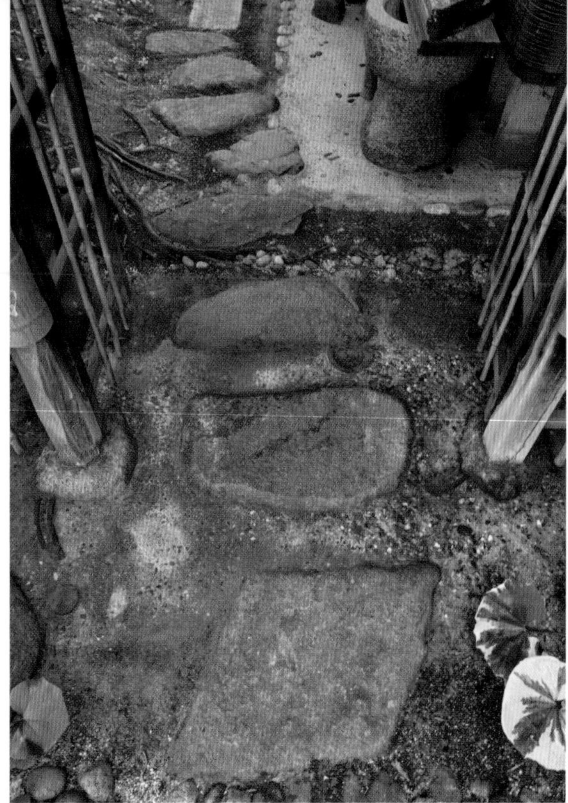

Above Selecting and placing stepping stones is a skill that comes with time but stability is the primary concern.

Below Wood boards define the curved shape of the *nobedan*. Stones are positioned then removed; a base of mortar is set and the stones are embedded.

While the majority of stone used in the garden is granite, I believe I am the first Japanese gardener to use limestone rock (*sekkaiseki*) extensively. Limestone is a little softer than granite but hard enough to make durable walls. Its benefit is that the interior and the surface of the stone are identical, giving more flexibility for chipping a shape without concern about glaring differences. It is also a lighter color overall than granite, which I find attractive.

Stepping stones (tobi ishi)

Stone, usually granite, is used to create stepping stones in the Japanese garden. Basically, the stones are embedded in soil or mortar such that only a small part remains above ground. The stones may be naturally flat or slightly rounded. Each stone should have enough girth to stick up between ¾ to 1½ inches (2 to 4 cm) above the ground. We never use slate or flagstone—which are too thin and have sharp edges—for stepping stones. There are an infinite number of arrangements for a stepping-stone path. As a general rule, the stones should be set one comfortable stride apart and slightly staggered to accommodate left and right foot. The stones must be stable and used on level ground. If there is a steep incline consider making stone steps instead. At a junction or when the stepping-stone path must diverge, it is common to insert a large dividing stone (*fumiwaki ishi*). Stones should all be set to the same height with no hills and valleys.

When arranging stepping stones in a path, avoid repetitive size and shape. In general, one stone should be large enough to accommodate one foot. Smaller supporting stones called *hikae ishi* are also used to break up patterns and add interest. Larger stones are used when the path comes upon an interesting view or when people walking in opposite directions will need to pass one another. In these cases, one or more stones large enough to accommodate one or two people standing still can be used.

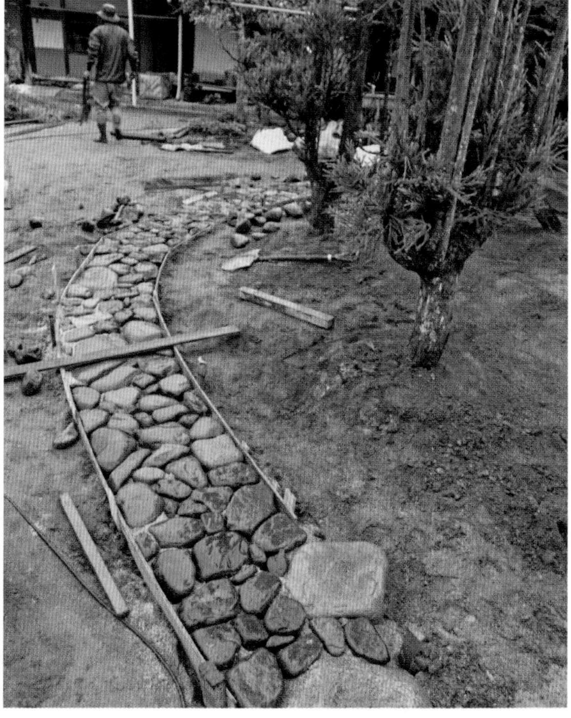

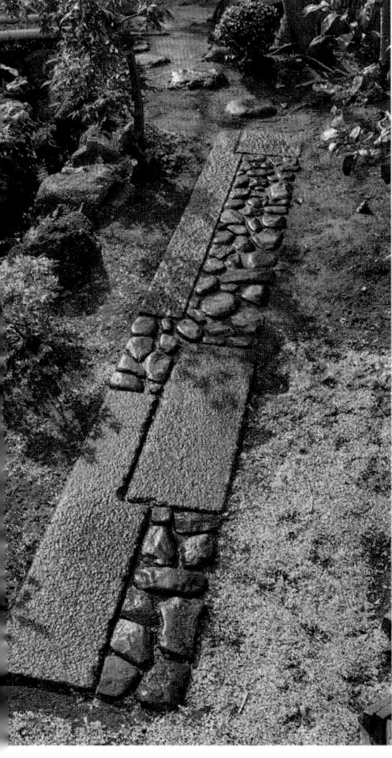

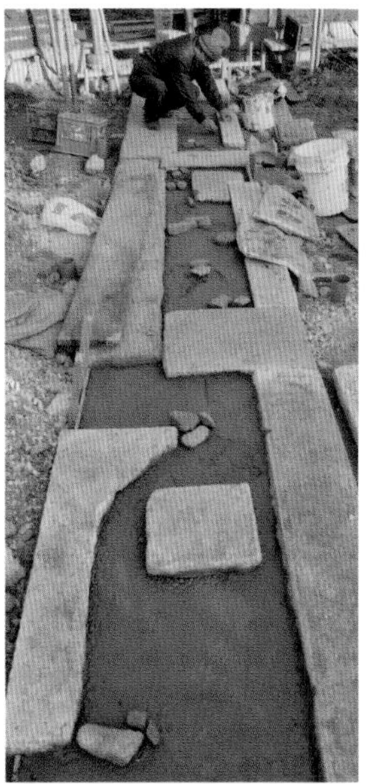

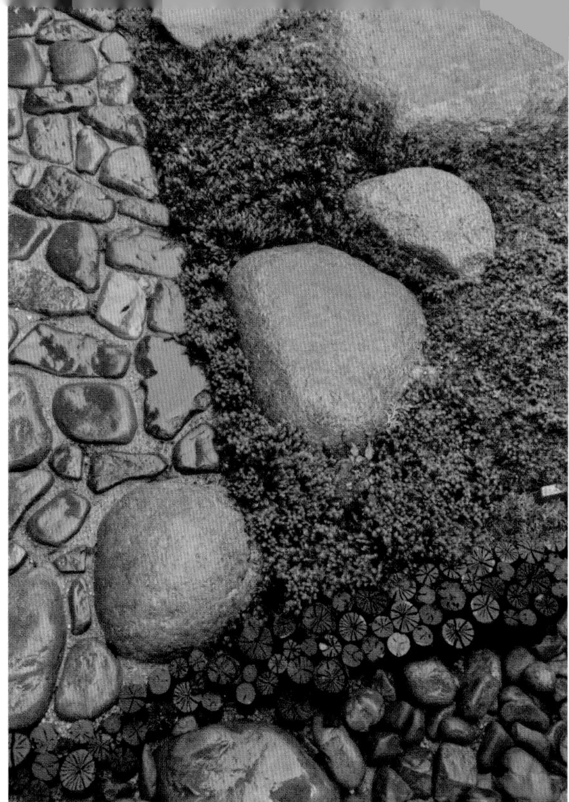

Above left A semi-formal mix of natural and cut stone. Center Cement holds the cut stone and creates a base for the exposed aggregate (*araidashi*). Right This *nobedan* walkway incorporates a stepping-stone path.

Walkways (nobedan)

When more than one person at a time will be walking, or when more formality is needed, we gather stones together to make a walkway called a *nobedan*. There are many such stone arrangements but they basically group as formal (*shin*), semi-formal (*gyo*), and informal or casual (*so*). Formal walkways use more geometric shapes, either natural or cut. The walkway may zigzag but the outside edge is always straight. Stone alone, or stone and clay combinations are used. The semi-formal style uses geometric and organic shapes with neither one dominant (organic shapes alone are sometimes used). The casual walkway uses only organic shapes and the outside edge may or may not be straight. Nobedan are often used to show off the style and skill of the gardener.

One style of formal walkway uses large, flat "label stones" (*tanzaku ishi*), and long, narrow stones (*obi ishi*). Stones are not all cut the same width, length, or shape. Some may be placed at angles and they vary from 2½ to 3 inches (4 to 6 cm) thick. The positions of the larger and the outer stones are decided first and they are set in place. The weight of the stones requires that they be embedded in concrete. Wooden boards are used to keep the concrete in place at edges with no stone. Enough space is allowed to cover the concrete on the top and sides with an inch of clay without exceeding the height and width of the stone.

Not only the stone but also the joint pattern of walkways should be interesting—especially on informal walkways. When making an informal walkway with many small stones, it is helpful to make the outside shape with thin boards nailed to stakes. Especially if you have a curved walkway, the boards help to maintain the overall shape and also the height of the stones. As with stone walls, there are no straight lines in informal walkways. Attention should be paid to the joint width and depth as well. A minimum of ⅜-inch (1-cm) width and about 1-inch (2.5-cm) depth or so is good. Recessed mortar is used in the joints.

With all walkways, observe two rules. First, the stones must be embedded deeply enough not to

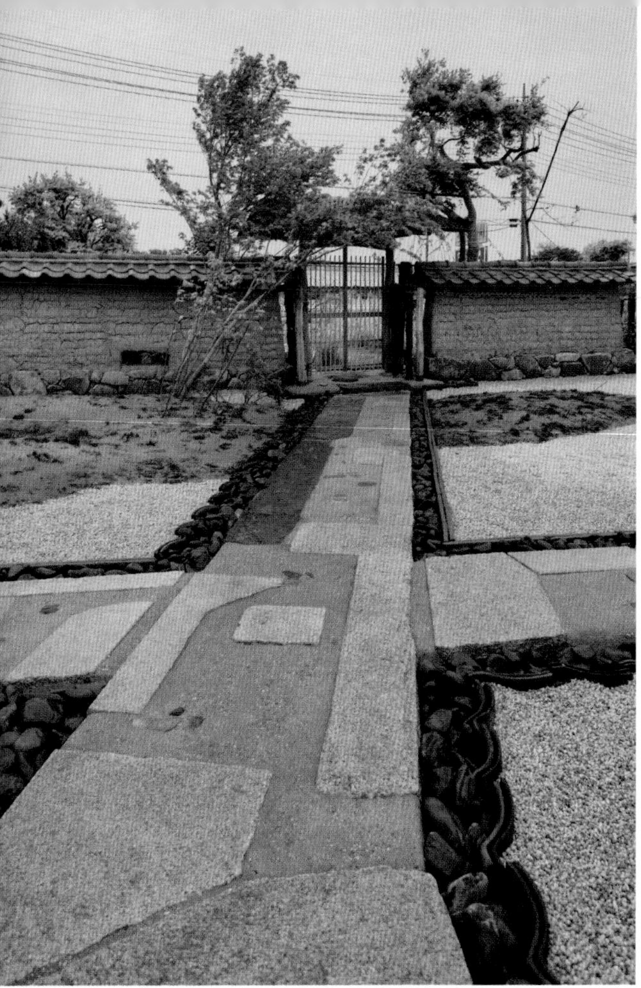

Left The *nobedan* walkway from page 133 (center), filled with exposed aggregate (*araidashi*) and finished with a border made of stone and roof tiles.

move when stepped on. This is particularly true of corner stones, which are more subject to movement. Corner and outer-edge stones especially should be at least 6 inches (15 cm) thick and well embedded in sand, clay, or mortar. The other rule is that no stone should stick up above any other as it may trip anyone walking on the nobedan. A two-by-four or long level can be used to check the height across the stones. The final considerations are drainage and silt. If the stone will sit in a bed of sand or soil, there should be no drainage issues, unless the ground outside the nobedan slopes towards it. If drainage is a problem, dig trenches a few inches deep on one or both sides of the walkway. Fill the trenches with gravel. Where you have problems with silt or mud sliding onto the walkway, bury ceramic tiles (*kawara*) along the edge of the trenches about 6 inches (15 cm) from the sides of the walkway, then fill with gravel or rounded stone. The tiles should be interlocked and stand several inches above the walkway to stop any mudflows.

Water basins (chozubachi)

A *chozubachi* is a water basin, usually made of stone. It is found in all types of Japanese gardens in all shapes and sizes. At the minimum it is a stone with a natural or cut crevice deep enough to hold water. It has no fixtures or drain. The water may enter through a hollowed out bamboo pole, one end of which has been placed in a stream or waterfall. Of course, these days a municipal water supply may be attached through a PVC pipe or flexible hose. The other method is to pour water from a pail.

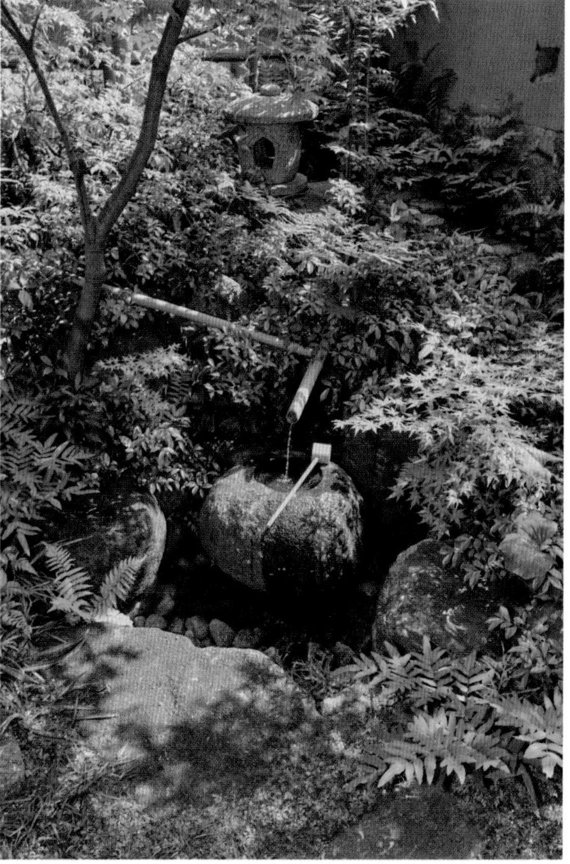

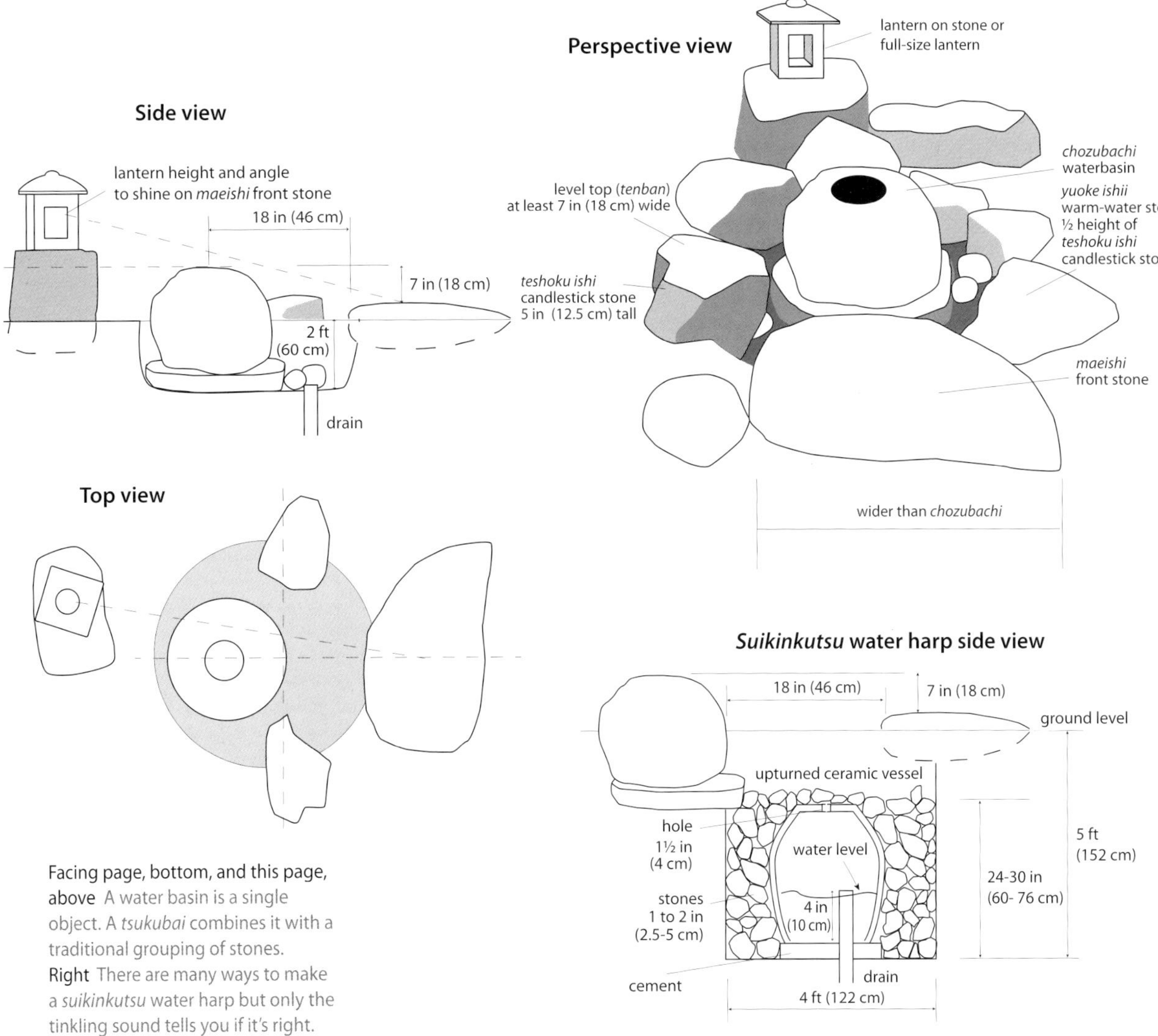

Facing page, bottom, and this page, above A water basin is a single object. A *tsukubai* combines it with a traditional grouping of stones.
Right There are many ways to make a *suikinkutsu* water harp but only the tinkling sound tells you if it's right.

Water-basin settings (tsukubai)

A *tsukubai* is an arrangement of a chozubachi water basin with other stones. *Tsukubai* means something like "crouching basin" which refers to the basin being set very low to the ground so that those using it must crouch or bow low. The act of hand washing is an act of ablution adopted from Shinto and Buddhist practices. To achieve the low height, a hole is dug in the ground and partially filled with rounded river stones. The stone basin is placed in the center or on the far edge directly on the river stones or on a stone used to adjust the height. The walls of the hole may be covered in clay or lined with stone.

Here is the typical arrangement of stones accompanying the water basin in the tsukubai: the front stone (*maeishi*), where a person crouches; the candlestick stone (*teshoku ishi*), usually placed to the left; the warm-water stone (*yuoke ishi*), for a small pot of water placed to the right. (The arrangement may depend on the school of tea that is practiced. For example, the Urasenke school favors the teshoku ishi on the right and yuoke ishi on the left.) A wooden or bamboo ladle with a long handle (*hishaku*) is also provided. Though not strictly speaking a part of the grouping, a stone lantern is usually placed behind the water basin in such a position and height that the light falls on the basin.

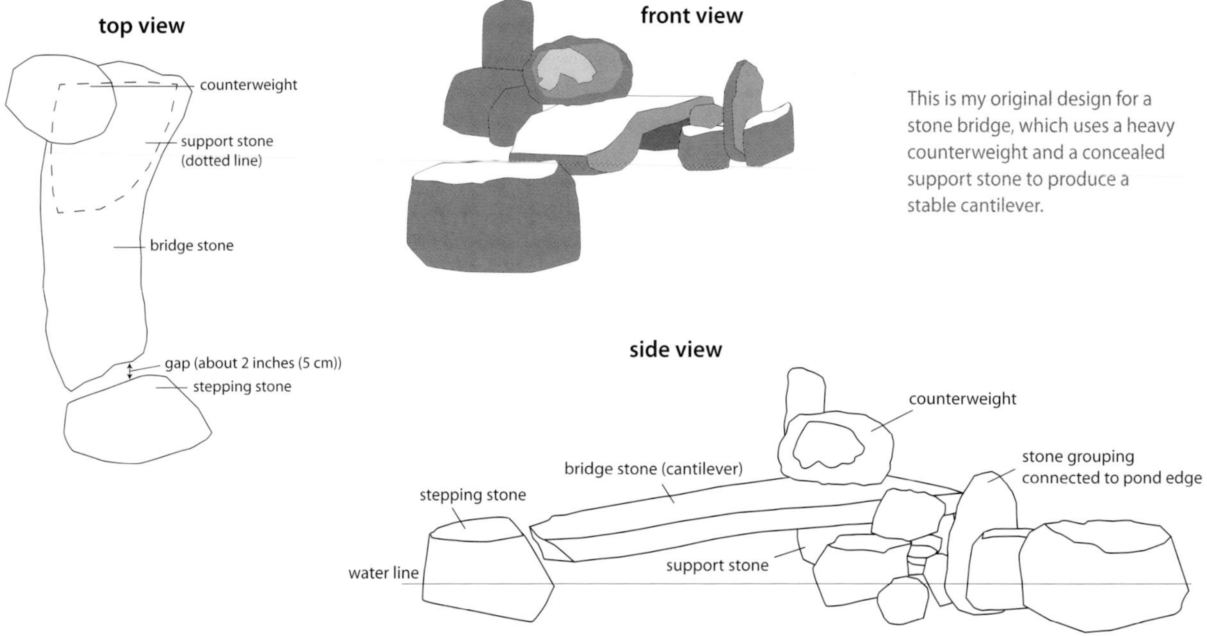

This is my original design for a stone bridge, which uses a heavy counterweight and a concealed support stone to produce a stable cantilever.

Water harp (suikinkutsu)

The *suikinkutsu*, called water harp or water koto in English, is not made of stone but it often accompanies water basins. The purpose is simply to produce agreeable sounds from the water dripping out of the chozubachi water basin. A hole is dug slightly to the front of the chozubachi, large and deep enough to bury a 2-foot (60-cm) tall ceramic planter, upside down. The mouth of the overturned planter is closed with mortar or stone and a drainage pipe inserted from the bottom to a height of about 4 inches (10 cm) from the bottom. Water drips though the small hole in the bottom (now, top) of the planter and strikes the water accumulated inside. Large stones are placed around the sides of the planter to enhance the echo of the dripping water. A ceramic sewer pipe, 1 by 3 feet (30 cm x 1 m) can also be used, in which case the bottom and top must be closed. In that case, a granite slab with a ¼-inch (6-mm) hole drilled in the center can be used as a lid. Stones are placed above the lid to disguise it.

Stone bridges (ishibashi)

Stone bridges are common in Japanese gardens, over streams and ponds and also in stone-and-sand gardens (*karesansui*) where an expanse of sand may be seen as symbolic for water. Stone bridges are made of one or two slabs of stone, usually granite, sometimes arched, either natural or cut. Other stones at the embankment or directly under the slabs support them. This discussion does not include engineered, arched bridges, which are a separate category beyond the usual scope of the gardener.

The simplest type of bridge is a single slab, up to 8 feet (2.4 m) long, 2 feet (60 cm) wide, and a minimum of 6 inches (15 cm) thick. A single, rectangular stone at each end is set into the embankments to support the slab. The classic *hashibasami* arrangement uses up to four stones placed at each of the corners of the slab. The stones support the slab, prevent lateral movement, and act as a guide for the person crossing. They also serve a decorative function. These stones vary in size and height with one stone usually higher than the rest—as much as 3 or 4 feet (1 or 1.2 m) tall.

Another bridge is the split type with two slabs meeting in the middle, supported by one or more large stones set into the pond or stream. The slabs may abut directly or they may be staggered. A small island of stone and soil may also be constructed in a pond and the ends of the bridge stones nested there. One other bridge, of my own design, which I call the "seesaw" bridge, is a cantilevered type. One end of the bridge is connected to the embankment and

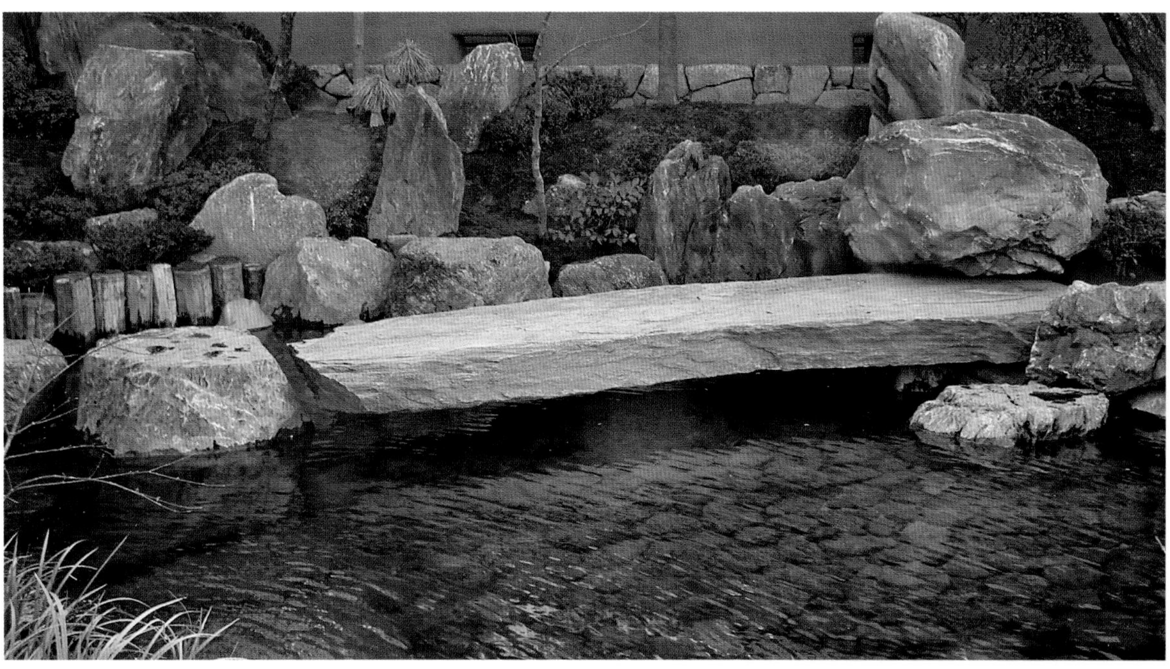

Above The "seesaw" bridge, with no apparent means of support, crosses the pond at Yushima Tenmangu Shrine (see page 72).

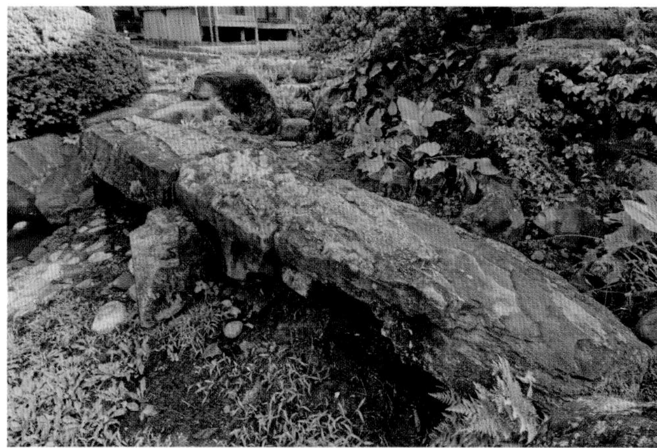

Right A split stone bridge, with a center "island" supporting the split halves, is typical of Japanese gardens.

supported by a large stone. On top of the slab, on the same end, another heavy stone is placed. The stone is placed to weigh on the slab but enough to the side that there is room to walk onto the bridge. The opposite end of the slab is unsupported. A large stone, the same height as the slab, is placed just past the end to allow the person to continue crossing. The gap between slab and stepping stone should be no more than a few inches.

Stone arrangements

Most of the stones we have talked about so far are purely functional. Such stones are generally classified as *yakuishi*. The terms *ishigumi* and *iwagumi* refer to stone arrangements that are generally symbolic or decorative but may also be functional. Both *iwa* and *ishi* mean stone and *gumi* means group. The most common ishigumi is the three-stone configuration. The most common of this group is called the Buddhist triad stones (*sanzonseki*). The group is comprised of a larger standing stone (*chusonseki*), flanked by two shorter "attendant stones" (*kyojiseki*), which are said to represent the Buddha and two bodhisattvas (*bosatsu*).

Two other common groupings are stones arranged to represent a turtle and a crane. Both of these groupings are often set on small islands such that a combination of mounded soil, stones, and plantings create a scenic and symbolic setting. Both groupings represent long life. The turtle is associated with the Chinese mythical island of Penglai (called Horai in Japanese), the Island of the Immortals, which was borne on the back of a giant turtle. Stones for the turtle usually comprise the head and legs, and those for the crane the head, wings, and tail.

Below A stone crane gracefully glides on the surface of a pond.

Bottom A "boat" stone on a sea of gravel carries good fortune from afar.

Right The Buddhist triad stone arrangement (*sanzonseki*) was first described in the eleventh century but may be much older.

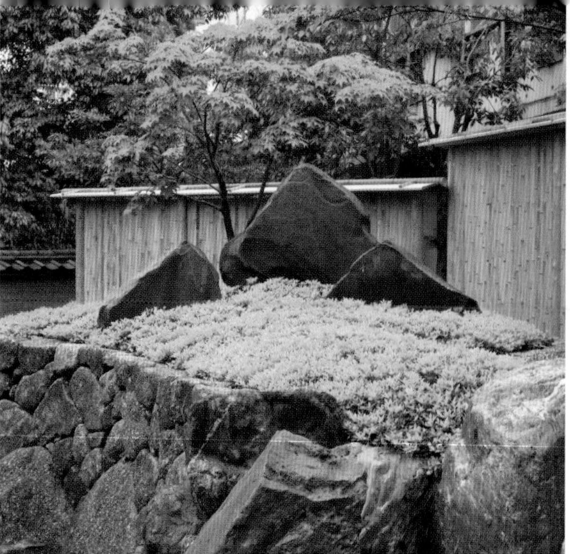

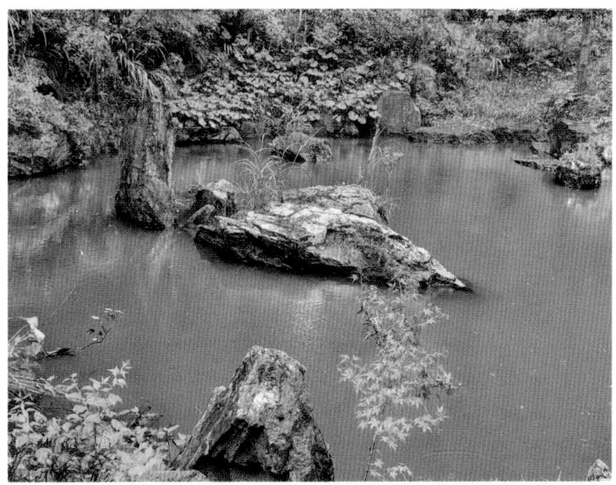

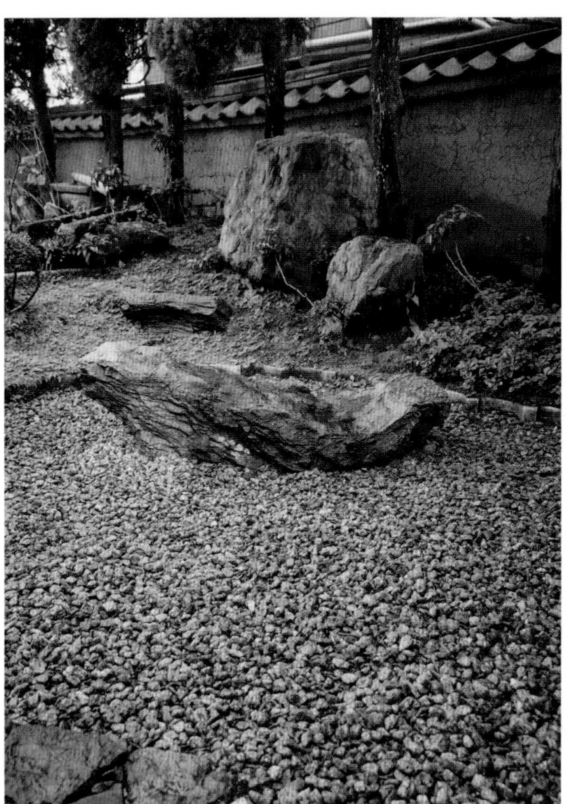

These island arrangements are found in both ponds and dry gardens. Pines, also a symbol of longevity, are often planted in these groupings.

When composing decorative groups of stones, layering and triangulation are important concepts. Triangulation refers to the idea that the bottom is always wider than the top—like a mountain. This lends an air of calm and stability. When stones are grouped, the relationship between the stones is more important than the characteristics of each one alone. Stones in an arrangement can be thought of as speaking to each other, like a group of friends, huddled together. Layering refers to grouping your stones so that all the stones are at least partially visible from the main viewing point. Although there are hidden stones that can only be seen by walking around the garden, generally speaking smaller stones are placed in front of larger ones, taller behind shorter, and so on.

Keishoseki (or *kazari ishi*), and *suteishi* are decorative stones which can be found separately or grouped. Some have symbolic meanings, such as the *funaishi* (see this page and page 141), but most are just for the purpose of achieving a good design, such as the *nejime ishi*. This is a stone placed near the base of a tree, sometimes with a low shrub. The purpose is to lend a sense of stability to the tree.

Waterfalls

Waterfalls are another type of stone arrangement that may be functional or symbolic or both. There are many types of waterfalls, characterized by the way in which they convey water. For example, the "cloth falls" (*nuno-ochi*) convey water falling like a sheet of linen. In Japanese *dan* means step, so with waterfalls we have the one-step falls, two-step falls (*ichidan*, *nidan*), etc. We also have the "Dragon's Gate" falls (*ryumonbaku*), based on Chinese folklore about a gate at the top of a waterfall guarded by dragons. A carp swims up the waterfall, outwitting the dragons to pass through the gate, thus becoming a dragon too, symbolizing the search for and attainment of enlightenment. This arrangement always includes a small stone at the base of the falls called the carp stone (*rigyoseki*).

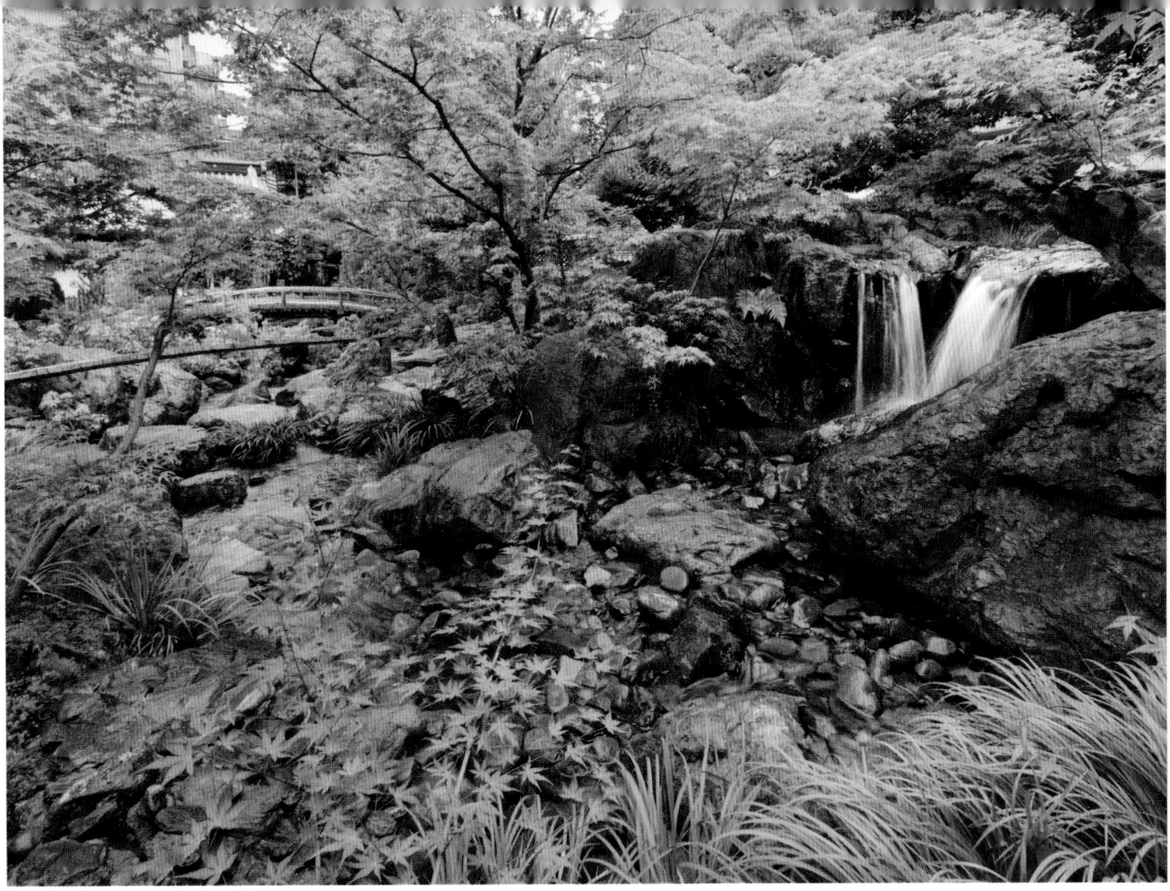

Another waterfall type begins with a tall, vertical stone called the *fudoseki*. This is an image of the Buddhist deity Fudomyo-o who stands immovable as protector of the Buddhist law and savior of souls. Next to this is the shorter, flatter, horizontal, mirror stone (*kagami ishi*). Water pools behind this stone and then cascades over it, leaving its surface shining like a mirror. The third stone (*oyaishi*) supports the mirror stone on the opposite side. It is also a large, standing stone but not as large as the fudoseki stone.

Above A massive waterfall is arranged over a concrete form. Carefully crafted, it seems to be formed by the hand of nature.

Below Not all falls are massive or tall. A natural stream contains many small drops and level changes.

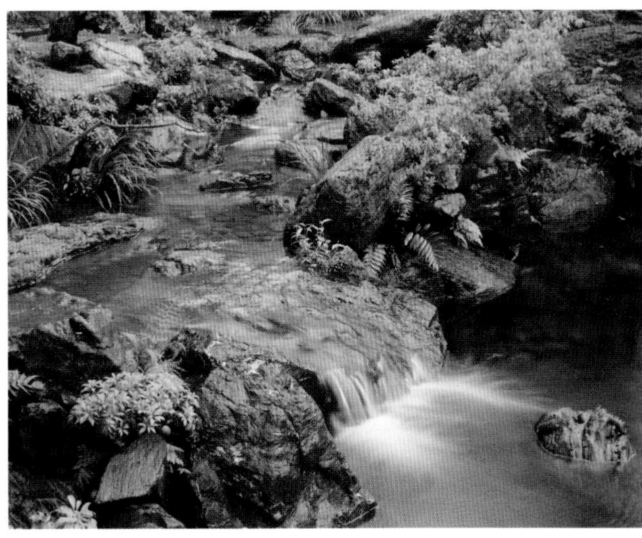

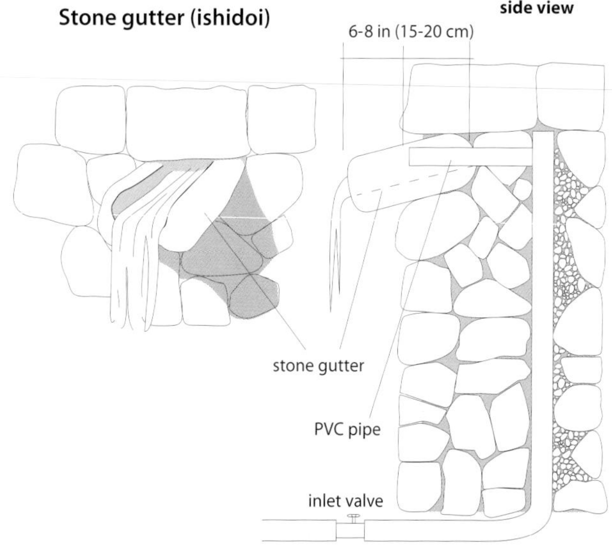

This is not the complete setting and it is subject to many variations. Often, another stone, called the water-dividing stone (*mizuwake ishi*) is included. It is similar to the carp stone, but the falling water is directed onto the water-dividing stone, which "divides" it and causes the water to spray.

Stone gutters (Ishidoi)

Another method of moving water in the garden is the stone gutter (*ishidoi*), usually in the form of a deep or shallow "U" shaped channel, cut from a single stone. Water enters the channel through a bamboo or PVC pipe. I often use small ishidoi built into a stone wall. The pipe is concealed in stone and only the gutter protrudes, usually at a slight downward angle, allowing water to stream from various points in the garden. It helps create a mountain atmosphere. Mountains are the source of water and one encounters many types of streams when hiking or searching for natural features to recreate in the garden. It's fairly easy to chisel a channel into a piece of stone and set it into a stone wall with mortar. A PVC pipe is set into the wall with a metal valve at an accessible point. The valve can be at the base of the wall or in a metal box with a lid set into the ground.

Funaishi boat stones

This boat-shaped, symbolic and decorative stone is usually found unaccompanied in gardens, with or without water, usually of medium size and often placed in a "sea" of gravel. It is considered to symbolize a passage through life, but some people see it as the treasure boat (*takarabune*) of the immortals. This depends somewhat on the era of interpretation. The origin of the *funaishi* is unclear and such a boat stone is not mentioned in any of the oldest writings on gardens. The most famous boat stone is at Daisen-in, a sub-temple of Daitokuji Temple in Kyoto. This garden is from the early

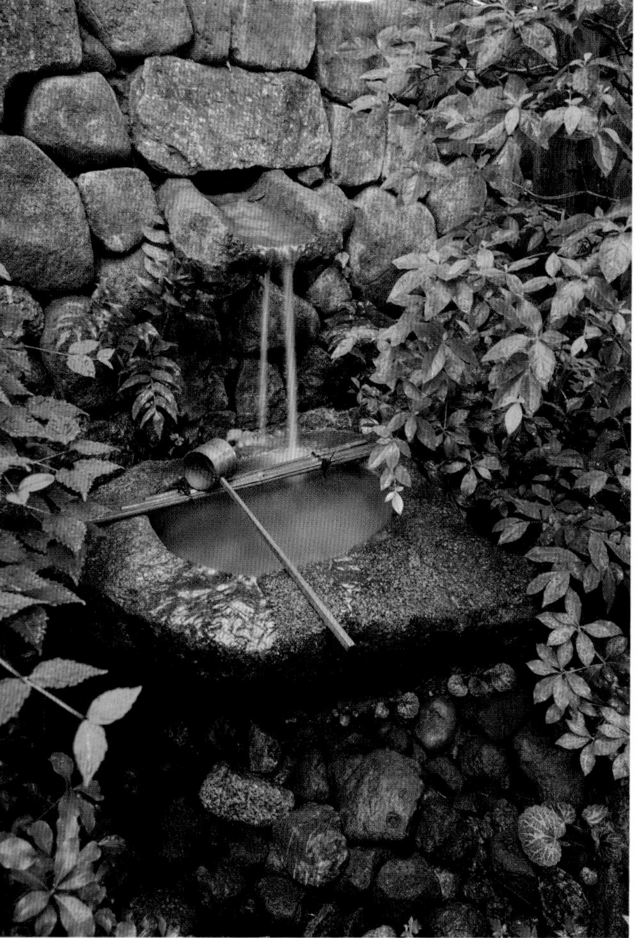

This small gutter pours water into a stone water basin that overflows into a drain concealed by small stones.

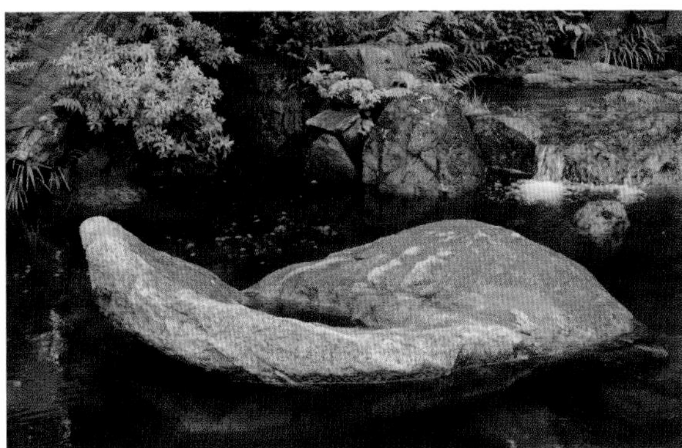

Left Another naturally shaped *funaishi* "boat" stone. This one is set on a stone-and-mortar base in a pond.

Below Essentials of stone handling: tripod and chain block, heavy wooden sled, steel or PVC pipes.

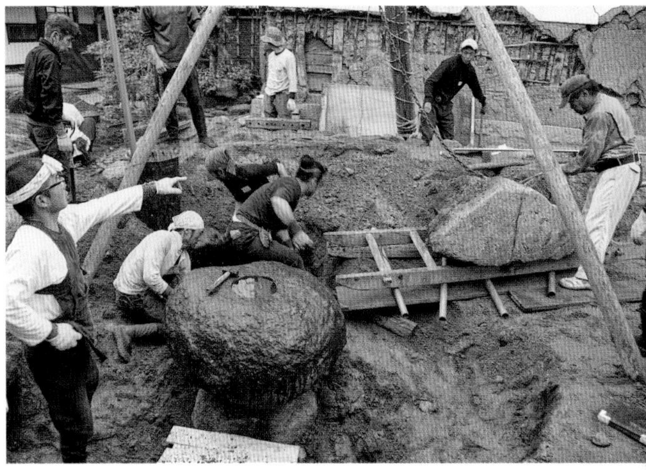

sixteenth century and influenced by Song-period Chinese culture, favoring the theory that its design was related to the Daoist obsession with immortality. This boat stone is said to have come from the garden of shogun Ashikaga Yoshimasa (1436–1490), which points to a history of boat stones from at least the fifteenth century. The boat stone is still a feature in Japanese gardens today.

Moving and lifting stones

I have mentioned that some stones can weigh a ton or more. But any stone of a few hundred pounds or more requires a few special tools to lift and set it in place. The most important of these are the wooden sled and the tripod with a chain block. A sled is made of two 6½-foot (2-m) boards of 2 x 6-inch (5 x 15-cm) lumber. One end of each board is cut in a curve like the prow of a ship. These are joined at five or six points along their length by 2 x 3-inch (5 x 7.5-cm) boards or 2½-inch poles. The space between the 6½-foot boards should be about 35 inches (90 cm). The joints should be glued and solid. The sled will be attached to a rope or heavy wire for pulling. Half-inch boards are used to create a path from the truck, where the stone is offloaded, to the final destination in the garden. Six or seven steel or PVC pipes about 2 inches (5 cm) in diameter are arranged on the boards. The sled is placed on top of the pipes, which act as rollers. Lift the stone from the truck with a crane or backhoe and place it on the middle of the sleigh. The sleigh is slowly pulled and pushed across the pipes. Take out the last pipe and put it in front of the sleigh. Continue like this until you reach the destination. Don't build up momentum because the sleigh is easy to roll and difficult to stop.

At your destination a tripod and chain block should be set up and waiting. The tripod is three long poles of about 6 inches (15 cm) diameter and tall enough to raise the stone to the desired height. The poles are wired together at one end, like the poles of a teepee. From the wire we hang a chain block or hoist. A wire cable with loops at each end is wrapped around the stone. Use cloth or some soft material between the cable and stone so as not to damage it. The cable is wrapped twice around the stone and the loops attached to the hook on the bottom of the chain block. Pull the chain and take up the slack slowly. The stone should be brought directly above the place where it will be placed. The final placement and direction of the stone is done by hand while it is still hanging. Keep pulling the chain and move the stone just high enough to clear any obstacles before setting it down. It requires several people to restrain the stone until you are ready to remove the cable.

Some Other Things You Should Know (2)

Mud on the Walls, Mud on the Floors

Mud is a convenient material that anyone can use. In the garden it has many applications for walls, floors, and other surfaces. Mud—more properly called clay—can be used alone or in combination with other materials. Correctly prepared and applied it is beautiful and durable. Clay has been used since ancient times in many different ways for structures all over the world. Adobe and cob are terms used outside Japan for clay mixed with sand and straw. We usually use soil dug from the site to make our clay. Since the clay content of the soil varies, the mix of sand, straw, and water will also vary. If the soil at your site is clay poor, you may need to purchase clay-rich soil. Clay is basically soil with a majority of very fine particles. Here, I will explain several of the applications we use in the Japanese garden.

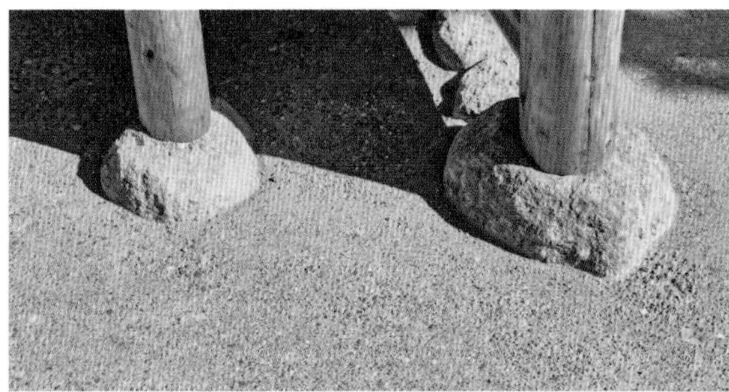

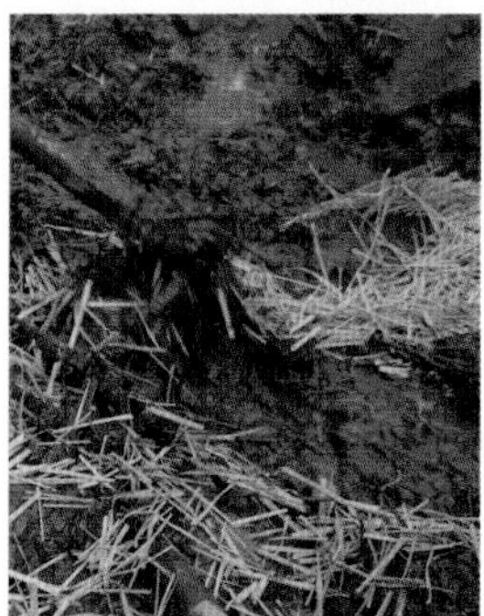

Above and top right *Araidashi* exposed aggregate: clay mixed with sand and fine stone.

Left Clay mixed with cut straw for a wall.

Far left Cut and natural stone embedded in a clay walkway.

Mud compositions

For floors (exposed aggregate):

- 3 parts small rounded gravel less than ⅜ inch (1 cm)
- 2 parts clay
- 1 part Portland cement

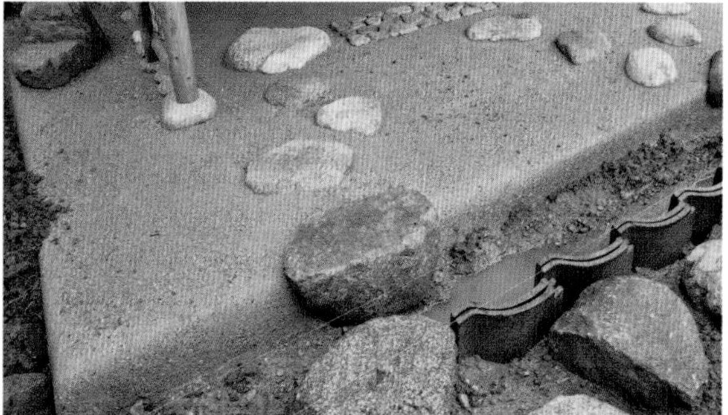

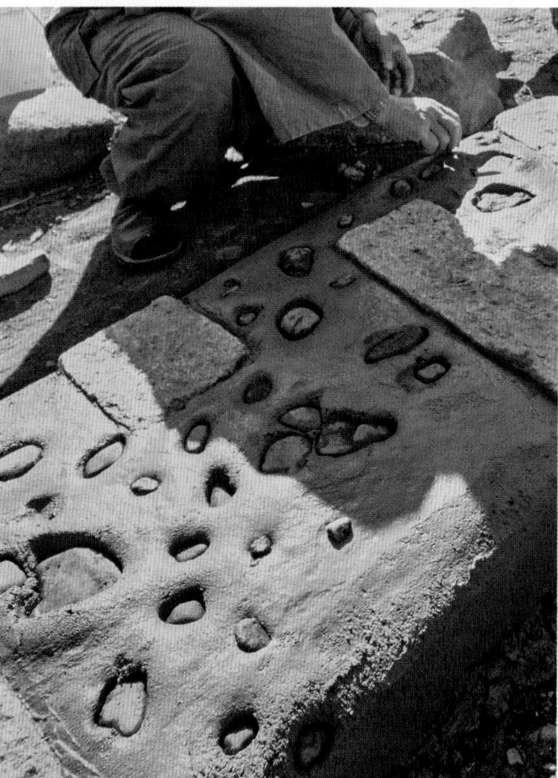

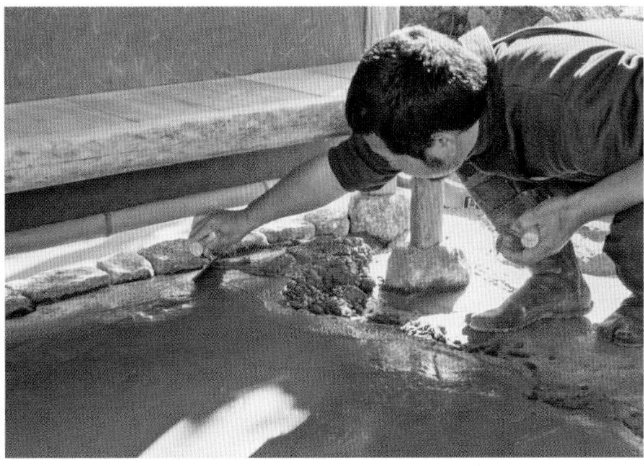

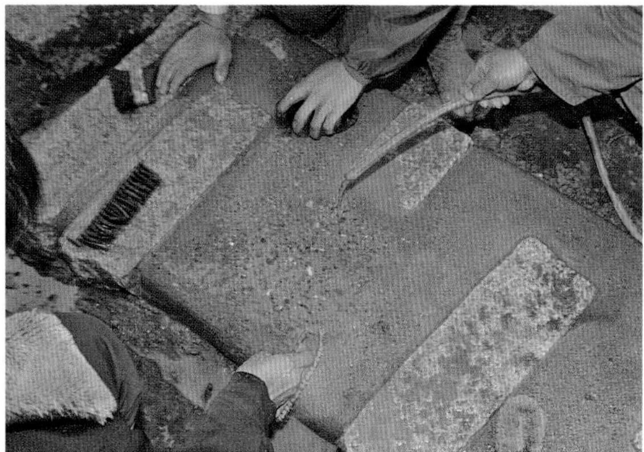

Above and right After the cement foundation and stones are set, thick clay is troweled on. The semi-dry clay is washed and scrubbed to expose the aggregate.

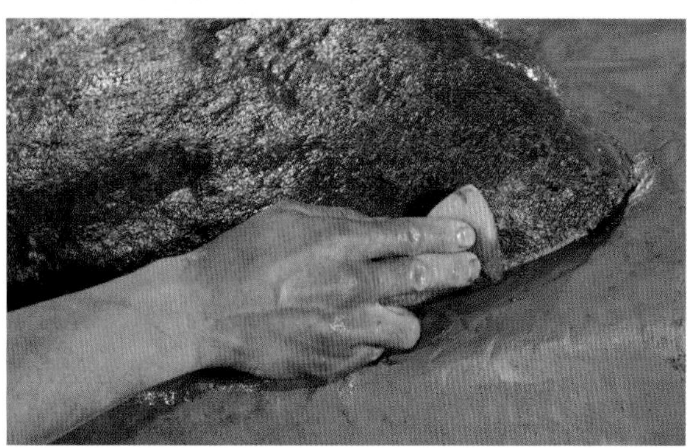

Bottom right Clay is carefully washed off any stone with a sponge before it dries.

This is a style that results in a pebble finish and is usually used for floors. The substrate can be flat and level, or rough and sloped. Where you need to use large stones, for the base of pillars, walls, etc., set the stones on the concrete substrate first, using mortar to anchor them. When the mortar is dry, the clay mix (above) is laid over the substrate with a trowel to a thickness of about 4 inches (10 cm). Any edges are rounded or beveled. When dry, use a soft bristle brush with slow-running water from a hose or sprayer. Scrub the surface with a soft brush to reveal the pebbles. Clean any clay from the large stones with a wet sponge. Then let the floor dry thoroughly before walking on it. Random stones of various sizes may be embedded into the wet clay, in a style known as *fukakusa*. Another style called *doma* is related to this. Doma is used on the interior of houses and was once the surface that covered much of the interior floor other than raised areas made of wood. Doma was used for kitchens, utility areas, and corridors and also became the name for these areas. The simplest of these floors were no more than pounded earth. The formula above is variable depending on need. For example, cement may be added in areas that are very wet or subject to greater pressure or wear but omitted in other cases.

For walls (*dobei*):

¾ to 1¼ pounds of straw or grass cut to 4–6 inch (10– 15 cm) lengths to 25 to 40 gallons (100 to 150 liters) of clay/sand mix

Make a frame of wood and bamboo on a base of stone. Mix the cut straw and clay with a lot of water and knead it until it is a sticky paste. Leave it covered for one day to one week to soften up the straw and knead it again. In older times, the mixture was stocked for a year or more and longer. This also depends partially on the quality of the clay (poor clay requires a longer standing time). Old clay walls can be broken up and remixed. Generally, mix about 1.5 times more material than the job demands. This applies to floors as well. The main reason is that every batch of clay will be a slightly different shade.

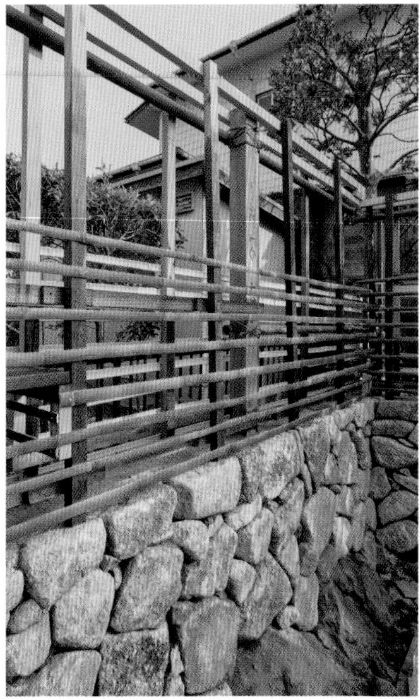

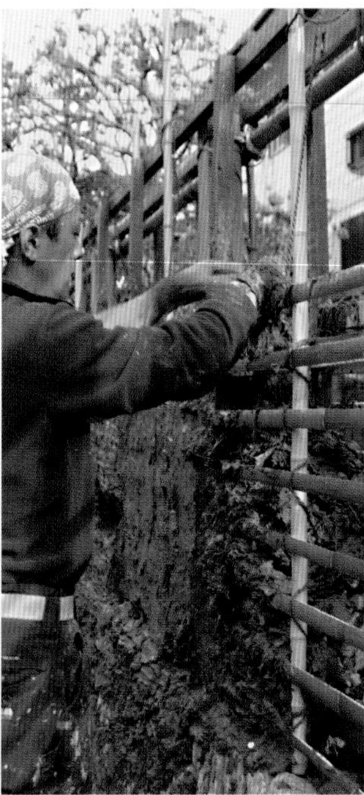

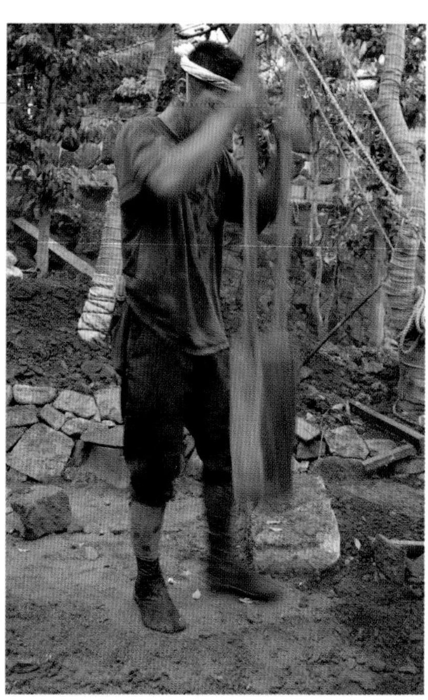

Above, left and center Split bamboo is nailed and tied over a wood frame. Clay fills and covers it.

Above Soil is pounded, in the traditional way, with a log of wood attached to long wooden handles.

The entire frame is filled to the surface with the clay. Keep the finished parts covered in plastic to keep them from drying too quickly. If the wall cannot be finished in a day, it should be finished in sections. Finish each section from the bottom to the top of the wall. The clay is applied with bare hands or wearing rubber gloves. For the final layer, fine sand can be added to the clay to create a mixture called *sunazuri*, and troweled on for a smoother surface. This also helps prevent cracking (the stickier the material the more it cracks on drying). The same mixture of sand and clay can be used to repair cracks. You may also allow the bamboo substructure to telegraph to the surface.

Tamped clay (*tataki*):

- 10 parts soil made up of decomposed granite (*masatsuchi*), volcanic loam (*akatsuchi*) and clay-rich soil (*arakida)* in equal parts
- 1 part limestone (*sekkai*)
- 1/10 part magnesium chloride (*nigari*) or calcium chloride
- A minimal amount of water

Another term for tataki is *sanwado* or *sanwa* soil. *San* means three and refers to the three primary materials. Originally, chloride was derived from seawater, and lime from crushed seashells. Tataki refers to tamping down the clay with blocks of wood (*tataku* means to hit or strike). Mix the clays and the limestone, while sprinkling the mixture lightly with water. Combine the chloride with water and add to the semi-dry mix. It should have enough moisture to clump together when squeezed in your hand. Pour out the mixture on a level base of gravel. Use a straight stick moved side-to-side and dragged to spread the clay evenly. Keep tamping until you have a flat and even build of about 4 to 6 inches (10 to 15 cm). The material should be applied in two or three layers. When finished, brush down the surface with water.

Rammed-earth wall (*hanchiku*):
arakida, decomposed granite (*masatsuchi*), *akatsuchi*, or other clay-rich soil
1 percent clean sand (*kawasuna*, *yamasuna*, etc.)

The *hanchiku* method was employed in China from around 3000 BC to make burial mounds, using silty soil with about 20 percent water content. From there, the practice spread to Korea and Japan. The Yoshinogari burial mound in northern Kyushu, built around 250 BC, is made in the *sochiku* style of compacted layers of soil. In our example, after a concrete foundation is poured and a stone base is set and leveled, we build a frame of two-by-fours and ½-inch (1.2-cm) marine-grade plywood. Reinforce with scaffolding pipe on long or tall walls to prevent bulging. The finished wall thickness here is about 20 inches (51 cm) but as little as 12 inches (30 cm) is possible when cement is added. Mix the materials with about 10 percent water by volume. The name *hanchiku* comes from the method of making the

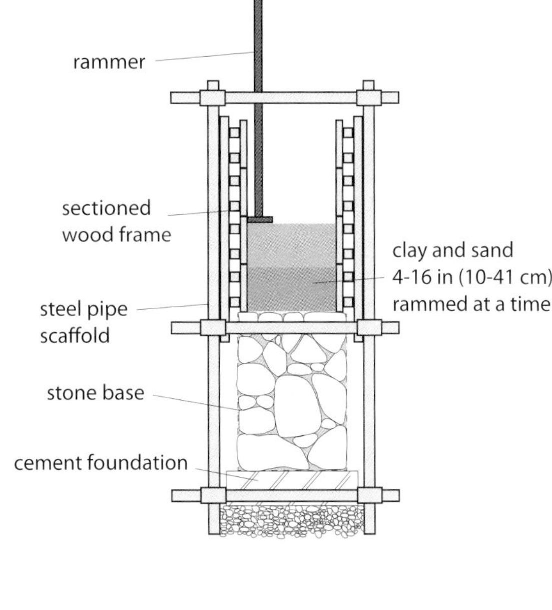

This page The *hanchiku* method uses a removable form into which a soil and sand mix is pounded.

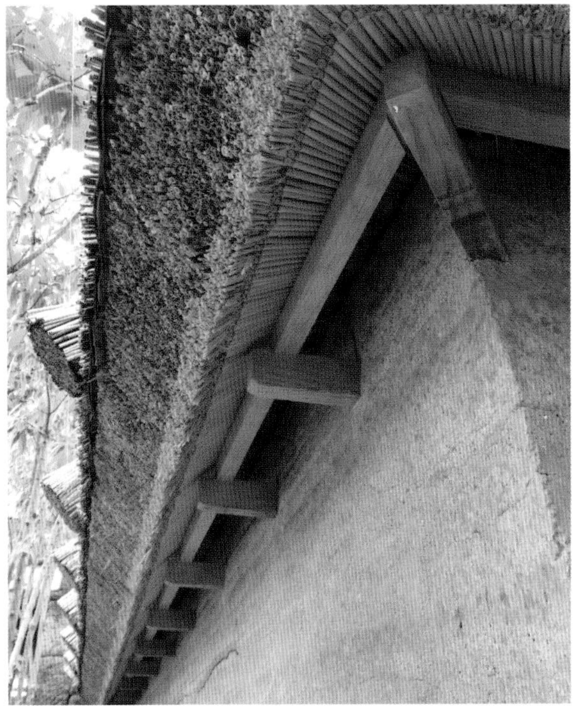

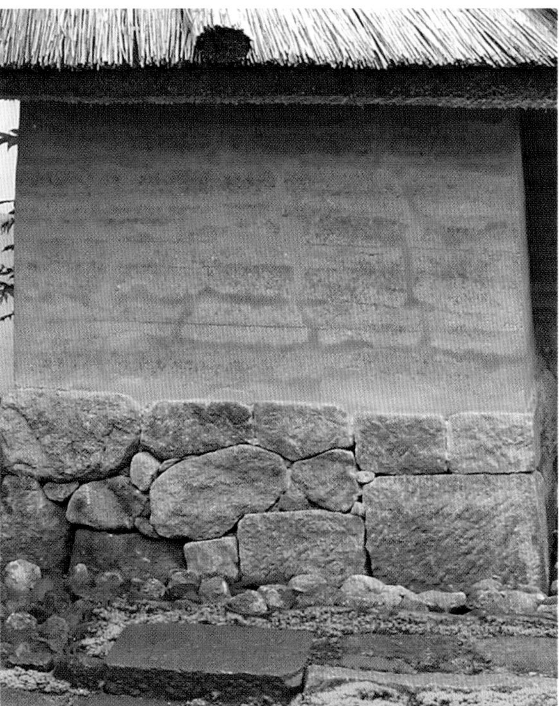

wall by ramming 4 to 16-inch (10 to 41-cm) sections at a time depending on the length of the wall. Add layers one at a time. Continue until the wall reaches the desired height. As with all mud or cement walls, this method should not be carried out in freezing weather or if it will freeze overnight. Carefully remove the form when the clay has set. If the form is made in sections, the section can be removed and used for the next level after the soil is rammed.

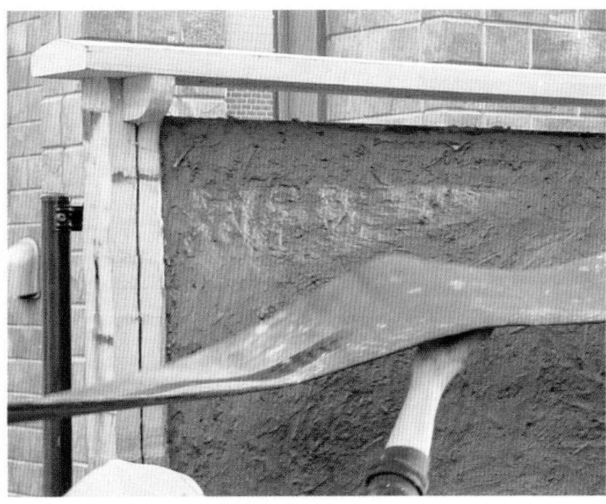

Clay surfacing for *nuri* and *arakabe* walls:

¾ to 1¼ pounds of straw or grass cut to 4–6 inch (10– 15 cm) lengths to 25 to 40 gallons (100 to 150 liters) of clay/sand mix

Build a frame of wood. Screw a lath made of split bamboo, tied with strong twine such as palm-fiber rope, to the frame. For one-sided walls, the lath may be screwed to the substrate. The mix of clay, sand, and straw is troweled onto and through the lath such that it bulges out the back side. Once the clay covers the lath, smooth it out and let dry. This is called an *arakabe*, which basically means "rough wall." The *arakabe* should develop cracks. For interior walls, various types of topcoat can be applied to produce a finished surface. These topcoats employ finer grades of clay, sand, bamboo grass (*sasa*), and may end in several coats of plaster. A *nuri* wall may be just a surfacing or a thin wall supported between posts, while a *dobei* is freestanding and at least 3 feet (1 m) thick.

For exterior and double-sided walls, the materi-

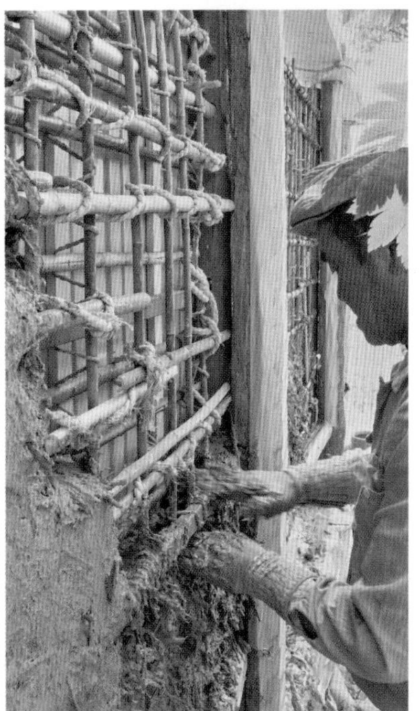

Above A pentagonal-shaped wooden roof is covered in tar paper before receiving a tile cap.

Left and right The single-sided wall is made with bamboo slats and poles. Steel pipe is used to support a corrugated metal surface on the opposite side. This was requested by a neighbor who shares the boundary line.

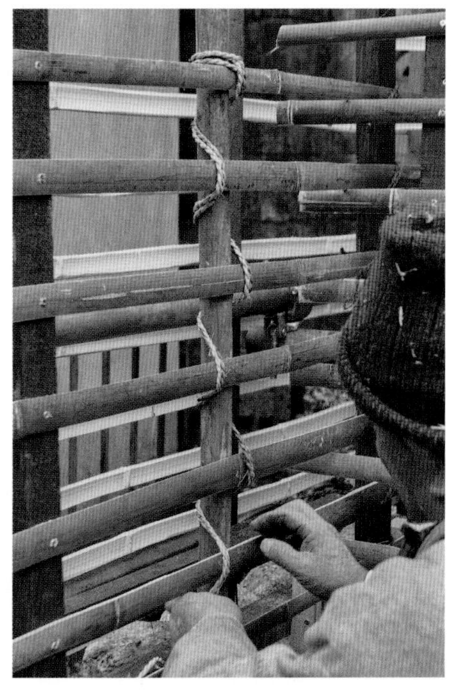

als and process are the same except that both sides of the wall need to be coated. Exterior walls are finished depending on the application. For example, barrier walls or walls around the boundaries of the garden are thicker and can be finished roughly. The bamboo lath may peek through at various points or the straw may show clearly on the surface. For walls around waiting benches, gazebos, and other more formal applications, the wall is thinner and a finer surface is common. No matter the size or finish, having a roof on an exterior wall is absolutely essential for extending its life. Roofs may be of ceramic tile, bamboo, or straw; over a wood substrate; or just wood without additional surfacing. The roof is best if it extends beyond the width of the wall such that rain drips without hitting the bottom of the wall. It is also common to arrange a small trench filled with round stones along the drip line.

Clay walls can be treated in may ways: finely textured between exposed wood; patterned textured and perforated; exposing the bamboo frame; using a variety of roof types from ceramic tile to bamboo and wood.

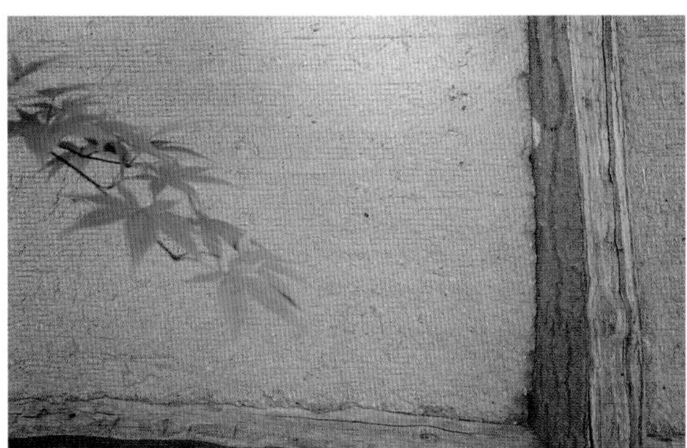

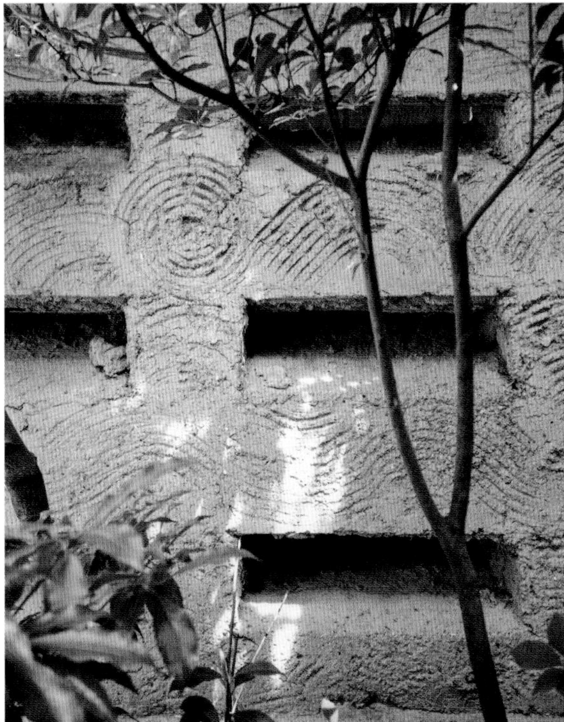

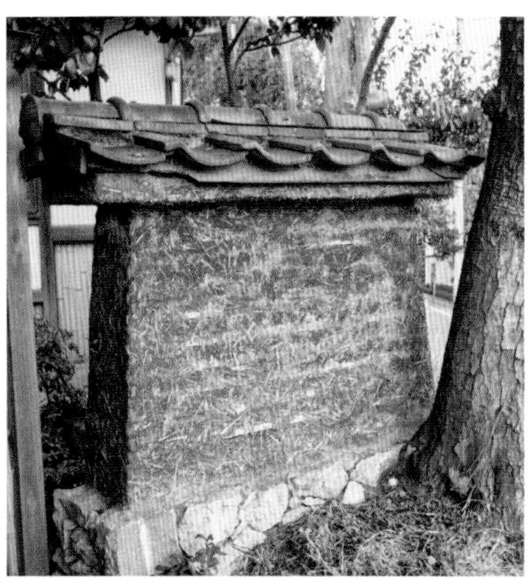

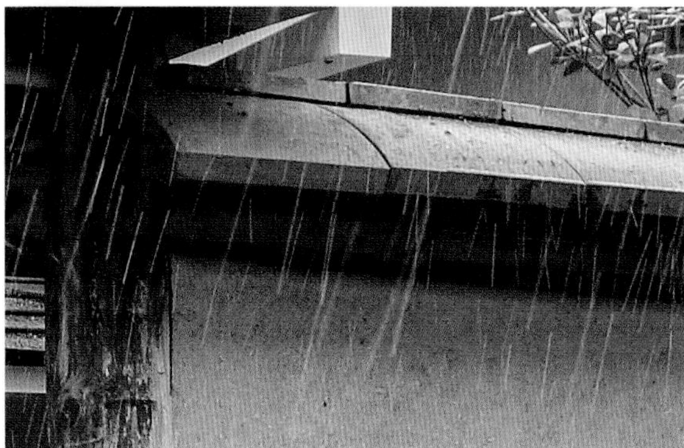

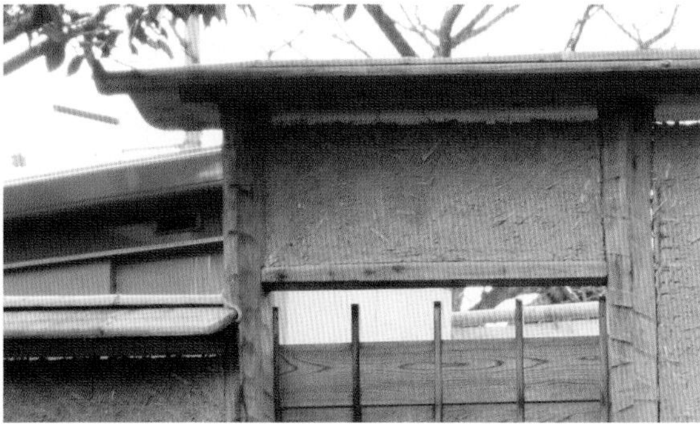

Some Other Things You Should Know (3)

Working with Bamboo

Even for me, a gardener who favors the use of stone and clay, bamboo is an essential material for building garden accessories. The obvious use is in fences: from the simple *yotsumegaki* to the more complex *koetsu-jigaki* (*gaki* means fence). But bamboo is an important construction material with many other uses that are less obvious. Here I give several uses of bamboo in the garden and some construction methods.

Bamboo should be cleaned

Bamboo is quite dirty, especially around the nodes, and should be cleaned before use. This can be done with a stiff brush and dishwashing liquid. If using bamboo for a structure where the branches are

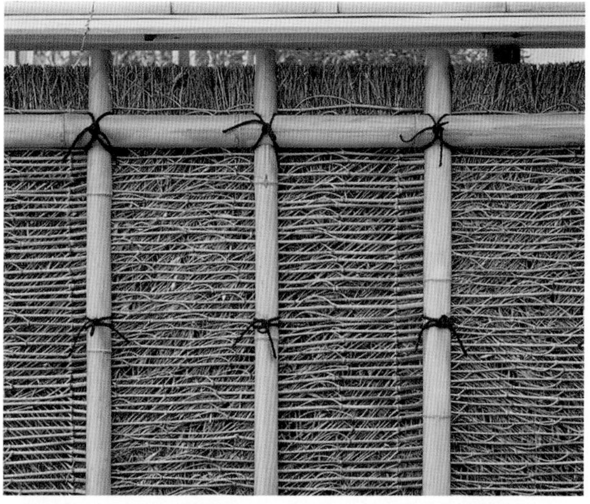

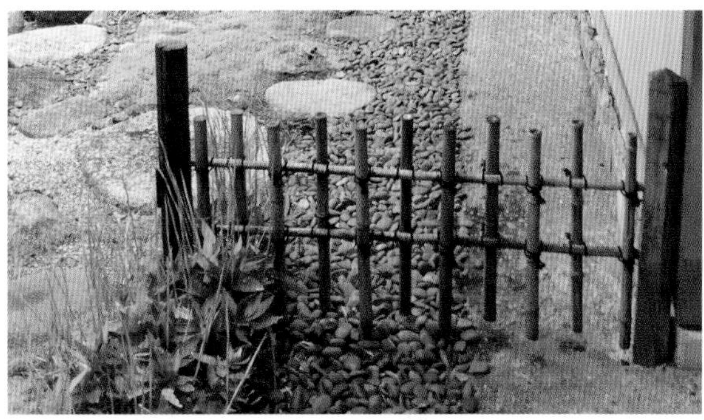

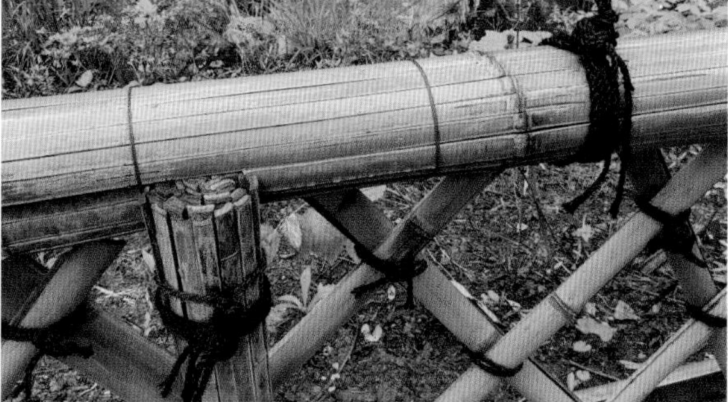

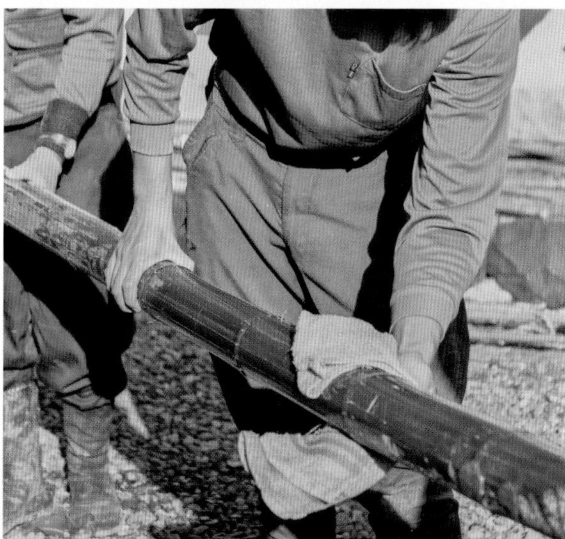

Above A small *yotsumegaki* fence consists of two narrow horizontal bamboo poles and a number of vertical poles tied front and back with *shuronawa* palm-fiber rope.

Right, top to bottom
A *katsuragaki* fence uses large bamboo cut in halves and tied either side of horizontal branches. The *koetsujigaki* fence wraps narrow bamboo strips around a wide core. Bamboo is usually heated and wiped to clean it but detergent in water will do.

included, such as a *katsuragaki* fence, or when it will be on the inside of a wall, it is not necessary to clean it first. To extend the life of bamboo, it can be heated to bring its natural oil to the surface. This oil can be used to polish the bamboo and help preserve it. Heating should be done over a coal brazier with the bamboo constantly rotated. As you rotate, the surface will begin to shine. Rub with a cloth a few times and return to heating. The green color will first turn dark and then light. The process is called *abura nuki*. The bamboo seller may be able to do this if requested. You can also use a propane torch, but take care not to burn the surface and brown it. It won't damage the bamboo but the color will become inconsistent. Bamboo that will be buried directly in the ground should be charred first.

Types of bamboo

There are many types of bamboo but in the garden we mostly use only several of them. Arrow bamboo (*yadake*) is narrow and straight. Traditionally used for fishing poles, we sometimes use it and black bamboo (*kurochiku*) in sleeve fences (*sodegaki*) because they are attractive. But their narrow size limits their applications. The types we use most are the so-called timber bamboos like *moso* and *madake*. These grow 40 to 50 feet (12 to 15 m) tall or more, and up to a diameter of 7 inches (18 cm). Madake is generally straighter and has a greater distance between the nodes, which makes it more useful. It also comes in narrow diameters (moso generally does not). Narrow bamboo of about 1 inch (2 to 3 cm) is lined up across the rafters of gates, waiting benches, etc. It is the first layer of roofing so it is visible when sitting or passing underneath.

Bamboo is used in the form of poles for structural applications as well as decorative ones such as in *tokonoma* alcoves where it is called a *tokobashira*. It is also used to create pipes for conducting water. For building structures, the main consideration is the size of the bamboo and its straightness. Tall bamboo will have slight curves but these can be straightened by bending in the opposite direction

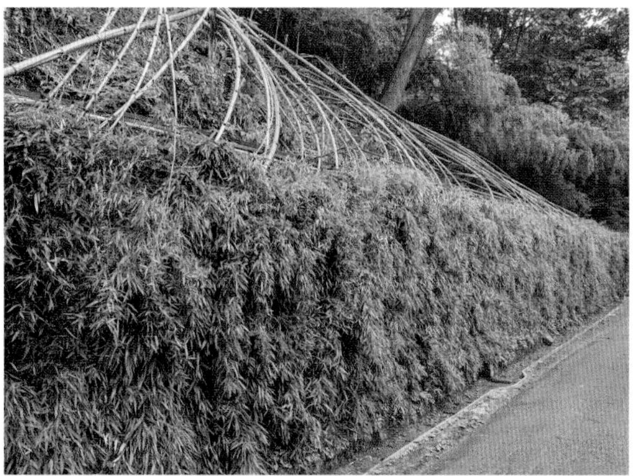

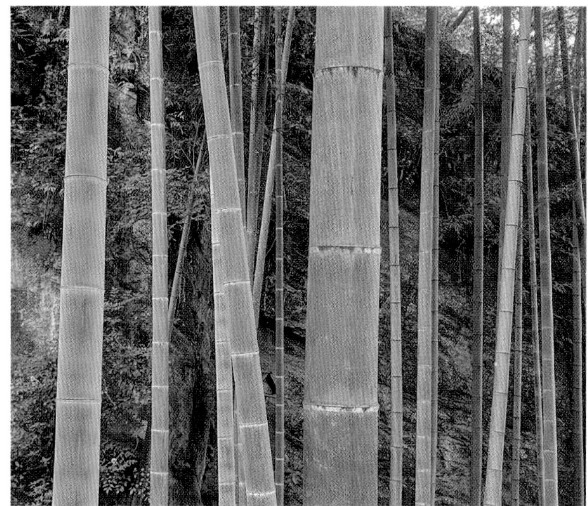

Top Originally, a *katsuragaki* is a living fence of bent bamboo tied to a frame, such as the one I made for Ryodenji Temple. Compare to the top photo on page 148.

Above A grove of *moso* bamboo at Ryodenji Temple.

Below A pipe saw is typically used to cut bamboo across the grain.

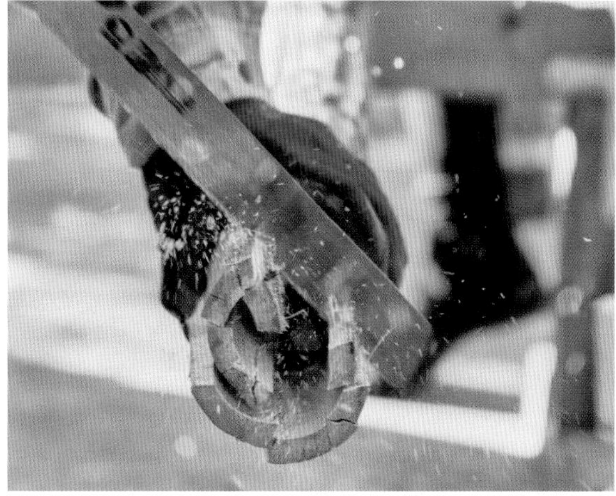

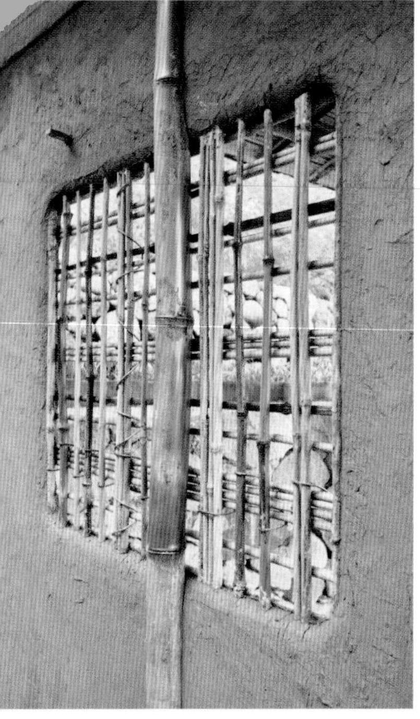

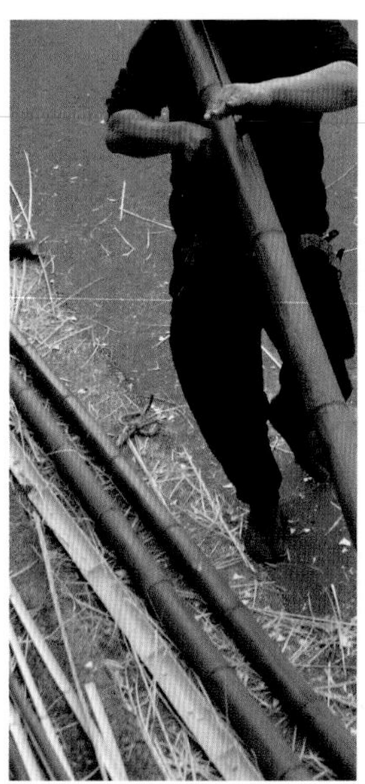

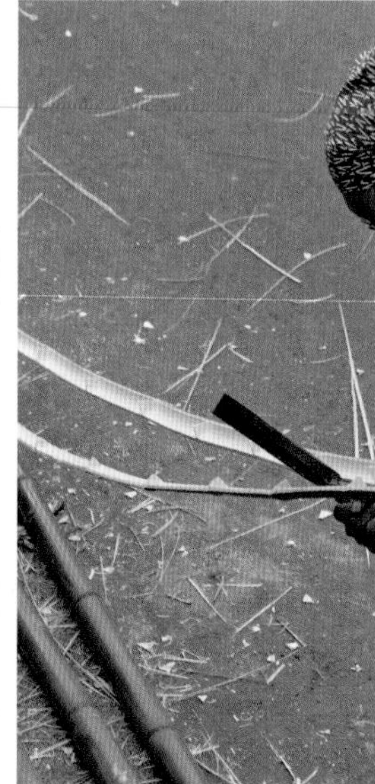

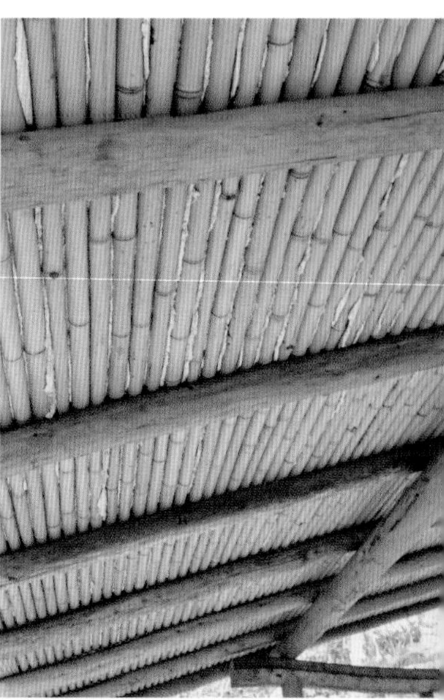

Above Tea-ceremony master Sen no Rikyu was the first to make the *shitaji mado*–style window by simply not filling part of the wall with clay.

Above, far right Whole bamboo is used in the ceiling of the waiting bench.

Above Bamboo is split lengthwise by centering the *nata* blade on one end and rapping it on the spine with a mallet or the palm of the hand.

especially while being heated. For decorative use, the beauty or rarity of the bamboo is a prime consideration. For example, turtle bamboo (*kame-take*) has a bulbous, twisting appearance, which is quite attractive when used as a single accent. Square bamboo that has been grown in a wooden form is novel.

Splitting and cutting bamboo

Most of the bamboo that we use in the garden is split anywhere from halves to twelfths. To split bamboo in half we use a mallet and a *nata,* a thick blade with a double bevel edge. Center the blade at one end of the bamboo and rap it with the mallet or palm of the hand. Once the bamboo is split through the first two or three nodes, pull it apart by hand. Hold it down on the ground with your foot and pull up on the top half. As you continue, the split will move off center. As one side becomes thinner, turn the bamboo over and pull on the other half to balance the split. Keep rotating until the split is complete. Short lengths will split without trouble. Alternatively, use the nata to split the bamboo from end to end. When you get to the end, there may be some shards, which need to be cleaned off with the nata. By the way, looking at the bamboo you will notice that the nodes at one end are close together. Several nodes at this end (*motoguchi*) should be cut off if it is hard to split.

Half-cut bamboo is often used in roofs in place of ceramic tile. It can be used to cap the ridge of the roof, or to cover the entire roof (see facing page, center left). To make an entire roof, lay pieces of half-split madake side by side on their backs (like turtles turned upside down). Add a second layer, turned to face downward, above the first, to cover all the joints. Hammer long, large head nails through both bamboos into the supporting wooden frame or substrate. Drill holes in the bamboo first. Cover the ridge with a long piece of madake closed at both ends, and notched to fit over the peak. This is not a waterproof roof and is intended mostly for exterior gates.

If you need to cut bamboo into smaller pieces

Below, top Nailing is done with care not to split the bamboo.

Below, center Half-cut bamboo, used as roofing tile on an entrance gate.

Below, bottom Bamboo is tied with *warabinawa* bracken-fern rope for a formal appearance.

Below, right Brushwood tied in bundles like torches and attached to a frame of bamboo and wood.

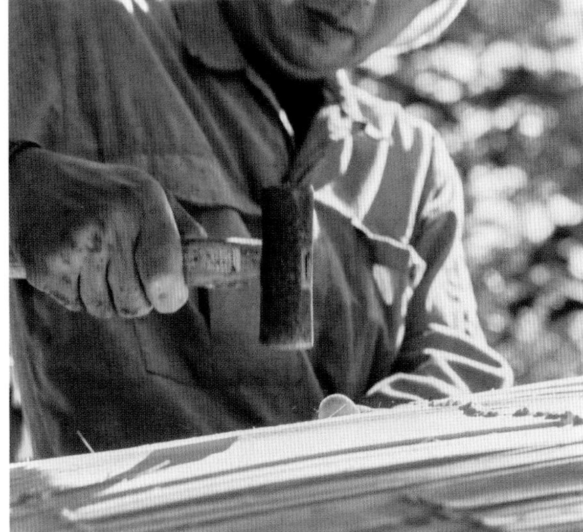

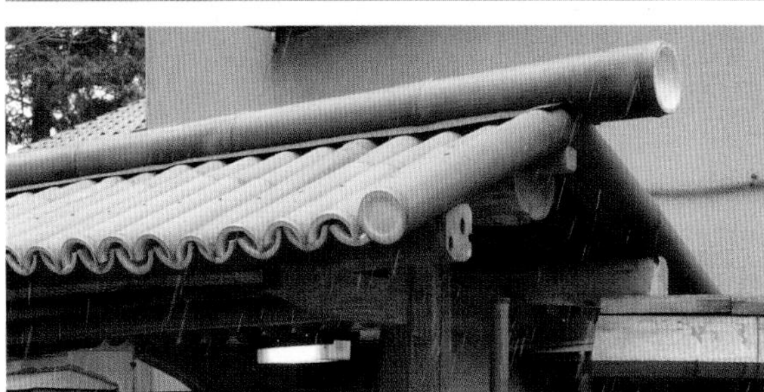

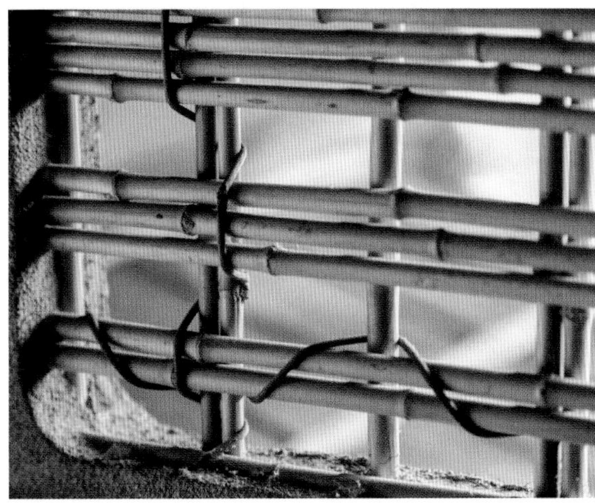

than halves it may be a good idea to use a commercial splitter. Put your splitter on one end of the bamboo and rap it with a mallet. After it gets going, hold the handles and bang the other end of the bamboo against the ground or the corner of a wall. After the split, you will need to remove the nodes with a rasp or knife. Another method is to use a piece of rebar before the bamboo is split. Rap the rebar at the end to punch through the first node. Pull the rebar up and down to clean out the node, and then continue through the next one. This is also the method to use when the bamboo will be used whole as a spout to transport water. For cutting the bamboo, a pipe saw or a saw with small teeth is best. A typical wood saw will tend to rip the bamboo, which is surprisingly stringy and difficult to cut. For shaping and trimming, a knife or file is used. If this all seems too daunting a task, bamboo can be purchased pre-split.

Tying, nailing and screwing

When constructing fences, palm-fiber rope (*shuro-nawa*) is used for tying the bamboo. Chocolate vine

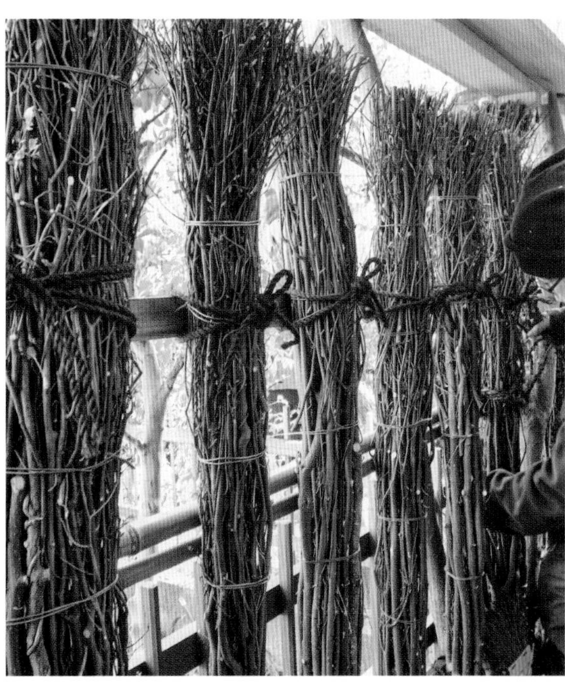

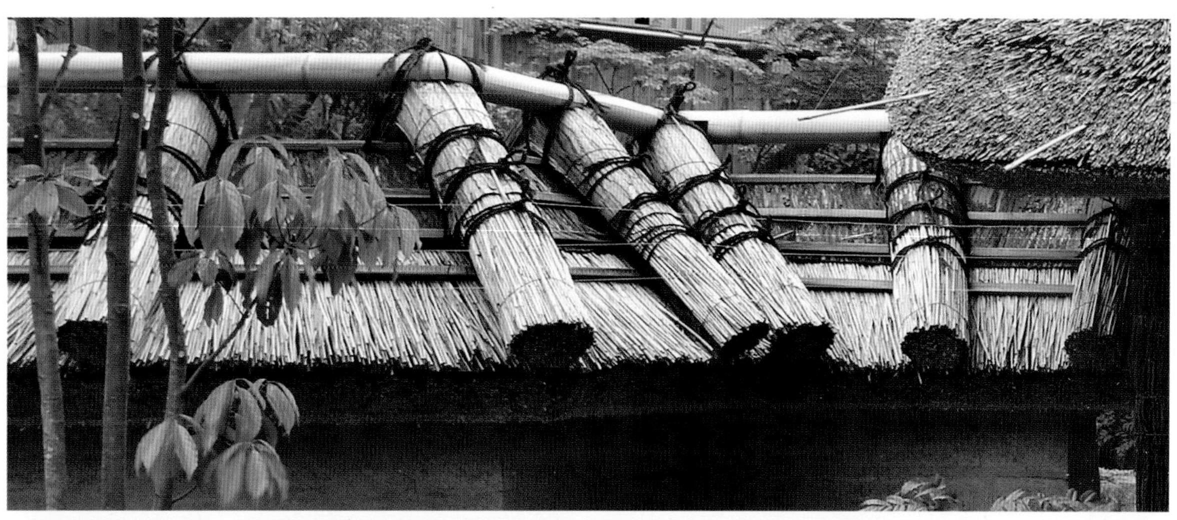

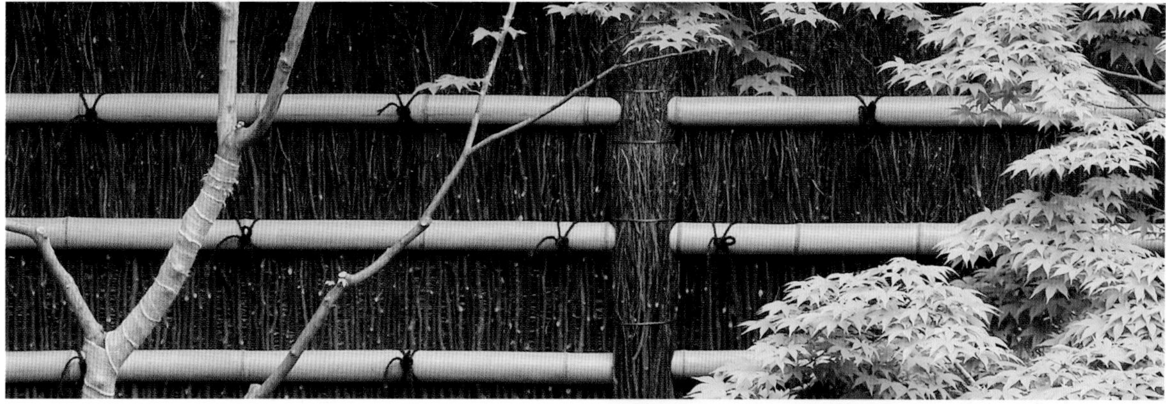

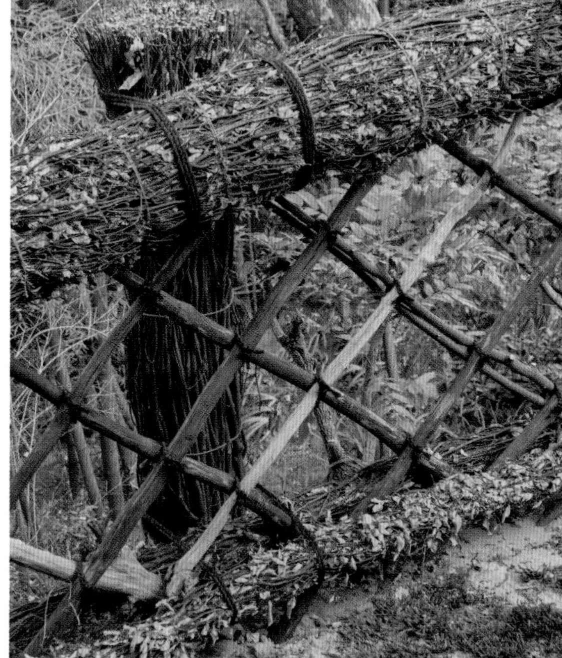

Top Miscanthus is used to cover the roof of the *hanchiku* wall and also tied in bundles to weigh it down.

Center Spicebush branches are held with half-cut bamboo in this *kuromojigaki* fence.

Right Normally made of bamboo, we made this *koetsujigaki* fence with spicebush and bush clover. The leaves are still attached but will eventually fall away.

Bamboo splits easily so, depending on the application, it needs to be drilled and nailed or screwed in place as it is here.

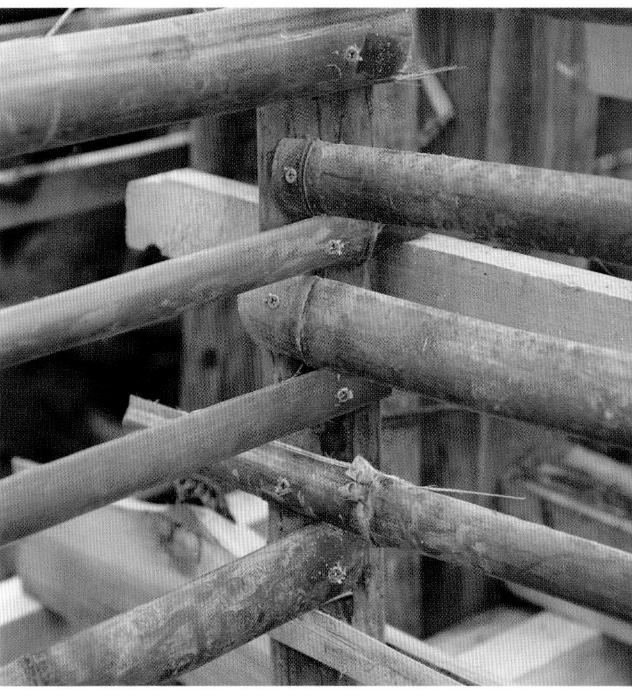

(*akebi*) and bracken fern (*warabinawa*) are also used. Shuronawa is first soaked in water, tied around the joints of the fence, and knotted on the front side. When it dries, it shrinks and tightens further than could be accomplished by hand. It is also used to tie bamboo frames that will later be covered with clay. For more formal or decorative work shuronawa dyed black (*somenawa*) is often used. The tying techniques can be mastered with some practice.

Wire is also used to tie fence joints and bundles of straw, pear wood, spicebush and bamboo used in fences. Wire is useful for strength and durability. We usually use aluminum wire or annealed copper wire (*namashi dosen*) which is soft and easily twisted and cut. Shuronawa is often used over the wire to disguise it. Wire is also used to attach ceramic tiles to the roof ridge of gates and walls. Japanese *kawara* curved ridge tiles each have a small hole in the top. The wire is attached to a nail head in the wood roof or a pipe running under the tile, pulled through the hole in the tile, and twisted into a knot.

Akebi vine is used like rope but mostly in more formal applications such as the windows of teahouses and waiting benches. Akebi is more difficult to twist and bend and should be soaked in hot water until it is pliable. Even then, it is not as pliable as rope and cannot be used for the tighter knots needed for fences. Warabinawa, made from the roots of the *warabi* bracken fern can be used like shuronawa but it is too expensive to be practical. Warabinawa is most famously used to tie around the stone placed on a footpath to indicate that entry is not permitted beyond that point. This is called a *sekimori ishi* and is typically found in tea gardens.

Screws, especially of stainless steel, are often used in the construction of wood and bamboo frames that will be covered in clay or other materials. In other words, screws are useful when they will not be seen. Nails are also indispensable for constructing frames and fences. In the case of bamboo, we often use nails with a wide head, or brass nails. The wide head helps to hold the springy bamboo, especially in split sections. Brass nails are used for their more formal appearance. Bamboo must be drilled before nailing because it cracks easily. When using screws with an impact driver it may not be necessary to drill first. Rapping the nail until it presses too hard against the bamboo will also make it crack. When the nail heads will be prominently displayed, be sure to line them up straight. When it is not desirable to see the nail head, tying shuronawa or somenawa over the top covers it nicely.

How to Make Some Simple Bamboo Fences

These fences are ideal for people who want to avoid a lot of knot tying.

Bamboo Kekkai

Basically, any type of barrier can be called *kekkai*—especially those which have no other specific name. Start with two wooden pegs about 2 feet (60 cm) long, and charred or coated to resist rot. The tops of the pegs should be flat or slightly concave. Hammer the pegs into the ground in a straight line around 32 inches (80 cm) apart. Cut a 4-foot (1.2-m) length of 4-inch (10-cm)-diameter bamboo. Attach the bamboo pole to the top of the pegs using 1½-inch (4-cm) strips of bamboo that have been heated and bent into a "U" shape. Wrap each strip around the bamboo pole, and screw it into the wooden peg. You can cover the screw head with shuronawa or use nails with decorative heads. Longer pegs can be used to make a taller border, up to about 36 inches (90 cm). Longer pegs need to be hammered deeper into the ground to ensure stability.

Bamboo Kekkai 2

The word *kekkai* is also used to denote a symbolic marker that tells the visitor that entry beyond a certain point is prohibited. It can be both a physical and spiritual distinction. The most famous kekkai of this type is the *sekimori ishi* often seen in the tea garden, simply a fist-size stone, wrapped with a piece of shuronawa or warabinawa bracken fern. But this type of kekkai can also be made of bamboo. I will mention two styles. The first is just two pieces of 4-inch (10-cm) diameter bamboo, cut to 1-foot lengths. Another piece, 30 inches (80 cm) long is laid across the shorter lengths and tied to them with rope to make a barrier that can easily be picked up and moved anywhere. Another style, which I think is more elegant, is the *namisaku kekkai*. This begins by splitting a 2-foot (60-cm) length of bamboo in half. Cut the ends at an angle as shown in the top photo on page 155. Take two 1 to 1½-inch (2 to 4 cm) strips of bamboo, about 2 feet (60 cm) long and bend them over heat. Mark the places on the half-cut bamboo where the bent bamboo strips will be inserted, and drill holes. Use a file to lengthen the holes enough to fit the ends of the bent bamboo. Overlap the two strips and tie with shuronawa.

Nanako fence

One of the simplest fences is actually just a border. Strips of bamboo about 1 x 36 inches (2.5 cm x 1 m) are arched and stuck in the ground. The arch will be about 8 inches (20 cm) high but up to 12 inches

Bottom, right and left Strips of bamboo are heated over charcoal and bent to shape.

Below The bent bamboo strips are used to secure a horizontal pole by nailing them to the sides of a wood peg pounded into the ground.

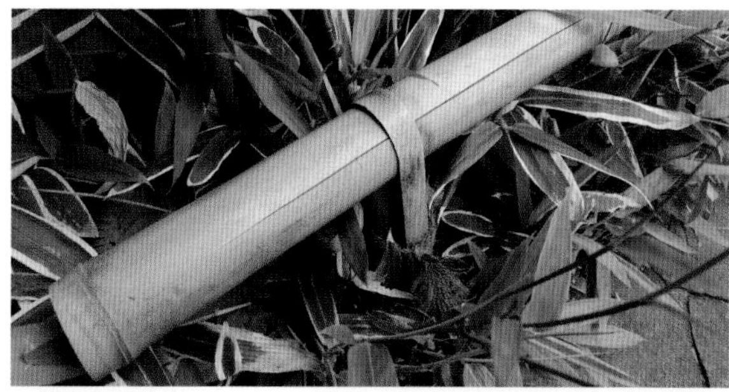

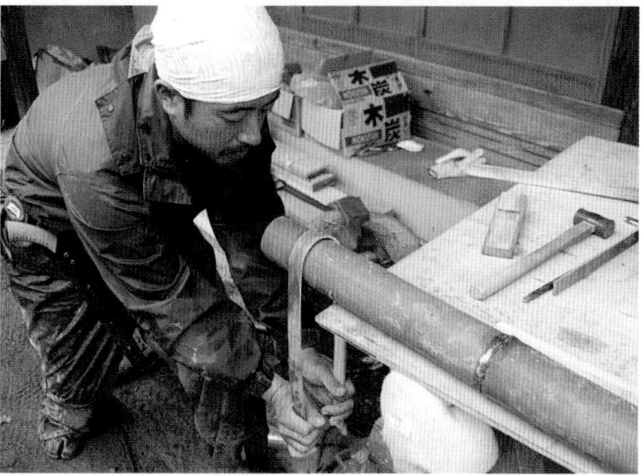

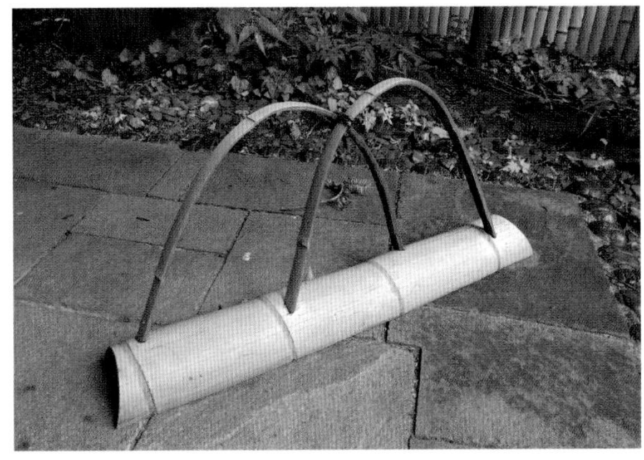

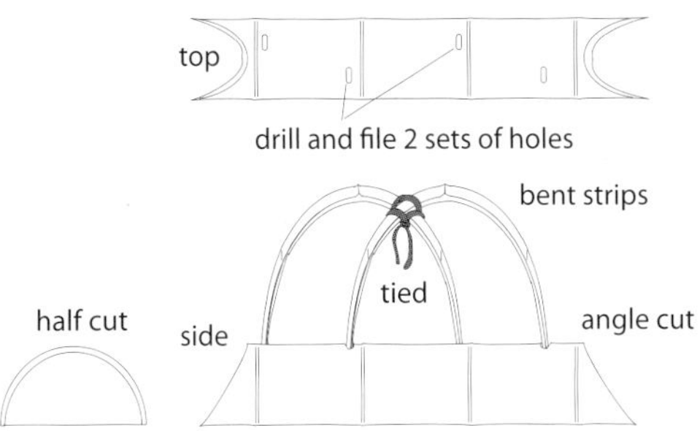

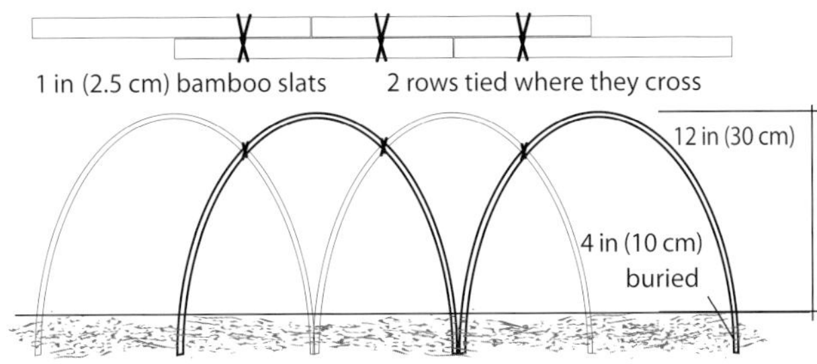

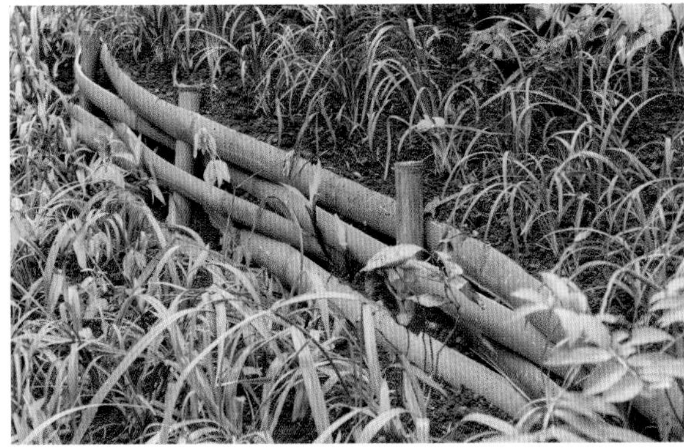

Top The *namisaku keikai* is a simple, elegant "barrier" that can be moved where needed.

Center A *nanako* fence is a simple border made from strips of bamboo.

Bottom A *shigara* is not unlike wattle fencing found anywhere in the world.

(30 cm) is okay, using longer strips. Use a knife to sharpen the ends like arrowheads. Push the ends into the dirt to overlap the next strips by about 4 inches (10 cm). The strips should be tied together with shuronowa or wire where they overlap near the top of the arch.

Shigara

This is not a fence but a temporary retaining wall. It is not intended to last but only help retain terraced dirt for several years until the plant's roots can hold the ground on their own. This is a quick and easy way to terrace a garden. It is attractive and inexpensive, and has the great merit of being flexible enough to form curves. Start by cutting 4-inch (10-cm)-diameter bamboo culms in 24 to 36-inch (60 to 90 cm) lengths to use as pegs. The culms should be closed on top and bottom. The length depends on the height of the retaining wall, which should be a maximum of about 16 inches (41 cm). The pegs should be hammered into the ground about 24 inches (60 cm) apart. Take long and wide bamboo poles (the maximum width and length you can find is good) and split them into quarters. Each strip will be about 4 inches (10 cm) wide. Start at the bottom of the pegs and weave the split bamboo between the front and the back of adjacent pegs. Finish on a peg and screw the strip in place. Add another strip and continue the row until you have the necessary length. Then, go back to the beginning and insert another strip directly above the first. The second strip begins and ends on the opposite side of the peg than the first. In this way, we create a sort of weave. Continue with two more strips and begin backfilling and planting.

LIST OF PLANTS APPEARING IN THIS BOOK

ENGLISH / JAPANESE / SCIENTIFIC

azalea **satsuki** *Rhododendron indicum*
bald cypress **nama sugi** *Taxodium distichum*
bamboo-leaf oak **shirakashi** *Quercus myrsinaefolia*
bay laurel **tabu no ki** *Machilus thunbergii*
bird-lime holly **mochi no ki** *Ilex integra*
bishop's hat **ikariso** *Epimedium grandiflorum var. thunbergianum*
black pine **kuromatsu** *Pinus thunbergii*
camellia otome **otome tsubaki** *Camellia japonica var. decumbens*
camellia sasanqua **sazanka** *Camellia sasanqua*
camphor **kusunoki** *Cinnamomum camphora*
cape jasmine **kuchinashi** *Gardenia jasminoides*
Chinese hackberry **enoki** *Celtis sinensis var. japonica*
Chinese juniper **ibuki** *Juniperus chinensis*
coral (Christmas) berry **manryo** *Ardisia crenata*
crape myrtle **sarusuberi** *Langerstroemia inica*
crested iris **shaga** *Iris japonica*
dwarf mondo grass (dragon's beard) **ryu no hige** *Ophiopogon japonicus*
evergreen azalea **tsutsuji** *Rhododendron tsutsusi*
evergreen camellia **kan tsubaki** *Camellia hiemalis*
false Japanese cleyera **mokkoku** *Ternstroemia gymnanthera*
fish pole bamboo **hote ichiku** *Phyllostachys aurea*
flowering cherry **sakura** *Prunus serrulata*
flowering dogwood **hanamizuki** *Cornus florida*
haircap moss **sugigoke** *Polytrichum*
Himalayan cedar **himalaya sugi** *Cedrus deodara*
holly osmanthus **hiragi mokusei** *Osmanthus heterophyllus*
horsetail **tokusa** *Equisetum*
hydrangea **ajisai** *Hydrangea spp.*
iron plant **haran** *Aspidistra elatior*
Japanese andromeda **asebi** *Pieris japonica*
Japanese arailia "paperplant" **yatsude** *Fatsia japonica*
Japanese aster **hani** *Kalimeris pinnatifica*
Japanese bitter orange **sudachi** *Citrus sudachi*
Japanese camellia **tsubaki** *Camellia japonica var hortensis*
Japanese cleyera **sakaki** *Cleyera japonica*
Japanese enkianthus **dodan tsutsuji** *Enkianthus perulatus*
Japanese eurya **hisakaki** *Eurya japonica*
Japanese flowering plum **ume** *Prunus mume*
Japanese holly fern **oniyabu sotetsu** *Aspidium falcatum (Cyrtomium falcatum)*
Japanese mahonia **hiragi nanten** *Mahonia japonica*
Japanese maple **iroha momiji** *Acer palmatum*
Japanese maple **yama momiji** *Acer matsumurae*
Japanese (osaka) maple **osakazuki momiji** *Acer palmatum "osakazuki"*
Japanese (osmunda) royal fern **zenmai** *Osmunda japonica*
Japanese photinia galbra "red robin" **beni kanamemochi** *Photinia glabra*
Japanese privet **nezumimochi** *Ligustrum japonicum*
Japanese sago palm **sotetsu** *Cycas revoluta*
Japanese stewartia **natsu tsubaki** *Stewartia pseudo-camellia*
Japanese stone oak **matebashi** *Lithocarpus edulis*
Japanese strawberry dogwood **yamaboshi** *Cornus kousa*
Japanese sweetflag **sekisho** *Acorus gramineus*
Japanese torreya (nutmeg yew) **kaya** *Torreya nucifera*
Japanese ume plum **shirokaga** *Prunus mume "shirokaga"*
Japanese white-bark magnolia **hounoki** *Magnolia obovata*
Japanese winterberry **umemodoki** *Iles serrata var sieboldii*
Japanese yew **inumaki** *Podocarpus macrophyllus*
kobushi magnolia **kobushi** *Magnolia kobus*
kumquat **kinkan** *Fortunella sp.*
lacquer tree **urushi no ki** *Toxicodendron vernicifluum*
lemon **lemon** *Citrus*
leopard plant **otsuwabuki** *Farfugium japonicum*
linden arrowwood **kamazumi** *Viburnum dilatatum*
magnolia **mokuren** *Magnolia quinquepeta*
marlberry **yabukoji** *Ardisia japonica*
mondo grass **oba ryu no hige** *Ophiopogon japonicus*
mono maple **itaya kaede** *Acer mono Maxim*
mountain camellia **yama tsubaki** *Camellia japonica*
mountain enkianthus **yama tsutsuji** *Enkianthus campanulatus*
mountain fern **yama itachi shida** *Dryopteris bissetiana*
mountain (pincushion) moss **yamagoke** *Leucobryum glaucum*
Nomura maple **nomura momiji** *Acer palmatum var. amoenum cv. Sanguineum*
orange **mikan** *Citrus unshiu*
peony **shakuyaku** *Paeonia lactiflora*
persimmon **kaki no ki** *Diospyros kaki*
red pine **akamatsu** *Pinus deniflora*
red plum **kobai ume** *Prunus mume "kobai"*
ring-cupped oak **arakashi** *Quercus glauca*
rose of Sharon **mukuge** *Hibiscus syriacus*
ruscus-leaved bamboo **okamezasa** *Shibataea kumasasa*
sarcandra glabra **senryo** *Sarcandra glabra*
spicebush **kuromoji** *Lindera umbellata*
susuki grass **kaya** *Miscanthus sinensis*
sweet osmanthus **kinmokusei** *Osmanthus aurantus*
sweet viburnum **sangoju** *Viburnum odoratissimum var. awabuki*
tokiwa dogwood **tokiwa** *Cornus hongkongensis*
ubame oak **ubamegashi** *Quercus phillyraeoides*
weeping cherry **shidare zakura** *Cerasus spachiana*
weeping maple **shidare momiji** *Acer palmatum Dissectum*
weeping plum **shidare ume** *Prunus mume Pendula*
white oak **shirakashi** *Quercus myrsinifolia*
wisteria **fuji** *Wisteria floribunda*
zelkova **keiyaki** *Zelkova Serrata*

INDEX

abura nuki, bamboo cleaning method 148–49
akatsuchi (volcanic loam), 11, 26, 31, 36, 60, 65, 81, 95, 144, 145
amigasa mon gate, 42–47, 62, 91, 93, 101, 103, 104, 106
araidashi (exposed aggregate), 25, 39–40, 41, 46, 58, 60, 61, 63–64, 84, 93–94, 118, 119, 125, 133–34, 142
arakida (clay-rich soil), 61, 71, 144, 145
azumaya (gazebo), 66–70

bamboo: cleaning, 148–49; *kekkai* (barrier), 153–54; *nanako* fence, 154–55; simple fences, 153–55; splitting/cutting, 150–51; structural applications of, 149–50; tying/nailing/screwing, 151–53; types of, 149–50
barrier (*kekkai*), 153–54
black soil (*kurotsuchi*), 95
"borrowed scenery" (*shakkei*); backyard, 51, 53–54; design principle, 12–13; in entranceway-theme garden, 23; refreshment-theme garden, 110, 113
bridge: constructing, 71, 80–82; husband-and-wife (*meoto*) bridge 30, 31; practical purposes of, 31; seesaw bridge, 136–37; split stone bridge, 137; stone bridges, 136–37; symbolism of, 31. *See also* earthen bridge
brushwood fence (*shibagaki*), 68, 104–5

caps (*hashigeta*), 78–79
carp, fish (*koi*), 28–31, 52, 139
chaniwa (tea garden), 42, 62, 122
chashitsu (teahouse), 102, 122
chaya (teahouse), 99
chi-sui-kafuu-kuu (Earth-Water-Fire-Wind-Void), design principle, 13
chozubachi (water basin), 16, 40, 41,56, 60, 109, 134–35, 136
clay: floors, 142–43; *doma*, 143; *fukakusa*-style floor, 143; rammed-earth wall (*hanchiku*), 83, 145–46, 152; *sunazuri* clay mixture, 144; surfacing, 146–47; tamped (*tataki*), 144–45; walls (*dobei*), 143–44, 146. *See also* clay wall
clay-rich soil (*arakida*), 61, 71, 144, 145
clay wall (*dobei*), 21, 33, 54, 89, 93–95, 106, 110,111, 115–16, 143–44, 146; *tsubashira kabe*, 107
"cloth falls" (*nuno-ochi*), 139
corridor (*engawa*), 12, 14, 16, 88–89
courtyard garden (*tsuboniwa*), 16, 62, 97, 108–9, 112, 114–17, 118–21
covered waiting bench (*koshikake machiai*), 61, 101, 125; arranging for, 102–3; constructing, 62–65
crossbeams (*keta*), 80–81
cypress wood (*sabi-maruta*), 84

Daitokuji Temple, 99, 140–41
Dazaifu Tenmangu Shrine, 73
deciduous tree garden (*zokibayashi*), 21, 62
deck, exterior (*nure-en*), 14, 16, 21, 49, 55, 112–13
design, principles for, 11–15
dobashira (earthen bridge), 69; large, 78–81; small, 71
dobei (clay wall), 21, 33, 54, 89, 93–95, 106, 110,111, 115–16, 143–44, 146
doma, floor style, 143
doors: *kugurido*, 107; sliding (*fusuma*), 122; wood plank (*tsunodo; sarudo*), 84, 107
double meaning (*mitate*), design principle, 12, 62
Dragon's Gate falls (*ryumonbaku*), 86, 139
drawing room (*shoin zukuri*), 99

Earth-Water-Fire-Wind-Void (*chi-sui-kafuu-kuu*), design principle, 13
earthen bridge (*dobashira*), 69; large, 78–81; small, 71
enclosure, design principle, 13
engawa (interior porch or corridor), 12, 14, 16, 88–89Engei High School (Tokyo Metropolitan Horticultural High School), 7
enkinkan (perspective), 112
ensaki chozubachi (water-basin stone), 89, 91
entranceway: *hikido*, 104; terrace entrance, 34–37; open driveway garden, 24–27; rice-terrace style (*tanada fu*), 38–41. See also *amigasa mon* gate
exposed aggregate (*araidashi*), 25, 39–40, 41, 46, 58, 60, 61, 63–64, 84, 93–94, 118, 119, 125, 133–34, 142

farmhouse (*minka*), 84, 104–5
fence. bamboo-branch fence (*takehogaki*), 99–101; brushwood fence (*shibagaki*), 68, 104–5; *katsuragaki*, 24, 28, 109, 111–12, 120, 148–49; *kekkai* (barrier), 153–54; *kenninjigaki*, 27; *koetsujigaki*, 148, 152; *kuromojigaki*, 84, 152; *namisaku kekkai*, 154, 155; *nanako* fence, 154–55; sleeve fence (*sodegaki*), 109, 149; *teppogaki*, 87; torch fence (*taimatsugaki*), 125; vertical split-bamboo (*tokusazuke*) fence, 83; *yotsumegaki* fence, 101, 148
feng shui, 29
finished/unfinished, design principle, 15
flat garden style (*hiraniwa*), 91
Fujimori, Meihosai, 124–25
fukakusa clay floor style, 143
fukiyose okarikomi, hedge style, 68
fusuma (sliding doors), 122
fuyodo (leaf mulch), 26, 36, 95

garden–home connection, design principle, 14
gates: *hikido*, 104; *shiorido*, 66; *sukiyamon*, 93; See also *amigasa mon* gate
gazebo (*azumaya*), 66–70
gojunoto (pagoda), 85
gorinto (pagoda), 13
granite, decomposed (*masatsuchi*), 30–31, 81, 144, 145
guest, primary, at tea ceremony (*shokyaku*) 103
gutters, stone, 30, 31, 35–37, 50, 52, 140

half-wall (*koshikabe*), 68
hanchiku (rammed-earth wall), 83, 145–46, 152
hashigeta (caps), 78–70
hatake no tsuchi (rice paddy soil), 60
hedge: *fukiyose o-karikomi*, 68; *ikegaki*, 112; ubame oak, 35–37; 112
hide-and-reveal (*miekakure*), 73; as design principle, 12
hikido entrance, 104
hill and pond garden (*tsukiyama*), 31, 62
hiraniwa (flat garden style), 91
hishaku (ladle), 135
history, design principle, 14
honzen ryori (cuisine style), 100
host, of tea ceremony (*teishu*), 103
hut (*soan*), 99

Ikkyu, 99
Ingen, 99–100
inlets, 30, 50, 52, 76. *See also* water
inner tea garden (*naka roji*), 114
ishidoi, *see* gutters, stone

jakago (snake baskets), 73, 76–77

kaiseki ryori (full-course meal), 98
kametake (turtle bamboo), 150
karesansui (stone-and-sand garden), 16, 49, 62, 97, 136
Katsura Imperial Villa, 79, 84, 108
kawara (ceramic roof tiles), 47, 110, 129, 134, 153
kawazuna (river sand), 61
kayushiki teien (stroll garden), 62
keta (crossbeams), 80–81
kirei-sabi, design style, 93–94
Kobori, Enshu, 42, 91, 93, 124
Kokin Wakashu poetry collection, 88
komisen (square pin), 80, 81
koi carp, 28–31, 52, 139
koshikake machiai (covered waiting bench), 61, 101, 125; arranging for, 102–3; constructing, 62–65
kugurido door, 107
kurotsuchi (black soil), 95
kusabi (wedges), 79
Kyoto Imperial Palace, 79

ladle (*hishaku*), 135
lanterns: *ishidoro* (stone lantern), 91, 97, 109; Kasuga, 91, 107; *nekoashi yukimi doro* (snow-viewing lantern), 52–53; *okidoro*, 105 107; Oribe, 91; Taihei, 52; *toro*, 56; *yukimi* 116.
last guest at tea ceremony (*tsume*), 103
laws, (knowing) design principle, 15
leaf mulch (*fuyodo*), 26, 36, 95
limestone (*sekkai*), 30, 81, 144

Manpukuji Temple, 100
Manyoshu poetry collection, 108
masatsuchi (decomposed granite), 30–31, 81, 144, 145
meisho, design principle, 12

meoto (husband-and-wife) bridge, 30, 31
miekakure hide-and-reveal design principle, 12, 73
miharashi dai (observation deck), 61
miniaturized landscape (*shukukei*), 12
minka (farmhouse), 84, 104–5
misogi (purification by water), 76
mitate, design principle, 12, 62
Miyukimon Gate, 83–84
mizubachi. See *chozubachi*
mizutani (shallow pond), 69
mizuya ("water house"), 92
"monk's hat" gate. See *amigasa mon*
mortar, 52, 61, 71, 126–34, 136, 140, 141, 143
mortises, open slot (*sammai-gumi*), 80
Mt. Sumeru, stone depiction of (*shumisenshiki iwagumi*), 85–86
Murata, Juko, 99
Mushanokojisenke school of tea, 42, 124
Myojo-in Temple, 82–87

nagare (stream), 56, 69
naka roji (inner tea garden), 114
namashi dosen (wire), 153
nata blade, 150
nijiriguchi teahouse entrance, 39, 100, 107, 117, 122
niju yane (second roof), 46
Niwa, Teizo, 7
Noami, 99
nobedan. See walkway
nodate chakai (outdoor tea ceremony), 104–5
nuki (tie beams), 79, 80, 81
numbers, design principle, 11
nuno-ochi ("cloth falls"), 139
nunozumi wall construction pattern, 126
nure-en (exterior deck), 14, 16, 21, 49, 55, 112–13

observation deck (*miharashi dai*), 61
Omotesenke school of tea, 124
outdoor tea ceremony (*nodate chakai*), 104–5
outer tea garden (*soto roji*), 101, 114
overflow gabions. *See* snake baskets

pagoda: *gojunoto*, 85; *gorinto* 13
permanent, design principle, 13
perspective (*enkinkan*), 112
philosophy, design principle, 14
pipes, unconventional use of, 59–60
ponds, 9, 28–33, 50–53, 69, 75–76, 79, 136–38, 141
pond, shallow (*mizutani*), 69
porch, interior (*engawa*), 12, 14, 16, 88–89
purification by water (*misogi*), 76

rapids (*seochi*), 52
Raymond, Antonin, 9
rebar, 51, 129–30, 151
rice paddy soil (*hatake no tsuchi*), 60
rice-terrace style (*tanada fu*) garden, 38–41
river sand (*kawazuna*), 61
roji (tea garden), 62, 97, 101–3, 114, 122
roof tiles, ceramic (*kawara*), 47, 110, 129, 134, 153
rope: bracken-fern (*warabinawa*), 151, 153, 154; black palm-fiber (*somenawa*), 153; palm-fiber (*shuronawa*), 65, 148, 151–154
"rough wall" (*arakabe*), 146
Ryodenji Temple, 123–24, 149
ryumonbaku ("Dragon's Gate" falls), 86, 139
ryureishiki tea room, 100

sabi-maruta (cypress wood), 84
Saito, Katsuo, 7, 9, 97
Sakuteiki garden-making treatise, 108
sammai-gumi (open-slot mortises), 80
sandbags, 60
sarudo wood plank door, 84, 107
seaweed glue (*tsunomata*), 46, 64
second roof (*niju yane*), 46
Sen no Rikyu, 97, 99, 122–23, 150
seochi (rapids), 52
sekkai (limestone), 30, 81, 144
shakkei ("borrowed scenery"); backyard, 51, 53–54; design principle, 12–13; in entranceway-theme garden, 23; refreshment-theme garden, 110, 113
shigara temporary retaining wall, 155
shinden zukuri, architecture style, 97
shitaji mado window, 65, 150
shoin zukuri (drawing room), 99
shokyaku (primary guest at tea ceremony) 103
Shomei, book, 124
shukukei (miniaturized landscape), 12
shuronawa (palm-fiber rope), 65, 148, 151–154
size, design principle, 12
sled, 141
snake baskets (*jakago*), 73, 76–77
snow cover, straw (*yukigakoi)*, 107
soan (hut), 99
sochiku, compacted layers of soil, 145
somenawa (black palm-fiber rope), 153
soto roji (outer tea garden), 101, 114
spirit/technique, design principle, 15
square pin (*komisen*), 80, 81
stepping stones, 22–23, 32,, 52, 53, 56, 61, 65, 84, 87, 94, 100, 103, 106, 112, 116, 122, 125, 132
stepping stone bridge (*sawatobi*), 74
stone-and-sand garden (*karesansui*), 16, 49, 62, 97, 136
stone gutters (*ishidoi*), 140
stones, arrangements: 137–38; Buddhist triad stones (*sanzonseki*), 85, 86, 137; fitting, 131; general terms, 127; *hashibasami*, 136; *ishigumi*, stone arrangement, 137; *iwagumi*, stone arrangement, 137; *koshikake machiai* arrangement, 102–3; *meoto* bridge, 30, 31; moving/lifting stones, 141; setting horizontally, 29; stepping stones (*tobi ishi*), 132; stone bridges (*ishibashi*), 136–37; stone gutters (*ishidoi*), 140; walkways (*nobedan*), 133–34; wash basin (*chozubachi*), 134–36; waterfall arrangement, 138–40
stones, decorative: boat stone (*funaishi*), 29, 33, 73, 138, 140–41; "crane" stones, 12, 137–38; *kazari ishi*, 138; *keishoseki*, 113, 138; pond-edge stones (*gogan*), 32; *shumisenshiki iwagumi* (stone depiction of Mt. Sumeru) 85–86; *suteishi*, 138; "turtle" stones, 12, 137–38
stones, types of: attendant stones (*kyojiseki*), 137; ballast stones, 89–91; bluish stone (*makuro ishi*), 106; boundary-guard stone (*sekimori ishi*), 153–54; candlestick stone (*teshoku ishi*), 107, 135; carp stone (*rigyoseki*), 139; dividing stone (*fumiwaki ishi*), 132; front stone (*maeishi*), 135; *fudoseki*, 14, 30, 139; guardian stone (*shugoseki*), 14; Kiso stone, 115, 116; *kurama ishi* stone, 84, 109; "label stone" (*tanzaku ishi*), 11, 93, 116, 133; limestone rock (*sekkaiseki*), 132; marital harmony stones (*meotoseki*), 14; mirror stone (*kagami ishi*), 139; *nejime ishi*, 138; *obi ishi*, 133; post stones, 63, 65; river stone, 31, 44, 61, 62, 74, 94, 134; rounded stones (*ise jari*), 52; shoe-removal stone (*kutsunugi ishi*), 11, 24, 86, 105, 112, 125; standing stone (*chusonseki*), 137; supporting stone (*hikae ishi*), 132; sword-hanging stone (*katanakake ishi*), 125; 132; *tsukuba ishi* stone, 67, 109; volcanic tuff (*oyaishi*), 34, 35 139; warm-water stone (*yuoke ishi*), 135; water-basin stone (*ensaki chozubachi*), 89, 91; water-dividing stone (*mizuwake ishi*), 140
stone walls: combination walls, 130; double-sided, 128–29; single-sided, 130; tall, 130
stream (*nagare*), 56, 69
stroll garden (*kayushiki teien*), 62
Sugawara, Michizane, 72
suikinkutsu (water harp), 94, 109, 112, 135–36
sukiya, architectural style, 122, 124
sukiya daiku carpenter, 122, 124–125
sunazuri (clay mixture), 144
sunlight, design principle, 13
symmetry, design principle, 11

Takahashi, Rikyo, 7
Takeno, Joo, 99
Tale of Genji, The, 15, 108
tamped clay (*tataki*), 35, 71, 73, 75, 144–45
tanada fu (rice-terrace style garden), 38–41
tataki (tamped clay), 35, 71, 73, 75, 144–45
tea ceremony, 12, 65, 98–107, 112, 114, 122–23
tea garden (*chaniwa/roji*), 42, 62, 91, 97, 99, 101–3, 114, 117, 122; for urban farmhouse, 104–7.
teahouse (*chaya/chashitsu*), 99, 102; reconstructing, 122–25
teishu (tea ceremony host), 103
Tenjin (god), 72–73
Tenyo-in Temple, 88–91
tie beams (*nuki*), 79, 80, 81
tobi ishi. See stepping stones

Tokyo Metropolitan Horticultural High School (Engei High School), 7
tomomachi (waiting bench), 106
tools: *koyasuke* (type of hammer), 130–31; *setto* (sledgehammer), 130–31
transient, design principle, 13
tsubashira kabe (clay wall), 107
tsuboniwa (courtyard garden), 16, 62, 97, 108–9, 112, 114–17, 118–21
tsukiyama (hill and pond garden), 31, 62
tsukubai (water-basin arrangement), 22–23, 40, 94–95, 100, 102–3, 106–7, 112, 116, 121, 122, 125–26, 134; construction, 135
tsume (last guest at tea ceremony), 103
tsunodo (wood plank door), 84, 107
tsunomata (seaweed glue), 46, 64
turtle bamboo (*kametake*), 150

Urasenke school of tea, 100, 114, 124, 135
view, design principle, 12
visibility, design principle, 14
volcanic loam (*akatsuchi*), 11, 26, 31, 36, 60, 65, 81, 95, 144, 145
wabi cha, tea-ceremony aesthetic, 99
waiting area of tea garden, inside, (*yoritsuki*) 101, 103
waiting bench (*tomomachi*), 106. *See also* covered waiting bench
walkway (*nobedan*), 21, 32, 93–95, 68–69, 75, 100, 103, 106–7, 112, 132; construction methods, 133–34
walls: clay wall (*dobei*), 21, 33, 54, 89, 93, 106, 146; construction methods, 126–127; half wall (*koshikabe*), 68–69; *neribei*, 25, 26; *nuri*, 146; *nunozumi* wall construction pattern, 126; rammed-earth wall (*hanchiku*), 83, 145–46, 152; retaining wall, temporary (*shigara*), 155
"rough wall"(*arakabe*), 146; *tsubashira kabe*, 107–8. *See also* stone walls
wall construction methods: *dobei*, 143–44; *karatsumi*, 127; *kuzurezumi*, 127; *nozurazumi*, 127
warabinawa bracken-fern rope, 151, 153, 154
water: capturing excess water, 60; flow direction, 13, 30; gravel stand-in, 12; knowing law, 15; overflow of, 75, 94, 140; presence of, 16; runoff, 15, 59; setting stones for, 32; symbolizing dragons, 30; symbolism, 14; "water house" (*mizuya*), 92
water basin (*chozubachi*), 16, 40, 41,56, 60, 109, 134–35, 136
water-basin arrangement/setting. See *tsukubai*
water-basin stone (*ensaki chozubachi*), 89, 91
waterfalls, 14, 28, 32, 52, 56, 86, 122, 138–40
water flow, design principle, 13
water harp (*suikinkutsu*), 94, 109, 112, 135–36
"water house" (*mizuya*), 92
wedges (*kusabi*), 79
well-being, design principle, 14–15
window (*shitaji mado*), 65, 150
wire (*namashi dosen*), 153

yoritsuki inside waiting area of tea garden, 101, 103
Yoshinaga, Yoshinobu, 7
Yoshinogari burial mound, 145
yukigakoi (straw snow cover), 107
Yushima Tenmangu Shrine, 72–77; 137; 159

zokibayashi (deciduous tree garden), 21, 62

GARDENS IN THIS BOOK THAT CAN BE VISITED

Buddha's Mountain Retreat of Moss and Stone (page 82)
Myojo-in Temple: 4-9-8 Shibakoen, Minato-ku, Tokyo 105-0011
• Not open to the public but may be viewed by appointment.

Garden of the Bell Tower (page 92)
Jutokuji Temple, 1282 Ueuchi, Kuki City, Saitama Prefecture 340-0211 • Open to the public. Accessible only by car.

The Garden of Plum Blossoms and Students' Prayers (page 72)
Yushima Tenmangu Shrine, 3-30-1 Yushima, Bunkyo-ku, Tokyo 113-0034 • Open to the public. The garden can be viewed from three sides but permission is required to enter it. Closes at 8 pm.

Garden for a Tea Get-together (page 98)
Kokonotsuido (tearooms): 1319 Tayacho, Sakae-ku, Yokohama 244-0844 • Open by reservation to customers. Tel: 045-851-6121 (Japanese only).

The Landslide that Became a Garden (page 58)
House of Flavors café: 3-2-10 Kamakurayama, Kamakura, Kanagawa Prefecture 248-0031
• Garden can be viewed by customers of the café by appointment. Accessible only by car. 11 am to 5 pm. Closed Wed. Tel: 0467-31-2636 (Japanese only).

The Tatsutagawa River Garden (page 88)
Tenyo-in Temple, 2-2-3 Shibakoen, Tokyo 105-0011
• Not open to the public but may be viewed by appointment.

A Tsuboniwa for Visvim (page 118)
Visvim, 1-22-1 Aobadai, Meguro-ku, Tokyo 153-0042
• Open to the public, access from inside the shop. Closes at 8 pm.

ACKNOWLEDGMENTS

Sadao Yasumoro has been building and designing gardens ever since he began assisting various professors while attending Tokyo Metropolitan High School, where he graduated in 1957. He is still creating and maintaining gardens today. He would like to thank all the people who supported him in his education and in his career throughout the years. He would also like to thank Joseph Cali, Hironori Tomino, and everyone else involved in the publication of this book.

Joseph Cali would like to acknowledge his coauthor and teacher of over twenty years, Sadao Yasumoro. He would also like to acknowledge Tatsuya Yamaguchi for his help with the gardens of Yushima Tenjin and Jutokuji, as well all the garden owners who graciously allowed the authors into their homes to photograph their gardens, and for sharing their stories. Finally, he would like to acknowledge Hironori Tomino who began photographing Yasumoro-sensei's work long before this book was conceived.

"Books to Span the East and West"

Tuttle Publishing was founded in 1832 in the small New England town of Rutland, Vermont (USA). Our core values remain as strong today as they were then—to publish best-in-class books which bring people together one page at a time. In 1948, we established a publishing outpost in Japan—and Tuttle is now a leader in publishing English-language books about the arts, languages and cultures of Asia. The world has become a much smaller place today and Asia's economic and cultural influence has grown. Yet the need for meaningful dialogue and information about this diverse region has never been greater. Over the past seven decades, Tuttle has published thousands of books on subjects ranging from martial arts and paper crafts to language learning and literature—and our talented authors, illustrators, designers and photographers have won many prestigious awards. We welcome you to explore the wealth of information available on Asia at **www.tuttlepublishing.com.**

Published by Tuttle Publishing, an imprint of Periplus Editions (HK) Ltd.

www.tuttlepublishing.com

All photographs by Hironori Tomino and Joseph Cali, except page 54–55 by Satoshi Askawa, and page 154 bottom right and left by Gunji Suda.

The poem on page 88 is taken from *Tale of Ise: Lyrical Episodes from the Tenth Century Japan, verse, no. 106,* translated by Helen Craig McCullough, Stamford University Press, 1968, p. 141

ISBN 978-4-8053-1614-6
ISBN 978-4-8053-1947-5 (for sale in Japan only)

Distributed by:
North America, Latin America & Europe
Tuttle Publishing
364 Innovation Drive, North Clarendon
VT 05759-9436 U.S.A.
Tel: 1 (802) 773-8930; Fax: 1 (802) 773-6993
info@tuttlepublishing.com
www.tuttlepublishing.com

Japan
Tuttle Publishing
Yaekari Building 3rd Floor
5-4-12 Osaki Shinagawa-ku, Tokyo 141 0032
Tel: (81) 3 5437-0171; Fax: (81) 3 5437-0755
sales@tuttle.co.jp
www.tuttle.co.jp

Asia Pacific
Berkeley Books Pte. Ltd.
3 Kallang Sector, #04-01, Singapore 349278
Tel: (65) 67412178; Fax: (65) 67412179
inquiries@periplus.com.sg
www.tuttlepublishing.com

Printed in China 2409EP

27 26 25 24 6 5 4 3

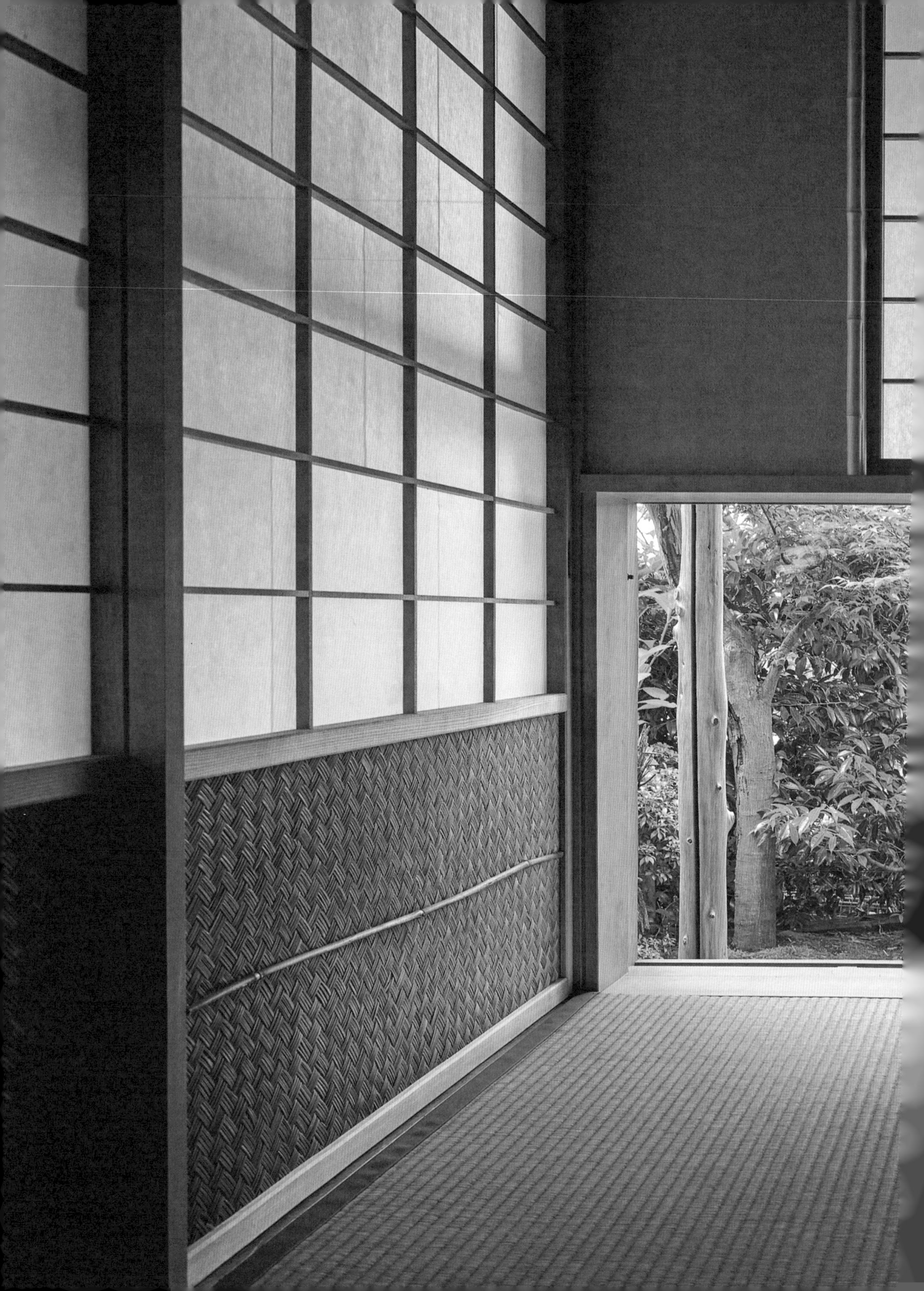